ROUTLEDGE LIBRARY EDITIONS: KOREAN STUDIES

Volume 2

HANYANG KUT

HANYANG KUT
Korean Shaman Ritual Music from Seoul

MARIA K. SEO

LONDON AND NEW YORK

First published in 2002 by Routledge

This edition first published in 2020
by Routledge
2 Park Square, Milton Park, Abingdon, Oxon OX14 4RN

and by Routledge
52 Vanderbilt Avenue, New York, NY 10017

Routledge is an imprint of the Taylor & Francis Group, an informa business

© 2002 Taylor & Francis Books, Inc.

All rights reserved. No part of this book may be reprinted or reproduced or utilised in any form or by any electronic, mechanical, or other means, now known or hereafter invented, including photocopying and recording, or in any information storage or retrieval system, without permission in writing from the publishers.

Trademark notice: Product or corporate names may be trademarks or registered trademarks, and are used only for identification and explanation without intent to infringe.

British Library Cataloguing in Publication Data
A catalogue record for this book is available from the British Library

ISBN: 978-1-138-38774-4 (Set)
ISBN: 978-0-429-28646-9 (Set) (ebk)
ISBN: 978-0-367-25267-0 (Volume 2) (hbk)
ISBN: 978-0-367-25271-7 (Volume 2) (pbk)
ISBN: 978-0-429-28690-2 (Volume 2) (ebk)

Publisher's Note
The publisher has gone to great lengths to ensure the quality of this reprint but points out that some imperfections in the original copies may be apparent.

Disclaimer
The publisher has made every effort to trace copyright holders and would welcome correspondence from those they have been unable to trace.

HANYANG KUT
Korean Shaman Ritual Music from Seoul

Maria K. Seo

Routledge
New York & London

Published in 2002 by
Routledge
29 West 35th Street
New York, NY 10001
www.routledge-ny.com

Published in Great Britain by
Routledge
11 New Fetter Lane
London EC4P 4EE
www.routledge.co.uk

Routledge is an imprint of the Taylor & Francis Group
Printed in the United States of America on acid-free paper.

Copyright © 2002 by Taylor & Francis Books, Inc.

All rights reserved. No part of this book may be reprinted or reproduced or utilized in any form or by any electronic, mechanical, or other means, now known or hereafter invented, including photocopying and recording, or in any information storage or retrieval system, without permission in writing from the publisher.

10 9 8 7 6 5 4 3 2 1

Library of Congress Cataloging-in-Publication Data

Cataloging-in-Publication information for this title is available from the Library of Congress

ISBN 0-415-94361-2

To my family and friends who stood by me.

Contents

List of Figures	xiii
List of Tables	xv
Acknowledgements	xvii
Note on Orthography	xix
Introduction	3
Chapter 1. The Path of a Native Fieldworker	11
Chapter 2. Korean Religious Practices	29
Chapter 3. *Musok* in View of Classic Shamanism	55
Chapter 4. Korean Shamans	67
Chapter 5. *Kut* in Sacred and Secular Contexts	97
Chapter 6. Musical Instruments Used in Hanyang *Kut*	123
Chapter 7. The Musicians of Hanyang *Kut*	135
Chapter 8. Music in Hanyang *Kut*	155
Chapter 9. *Ch'ŏnshin Kut* and Music	181
Chapter 10. Seoul *Saenam Kut* and Music	217
Conclusion	235
Appendix A. Plates	249
Appendix B. Audio CD Notes	275
Glossary	279
References	301
Index	315

Figures

1. Three kingdom periods   33
2. Kim Sun-Bong and his family musicians   143
3. Lineage of teachers, students and family musicians of Kim Chŏm-Sŏk   144
4. Hŏ Yong-Ŏp and his family musicians   146
5. Hŏ Yong-Ŏp's teachers and various instruments he has learned   146
6. Kim Ch'an-Sŏp and his family musicians   148
7. Yang Hwa-Yŏng and his family musicians   149
8. Yang Kyŏng-Wŏn and his students   150
9. Yi Ki-Jŏng's teachers   151
10. Column of Korean notation   168
11. *Kutkŏri changdan* in Korean notation   169
12. *Kutkŏri changdan* in Western notation   169
13. *Kutkŏri changdan* in *kuŭm* (onomatopoeic words)   169
14. *Chegŭm* (cymbals) pattern for *kutkŏri changdan* in Korean notation   170
15. *Chegŭm* (cymbals) pattern for *kutkŏri changdan* in Western notation   170
16. *Pyŏlsang changdan* in Korean notation   170
17. *Pyŏlsang changdan* in Western notation   170
18. *Pyŏlsang changdan* in *kuŭm* (onomatopoeic words)   170
19. *Chegŭm* (cymbals) pattern for *pyŏlsang changdan* in Korean notation   171
20. *Chegŭm* (cymbals) pattern for *pyŏlsang changdan* in Western notation   171
21. *Tangak changdan* in Korean notation   171
22. *Tangak changdan* in Western notation   171
23. *Tangak changdan* in *kuŭm* (onomatopoeic words)   172
24. *Chegŭm* (cymbals) pattern for *tangak changdan* in Korean notation   172
25. *Chegŭm* (cymbals) pattern for *tangak changdan* in Western notation   172
26. *Ŏtmori changdan* in Korean notation   172
27. *Ŏtmori changdan* in Western notation   172
28. Combination of 5-beat and 8-beat patterns in *shijo changdan*   173
29. Five-beat pattern of *shijo changdan* in Korean notation   173
30. Five-beat pattern of *shijo changdan* in Western notation   173

31. Eight-beat pattern of *shijo changdan* in Korean notation   173
32. Eight-beat pattern of *shijo changdan* in Western notation   174
33. *Chajin Hwanip* in Korean notation   174
34. *Chajin Hwanip* in Western notation   174
35. *Seryŏngsan* in Korean notation   175
36. *Seryŏngsan* in Western notation   175
37. *Yŏmbul changdan* in Korean notation   175
38. *Yŏmbul changdan* in Western notation   175
39. *Pan Yŏmbul changdan* in Korean notation   176
40. *Pan Yŏmbul changdan* in Western notation   176
41. *Chegŭm* (cymbals) pattern for *Pan Yŏmbul* in Korean notation   176
42. *Chegŭm* (cymbals) pattern for *Pan Yŏmbul* in Western notation 176
43. *Ch'wit'ae* in Korean notation   177
44. *Ch'wit'ae* in Western notation   177
45. *Kil Kunak* in Korean notation   177
46. *Kil Kunak* in Western notation   177
47. *Tossam Kŏri* and ritual knives   231
48. *Tossam* dance   232
49. Ending *Tossam Kŏri*   232
50. Map of classic shamanism areas in Asia by Ter Ellingson   237
51. *Hoeori param munyang* (whirlwind pattern)   239

Tables

1. Hyangp'unghoe members and their *shindang* (shrine room) names	91
2. *Kut* designated as Intangible Cultural Properties	118
3. Instrumental ensembles for Hanyang *kut*	131
4. Hŏ Yong-Ŏp's teachers on various instruments	147
5. Other musicians involved in Hanyang *kut* ritual music	152
6. Basic drum strokes on *changgu*	167
7. The twelve *kŏri* (sections) of Hanyang *ch'ŏnshin kut*	182
8. Sections of *kut* (ritual)	184
9. Eight actemes (action units) of Hanyang *kut*	188
10. Artists designated for Seoul *Saenam Kut*	219
11. Order of *ch'ŏnshin kut* and *andang sagyŏng maji kut*	222

Acknowledgements

I would like to acknowledge and show my appreciation to those who gave me tremendous encouragement on both sides of the Pacific Ocean.

This work is here with the help of my family and friends. I would like to thank Jennee Osburn, a colleague I met on my first day of classes at the University of Washington, who saw me through with her scholarship and generous friendship. I would also like to thank Mr. and Mrs. Yi Sang-Min, devout Protestants who helped my study of *musok* in Seoul despite religious differences.

I applaud and give thanks to the many shamans, ritual musicians, and *musok* believers who opened their world to me. In particular, I would like to express my gratitude to Mr. Kim Chŏm-Sŏk, a ritual musician, and Ms. Yi Sang-Sun, a *kangshinmu* (spirit-possessed shaman), who have become family friends.

Mr. Park Hung-Ju [Pak Hŭng-Ju], the director of Kut Research Institute, shared his knowledge and wisdom gained through many years of his own field experience. I appreciate his friendship and kind assurances. I would like to give credit to Ms. Chung Su-Mi [Chŏng Su-Mi] for the photograph of *sam t'aegŭk*.

My thanks go to my professors—Ter Ellingson, Linda Iltis, Lorraine Sakata, Clark Sorensen, Christopher Waterman, and Lee Hye-Ku—for guiding me, as well as staff at the University of Washington—Jackie Duggins, Diana Reed, Laurel Sercombe, John Gibbs, Deborah Pierce, and David Bilski. I would also like to thank Paul Johnson, Jennifer Post, and Damian Treffs at Routledge.

This work is a creation by my family. I wrote the text, took photographs, and recorded the ritual music, but the music notations were produced by Michael Sung Park, the tables by Ioana Park, the drawings by Deborah Gassner Park and Joseph Chin Park, and the CD by Peter Joon Park.

To everyone who has touched my life passively or actively (*ŭm/yang ŭro*), I thank you.

陰陽 으로 도움을 주신 여러분께 眞心 으로 感謝 드립니다.

徐 公珠

Note on Orthography

Korean names and terms are presented here following the rules of McCune-Reischauer romanization, unless they are considered well known to English readers, such as Seoul. I have provided an additional romanized word in brackets when they first appear for clarification, for example, Seoul [Sŏul] or Park Chung Hee [Pak Chŏng-Hŭi].

Asian names—Chinese, Japanese, and Korean names—are presented with the family name first. If the name has been anglicized, the family name is presented last. Since Korean given names are usually made up of two words, they are presented with hyphenation between the two, both beginning with capital letters. But if the given name has only one word, a comma is placed after the family name for clarification. For example Pak, Kim indicates that Kim is a given name.

Several words are romanized with emphasis on Korean spelling. For example, the word for hereditary *mudang* is pronounced "*sesŭmmu*" but for this work it is spelled "*sesŭpmu*" to guide readers to the correct Korean spellings. Other words spelled in this manner include: Chongro (pronounced Chongno), *haksŭpmu* (*haksŭmmu*), *kukmu* (*kungmu*), and so on.

Koreans in general use the same word for singular and plural forms of a noun. For this work, I italicized Korean words and clarified whether they should be understood as singular or plural nouns by adding appropriate verb conjugation in English. For example, *kangshinmu* (spirit-possessed shaman) dances alone while *kangshinmu* (spirit-possessed shamans) sing together.

The different ways of pronouncing the "o" and "ŏ," as well as "u" and "ŭ," are as follows:

"o" as in o̱asis
"ŏ" as in bro̱ther
"u" as in flu̱te
"ŭ" as in pu̱t

In Korean, certain consonants are unvoiced and unaspirated. They are romanized as *j*, *k*, *p*, and *t*. Certain consonants are aspirated and romanized with an apostrophe as *ch'*, *k'*, *p'*, and *t'*.

jo, unaspirated, is similar to <u>J</u>oe
ch'u, aspirated, is similar to <u>ch</u>ew
ko, unaspirated, is similar to <u>g</u>o
k'a, aspirated, is similar to <u>c</u>ar
puk, unaspirated, is similar to <u>b</u>ook
p'ul, aspirated, is similar to <u>p</u>ool
ton, unaspirated, is similar to <u>d</u>one
t'on, aspirated, is similar to <u>t</u>on

In English, the consonants *k*, *p*, and *t* are usually aspirated when they appear before a vowel. For English readers, the *t* in *ton* may look like it should sound like the beginning of "Tony," but it is meant to sound like the *t* at the end of "not." Thus *g*, *b*, and *d* may seem more appropriate because they are not aspirated, but they are not generally used because they are voiced (the difference between voiced and unvoiced can be heard in the endings of "bid" versus "bit").

Hanyang Kut

Introduction

As a person born in Korea and trained as an ethnomusicologist in the United States of America, I wish to examine how Korean music is created, how it changes, and how it functions in Korea, as well as to learn about the musicians, performance practices, cultural context, and other issues important in the field of ethnomusicology. My focus for this work is the ritual music of the Hanyang *kut* performed in the Seoul area in both sacred and secular contexts.

Kut is commonly understood as a large-scale ritual performance with music and dance, but small-scale seasonal offerings by a housewife for the spirits of her family ancestors without any music may also be referred to as a *kut*. Large-scale *kut* with music and dance may be divided broadly into two types—*p'ungmul kut* led by secular musicians who play percussion instruments and *hojŏk* (conical oboe), and *mudang kut* led by musically trained *mudang* (ritual specialists) and *chaebi* (ritual musicians).

Kut is associated with *mu*, which is generally considered to be the oldest indigenous religion of Korea. For centuries *mu* has provided an overarching framework of moral, social, and cultural meaning to individuals, families, and communities in Korea. Many Koreans today still believe in *mu*. But many other Koreans reject *mu*, considering it "backward," and refer to it as *mishin* (superstition). Yet the customs and lifestyles of many Koreans (both *mu* believers and non-believers) continue to reflect much of the worldview of *mu*.

Mu advocates the harmony of the universe, created by a perfect balance of *samjae* (three elements): *ch'ŏn* (heaven), *chi* (earth), and *in* (humans). The belief system of *mu* includes belief in many types of *shin* (spirits). Most spirits are benevolent spirits (*shin*), but some are malevolent spirits (*kwi shin*).

"*Mu*" is written with the Sino-Korean ideograph 巫, which elucidates the fundamental elements of *mu*. The horizontal upper and lower bars (—) represent heaven and earth, respectively, while the vertical bar (|) symbolizes the practice of *mu*, including the ritual specialists. Although the two characters on either side of the vertical bar are often interpreted as the sleeves of dancers, it seems to me that they represent human beings with the Sino-Korean ideograph *in* (人, human being). Thus the ideograph 巫 (*mu*) depicts *mu*, the indigenous belief system which advocates the harmony of the universe, created by a perfect balance of heaven, earth, and humans, mediated by ritual specialists.

The concept of reciprocity between spirits and humans is central to *mu*. Illness, misfortune, or difficulties in life are believed to be caused by an imbalance of *samjae* (heaven, earth, and humans). When the balance is disturbed, the indigenous Korean way of restoring universal harmony is through a large-scale *kut*, a ritual in which music plays an essential part. During the *kut* (ritual), *mudang* (ritual specialists) and *chaebi* (ritual musicians) offer prayers, food, and money, as well as dances, songs, and instrumental music to the spirits. *Mu* practitioners believe that if the spirits are content with the elaborate *kut* provided for them, they will grant any wishes the *mudang* (ritual specialist) may relay on behalf of the *chegajip* (sponsor) of the *kut*. It is similar to a situation in which someone treats a powerful benefactor to a banquet and entertainment in order to create good feelings. In a *kut*, the ritual music is of central importance for it is offered as entertainment for the spirits in order to please them so that they will help the sponsor of the *kut*.

Mu is also known as *musok*. The term "*musok*" may be relatively recent,[1] but it refers to *mu*, which has a long history in Korean culture. Some scholars object to using the term "*musok*," as its early usage was derogatory, being used by upper class people who considered the *mu* to be a lower class citizens' activity. However, most of the *mudang* (ritual specialists), *chaebi* (ritual musicians), *chegajip* (ritual sponsors), and scholars whom I have met in the field in recent years use the term "*musok*" in a non-derogatory way, and I have decided to follow their practice.

The term "*musok*" consists of two words: *mu* (巫) and *sok* (俗). The meaning of *mu* was discussed above. The word "*sok*" can be translated as "folk customs." I think it is acceptable to add it to "*mu*," because *mu* has been the central religious view of the majority of Koreans from early years and its concepts have been embedded in daily life and customs for centuries.

Mudang (ritual specialists of *musok*) may be broadly grouped into three types: *sesŭpmu* (hereditary *mudang*), *haksŭpmu* (apprenticed *mudang*), or *kangshinmu*[2] (spirit-possessed *mudang*).[3] Only *mudang* of the third type are actually shamans, according to Johan Reinhard's definition of shaman.[4] In his

---

[1] One of the first uses of the term "*musok*" is in the title of Yi Nŭng-Hwa's work *Chosŏn Musok-ko*, published in 1927.

[2] *Kangshinmu* (spirit-possessed *mudang*) are also known as *pingŭimu*, *chŏpshinmu*, *naerin mudang*, *shin naerin mudang*, and *shindŭllin mudang* (Lim J.H. 1999:120). Some translate *kangshinmu* into English as charismatic shaman or god-descended shaman.

[3] Although the terms *sesŭpmu*, *haksŭpmu*, and *kangshinmu* are relatively recent and developed by scholars, many *mudang* have read the scholars' works and nowadays most *mudang* use these terms themselves. See chapter 2 for more terms for *mudang*.

[4] For a discussion of various definitions of shaman and shamanism see chapter 3.

essay about the problems of defining the term "shaman," Reinhard includes spirit possession as a main criterion:

> A shaman is a person who at his will can enter into a non-ordinary psychic state (in which he either has his soul undertake a journey to the spirit world or he becomes possessed by a spirit) in order to make contact with the spirit world on behalf of members of his community. (Reinhard 1976:16)

Among Korean *mudang*, only *kangshinmu* can become spirit-possessed. This distinction is important and yet it is often overlooked or ignored. Many scholars refer to all *mudang* as "shamans," even though only one of the three types is actually spirit-possessed.

Another common misunderstanding of *mudang* has to do with gender. The term "*mudang*" is often translated as "female ritual specialist," but there are also male *mudang*. Male *kangshinmu* (spirit-possessed *mudang*) are known as *paksu*. During my fieldwork, I have met many *paksu*. Some scholars suggest that *musok* is a religion for women, as a complement to Confucianism for men. But men also are involved in *musok* as *mudang* (ritual specialists), *chaebi* (ritual musicians), and clients.

"*Musok*" is often translated into English as "Korean shamanism." The use of the term "shamanism" to refer to Korean *musok* first appeared in late 19th century writings in English by Westerners.[5] Ch'oe Nam-Sŏn (1927) incorporated the term "shaman" into his Sino-Korean writings about *musok*, calling it *salman'gyo* (薩滿敎 shaman religion). Many scholars (Korean and non-Korean) continue to use the term "shamanism" to refer to the Korean indigenous religion.

Although Korean *musok* shares much of the belief system and rite techniques of "classic" Inner Asian shamanism, many features of *musok* are distinctive, prompting many scholars to prefer terms like *mu* (Cho Hung-youn [Cho Hŭng-Yun] 1990),[6] *musok* (folk practice of *mu*: Kim T'aegon 1991, 1998;[7] Kim In-Hoe 1993; Ch'oe Kil-Sŏng 1990; et al.), *muism* (Yim Suk-Jay [Yim Sŏk-Chae] 1971), *mugyo* (literally, *mu* religion: Ryu Tong-Sik 1989; Pak Yong-Suk 1988; Ch'a Ok-Sung 1997), *sinkyo* (spirit worship: Clark [1932] 1961), *shin kyo* (literally, religion of spirits: Yi Nŭng-Hwa [1927] 1991; Kim Duk-Hwan

---

[5] Boudewijn Walraven (1998:62) traces the first use of "shamanism" for the Korean "mudang creed" to an anonymous author in the Korea Repository published in 1895 by missionaries. Walraven (1998:72 n. 25) also mentions that Landis had used the term "shamanism" in his article published in 1895.

[6] In his most recent publication, Cho Hung-youn uses the term "*mu*" interchangeably with "Korean shamanism" (1999).

[7] Although Kim T'aegon used the terms *musok* and *mugyo*, Chang Soo-Kyung, who translated Kim's work into English after Kim's death, replaced them with *mu* and *muism*.

1988; Lee Jung-Young 1981), and *kut* (ritual: Park H.J. 1991). The debate regarding the choice of a term for the Korean indigenous belief system, religion, and worldview continues among scholars, and agreement on a single term has not yet been reached.

It is interesting to note the terms used in the names of organizations of scholars and researchers in various fields studying *min'gan shinang* (folk religions of the general populace) in Korea: "*Han'guk Musok Hakhoe* (Association for Korean Shamanistic Studies)" (1998), "*Han'guk Shamanism Hakhoe* (Korean Society for Shamanism Studies)" (1997), and "*Kut Yŏn'guso* (*Kut* Research Institute)" (1991). Terms like "*musok*," "shamanism," and "*kut*" have been used interchangeably by members of these organizations and their common interest of research is the Korean indigenous worldview.

Since many *mudang* (ritual specialists) read and follow what Korean scholars have written about *mu* and its ritual practitioners, some now adopt scholarly terms and concepts to discuss their work. For example, most of my informants refer to themselves as *kangshinmu* (spirit-possessed *mudang*). Some call themselves "shaman" and refer to their religious practice as "shamanism".[8]

Some *mudang* have been recommended by scholars for recognition by the Korean government for their ritual knowledge and skills. Since the Park Chung Hee (Pak Chŏng-Hŭi) government (1963–1979) introduced legislation in the 1960s for the "preservation" (*pojon*) of "important intangible cultural properties" (*chungyo muhyŏng munhwajae*) to strengthen national identity, a number of *musok* rituals have been designated as Important Intangible Cultural Properties and presented on the public stage as the "original form" (*wŏnhyŏng*) of Korean traditional (*chŏnt'ong*) arts (see chapter 5).

Although *musok* is found throughout Korea, there are regional variations. Ritual specialists from various regions have distinctive ways of presenting *kut*, reflecting the aesthetics of the people who live in a given area. The differences may be noted, for example, in food offerings, costumes, songs, dances, and music for the rituals.

In Seoul, the capital of South Korea, a large number of styles of *kut* from various regions of Korea are performed in sacred and secular contexts. Seoul is located in the central part of the Korean peninsula (126°59' North Latitude and 37°33' East Longitude) along the lower Han River. *Kut* from North Korea— Hwanghae, P'yŏngan, and Hamgyŏng Provinces—are performed in Seoul by *kangshinmu* (spirit-possessed *mudang*) who moved from North to South Korea during the Korean War (1950–1953). *Kut* from various South Korean regions— Cheju, Chŏlla, Ch'ungch'ŏng, Kangwŏn, Kyŏnggi, and Kyŏngsang Provinces— are also performed in Seoul, mostly by *sesŭpmu* (hereditary *mudang*).

Among the many types of *kut* found in Seoul, I have chosen to focus my studies on the Hanyang *kut*, the rituals originating in the Seoul area and

---

[8] "Shaman" is transliterated as "샤만" in Korean and "shamanism" as "샤마니즘."

performed by *kangshinmu* (spirit-possessed *mudang*). The capital of Korea since 1394, Seoul was known as Hanyang or Hansŏng during the Chosŏn Dynasty (1392–1910)[9] and as Kyŏngsŏng[10] during the Japanese occupation (1910–1945). Although Hanyang *kut* are also often referred to as Seoul *kut*, I will refer to them as Hanyang *kut* in this work in order to distinguish them clearly from other regional styles of *kut* held in Seoul. Hanyang *kut* are formal, elegant, and complex. Hanyang *kut* have been so carefully guarded by their practitioners that few scholars have been able to study them.

Most scholars of Korean *musok* from abroad have studied the rituals by *kangshinmu* (spirit-possessed *mudang*) from the northwestern regions—Hwanghae and P'yŏngan Provinces—or by *sesŭpmu* (hereditary *mudang*) from the southern provinces—Ch'ungch'ŏng, Chŏlla, Kangwŏn, and Kyŏngsang Provinces. Among the authors who have produced works in English about Korean shamanism and its rituals, Alan Carter Covell, Jon Carter Covell, Hyun-Key Kim Hogarth, Halla Pai Huhm, and Boudewijn Walraven have worked with *kangshinmu* who practice Seoul, Hwanghae Province, and P'yŏngan Province style *kut*. Laurel Kendall worked in Enduring Pine Village (fictitious name) in Kyŏnggi Province while Alexandre Guillemoz studied in Mipo (fictitious name), a fishing village in the southeastern coastal region of Korea. Keith Howard, Park Mikyung [Pak Mi-Kyŏng], and Nathan Hesselink have studied Chŏlla Province *sesŭpmu* (hereditary *mudang*) rituals while Kim Seung Nae has focused on the Cheju Island tradition.

Among the many published works on Korean *musok*, several scholars discuss Hanyang *kut* by spirit-possessed shamans, but the coverage of ritual music is quite limited. Akamatsu and Akiba include three songs—*Chesŏk Ch'ŏngbae, Chesŏk Shin'ga* and *Ch'angbu T'aryŏng*—transcribed in Western notation by Yi Chong-Tae in their work ([1938] 1991, 2:237–238) while Akiba discusses four musical instruments—*changgu, ching, koritchak*, and *chegŭm*—used in Hanyang *kut* ([1950] 1987:152–154). Kim T'aegon includes one song from Hanyang *kut* transcribed by Yi Po-Hyŏng (1979:251) while Yi Po-Hyŏng writes on Korean ritual music in general, including Hanyang *kut* (1993:92–101). Cho Hung-Youn discusses the symbolism of musical instruments (1990:73–77) and Halla Pai Huhm has notation for three Hanyang *kut* songs and three pieces for *p'iri* and *changgu* (1980:23–31). Kukrip [Kungnip] Munhwajae Yŏn'guso published *Seoul Saenam Kut*, introducing the repertoire of Seoul *Saenam Kut* and providing a brief explanation of the instrumental pieces, as well as four *changdan* (rhythmic cycles) used for Seoul *Saenam Kut* (1998:133–141). The National Center for Korean Traditional Performing Arts produced *Korean*

---

[9] Hanyang was established as the capital of the Chosŏn Dynasty in 1394 by the dynasty's founder T'aejo (Yi Sŏng-Gye) because it was considered to be an auspicious site. Hanyang was a city located in Hansŏng county district.

[10] Kyŏngsŏng was pronounced Keijō in Japanese.

Shaman Music: Seoul Jaesu Kut and Jinogwi Kut with accompanying CDs, introducing song texts and transcription of songs of the two Seoul area *kut*, *jaesu* [*chaesu*] *kut* for the living and *jinogwi* [*chinogwi*] *kut* for the departed (1995).

When Korean ritual music is discussed, it is usually music of the southeastern or southwestern regional traditions. I felt challenged to learn more about the Hanyang *kut*, its musical practices, and its musicians. Since 1991, I have been fortunate to be accepted by more than one hundred *kangshinmu* (spirit-possessed *mudang*) in Seoul, including dozens of *paksu* (male *kangshinmu*), and many *chaebi* (ritual musicians). I have been able to observe more than one hundred *kut* (rituals). The *kangshinmu* and *chaebi* taught me esoteric knowledge and techniques, ranging from prayers and songs to the minute details of taboos and ritual preparations.

During the past nine years, I went to Korea once or twice a year, usually staying there for three months each time. I went to the field at different times of the year to observe and experience the various seasonal activities among the shamans and their clients. My returning to the field every year gave me the opportunity to observe numerous changes in *musok* practice and resulted in earning the trust of many *kangshinmu* (spirit-possessed *mudang*) and *chaebi* (ritual musicians) because they perceived my interest in *musok* to be sincere and lasting. The more time I spent with shamans and musicians, the more willing they were to share their esoteric knowledge with me.

Unlike *sesŭpmu* (hereditary *mudang* who are born into musician families), the *kangshinmu* (spirit-possessed *mudang*) begin their musical training after their initiations. In most cases, they are not familiar with any *musok* related activities and so must start at the beginning. They memorize prayers and song texts, learn to sing songs, play cymbals and drums, and learn ritual techniques. *Kangshinmu* learn individually from their spirit parents or through group instruction at shaman schools in Seoul (see chapter 4). It takes many years of rigorous training to become a shaman performing at large-scale rituals, singing, dancing, playing instruments, and making clients cry or laugh. As I learned how much time and energy the *kangshinmu* and musicians must invest to properly perform in *kut*, I saw the value of sharing the insights that I gained through my fieldwork. In this work, I shall attempt to show how ritual music is used in Hanyang *kut*, as well as how it influences secular music in contemporary South Korea.

In order to provide a context for my study of Hanyang *kut*, I will begin by recounting the path that led me to Seoul as a native fieldworker (chapter 1). I will introduce the nation's creation myth and discuss *musok* (chapter 2) and then consider *musok* in view of the "classic" shamanism of Inner Asia and *kangshinmu* (spirit-possessed shamans) as "classic" shamans, pointing out similarities and differences (chapter 3). Present-day *kangshinmu*'s roles and socio-political activities will be discussed by introducing organizations of *kangshinmu* and a school for *kangshinmu* (chapter 4). In the following chapter, *kut* (rituals) by *kangshinmu* performed in contemporary Seoul in sacred and secular contexts will be surveyed, as well as a play, a parody, and folk singers' concerts that have *kut* by *kangshinmu* as their central theme. In addition, government policies designating *musok* rituals as Important Intangible Cultural Properties will be discussed (chapter 5). The musical instruments used in the Hanyang *kut* (chapter 6), the musicians and ensembles involved in the Hanyang *kut* (chapter 7), and the vocal and instrumental music repertoire of the Hanyang *kut* will be presented (chapter 8). Two Hanyang *kut*—*ch'ŏnshin kut* and Seoul *Saenam Kut*—which are held for the living and the dead, respectively, will be examined, showing how intrinsic ritual music is to the *kut* (chapters 9 and 10). I will then discuss *musok* and its ritual music as an essential part of Korean identity in the concluding chapter.

I have included photographs to show how shamans and musicians work together to present splendid ritual performances (see appendix A). Throughout my fieldwork, I have photographed and videotaped many *kut* after obtaining permission from the *kangshinmu* (spirit-possessed shamans), *chaebi* (ritual musicians), and *chegajip* (sponsors). The photographs of shamans and musicians in this work portray those who encouraged me to present the information correctly. Consequently their names and efforts are acknowledged in appreciation (while respecting the wishes of those who prefer to remain anonymous). I have also provided an accompanying audio compact disc of ritual music performed at various Hanyang *kut* that I attended and recorded after obtaining permission (see appendix B for CD liner notes).

CHAPTER 1

The Path of a Native Fieldworker

1. From the Beginning

The deafening sounds of cymbals and drums, the *mudang*'s fierce looking face, colorful banners, twirling knives and swords in the air—these are my recollections of a *kut* (ritual) that I attended in North Korea when I was six years old. I still remember the *kut* and the *mudang* (ritual specialist) with considerable fear.

My family warned me not to stir while the *mudang* was in trance because absolute silence was necessary for the *mudang*'s soul to return to his body. Otherwise, the *mudang*'s soul might wander or capture an audience member, forcing them to become a *mudang*. I did not know what it meant to be a *mudang*, but I knew intuitively that I did not want to become one.

Much Later

My husband and I were both born in Korea. We were married in May 1961 in Seoul, the capital of South Korea, and moved to Canada that September because my husband, a nuclear physicist, had been offered a position as a research scientist. We made our home in Canada and raised three sons. Living in North America for thirty-nine years, I often wished to return to my native country.

My husband became a naturalized Canadian citizen within a few years, but I hesitated because I missed my family, my friends, and my country. I simply missed being a Korean living in Korea. Although I appeared to adjust rather well to the North American way of life, my longing for "home" grew deeper as the years passed.

My ambivalence about my identity and ethnicity began to challenge me. I had lived in Korea for twenty-three years, but I have been living in North America for more than thirty-nine years. My physical appearance is that of a Korean, but my worldview is that of a "transnational" due to my life as an immigrant in a foreign land, an issue discussed by Slote (1993:69).

In order to learn more about my Korean heritage, I often read books about Korea. Most of the books and articles I read seemed to suggest that Korean cultural identity was formed by Confucian ideals and/or the worldview of *musok*, the Korean indigenous religion. About a decade ago, the literature concerning Korean shamanism was not readily available to me and too limited to satisfy my intense curiosity.

A Letter from Seoul

In the spring of 1991 in Seattle, my parents were visiting me from Seoul. One day in March my parents received a letter from their neighbor in Seoul. They were stunned by the news contained in that letter. The neighbor, a young man, expressed his anger and despair because his wife had to become a *kangshinmu*, a spirit-possessed *mudang*. My parents were so distressed and saddened by this tragic news that they seemed unable to recover from the shock for a long time.

My parents, then in their seventies, had known several *mudang* (ritual specialists) during their lives, but this was their first experience of personally knowing someone who was transformed from an ordinary housewife to a spirit-possessed *mudang*. Disasters in life are thought to happen to others whom we read about in the papers or hear about on the news. My parents could not articulate the reasons why becoming a spirit-possessed *mudang* was so upsetting. They simply knew it was "the end" of the young couple's life, and they were deeply saddened. My heart sank instantly, too. We felt deep sympathy for the couple. What a tragedy to have someone in the family become a *kangshinmu,* a spirit-possessed *mudang!* We felt sorry for the wife, but we also worried about the husband and the family. What would become of the couple, their children, their relatives, and friends? How would they cope with this tragic situation? We perceived the difficulty of this family, but none of us had any logical explanation for our feeling this way. I wanted to know what really caused my parents and me such grief for the couple and their family. I hoped to find answers to the many puzzling questions—What is a *mudang*? Why does our friend have to face such a tragic fate against her will? What is really happening and why?

A Visit to Seoul

In September 1991, I visited Seoul with my sons and a friend for the first time since 1981. Enormous changes had taken place in Seoul in those ten years. New highways from the airport to downtown were multi-laned like those in Europe and North America. Seoul had expanded across the Han River toward the south, creating a gigantic metropolis. The city skyline had risen with tall skyscrapers as if it wanted to boast the surging energy of its people. Streets and highways were filled with cars. There were many times when no cars moved, as if they were in a huge parking lot where an attendant had piled up the cars to the maximum capacity with no room to spare. There were too many vehicles on the road, causing traffic jams and parking problems everywhere. I felt that too much Western influence was choking the flow of Korean life.

It was only after we crossed the Han River, northbound toward downtown Seoul, that some of the old buildings and streets began to look familiar. Amid the high-rise buildings and modern structures along the main roads, I noticed numerous signs advertising *musok* practices. The wording of the signs was not straightforward, but if one read between the lines, it was clear that *musok* practices were being offered. I was pleasantly surprised to learn that *musok* is a living tradition, readily accessible, contrary to what I had assumed from the readings. I was glad that I had decided to come home—to observe, to experience, and to learn firsthand.

Mrs. A, the First *Kangshinmu* I Met

The first *kangshinmu* (spirit-possessed *mudang*) I met was Mrs. A, my parents' friend and neighbor who first became spirit-possessed earlier that year (I have called her Mrs. A in accordance with her wish to remain anonymous). When my sons, a Canadian friend, and I visited Korea in September, Mr. and Mrs. A invited us to their home. We felt rather uneasy about meeting a *kangshinmu*. My parents convinced us that no harm would come to us, because the neighbors were a very nice couple. Mr. A greeted us at the door and guided us to a room where we waited for Mrs. A.

When she entered the room, I was so struck by her beauty that I needed a few moments to compose myself before I could greet her. I could not believe that this young woman, the mother of two daughters, was a *kangshinmu*. Her manner and attire were so elegant that she did not conform to the image of a *kangshinmu* that I had formed, based on my childhood memory. There was absolutely no evidence that would cause anyone to suspect her of being a spirit-possessed *mudang*.

Mrs. A was in her early thirties. She wore traditional Korean women's clothing. Her long skirt flowed gently to the floor and her movements were graceful. Her hair was done up in the traditional married woman's style—parted in the middle with the hair tied neatly in a knot at the nape of the neck and fastened with a *pinyŏ*, a hair ornament about six inches long.

The First Experience of Divination

Since it is commonly known among Koreans that a neophyte *kangshinmu*'s power of divination is particularly strong and accurate, my whole entourage decided to ask Mrs. A to tell our fortunes. No one knew quite what to expect. Mrs. A invited us one by one into her *shindang* (shrine room), to discuss the fortunes privately. She invited me to stay as an interpreter because my sons and our friend did not understand much Korean. She also kindly permitted me to tape record her fortune-telling and our conversations. Before the fortune-telling session began, my mother offered an envelope to Mrs. A and left the room. My mother later told me that there was 50,000 *wŏn* (about $70.00 in US funds in 1991) in that envelope.

The shrine room was rectangular with windows on one side and a door opposite. Paintings of various spirits hung on one long wall. Some spirits looked fierce, some gentle. Below the paintings was an altar where several images of spirits were displayed. Rice, fruits, candies, cigarettes, and money were piled up before these images as offerings. Several tall candles were lit and incense burned in several small ornate vessels (see plate 1).[1]

Mrs. A sat near the doorway, placing a small table between herself and her client (see plate 2). She wanted to know where the client lived and the time, date, month, and year of birth. Remembering that divination is done according to lunar calendar dates, I apologized for knowing this vital information only by the Gregorian calendar. She smiled gently and proceeded immediately to consult a book in order to find the corresponding dates for the lunar calendar.

The information given, Mrs. A closed her eyes and began to summon her spirits, asking them to descend and help her. She held a bell in her right hand, shaking it intermittently whenever she seemed to need to take a breath. She announced her client to the spirits, mentioning the client's name, residence, and the *saju* (the four columns of life—the time, date, month, and year of birth).

Mrs. A had a dozen large *yŏpchŏn* (brass coins about two inches in diameter with a quarter-inch hole in the center). She rolled the *yŏpchŏn* on the table several times for each client. At each roll the *yŏpchŏn* created a different configuration. Some *yŏpchŏn* stayed in isolated piles, others rolled off the table. Mrs. A interpreted each client's fortune according to the configuration. When she said someone was away, for example, she pointed to a coin fallen from the

---

[1] Plates (i.e. photographs) are in appendix A.

table. Gesturing toward two coins close together, she said that the couple was happy, and so on.

Mrs. A also confided in us that she could feel the physical pain of the client and pointed to one of my sons, saying that he was suffering from a stomach ache. My son later told me that it was true.

When my turn came, I asked Mrs. A if and when I would receive my Ph.D. degree and return to Korea. She told me that I would be returning to Korea without completing the degree. Since for many decades I had dreamed of returning home with the degree, I felt completely shattered.

We took several snapshots with Mrs. A in her shrine room and hurried home to discuss the experience among ourselves. Everyone thought it had been fun but most gave little weight to what Mrs. A had said. But I was so disturbed and hurt that I began to doubt her ability. I refused to believe her, because she did not tell me what I wanted to hear.

Mrs. A and Her Family

After that first visit to Mrs. A's shrine, I began to get acquainted with Mr. and Mrs. A. I wanted to get to know the couple and their family members better so that I might learn more about the stages of development in Mrs. A's career as a *kangshinmu* (spirit-possessed *mudang*), but she seemed to avoid me. Although I saw the husband often, I was allowed to visit Mrs. A only by infrequent invitation.

Mrs. A's mother looked after the two granddaughters. One girl was a junior in high school, the other a first grader in a private school. Leaving the two daughters in the family home under the grandmother's care, Mrs. A and her husband had moved to another area of Seoul where no one knew them in order to establish new identities. Mrs. A visited her children late at night two or three times a week, but the children were not permitted to visit their parents in their new home. Mr. A was seen in both neighborhoods, but the family was never seen together in public after Mrs. A became a *kangshinmu*. These measures were taken to protect the children from gossip. It was difficult for all parties concerned. I was amazed to observe how well the youngest member of the family, the seven-year-old girl, was adjusting to this drastic change of life.

When one becomes a *kangshinmu*, one's family and even friends are often shunned by outsiders. Within the family, many *kangshinmu* lose their original family ties due to the conflicts arising from their status as *kangshinmu*. The *kangshinmu*'s spouse, parents, and relatives often terminate their relationships with the neophyte and go their separate ways, because they find the situation too difficult to handle. Some *kangshinmu* families move away together to a new place, attempting to keep the family unit intact. Few *kangshinmu* keep in touch with their relatives openly. Most of them prefer to maintain a low profile in order to protect their families and relatives from ostracism.[2]

Back to School in the US

Unfortunately, my three-week holiday was quickly over and we had to return to America. The last I heard, Mrs. A was extremely busy with her clients and her newfound interest in Korean traditional music. She was learning Korean traditional songs and drumming through evening classes and progressing rather well. Since Mrs. A was busy with her work and the daily lessons, we left Korea without saying good-bye to her in person.

Back in Seattle I resumed my studies. Unfortunately, I often remembered Mrs. A's discouraging remarks that I would return to Korea without finishing my degree. Whenever her remark disturbed me, I struggled to focus on my studies. I was a fairly diligent student at school. Why on earth should I not finish the degree? She had to be wrong. I wanted so much to prove her wrong.

Back to Seoul, as Predicted

One day in early December 1991, I received a telephone call from a family friend in Seoul. He told me that my father, who had planned to spend the Christmas holidays in Seattle, was seriously ill. When I called my father's physician in Seoul, he urged me to return to Korea as soon as possible, expressing his concern that my father had only three weeks to live due to liver cancer. The next day I left Seattle to return home to care for my father. The day after I arrived in Seoul, he was rushed to the intensive care unit of the hospital where I remained with him. A week or so later, I realized I had returned to Korea without a degree as Mrs. A had predicted!

While in Seoul, I remembered that I had an appointment with my doctor in Canada to receive treatment for a chronic eye condition. My father's physicians assured me that my father would live for a while longer, allowing the time for me to go to Canada, receive the injection, and return. I was to leave Seoul on the 10th of January and return the 15th.

However, afraid to leave my ailing father, I decided to consult a *kangshinmu* (spirit-possessed *mudang*) as many a desperate Korean would do. Since I knew only one *kangshinmu* at that point, I looked to Mrs. A for advice. She told me not to make the trip. She did not give me any explanation, but her

---

[2] For example, Cho Cha-Ryong, a *kangshinmu*, recounts his personal experiences concerning his family and relatives in his autobiography *Shin ŭl T'aekhan Namja* [A man who chose the spirits] (1996).

tone of voice somehow convinced me to cancel my appointment with the Canadian doctor and remain in Seoul. My father passed away on the 13th of January. I was grateful that Mrs. A had suggested that I remain in Seoul. Had I not consulted her, I surely would have missed the chance to be with my father on his deathbed.

At the Hospital

It is required in most Korean hospitals that family members look after the patient to reduce nursing costs. Food and medical care are provided by the hospital, but other types of care are the family's responsibility.

My father was a successful businessman. Although known for his wit and his love of life, he seldom spoke while in the hospital. His gentle glance expressed how deeply he appreciated those who visited him, especially his three grandchildren who had come from Canada. He often held my hand and kissed it gently without a word, his eyes closed. Words seemed absolutely unnecessary, even useless, during those painful and distressing hours.

It is considered a great tribute to the patient if a friend or relative spends the night at the hospital. I protested that my father needed a good night's sleep, but Korean custom prevailed, and my father had visitors honoring him day and night throughout his hospital stay. Since Mr. A was a good friend of my parents, he came and spent every Saturday night with my father, giving my mother and me a chance to sleep. One Saturday, however, Mr. A told me that he could not come to the hospital that night. I managed to stay up with my father through the night looking after him alone while my mother rested. My father said that he was glad to be alone with me. After all it was the first night without a visitor since he had been hospitalized. He needed to tell me many things. He seemed to know he was dying despite every effort to convince him otherwise.

A Hospital Policy—Discharging a Patient at Death's Door

The next night, Sunday at about eleven o'clock, my father's condition began to deteriorate rapidly. His doctors began to rush through the paperwork necessary to discharge him from the hospital.

According to Korean custom, it is preferable to die in one's own bed, and the doctors were doing their best to let my father face death at home. I was heavyhearted to learn that we must take my father home because it meant that we were accepting his death. Shortly after midnight, an ambulance with a doctor in attendance rushed my father home where he passed away in the early hours of Monday morning, January 13, 1992. My father looked slowly, one by one, at everyone who was hovering over him before he closed his eyes. He died in peace among those who loved and mourned for him.

Mr. A, the *kangshinmu*'s husband, explained that Mrs. A had told him not to go to the hospital that last Saturday night. She said that my father needed those last few hours alone with his only child—me. I am grateful that Mr. and Mrs. A gave me the opportunity to be with my father for our last intimate conversation. The night was too short, but I shall remember always what my father shared with me that night.

After my father's funeral, I returned to Seattle with my mother and my sons. Many events that had happened in Seoul stirred me, and I felt deeply intrigued. I had the personal experience of having my fortune told and being safeguarded by a *kangshinmu*. I observed the doctors in a western-style university hospital desperately attempting to discharge a patient so that he could die in his own bed. I knew that Koreans in general dread the thought of dying outside of their own homes, but I did not know why.

Much later I learned that *musok* followers believe that the soul can rest in peace only if one dies at home. If one dies unnaturally, unexpectedly, unfulfilled,[3] or not at home, the soul is condemned to wander forever and might haunt living family members. In *musok,* ancestors are venerated, and reciprocal caring relationships continue even after the members are separated by death. A Korean hopes to face death at home in order to ensure peace in the family he leaves behind. One tries to avoid becoming a wandering spirit (*kaek kwi*) haunting the family he loves. My experience in Seoul gave me a glimpse of how much the worldview of *musok* has penetrated Koreans' daily lives, and how often they unconsciously "practice *musok*" because traditions and customs are rooted deeply in the *musok* religion.

2. In the Field as a Native Korean

When I returned to Korea in 1992 to learn more about *musok*, I was anxious to visit with Mrs. A, the first *kangshinmu* (spirit-possessed *mudang*) I had met. Unfortunately, I was told that Mrs. A was too busy to see me because she, as a diviner and ritual specialist, was in great demand by her clients. In addition to her work, Mrs. A was pursuing her interest in Korean traditional music and dance in daily classes. Since I was interested in learning more about Korean traditional music, I asked Mr. A where the classes were held, who her teachers were, what repertoire she was learning, and so on. Mr. A's answers were always vague and he usually managed to change the subject. The only information I

---

[3] People who are not married are considered unfulfilled, as are those who are married but have not produced a son.

received was that this school was located not far from our neighborhood and that Mrs. A was learning a lot from a wonderful teacher in daily evening classes.

Seeing that Mrs. A was not going to help me, I felt the need to look for other *kangshinmu*. I asked everyone around me—relatives, friends, neighbors, and acquaintances—if they knew any *kangshinmu*. Their answers were always an emphatic "No!" and telling me that *musok* no longer exists in modern Korea. Some friends were sympathetic toward my ignorance. They even made excuses on my behalf, saying that my long absence from Korea had caused me to be unaware of these changes.

Realizing that my interest in *musok* was serious, some of my close friends were upset, suggesting that I return to my career as a concert pianist. They expressed their disappointment openly. My friends who had attended Catholic girls' school with me were quick to point out that my interest in *musok* was against my religion, warning me that I would become spirit-possessed if I continued "this nonsense" and got involved in the "devil's activities." Some began to pray for me, the renegade friend, while others chose to avoid me. Involvement with *musok* was not "politically correct." I was making people around me uncomfortable. Even though I was in Korea surrounded by my family and friends, I felt alone and isolated at times because of my interest in *musok*.

When I realized that no one around me appeared to know much about *musok*, I decided to contact Mr. B, a Korean scholar who had lectured and published many articles about *musok*. When we were introduced, he told me how glad he was to meet me in person, because he had known of me as a pianist during his college years. He said he would call me to arrange a time and meeting place so that we could attend a *kut* (ritual) that weekend. He never called. Whenever I see how most Koreans, including *kangshinmu* and musicians, are willing to help foreign scholars but not native ones, I cannot help remembering Mr. B who dismissed me although he is known among foreign scholars for his willingness to assist researchers from abroad. I felt discriminated against for being a native Korean.

In 1994, I often met a Korean scholar who was doing her field research in social anthropology. When we were both present at the same functions in Seoul—rituals, private and public gatherings—it was evident that people were treating her better than me. Apparently she, too, knew she was treated differently, as she recounts her experience with Kim Kŭm-Hwa, a *kangshinmu*, and others:

> I could not help remembering how friendly she had been to me and my husband in 1989, obviously mistaking me for a foreigner as well. All my life, I have frequently been mistaken for a foreigner, because of my facial complexion and features which are not typically Korean, and my long absence from Korea

might have possibly accentuated the illusion. Since *sadaesasang*[4] towards foreigners, particularly westerners, was rampant, among the shamans, as well as ordinary Koreans, I was often a recipient of unexpected kind gestures and special treatment. Even after I corrected their mistake, in most cases, I continued to enjoy similar privileges, as someone who lived in England, and therefore with the status of 'guest'. Those who did not come into regular contact with westerners were convinced that I was playacting, when I told them I was a 'pure Korean'. They often treated me doubly well, asking, 'Where did you learn to speak Korean so well?' This, I soon found out, was a great advantage for me from the financial point of view. As a 'foreign scholar' of limited means, I was spared having to donate large sums of money to the shamans/spirits. (Hogarth 1995:23)

Several *kangshinmu* (spirit-possessed shamans) told me that they were comfortable being interviewed by foreigners, because they felt safe knowing that the taped conversations or photographs would be carried to far away places with no effect on their life in Korea. But one day Ms. C, a *kangshinmu*, told me and a few of her *kangshinmu* friends how she was scolded by her New York City relatives for hours over the telephone. The relatives recognized Ms. C on a TV program shown there. It was bad enough that Ms. C was a *kangshinmu*, but they could not forgive her for appearing on public television. Deeply hurt, Ms. C was crying as she warned others not to trust foreigners.

On one occasion I witnessed an unusual incident at a *kuttang* (ritual hall) located in Uidong where a *naerim kut* (initiation ritual) was underway. Foreigners—a young woman, two cameramen, and an interpreter—barged in while the *kut* was in progress.

The intruders were anxious to wrap up their project quickly so that they could be on their way to the airport. They were annoyed that the *kut* had stopped. This group behaved rudely and made unkind remarks, probably assuming that no one present could understand French, while I observed them in silence. When they had abruptly opened the door of the ritual hall, naturally the *kut* (ritual) was interrupted.[5] The French woman presented questions in English to an American, the interpreter hired for the occasion, so that he could relay questions to the *kangshinmu* (spirit-possessed *mudang*) in his limited Korean. The questions were about prostitution and homosexuality among *kangshinmu*. They were

---

[4] *Sadaesasang*, "[o]ften translated as 'flunkeyism' or 'toadyism,' it literally means 'the idea of submitting to the stronger' or 'looking up to the greater.' Thus foreigners, particularly westerners, are given special treatment to an extraordinary extent" (Hogarth 1995:43).

[5] Despite the fact that the doors of the ritual hall are usually closed during a *kut*, people go quietly in and out. The reason for stopping this *kut* in progress was the amount of commotion the group had created.

pushing for quick answers, but *kangshinmu* Lee and others were perplexed by such questions. Realizing the difficulty of obtaining any comments from the *kangshinmu*, they urged that the ritual be continued so that they might film, which the *kangshinmu* obliged. They filmed for about ten minutes and left (February 1994).

After they left, I asked if any *kangshinmu* would have tolerated such behavior from native Koreans. The three *kangshinmu* answered in unison without hesitation, "Absolutely not!" I could see the benefit of communicating between *kangshinmu* and native scholars since both could articulate ideas better in their own language, thus reducing the errors caused by misinterpretation. At times I find misleading statements about *musok* written by authors from abroad who have reached conclusions without grasping the layers of esoteric knowledge guarded by *kangshinmu*. In reality, most scholars from abroad do their research in Korea with limited time and budget, and some are handicapped by inadequate language skills.

Before I began my fieldwork, I felt fortunate to be Korean. As a native Korean speaker, I felt no need to acquire a field language as my colleagues were required to do. It certainly was a challenge for me to pass the English test to be admitted to the University of Washington as a graduate student, as well as the two foreign language examinations—French and German—for my doctoral work. I had simply assumed that my fieldwork in Korean would be easier than the course work I did in English. The first fact I had to face, however, was the modifications in the Korean language by the Korean government since 1961. I had to learn new words and idioms, as well as spellings revised by the government. For example, *pihaengjang* (airport) was replaced by *konghang* and *sunsa* (police) by *kyŏngch'al*.

Since a *kut* (ritual) lasts usually from a whole day to several days, there are many breaks and meal times during which musicians and *mudang* (ritual specialists) chat. The musicians always invited me to join in, but I could not follow their conversation fully because they used words and phrases I was not familiar with. Initially I was self-conscious about not understanding everything, but later I realized that many words and phrases have exclusive meanings for *kangshinmu* (spirit-possessed *mudang*) and *chaebi* (musicians). Over the years I was able to decipher some of their codes and euphemisms, but I am sure many more remain for me to comprehend. I decided not to ask for direct explanations, convinced that they would not use *ŭnŏ*, a language exclusively used among *musok* practitioners, if they wanted me to understand. Whenever they realized I had caught the meaning of their words, they smiled knowingly. It was "our little secret." With these subtle gestures, I knew I was slowly being accepted. A few told me that they appreciated my being discreet, but I must confess that my frustration was not easy to handle at times. Contrary to my earlier hopes, I had to learn many new words and phrases in both sacred and secular contexts in the field.

Once *ŭnŏ* is known to outsiders, the words become "*saŏ* (dead words)," and the person considered responsible for the slip is scolded by members of the group (Ch'oe K.S. 1990:32–33). For those interested in *ŭnŏ* as used in the 1970s, Ch'oe provides about two hundred words in ten categories—body parts, clothing, food, pronouns, *musok* practices, awards/penalties, fees, emotions, sex, and animals, as well as inanimate objects (Ch'oe K.S. 1990:37–38).

As the years go by, most of the *kangshinmu* (spirit-possessed *mudang*) I have met have become friendlier and more willing to guide me in the right direction. Several *kangshinmu* and musicians told me they often felt annoyed, used, and violated by those who intrude into their sacred world, describing a few scholars as people who observe, take pictures, record, ask questions, write dissertations, acquire degrees, and think they know it all. On the other hand, they respect and appreciate the scholars who make valuable contributions through their writings and lectures with a genuine interest in *musok*. Several *kangshinmu* actually urged me to record and publish, promising that they would guide me. It appears to me that most *kangshinmu* and musicians are truly concerned about the correct presentation of their world.

Following Professor Lee Hye-Ku's advice, I tried to present the same questions to the same people at least three times.[6] Gradually I began to notice discrepancies in the answers given by several *kangshinmu* (spirit-possessed *mudang*) and musicians. Whenever I asked them why the answers vary so greatly, they laughed and said that they do not share anything with those who come around only once or twice. The several sets of answers to the same inquiries I collected through the years seem to verify that I am getting closer to what I have been seeking. My quest for the *musok* world was motivated by my desire to know more about my roots. I have taken time, letting *kangshinmu* and musicians share information with me on their own terms when they are ready.

I have not walked in "off the street" to meet any *kangshinmu*[7] or "gate crashed" at rituals,[8] but have always waited to be properly introduced to *kangshinmu* and musicians, and invited by them to their sacred world. Yet once in 1993, I had to leave the *kuttang* (ritual hall) because the sponsor of a ritual felt uncomfortable. I had been invited to this ritual by the *kangshinmu* and musicians. The *kut* was held in the largest room at Pohyŏn Sanshin'gak where three *kangshinmu*, three musicians, one woman (the sponsor), and I were

---

[6] This advice was given to me by Professor Lee when I was a graduate student at Seoul National University in 1960.

[7] Youngsook Kim Harvey relates experiences of walking in "off the street" to meet shamans (1984:35).

[8] Hyun-key Kim Hogarth describes how her reception at the *kut* into which she "gatecrashed" varied from "that of hostility to extreme friendliness" (Hogarth 1995:36).

present.⁹ Since the sponsor was a regular client of one of the *kangshinmu*, she had become acquainted with his group of *kangshinmu* and musicians over the years. Noticing me, the sponsor told one of the *kangshinmu* that she was extremely uncomfortable having me, an outsider, present there. Since everyone else knew me, they all tried to persuade her to let me stay, but to no avail. I had to leave. This happened only once during my nine years of fieldwork, but the experience made me appreciate all the more those who opened their doors to me. When I photograph or videotape, I have been cautious not to include sponsors. When sponsors request copies of my recordings, I have always obliged them.

During my fieldwork, I have adopted the manner of participant observer.¹⁰ When asked, I played cymbals during the ritual. I received *kongsu* (message from the spirit) and drank ritual wine when offered. I sometimes folded the ritual clothing. I often attended rituals without notepad, tape recorder, or video camera until the *kangshinmu* (spirit-possessed *mudang*) felt comfortable. Several *kangshinmu* even asked me why I was not taking any pictures or videos like others. The extra time and effort that I spent to get to know *kangshinmu* has earned their trust and resulted in many friendships.

When I first began my fieldwork, I turned for advice to other scholars involved in *musok* research, hoping to get a lead in locating some musically outstanding shamans. Their responses were always discouraging. They told me that there was no music, only loud cacophony in any *kut* held by Seoul-area *kangshinmu*. Several scholars advised me that I should consider studying *kut* in the *sesŭpmu* (hereditary *mudang*) tradition like the *ssikkim kut* in Chindo Island because their *kut* are filled with wonderful music. They asserted that there could hardly be anything musically interesting for an ethnomusicologist in the *kangshinmu kut*. Since I, too, remembered the *kut* with its deafening sound of cymbals and drums from my childhood, I was troubled.

But one day in 1993 I met Professor Kim T'aegon (1936–1996), a well-known Korean folklorist and scholar of Korean *musok*, who had collected *muga* (texts of shaman songs) for nearly three decades. He encouraged me to explore *muak* (ritual music of *musok*) for he, too, was interested in the *kangshinmu* ritual music. One day he invited me to the Kuksadang¹¹ ritual hall to introduce some musicians to me. The Kuksadang is located on top of Mt. Inwang in the

---

⁹ Pohyŏn Sanshin'gak, a ritual hall (*kuttang*), is located in P'yŏngch'ang Dong, a wealthy neighborhood in Seoul, and has twelve separate ritual rooms.

¹⁰ Participant observation is a method of social research in which the researcher becomes a participant in a social activity. Participant observation is "an especially useful method where the social action being researched is deviant or covert. Participant observation can be described as a 'discovery-based approach' as well as a means of testing propositions" (Jary and Jary 1991:355).

¹¹ Kuksadang is also known as Sŏn Pawui.

northwestern part of Seoul.[12] After you reach the parking area, you must climb one hundred and thirty-six uneven steps to the Kuksadang. In the parking lot, a large information board indicates that nineteen Buddhist temples are nestled along the path to the Kuksadang. Each temple was marked on the map with names as well as the locations of public phones and rest rooms. Yet I found no information on the board for the Kuksadang itself, the largest structure situated on the mountain.

About halfway to the Kuksadang, I began to hear sounds coming down from up on the mountain. The rhythmic pattern of drums and cymbals was unclear, but the sound became louder as we approached the building. As we entered the ritual hall, I was shocked to see two *kut* simultaneously in progress side by side. The two *kut* were held for different purposes—the *chaesu kut* to bring good fortune to a family and the *naerim kut* (initiation ritual) for a young man.

We stayed inside the hall, but the instrumental music from the two ensembles was so loud that no one could converse. We exchanged *myŏngham* (business cards) with the musicians whose gestures I understood to mean that they would call me sometime and left the building, bowing to bid goodbye. There certainly were musicians at Kuksadang and I had observed two *kangshinmu* singing their songs inside the ritual hall, accompanied by their respective instrumental ensembles, including aerophones [13] like the *p'iri* (cylindrical oboe) and *hojŏk* (conical oboe). As soon as we closed the doors and left the building, the singing voices of the *kangshinmu* faded while the percussion sounds remained audible for a long time as we walked down the stairs. Had I not been inside the ritual hall, I would have agreed that there is little music, only disorganized sound in the *kangshinmu kut*.

A few days later, Mr. D called me at seven in the morning, asking if I would like to attend a *kut* that morning. I was to meet him at eight. When we met, he told me that he would not attend the *kut* with me but had arranged it so that I would be welcome at the ritual. He was one of the musicians that I had met at Kuksadang with Professor Kim T'aegon. Mr. D told me that he had made this arrangement because he knew I was interested in ritual music. He wanted me to meet "first-rate musicians" (*cheil kanŭn chaebidŭl*) at this *kut*, saying humbly that he himself was a musician of modest skill. He emphasized that I should get to know Mr. Kim Chŏm-Sŏk, one of the outstanding *chaebi* (ritual musicians) of the Hanyang *kut*.

---

[12] Since I do not own a car in Korea, I am often given rides by two neighbors who seem to know every corner of Seoul. Neither neighbor, one of whom has been a taxi driver in Seoul for nearly two decades, knew where Kuksadang was located. It was amazing to me that I had to show the way to Kuksadang to both neighbors, as well as to other taxi drivers in the city.

[13] Aerophones are wind instruments.

As we were chatting, a car pulled up. Mr. D talked to the people inside the car and told me to get into the backseat. The car drove away immediately and I rode with one shaman and two musicians. One of the musicians was Mr. Kim Chŏm-Sŏk who from that day willingly became my principal informant on ritual music of the Hanyang *kut*.

Although no one explained to me where we were going or what type of ritual I was going to attend, I found out later that we were there to celebrate Mr. E's sixth anniversary as a shaman. The shaman who had driven us there began the *kut* with *pujŏng kŏri* by singing while accompanying himself on the *changgu*, the hourglass-shaped drum. Four musicians began to play with him and I was impressed with their music. After the *pujŏng kŏri*, I was told to go to another place with the musicians. We walked about five minutes to reach another private home of Mr. E. I then realized that the first home was his *shindang* (shrine room) and the second one was his family residence which was much larger and elegant. When we arrived there, I noticed that a man was reciting prayers seated in front of the altar, accompanying himself on the *changgu* (hourglass-shaped drum) and *ching* (large gong).[14] A huge breakfast was offered to the musicians and me. Two female *kangshinmu* joined and the *kut* continued after breakfast. All the shamans and instrumentalists were good musicians and it was indeed a great experience for me to listen to the ritual music in sacred context all day long.

Since then I have attended many *kut*. I found each ritual to be a unique experience because rituals are presented with many variations. Looking back on my days in the field, several rituals stand out in my memory. One ritual I attended in March 1994 was unusual because Mrs. Kang was the sole *kangshinmu* at her *chinjŏk kut*.[15] The ritual was filled with the music of *samhyŏn yukkak*, an ensemble of six musicians[16] (see CD tracks 6–9).[17] She did not sing any songs, but simply danced all day to the accompaniment of the instrumental music, giving *kongsu* (messages from spirits) to her clients from time to time. She changed into the appropriate ritual costumes to honor the specific spirits and

---

[14] The shaman did a *tokkyŏng* (recitation) while playing one head (*kung p'yŏn*) of the *changgu* (drum) with a *pangmangi* (wooden stick) held in his right hand and playing the *ching* (gong) placed on the floor with *ching ch'ae* (wooden stick wrapped with cloth at one end) held in his left hand.

[15] Most *chinjŏk kut* (rituals sponsored by *kangshinmu*) are usually performed with at least three *kangshinmu*.

[16] The musicians in a *samhyŏn yukkak* ensemble usually play two *p'iri* (bamboo oboes), *haegŭm* (two-string fiddle), *taegŭm* (transverse bamboo flute), *changgu* (hourglass-shaped drum), and *puk* (double-headed barrel drum). On this occasion, *ajaeng* (bowed zither) was played instead of *haegŭm*. The two musicians playing *p'iri* also played *hojŏk* (conical oboes) (see CD tracks 26–27).

[17] See also appendix B for more information about the accompanying compact disc.

danced at the Kuksadang ritual hall. She is one of the *chŏnnae*[18] *kangshinmu* who specialize in divination.

Another unforgettable ritual filled with wonderful music was a Seoul *Saenam Kut* held in March 1994 for a *kangshinmu* who passed away in her eighties. I received a phone call from Mr. Kim Chŏm-Sŏk who had kindly obtained permission for me to attend this *kut*, saying that I should experience this ritual, even though he was not going to be there. Apparently the *tangju* (the *kangshinmu* responsible for organizing the ritual) had asked for my birth date before she agreed that I might attend. When I climbed to the Kuksadang ritual hall about ten in the morning, more than twenty people with cameras and video camcorders were already there. Crews with much equipment from various TV stations were also there. People were quick to tell me that no one would be admitted to the ritual hall, but they were going to wait because part of the ritual would be held outdoors later. I did not know what to do but wait. Within about ten minutes, a woman appeared and whispered to me to follow her.

When we entered the ritual hall, I was given a place where I could comfortably videotape the entire ritual. No other outsiders were allowed in. The ritual hall was packed with family and *kangshinmu* who had come to pay their respects to their departed friend. Since I had never seen the Seoul *Saenam Kut* before, I decided to videotape the entire ritual. The ritual began, but more *kangshinmu* were still coming in. The shamans—Pak Chong-Bok, Chu Pok-Hŭi, and Yi Sang-Sun—and instrumentalists—Kim Chŏng-Gil, Pak Yŏng-Bong, and a musician F who wished to remain anonymous—were all fine musicians. There were songs I had never heard before.[19] The splendid ritual costume of Pari Kongju was impressive. About seven in the evening, another offering table was set on the ground outside. When I went outside the ritual hall, I was surprised to see people still waiting. I later learned that these professional photographers and videographers had known the importance of this ritual. Despite the fact that they were not admitted to the ritual hall, they were treated well with food and drinks as at any other *kut*. When it began to get dark, I was ready to put my camera away since my video camera did not have a light attachment. Suddenly a man I had noticed before at other rituals grabbed my camera and began to tape, saying something about how precious this ritual was. He closely followed the shamans and family members in their ritual circumambulation around the table. The musicians came outside and played in the dark. The ritual was splendid and the music truly moving.[20]

The ritual was still going at eleven in the evening when my friend came to pick me up. I got my camera back and began to go down the mountain. On the way several people from different TV stations offered to buy the tape I had

---

[18] *Chŏnnae* are those who devote themselves to divination and small-scale rituals.

[19] I later learned that one of the songs was called "*Chungdi Patsan*."

[20] I later gave a copy of the music to the man who had recorded it with my video camera.

made inside the ritual hall. Perhaps I was the last one to record the shaman Pak Chong-Bok singing *Pari Kongju* in a sacred context (see CD track 33).

Later, the Seoul *Saenam Kut* was staged for public performance in September 1994 at the Seoul Nori Madang with Pak Chong-Bok, Kim Sang-Sŏl, and Han Pu-Jŏn and at the Kyŏngbok Palace in 1995 by a different group of shamans. The performance of the latter group, carried out by Kim Yu-Gam, Han Pu-Jŏn, Yi Sang-Sun, and Kang Yun-Gwŏn, was discovered by Cho Hŭng-Yun and Kim Sŏn-P'ung [21] who recommended that the Seoul *Saenam Kut* be considered as an Important Intangible Cultural Property. Music for both performances of Seoul *Saenam Kut* (1994 and 1995) were provided by the same three musicians—Kim Chŏm-Sŏk, Kim Chŏng-Gil, and Hŏ Yong-Ŏp—who were recommended by Cho and Kim to be considered as the members of the *poyu tanch'e* (designated group) for Seoul *Saenam Kut*. In 1996, the government designated the Seoul *Saenam Kut* as Important Intangible Cultural Property number 104. Since then the Seoul *Saenam Kut* has been performed annually on a public stage.

In the research report, Kim Sŏn-P'ung states the fact that Yi Sang-Sun is the only *kangshinmu* who can sing the ritual song *Chungdi Patsan* (1995:55). Since I had enjoyed listening to Yi Sang-Sun sing *Chungdi Patsan* at a ritual in March 1994, I wished to work with her but had to wait for several years until she was willing (see CD tracks 30–32). It was in May of 1998 when she asked for me and suggested working together. When I asked why it took so long for her to call, she told me because "now is the right time." She became my main informant on the rituals while Kim Chŏm-Sŏk continued to be my principal informant on the ritual music of the Hanyang *kut*. Both Yi Sang-Sun and Kim Chŏm-Sŏk were appointed by the government in 1996 as *chŏnsu kyoyuk pojoja*, responsible for the education and transmission of the Seoul *Saenam Kut*. I feel fortunate that I was able to work with Yi and Kim who are both honored by the government for their ritual skills and knowledge of the Seoul *Saenam Kut*, a type of Hanyang *kut* (see chapter 10).

I have met many *kangshinmu* but I keep in touch with about one hundred *kangshinmu* and twenty musicians in the greater Seoul area. Over the years, I have been able to watch several neophyte *kangshinmu* become respected ritual specialists in the community, while some instrumentalists have become better musicians. It is interesting also to observe how in-groups among *kangshinmu* and musicians are created and sustain or fail and how the rituals and *musok* practices change in tune with the modernizing world. It was sad to lose several well known *kangshinmu* to the other world and to observe a few becoming too ill or frail to perform any longer.

---

[21] Cho Hŭng-Yun and Kim Sŏn-P'ung were the government-appointed official and consultant (*munhwajae wiwŏn* and *munhwajae chŏnmun wiwŏn*), respectively.

Despite the fact that I was confused and frightened at the beginning of my research, I am no longer afraid of spirit-possessed *kangshinmu* or *musok*. If I can persuade a few through this work to tolerate *musok* without fear and prejudice, I will consider myself fortunate. This report of my quest offers the findings that I am able to share without revealing things considered secret by those who opened their hearts and taught me.

CHAPTER 2

Korean Religious Practices

Let me begin with a brief introduction to Korea, its history, its foundation myth, and its religions in order to provide a context for our discussion of *musok*, the Korean indigenous religion.

1. Korea

The Korean peninsula is often referred to as the "Land of the Morning Calm"[1] or the "Land of Bright Morning" in the poetic rendition of the word "Chosŏn" from the Chosŏn Dynasty (1392–1910).[2] "Korea" (or "Corea") and "Coreé" are attempted transliterations into English and French, respectively, of the word "Koryŏ" referring to the Koryŏ Dynasty (918–1392).[3] Throughout Korean history, the peninsula has been at times overrun by neighboring peoples—Mongols, Manchus, Russians, Chinese, and Japanese. Thus Korea has long attempted to isolate itself from contact with other nations. In the early 1800s Korea was known in the West as the "Hermit Kingdom" as a result of failed attempts by America and several European nations to open trade or

---

[1] The term "Land of Morning Calm" first appeared in 1885 in *Chosŏn* by Percival Lowell (Pratt and Rutt 1999:232).

[2] "Chosŏn" is written as 朝鮮 in Sino-Korean ideographs. The etymology of the name Chosŏn, according to *Shih Chih So-Yin* [Hidden meanings to the *Historical Records* explained] written by Ssu-ma about 720, is as follows: the Chinese ideograph *"cho"* (morning) in "Chosŏn" is pronounced the same way in Chinese as the one for "tide," and the graph *"sŏn"* (fresh) is pronounced the same way as the one for "a river teeming with fish." Thus "Korea was named 'Chosŏn' because it has waters teeming with fish" (Lee, P. 1996:236).

[3] Koryŏ is written as 高麗 in Sino-Korean ideographs.

diplomatic relations (Coleman 1997:29). China held Korea as a tributary state for centuries, finally relinquishing her power to Japanese forces who won the Sino-Japanese War (1894–1895). Japan, defeating Russia in the Russo-Japanese War (1904–1905), made Korea her protectorate on November 17, 1905, and ruled Korea from 1910 to 1945. Liberated from Japan after World War II, Korea was divided into two nation states—the Republic of Korea (South Korea) and the Democratic People's Republic of Korea (North Korea). Their official Korean names are Taehan Min'guk (South Korea) and Chosŏn Minjujuŭi Inmin Konghwaguk (North Korea). Their capitals are Seoul and P'yŏngyang, respectively.

In spite of a five thousand year history of ethnic homogeneity, the two nations were separated at the 38th parallel, torn apart by political ideology. Neither government has allowed its people to cross the border or to communicate beyond the boundary since 1945, forcing many families, relatives, and friends to remain in mutual isolation.[4] About 45.9 million people lived in South Korea (38,452 sq. miles) in 1997 and 22.4 million people in North Korea (46,814 sq. miles) in 1996 (Korean Overseas Cultural Information Service 1998:11).

Nowadays Koreans live not only on the Korean peninsula but also in more than 90 nations on all six inhabited continents—Asia, Africa, Australia, Europe, North America, and South America.[5] In 1993 the number of Koreans living outside the Korean peninsula exceeded five million, equal to about 8.3 percent of the total population of the Korean peninsula, according to Lee Kwang-Kyu (1993:7). For the purposes of this work, I will focus on Koreans living in South Korea and in the United States of America.

---

[4] During the Korean War (1950–1953) many Koreans migrated from the North to the South, including many *musok* ritual specialists and musicians who settled in Seoul or in Inch'ŏn, a harbor city on the midwestern coast. Through the years, several attempts have been made to establish communication between separated family members living in the North and the South by international organizations including the Red Cross. A few family members have met in China or the United States, but most have not been so fortunate. The first summit meeting between the two leaders, Kim Dae-Jung of South Korea and Kim Chŏng-Il of North Korea, took place in P'yŏngyang, the capital of North Korea, in June 2000.

[5] In 1901 the government introduced a policy of emigration for Koreans. As severe drought and famine had struck the nation, the emigration law allowed Koreans to leave the country for economic reasons (Lyu 1977:33).

2. The Creation Myth of Korea

The Tan'gun creation myth has long been a part of the Korean heritage. It is said that many years ago, the heavenly God Hwan In granted his son Hwan Ung's wish to live among men. Hwan Ung descended from heaven with three thousand followers along with the Earl of Wind and the Masters of Rain and Clouds.

Peter Lee translates a version of this myth, which appears as a passage in the *Samguk Yusa* (*Memorabilia of the Three Kingdoms*)[6] written by the Buddhist Monk Iryŏn (1206–1289)[7] during the reign of King Ch'ungnyŏl (1274–1308) of the Koryŏ Dynasty (918–1392), as follows:

> At that time a bear and a tiger who were living in the same cave prayed to Hwanung to transform them into human beings. The king gave them a bundle of sacred mugwort and twenty cloves of garlic and said, "If you eat these and shun the sunlight for one hundred days, you will assume human forms." Both animals ate the herbs and avoided the sun. After twenty-one days the bear became a woman, but the tiger, unable to observe the taboo, remained a tiger. Unable to find a husband, the bear-woman prayed under the sandalwood tree for a child. Hwanung metamorphosed himself, lay with her, and begot a son called Tan'gun Wanggom. (Lee, P. 1981:4)

The content of the foundation myth—the Tan'gun legend—as described above is illustrated on stone slabs in the Wu family shrine built in 147 C.E. in Chia-hsiang hsien, Shantung, China (Lee, P. 1993:5).

Tan'gun,[8] the legendary founder of Korea, is said to have ruled Korea from 2333 B.C.E. Since the traditional calendar, *tan'gi*, begins from that year, the year 2000 C.E. is the year 4333 according to *tan'gi*. Koreans use both the Gregorian calendar and *tan'gi* in their daily lives, even though the *tan'gi* was officially replaced by the Western calendar in 1962.[9] The term *"tan'gi"* (檀紀) is

---

[6] *Samguk Yusa* is referred to as "Memorabilia of the Three Kingdoms" by Peter Lee (1981), as "Remnants of the Three Kingdoms" by Boudewijn Walraven (1994), and as "Legends and History of the Three Kingdoms of Ancient Korea" by Ha T.H. and C.K. Mintz (Iryŏn 1972).

[7] Iryŏn [Il-Yŏn, 一然]'s birth name was Kim Kyŏn-Myŏng.

[8] Tan'gun in *Samguk Yusa* was expressed as 壇君 but later changed to 檀君 (Yi [1959] 1977:33).

[9] *Tan'gi* was accepted as the official calendar by Law No. 4 in 1948 during the First Republic, but Law No. 775 during the Second Republic designated the Western calendar as official beginning on January 1, 1962 (*Kwanbo* [Government gazette] no. 3014, 1 December 1961, cited by Kang Tong-Gu [1998:121]).

made up of two words: *tan* (檀) from Tan'gun (檀君) and *gi* (紀 calendar). The Gregorian calendar is called *sŏgi* (西紀), meaning a calendar from the West (西).

According to legend, Tan'gun ruled Tan'gun Chosŏn[10] for fifteen hundred years from 2333 B.C.E. and became a mountain spirit upon reaching 1,908 years of age. Tan'gun, the first politico-religious leader of Korea, is hailed as the mythical founder of *musok*, the indigenous religion of Korea, and is considered the first Korean *mudang* (ritual specialist). In 1948 the Korean government designated October the 3rd as *Kaech'ŏnjŏl* (literally, the "Day of Heaven's Opening"), a public holiday acknowledging Tan'gun as the founder of Korea, who, it is said, opened the Gate of Heaven to descend to Mt. Paekdu in order to establish the nation.

3. Religious Practices Among Koreans

From early times, Koreans have celebrated harvest festivals to give thanks to heaven for plentiful crops. With agriculture as their economic basis, they have believed in the supernatural powers of nature. They have prayed for good crops in the spring after the planting, for rain and good weather for all seasons, and thanked heaven in the fall with offerings of food, drink, music, and dance.

For example, the *yŏnggo* (literally, "spirit-invoking drums," here referring to a festival) of Puyŏ state (18 B.C.E.–660), held in the twelfth lunar month, as well as *tongmaeng* (worship of Chumong, the founder of Koguryŏ) of Koguryŏ (37 B.C.E.–668) and *much'ŏn* (literally, "dance to heaven") of the Eastern Ye, both held in the tenth lunar month, were harvest festivals. Two celebrations in Samhan (the three Han states),[11] which took place in the fifth lunar month after seed had been sown and in the tenth lunar month as a thanksgiving festival, were religious observances (Lee K.B. 1984:33).

During the Samhan period, religious festivals were led by ritual masters known as *ch'ŏn'gun* (Heavenly Prince or Master of Heaven). It is believed that religious and political functions were one in early Korea as the leaders were known as *kŏsŏgan*, *ch'ach'aung*, and *isagŭm*, meaning "chief," "shaman," and "successor prince," respectively (Lee K.B. 1984:29). As Daniel Kister tells us, "king and shaman were one" during the period when Buddhism and Confucianism first appeared in Korea (1997:3). Through the years, religious services were gradually entrusted to ritual masters by the ruling class who enjoyed secular and political powers.

---

[10] Tan'gun Chosŏn is different from the Chosŏn Dynasty founded in 1392 by Yi Sŏng-Gye.

[11] Samhan refers to Mahan, Chinhan, and Pyŏnhan of the Korean confederated kingdoms period about the 1st to 3rd centuries (Lee K.B. 1984:24–25).

Confucianism, Buddhism, and Taoism came to Korea during the Three Kingdoms (Koguryŏ, Paekche, and Shilla) period. The Three Kingdoms period began in the first century B.C.E. and ended in 668 when Shilla united the three kingdoms and began to govern the Korean peninsula as one nation for the first time under the name Unified Shilla. See Figure 1 for the dates of the individual kingdoms.

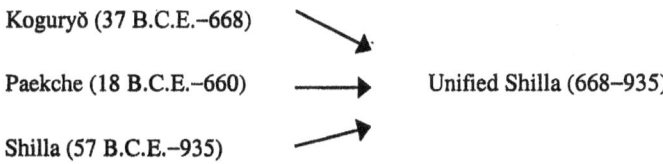

Figure 1. The Three Kingdom Periods

Buddhism imported during the Three Kingdoms period seems to have been influenced by *musok* (indigenous religion), which regards *kukt'ae minan* (peace for the nation and its people) as important. Consequently the Mahayana belief merged with autochthonous *musok* forming the unique *hoguk pulgyo* ("state-protection Buddhism") that was thereafter to characterize Korean Buddhism (Kim Y.H. 1993:2–3). As Lee Ki-Baik explains:

[T]he aspect of Buddhism as a doctrine for the protection of the state was a powerful attraction of that faith in the Three Kingdom period. Buddhism of course also was a vehicle for seeking the well-being of the individual, for example through prayers for recovery from illness or for having children, but its practice as a faith assuring the well-being of the state is still more strongly in evidence. (Lee K.B. 1984:60)

The ruling classes have influenced the religious practice of the common people throughout history. During the Shilla period, the *p'algwanhoe* (Festival of the Eight Vows) sought national peace; the *yŏndŭnghoe* (literally, Lotus Lantern Festival),[12] introduced during Koryŏ, sought the blessings of Buddha; and the *narye* (annual exorcism of the court)[13] was instituted in early Koryŏ and influenced by Chinese models (Pihl 1994:18). During the Koryŏ Dynasty (918–

---

[12] *Yŏndŭnghoe*, a Buddhist occasion, was held on the fifteenth day of the first month. It involved music, dance, and processions with lighted lanterns (Pratt and Rutt 1999:529).

[13] *Narye*, instituted in the early Koryŏ period and influenced by Chinese models, served as the annual exorcism of the court (Heyman 1993:19).

1392), Buddhism and Taoism[14] were encouraged by the court, but both were officially banned during the Chosŏn Dynasty (1392–1910) because the ruling classes of Chosŏn embraced Confucianism and Neo-Confucianism as the state ideology.

When Japan ruled the Korean nation (1910–1945), Koreans were forced to practice Japanese Shintoism, for instance, by participating in the *shinsa ch'ambae* (attending services at Shinto shrines). In order to clear land to build a Shinto shrine, the Japanese government moved Kuksadang, the ritual hall built by the first King T'aejo of the Chosŏn Dynasty, from Mokmyŏk Mountain (present-day Namsan, the South Mountain) to Inwang Mountain in July 1925 (Yi C.G. 1996:202).

When the country gained independence from Japan in 1945 at the end of World War II, Korea was divided into two nation states, as mentioned earlier. Under the influence of communism, religious activities in North Korea were restricted, but the South Korean people were free to practice the religion of their choice, resulting in religious pluralism. In addition to indigenous religions (Musok, Ch'ŏndogyo,[15] Chŭngsan'gyo, Hanŏlgyo, Taejonggyo, T'ongilgyo, Wŏn Pulgyo [16]) and imported ones (Christianity, Buddhism, Taoism, Confucianism, Islam), more than 240 religious movements sprang up throughout South Korea in the 20th century (Korean Overseas Cultural and Information Service 1998:172).

Despite the fact that a 1995 survey indicated that religious adherents in South Korea numbered 22.78 million, 51.1% of the nation's total population (Yun S.Y. 1997:9), it has been difficult to obtain an accurate number of practitioners of each religion existing in Korea because, as Homer B. Hulbert[17] observed:

> As a general thing, we may say that the all-round Korean will be a Confucianist when in society, a Buddhist when he philosophises and a spirit-

---

[14] In the seventh century, as part of diplomatic relations with T'ang China, the Koguryŏ (37 B.C.E. to 668) government adopted the use of T'ang state rituals (Chinese *chiao*) for the protection of the royal family and the state. Religious Taoism remained the official state ideology during the Koryŏ period (918–1392).

[15] Ch'ŏndogyo was founded by Ch'oe Che-U (1824–1864) as Tonghak in 1860 (Kim C.S. 1993:224).

[16] New religions were founded by Korean religious leaders, for example, Chŭngsan'gyo in 1901, Taejonggyo in 1909, Wŏn Pulgyo in 1916, T'ongilgyo in 1945, and Hanŏlgyo in 1965.

[17] Hulbert was an American missionary educator who lived in Korea for twenty-one years between 1886 and 1907 and died in Seoul during a visit in 1949. He was "buried in the Seoul Foreign Cemetery in Hap Chung Dong, where his epitaph, spoken by himself, is 'I would rather be buried in Korea than in Westminster Abbey'" (Paik L.G. 1969:4).

worshipper when he is in trouble. Now, if you want to know what a man's religion is, you must watch him when he is in trouble. Then his genuine religion will come out, if he has any. It is for this reason that I conclude that the underlying religion of the Korean, the foundation upon which all else is mere superstructure, is his original spirit-worship. ([1906] 1969:403-404)

4. *Musok*

In *musok* (indigenous religion of Korea), various myths are aurally transmitted through *muga* (ritual songs) sung or narrated by *mudang* (ritual specialists). *Musok* believers observe calendrical rituals as well as crisis rituals to maintain harmonious order in their lives. Koreans believe that Samshin (literally, three spirits)—Hwan In, Hwan Ung, and Tan'gun—are the most important spirits. Hwan In is worshipped as the supreme God, the creator, and referred to as Hananim (literally, the Only God), Hanŭnim or Ch'ŏn-Shin (both meaning Heavenly God),[18] Okhwang Sangje (Jade Emperor of Heaven), or Chesŏk Nim.[19]

In addition to Hananim, a pantheon of gods[20] of nature, spirits, Buddhas, Taoist saints, historical heroes, and deified ancestors are worshipped. The pantheon worshipped by *shimbang* (*musok* ritual specialists) on Cheju Island consists of more than 18,000 spirits (Ch'oe C.S. 1996:43). The spirits worshipped in contemporary *musok* include those from Taoist and Buddhist

---

[18] The name *Hananim* in Korean may be interpreted as "Hana (One) Nim (honorific), or as Han-Al (One Egg) Nim, or Han-Wul (One World) Nim, or Hanul (Sky) Nim. In the old historical records it was read as Han-In [Hwan In] and interpreted as Hwan (Bright) Nim" (Zozayong 1982:44). Zozayong [Cho Cha-Ryong] also states that *Ch'ŏn-Shin* is a Confucian expression. *Ch'ŏn* (heaven) is mentioned throughout the classical Confucian book *Sŏkyŏng*. *Ch'ŏn-Shin* is of Chinese origin and equivalent to the Korean term *Hananim* (ibid.).

[19] The term "Okhwang Sangje" (Jade Emperor of Heaven) comes from Taoism while "Chesŏk" comes from Hinduism. "The Hindu Indra-Vanin merged with the Korean Whan-In, causing a great deal of confusion in Korea. Ilyŏn, the author of the book *Samguk-Yusa*, stated in a footnote that Hwan-In is the same as Vanin, calling him Chesŏk. He used the Hindu-related term Chesŏk instead of the Confucian term Ch'ŏn-shin or the Taoist term Okhwang Sangje to express the Korean concept of Hananim" (Zozayong 1982:44-45).

[20] The term "gods" is defined by William Paden, a scholar in the comparative study of religion, as a "thematic label to include any beings that humans engage in a religious manner: buddhas, ancestors, spirits, gurus, as well as what we in the West usually think of as gods" (1994:9).

traditions: Okhwang Sangje, Ch'ilsŏng (Seven Star Spirits), and Obang Shinjang (Protector of Five Directions) from Taoism, and Buddhas and Boddhisattvas from Buddhism. Deified ancestors include Korean kings, queens, and war heroes, as well as Chinese scholars and war heroes.[21]

Many scholars have attempted to understand the world of spirits through years of research, but no completely satisfactory conclusions have been reached to date. For example, the late Kim T'aegon who did extensive fieldwork among Korean shamans, identified 273 gods and spirits worshipped in *musok*. He grouped these gods and spirits into two classes—nature spirits and ancestor spirits—subdividing the former into twenty-two and the latter into eleven types of spirits (Kim 1991:285; Kim, ed. 1991:55). Several scholars have classified spirits in a hierarchy according to their roles. Yang Jongsung [Yang Chong-Sŭng], a folklorist who has studied rituals of the *kangshinmu* (spirit-possessed *mudang*) and *sesŭpmu* (hereditary *mudang*) traditions,[22] asserts that it is not correct for scholars to consider spirits in terms of a hierarchy, because they simply coexist, each carrying out his own responsibility without cooperating or interfering with others (1999b:16). For example, various spirits are known to have powers to protect families (San Manura and Kunung), prevent misfortunes (Pyŏlsang and Hogu), grant wishes for wealth (Taegam), long life (Chesŏk), and peace (Sŏngju) (Ryu T.S. 1989:318).[23]

The ways *kangshinmu* worship their spirits are varied, as suggested by the saying, "*Sŏngsubon ŭn hanbon iyo chejabon ŭn kakbon ida*" (Spirits have one way of being worshipped, but each *kangshinmu* has their own way of worshipping). No two *kangshinmu* have an identical number of *momju* (body-governing spirits) nor are they spirit-possessed by the same spirits in the same order. These are the main reasons why a clear picture of the entire pantheon of spirits in *musok* is not available.

Kim, a spirit-possessed shaman, told me that *kangshinmu*, however, generally divide spirits into three groups: *chŏngshin*, the spirits regularly venerated through rituals; *chosang*, family ancestors including those who died young; and *chapkwi* or *chapshin*, low miscellaneous spirits (personal communication, 1994). All three types of spirits are treated with respect during the rituals. They will each be discussed in detail later.

---

[21] In recent years, some shamans are possessed by the American General Douglas MacArthur (Howard 1998a:12). Koreans admire General MacArthur, who helped South Koreans by successfully launching the invasion at Inch'ŏn on September 15, 1950, during the Korean War.

[22] Yang studied under *sesŭpmu* from 1967 through 1970 and under *kangshinmu* of Hwanghae province from 1976 to 1982 (1999b:9).

[23] This makes me think about patron saints in Catholic faith. For example, St. Cecilia for musicians; St. Christopher for travelers; St. Thomas Aquinas for students; and St. Gregory the Great for teachers.

Musok believers gather and pray with shamans [24] and at rituals for supplication and benediction while observing various taboos in their daily lives. In *musok*, there are no written guidelines such as the Ten Commandments of Christianity[25] or the Eight-fold Path of Buddhism.[26]

Through the years, *musok* has managed to select, transform, and adapt concepts and practices from other major religious traditions. The guidelines for *musok* believers are greatly influenced by *samgang oryun*, a traditional Confucian concept deeply rooted among Koreans as the principle for human relationships. As Martina Deuchler explains, *samgang* (three cardinal human relationships)—the relationships between ruler and subject, father and son, and husband and wife—provided human society with a fundamental and unchangeable structure (1980:82–83).

> They [the three relationships] were reinforced by the moral imperatives (*illyun* or *oryun*) that guided interpersonal relationships: righteousness (*ŭi*) between sovereign and subject; proper rapport (*ch'in*) between father and son; separation of functions (*pyŏl*) between husband and wife; sequence of birth (*sŏ*) between elder and younger brothers; and faithfulness (*sin*) between senior and junior. (Deuchler 1980:82–83)

---

[24] *Musok* believers gather at their shamans' places at least once a month on the first day of each lunar month. Some visit twice a month, on the first and fifteenth days.

[25] The first four of the Ten Commandments according to Exodus 20 in the Old Testament are concerned with the relationship between people and God; the remaining six with people, families, and neighbors. The commandments are as follows: "[1] You shall have no other gods before me. [2] You shall not make for yourself an idol in the form of anything in heaven above or on the earth beneath or in the waters below. . . . [3] You shall not misuse the name of the Lord your God, for the Lord will not hold anyone guiltless who misuses his name. [4] Remember the Sabbath day by keeping it holy. . . . [5] Honor your father and your mother, so that you may live long in the land the Lord your God is giving you. [6] You shall not murder. [7] You shall not commit adultery. [8] You shall not steal. [9] You shall not give false testimony against your neighbor. [10] You shall not covet your neighbor's house . . . or anything that belongs to your neighbor" (New International Version 1997:112–3).

[26] In the *Mahaparinirvana Sutra* and in many other sutras, the Buddha described the path to Nirvana as three higher trainings—ethics, concentration, and wisdom. He also enumerated the noble eightfold path, which can be subsumed in the three higher trainings: correct action, correct speech, and correct livelihood for higher training in ethics; correct effort, correct mindfulness, and correct concentration for higher training in concentration; correct view and correct realization for higher training in wisdom (Chodron 1992:60–61).

One may hear these principles for relationships in many shaman songs, as in the following passage, wishing the best for a child:

Nara enŭn ch'ungshindongi,
  Be a faithful servant to the country,
Pumo enŭn hyojadongi,
  Be a filial child to your parents,
Iut enŭn hwamokdongi.
  Be a friendly person with your neighbors.

In addition to maintaining harmonious relationships with people, *musok* believers are encouraged to make every effort to maintain good relationships with nature and the spirits. Reciprocity is a central concept in *musok*—they believe that if one is good to nature and the spirits, they in turn will be good to humans. Caring relationships among humans, including the unborn and the departed, are considered essential to keep life harmonious in this world. Among the believers, *musok* is considered a religion of striving for universal harmony. Several *kangshinmu* told me that *musok* is a religion of peace and harmony. They do not hesitate to point out the fact that *musok* has not objected to or rejected other religions, but accepted them into itself throughout Korean history.

As mentioned earlier, *musok* interprets an imbalance of *samjae* (heaven, earth, and humans) as the cause of illness and misfortune in life. I was told by one of my informants that the spirit-possessed shamans believe heaven to be filled with spirits and earth with ancestor souls. If spirits or ancestor souls are angry about something, they will let humans know by causing sickness, conflicts in the family, or financial difficulties. When this happens, the *kangshinmu* attempts to mediate and restore peace by inviting and entertaining the spirits and ancestor souls during a ritual with offerings to please them, asking forgiveness on behalf of the afflicted clients.

5. *Mudang*, Ritual Specialist

The most commonly accepted term for a ritual specialist in *musok* is *mudang*. There are several hypotheses concerning the etymology of *mudang*.[27]

---

[27] As an example of early Western writings, I would like to quote Hulbert, an American missionary educator and linguist who stated that "[t]he word *mudang* means 'deceiving crowd,' and *p'ansu* means 'decider of destiny.' The former name is specially appropriate" (Hulbert [1906] 1969:413). Since Hulbert did not provide any reference, I assume that he misunderstood both terms, *mudang* and *p'ansu*. Clark, another American, interprets *mudang* as follows: "'Moo' is the Chinese character meaning 'deceiving,' and

Chijo Akamatsu and Takashi Akiba postulated that the term *mudang* came from *ootan*, a variant of *udagan*, an Altaic word referring to a female shaman ([1938] 1991, 2:38).

Conforming to V.F. Troshchanski's theory, they thought *ootan* became *mootan* (*mudang*) when the *m* sound was added in Korea. The linguistic evidence of the widespread use of the term *udagan* (female shaman) and its variants in the Altaic languages convinced Troshchanski that shamans were originally women and that male shamans appeared later.

> Among the Mongols, Buryat, Yakut, Altaians, Torgout, Kidan, Kirgis, there is one general term for a woman-shaman, which has a slightly different form in each tribe: *utagan, udagan, udaghan, ubakhan, utygan, utiugun, iduan* (*duana*); whereas the word for man-shaman is different in each of these tribes. (Troshchanski 1902:118)

Yongsiyebu Rinchen, a Mongolian scholar, looks at the root meaning of the Mongol word *udagan*, which is built up in such a way that its morphology reveals its inner meaning. Rinchen states that "[t]he term *udagan* is made up of a root *ud-*, from the Turkic *ut* (fire), followed by *-a-* (vowel without meaning regularly added between consonants), followed by *-ga-*, a suffix meaning 'the one who does something', followed by *-n*, a suffix meaning a person or a thing. *Ud + a + ga + n* therefore means 'a person who produces fire'" (Rinchen 1977:149–150).

Korean *mudang* worship fire spirits and burn *soji* (sacred papers) during rituals as offerings to heaven or for the purification of ritual areas. Sometimes they use holy water mixed with ashes from burned sacred papers for healing and for purification.

Continuing to hypothesize regarding the development of the word *mudang* from *udagan/ootan/mootan*, it is suggested that the Chinese characters used for *ootan* (巫堂) were borrowed in earlier days by Koreans to refer to the ritual specialist. The Sino-Korean character (巫) is pronounced *wu* in Chinese, but *mu* in Korean (Ryu 1989:276). According to Mingyue Liang,

> the ancient pictograph for dance-wu (𣦏, in modern form 舞) is related to the modern ideogram for shamanness-wu (巫). The archaic pictorial element wu symbolizes a woman in dance movement wearing either a long-sleeved garment or ornaments (charms or feathers). The shaman(ness) whose job was to act as a mediator between the world of the gods and the world of man presided over religious matters such as ceremonies and sacrifices. An important

---

'tang' might be translated 'company'" (Clark [1932] 1961:184). Clark refers to two sources: (1) *Korea Review*, 1903:145 and (2) Bishop, *Korea and Her Neighbors*, [1898] 1970:409. I did not find any evidence in Bishop's book to support Clark's assertion.

qualification for a shaman(ness) was to be a competent dancer and musician. (1985:49)

Considering the etymology of *dang*, Seich Izumi has suggested that when the number of people involved in *mu* increased, the Chinese ideograph *dang* (堂) was added to the word *mu* to indicate that there are many female *mu* practitioners (Izumi 1969:57). Lee, on the other hand, interprets *dang* as "an altar or a shrine" (Lee J.Y. 1981:3). Some scholars have interpreted *dang* as "company" (Clark [1932] 1962:184) or a "place" (Yi N.H. [1927] 1991:13). It may be that *dang* was added after *mu* as an honorific.[28] Thus the term *mudang*, referring to *musok* ritual specialists, may be written with either Korean characters (무당) or with Sino-Korean ideographs (巫堂), while the meaning of *dang* is interpreted in several ways for lack of historical evidence and agreement among scholars.

Three Types of *Mudang* (Ritual Specialists)

Korean *musok* ritual specialists, generally known as *mudang*, may be broadly grouped into three types: *kangshinmu* (spirit-possessed *mudang*), *sesŭpmu* (hereditary *mudang*), and *haksŭpmu* (apprenticed *mudang*). Most Koreans and foreigners refer to *musok* ritual specialists as *mudang, manshin,* or shamans, without acknowledging the differences in their roles and capacities.

Kangshinmu (spirit-possessed *mudang*) are male or female shamans chosen by the spirits. *Sesŭpmu* (hereditary *mudang*) are mostly females who have inherited the role of *mudang* from previous generations of family members. *Haksŭpmu* (apprenticed *mudang*) are males or females who choose to become involved in *musok*.

In general, numerous *kangshinmu* reside in Seoul and north of the Han River[29] while *sesŭpmu* live either south of the Han River or in the eastern part of the Korean peninsula. *Haksŭpmu* are found throughout the country. On the island of Cheju, located in the far south, ritual specialists, both hereditary and spirit-possessed, are known as *shimbang*. It is interesting to note that male *shimbang* outnumber female *shimbang* on Cheju Island, unlike the rest of the

---

[28] According to *Kukŏ Taesajŏn*, a Korean dictionary, *dang* (堂) is used after names of buildings or pen names (Yi H.S. 1998:843). For example, Yim Yi-Hwan (1544–1610) was called Samyŏngdang (also Samyŏng Taesa), while the mother of Yulgok, a Confucian scholar, and a gifted woman of arts and letters was called Shin Saimdang (1504–1551). In everyday language, Koreans refer to someone else's mother as *chadang* to show respect.

[29] The Han River, 514 km long, flows through Seoul, providing water for irrigation and industrial use.

peninsula where the majority of *sesŭpmu* (hereditary *mudang*) are female (Ch'oe K.S. 1992, 2:257).

Korean *sesŭpmu* (hereditary *mudang*) are often mistaken for shamans. *Sesŭpmu* offer prayers and rituals to gods, spirits, and ancestors on behalf of the community, but they do not have means to communicate with them directly. They are not spirit-possessed. We may consider *sesŭpmu* as priest, following Lowie's distinction between shaman and priest.

> Whereas a shaman by definition acquires his status through a personal communication by supernatural beings, the priest need not have this face-to-face relationship with the spirit world but must have competence in conducting ritual. (Lowie 1958:413)

In other parts of the world, an individual may elect to become a shaman, for example, among the Altaic, Turkic, Tamang, and Jivaro peoples. In some cases a shaman is chosen by the will of the clan as among the Tungus and Tamang people.[30] In Korea, one may study and become a *haksŭpmu* (apprenticed *mudang*)[31] by choice. But one does not choose to become a *kangshinmu* (spirit-possessed *mudang*). *Kangshinmu* are elected by the spirits.

Haksŭpmu are also referred to as *chŏmjaengi* (diviner), *ch'ŏlhakka* (literally, philosopher), *kidae* (trained musician), *kyŏngjangi* (sutra readers), *p'ansu* (blind diviner and/or sutra readers), *pŏpsa* (sutra readers), *posal* (literally, female Buddhist), *tosa* (literally, Taoist) and so on. Except for the term *kidae*, which is reserved for musically trained *haksŭpmu*, all the others refer to *haksŭpmu* who as a rule specialize in *tokkyŏng chŏmbok* (ritual incantations/sutra reading and divination). They are known as sutra readers (*kyŏngjangi*) or diviners (*chŏmjaengi*) for their specialties, but often by a euphemism—philosopher, Taoist, Buddhist, and so on.

In order to specialize in *tokkyŏng* (reading of incantations), *haksŭpmu* must memorize many *mugyŏng* (*musok* prayers and incantations) suitable for various occasions. The texts of *mugyŏng* borrow heavily from Taoist and Buddhist scriptures. *Okch'ugyŏng*, for example, originated in the Taoist tradition, while *Pulsŏl ch'ŏnji p'alyanggyŏng* and *Pulsŏl ch'ŏnsugyŏng* are two of many prayers derived from Buddhist texts (Akamatsu and Akiba [1938] 1991, 2:240).

For ritual recitation, the *haksŭpmu* (apprenticed *mudang*) accompanies himself with a percussive musical instrument such as a *mokt'ak* (a wooden idiophone),[32] *ching* (large brass gong), *kkwaenggwari* (small brass gong), *puk*

---

[30] For discussions of Nepali and Jivaro shamans, see Maskarinec 1995 and Harner 1973, respectively.

[31] *Haksŭpmu* (apprenticed *mudang*) are also referred to as *sŭpdŭkmu* (Ryu T.S. 1989:280).

[32] *Mokt'ak* is a wooden instrument made in the shape of a fish and struck with a wooden mallet. Idiophones, according to the classification of musical instruments by Erich M.

(double-headed barrel drum), or *changgu* (hourglass-shaped drum). Sometimes a *kkwaenggwari* (small gong) is attached to the *changgu* (drum) so one *haksŭpmu* may play both instruments. At times a *ching* (large gong) is placed on the floor so that one *haksŭpmu* may play both the *ching* and *changgu*.

In addition to various *mugyŏng* (prayers and incantations), some *haksŭpmu* learn to sing ritual songs and to play *changgu* (drum) so that they may be hired for *kut* (rituals) officiated by *kangshinmu* (spirit-possessed shamans). A musician *haksŭpmu*, known as *kidae*, often stands in for a *kangshinmu* who might lack the musical skills for rituals. In contemporary Korea, however, a few professional folk singers have become *haksŭpmu*, learning *musok* ritual songs in order to present *kut* in concerts in secular contexts. Unlike *kidae*, these folk singer *haksŭpmu* are not expected to participate in rituals in sacred context. *Kut* performances by folk singers will be discussed in chapter five.

Since most *haksŭpmu* (apprenticed *mudang*) begin their careers in hope of economic gain, they actively promote their services through newspaper and magazine advertisements. They place signs outside their offices or residences to attract walk-in clients. Some have private practices in rented "office-tels"[33] in high-rise buildings and work with clients only by appointment, carrying on their activities unnoticed by neighbors. Some *haksŭpmu* indicate their business indirectly by displaying signs with the *man* symbol (卍) or signs that read *ch'ŏlhakkwan* (literally, a building for philosophy).

The *man* symbol (卍) is a swastika. "The Swastika is a cross with each of its four arms turned at a right angle, either clockwise or counterclockwise" (Sullivan 1997:223). Although the swastika with arms turned clockwise was used as a symbol for the Nazi party (and called *Hakenkreuz*—literally, hooked cross), the swastika is more widely used as an auspicious symbol in Hinduism and Buddhism. Swastika (or *Svastika*) comes from Sanskrit (su + asti + ka), meaning "marker of goodness" in many parts of the world (Sullivan 1997:223). Professor Ter Ellingson explained to me that *su* means good or well, *asti* refers to a being, and *ka* works as a modifier (personal communication, 2000).

About the *swastika*, Hans Biederman explains further that

---

von Hornbostel and Curt Sachs, are musical instruments made of solid and non-stretchable materials, played by ways of "concussion, striking, stamping, shaking, scraping, friction and plucking" (Dournon 1992:258). *Mokt'ak* is known as *muyu* in China.

[33] *Office-tel* is a "*Konglish*" (Koreanized English) word referring to a one-room apartment in a high-rise building with no separate bedroom, similar to a studio apartment in North America. As the name office-tel (office + hotel) indicates, it may be used as home and office or solely for business, but many singles and newly married couples make their homes in office-tels.

It has been documented in the pre-Aryan civilization of Mohenjo-Daro on the Indus River (ca. 2000 B.C.); in ancient China the swastika (*wan tsu*) is symbol of the four points of the compass. Since ca. A.D. 700 the Chinese have also associated it with the number 10,000, or infinity. In the Buddhist tradition of India it is referred to as the "seal on Buddha's heart"; in Tibet, too, it is associated with good fortune and serves as a talisman. (Biederman 1992:334)

The Sino-Korean ideograph for the number 10,000 is 萬 (*man*) and the term *manshin* (ritual specialist) is expressed with Sino-Korean ideographs as 萬 神 or 卍 神, where 神 (*shin*) means spirits. In general, the symbol 卍 (*man*) is used as an emblem for Buddhist temples in Korea. Borrowing from the Buddhist tradition, it is also used nowadays to indicate *musok shindang* (shrine rooms). The *man* symbol (卍) is considered an emblem of good fortune (*kilsang*) and is believed to gather *manbok subok*, great fortune and long life (Park H.J. 1999:78).

Many *haksŭpmu* have mastered the skills of divination or ritual recitation, but others are relatively untrained. Since it is difficult to verify the qualifications of *haksŭpmu*, would-be clients must rely on reputation or personal experience. In addition, some *haksŭpmu* pretend to be spirit-possessed, making it hard for the potential client to distinguish between *haksŭpmu* (apprenticed *mudang*) and *kangshinmu* (spirit-possessed *mudang*) who specialize in *tokkyŏng chŏmbok* (ritual incantations/sutra reading and divination).

During the Chosŏn Dynasty (1392–1910), when society was divided into four classes—*yangban* (elite class), *chungin* (literally, middle people), *sangin* (commoners), and *ch'ŏnmin* (base people)—*mudang* belonged to the "base people" who were engaged in eight types of work (*p'alch'ŏn* or *p'albansach'ŏn*) as listed below:

1. private slaves (*sanobi*)
2. Buddhist monks (*sŭngryŏ*)
3. butchers (*paekjŏng*)
4. shamans (*mudang*)
5. musicians (*kwangdae*)
6. funeral attendants, pallbearers (*sangyŏkkun*)
7. female entertainers (*kisaeng*)
8. artisans (*kongjang*)

Although the status of *ch'ŏnmin* (base people) was officially abolished in 1894 and, as Clark Sorensen puts it, "the category has now melted into the rest of the population" (1989:165); the concept of "low class citizen" lingers on and *mudang* are still generally looked down upon by Korean society.

After the fall of the Chosŏn Dynasty in 1910, Japan ruled Korea until 1945. During that period, Japanese rulers discouraged *musok* practice in Korea, claiming that *musok* was superstition (*mishin*). Regarding their own folk belief system as superstition, the Japanese government had issued a decree prohibiting shamanic rituals in Japan in 1873 during the Meiji Period (1868–1911) (Sasamori 1997:94). Despite the Japanese government's attempt to eradicate *musok* in Korea, it went underground and survived in seclusion for thirty-six years.

After Korea was liberated from Japan in 1945, she began to modernize, aspiring to meet the standards of the Western world. The new government frowned on anything traditional, whether political ideology or religious outlook. All calendrical rituals were banned, while traditional weddings and funeral rites were scaled down to a minimum following the government regulation known as *Kajŏng Ŭirye Chunch'ik* (Standard rules for family ceremonies) first established in 1969 but revised and reinforced in 1973 (Choi C. 1997:26).

Historical evidence attests that *musok* has been marginalized by the governing powers and the upper classes who preferred imported religions and cultures. *Musok*, however, has thrived as *min'gan shinang* (religion among people) for nearly five thousand years in Korea under varying degrees of adversity.

Under the influence of imported religions from the West, many converted Korean Christians oppose *musok* (Korean indigenous religion) practice, and *mudang* (ritual specialists of *musok*) have been ostracized and treated harshly by the general public. Although marginalized and restricted, *musok* survives in modern Korea and *mudang* (including *kangshinmu*) continue to serve the needs of the people.

Various Terms for *Mudang*, Korean Ritual Specialists

As mentioned earlier, *musok* ritual specialists are generally known as *mudang*, but various other terms are used as well. Some of the terms presented here reflect the gender, specialty, or regional background of the *mudang* while others are euphemistic. Korean ritual specialists may be referred to as: *cheja, ch'ilsŏng halmŏm, chŏnnae, hosemi, hunjang, hwarang, hwaraengi, kangshinmu, kija, kimu, kukmu, kwangdae, kyeja, kyŏk, kyŏngjangi, maenggyŏk, manshin, mu, mudang, mugyŏk, muja, munyŏ, musokin, myŏngdu, naerin mudang, namgyŏk, namnu, nangjung, naramudang, osimi, paksa, paksu, p'ansu, pŏpsa, poksa, posal, saet'ani, salman, samu, sani, sesŭpmu, shimbang, shinbang, shinjang halmŏm, shinsŏn, sŏn'ga, sŏn'gwan, sŏnmudang, sŏnp'ung, sukmu, sŭnbang, sŭsŭng, t'aeju mudang, tan'gol, tan'golle, tongja mudang, tosa, t'osaebi, yangjung, yŏmu, yŏngmae*, and so on. For each term mentioned above, a brief explanation is provided in the glossary.

As mentioned earlier, there are different types of *kangshinmu* (spirit-possessed shamans) according to their musical skills.³⁴ Not all *mudang* perform *kut* (large-scale rituals). *Ch'ilsŏng halmŏm, chŏnnae, hosemi, hunjang, kyŏngjangi, maenggyŏk, miji, myŏngdu, osimi, p'ansu, pŏpsa, poksa, posal, shinjang halmŏm, shinsŏn, t'aeju mudang,* and *tosa* do not perform *kut* (large-scale rituals), but engage mostly in small-scale rituals involving *tokkyŏng poksul* (recitation of incantation and divination). Some who claim mighty powers of direct communication with the spirits (*mubult'ongshin*) specialize only in divination.

Posal

Kangshinmu (spirit-possessed shamans) often conceal their identities by using pseudonyms. For example, *"posal"* is a Korean word for the Sanskrit term "Boddhisattva," referring to a Buddhist lay woman who strives for the enlightenment of all human beings including herself,³⁵ but *"posal"* is also used euphemistically to refer to female *kangshinmu*, making it difficult to distinguish them from women Buddhist believers.

Many *musok* believers call their *kangshinmu "posal"* in order to avoid unwanted attention from outsiders. Early in my fieldwork, I thought shamans used the term *posal* because of the many elements of Buddhism incorporated into *musok* practice, but I learned later that *posal* is not used within the circle of family, friends, and clients of well-established *musok* practitioners. Many shamans have business cards printed with names like Kim Posal or Yi Posal and their telephone numbers. Since Kim, Yi, and Pak are common family names in Korea, it is easy for *kangshinmu* to conceal their identities.

Manshin

Manshin is another term used for *kangshinmu*.³⁶ Since the word *manshin* (literally, ten thousand spirits) suggests the multiplicity of spirits worshipped in *musok*, the term *manshin* is used contemptuously by some Koreans who view

---

³⁴ Akamatsu and Akiba distinguish musician *kangshinmu* from the others by calling them *sukmu* [*sungmu*] while calling the neophytes *saeng mu* or *sŏn mudang* ([1937] 1991, 1:42–43).

³⁵ The designation used in Korea for Buddhist laywomen is *posal* ("boddhisattva") while laymen are known as *ch'ŏsa* ("householders") (Buswell 1997:115).

³⁶ *"Manshin"* is sometimes romanized as *"mansin."* *"Manshin"* is closer to pronunciation.

world religions in evolutionary terms, placing polytheism on the bottom of the religious hierarchy and monotheism on top.

In 1985, however, when the Korean government honored Kim Kŭm-Hwa, a *manshin* (spirit-possessed shaman) from Hwanghae Province, as the *poyuja*[37] (designated performer) of Important Intangible Cultural Properties number 82 *na* [b],[38] the term *manshin* began to gain more respect and recognition. *Manshin* is a preferred term for *kangshinmu* in Hwanghae Province where Kim was born. The designated performers (*poyuja*) of Important Intangible Cultural Properties are generally known as *in'gan munhwajae* ("human cultural property" or "living cultural treasure") and are greatly admired. Because Kim Kŭm-Hwa was recognized by the government as an *in'gan munhwajae*, "*manshin*" has become a synonym for "*kangshinmu*" and has come to symbolize the power of the *kangshinmu* (spirit-possessed shaman) to tame and communicate with ten thousand spirits.

In the West, several researchers have written about female *manshin* they worked with in Korea, creating the impression that *manshin* means a female *mudang*. But in fact, *manshin* refers to both female and male *kangshinmu* (spirit-possessed shamans), while excluding all male and female *sesŭpmu* (hereditary *mudang*) and *haksŭpmu* (apprenticed *mudang*).

Paksu

The male *manshin* (spirit-possessed shaman) is also referred to as *mugyŏk, paksu, paksa, mudang,* and *kangshinmu*. He is a healer, a diviner, and a keeper of shaman songs, rituals, and oral traditions. In many cultures, the ritual specialists of secret magico-religious traditions are referred to by terms indicating their special knowledge or wisdom. "*Paksu*," in Korean, also suggests this knowledge and skill. It is interesting to note that two different sets of Sino-Korean characters were assigned to *paksu*: 拍手[39] by Akamatsu and Akiba ([1938] 1991, 2:40) and 博數[40] by Yi Nŭng-Hwa ([1927] 1991:14) who postulated that "*paksu*" may have originated from either "*paksa*" or "*poksa*." Yi, however, asserted later that "*paksu*" came from "*pokpaksa*" (卜博士), the

---

[37] *Poyuja* literally means a holder or retainer. For this work, I will translate it as a designated performer of the rituals when discussing Important Intangible Cultural Properties.

[38] The Important Intangible Cultural Properties number 82 *na* [b] are *Sŏhaean Paeyŏnshin Kut* and *Taedong Kut* from Hwanghae Province in North Korea.

[39] *Paksu* expressed in Sino-Korean as 拍手 literally means "applause."

[40] *Paksu*, written in Sino Korean as 博數 (literally, "knowing numbers well," perhaps referring to divination), actually refers to a male *kangshinmu*.

term used for male *mudang* from the Shilla and Koryŏ periods ([1959] 1977:265).

In contemporary Korea, *"paksu"* (博數) means a male *kangshinmu* (spirit-possessed shaman) and *"poksa"* (卜師) means a male divination specialist. Despite the fact that the term *"paksa"* (博士) was used for male shamans in earlier days, it no longer refers to a ritual specialist but rather to a person who has earned the highest degree conferred by academia, the Doctor of Philosophy. The word *"paksa"* (博士) is also used in everyday language to compliment a person excelling in something, for example "computer *paksa*," "chess *paksa*," and so on. There is even a restaurant franchise called *"mandu paksa,"* *mandu* being a dumpling dish.

In Central Asian cultures, the *baxsi* is regarded as a man of great expertise who possesses the power of magic; he is doctor, musician, and poet. Karl Reichl postulated the following etymology:

> The most likely etymology for this word is Ancient Chinese *pak-si* (Modern Chinese *bo-shi*), "master, teacher." What is interesting about the word *baxsi* is that it has two senses in those modern Turkic languages that have preserved it. In Uzbek, Turkmen, and Karakalpak the term *baxsi* (and its phonetic variants) denotes the singer of oral epic poetry, in Karakalpak more narrowly one type of singer. In Kirghiz and Kazakh, however, *baxsi/baqsi* means "shaman, sorcerer, quack." Once again singer and shaman are associated in terminology. Although no known Uzbek *baxsi* of this century combined the art of singing with the art of healing, older singers in the 1940s still remember such a union of singer and shaman in former times. (Reichl 1992:65)

The Korean *paksu*, as healer and musician, sings while accompanying himself on the *changgu* (hourglass-shaped drum) like the *bakhshy*, the doctor and musician among the Uighur, whose "hallmark is a drum *(dap-doira)*" (Zeranska-Kominek 1992:304).

According to Troshchanski, a male shaman is called *"baksa (baksy)"* in Kirgis (Troshchanski 1902:118). Considering Korea's historical ties with neighboring countries—China, Siberia, Mongolia, and Manchuria—it is reasonable to speculate that the term *paksu* may be related to the Inner Asian terms *baxsi, baqsi, bakhshy, baksa (baksy), bagsi,* and/or *baghshi*.

Some authors, unfortunately, believe that *paksu*—spirit-possessed male shamans in Korea—are rare and that they appear to be female impersonators.

> In Korea, all shamans are women, or occasionally men dressed as women, and the Korean shaman has been called "a woman among women, a ritual expert of and for housewives." (Vitebsky 1995:33)

In Korea, at least for the last few hundred years, however, all those termed shamans are females or, if male, dressed as a female while practicing. (Paper 1997:104)

Since both Piers Vitebsky and J. Paper refer to Laurel Kendall's work, I would like to comment here on a paragraph from Kendall's *Shamans, Housewives, and Other Restless Spirits: Women in Korean Ritual Life*:

[M]ost *mansin* are women, and all *mansin* minister directly to women. The rare male shaman in Korea (*paksu mudang*) performs *kut* wearing women's clothing, down to the pantaloons that hide beneath his billowing skirt and slip. (Kendall 1987:27)

In another work, Keith Pratt and Richard Rutt state that "[t]he *mudang* dresses in the clothes of the opposite sex, often with iron ornaments," referring to another publication by Kendall[41] (Pratt and Rutt 1999:296).

It is generally believed that Korean female shamans outnumber males and that about 20% of spirit-possessed *kangshinmu* are *paksu* (male shamans) (Hogarth 1995:183). Considering the fact that there are over 90,000 registered shamans in contemporary Korea (Hogarth 1995:183),[42] we can estimate that roughly 18,000 (20% of 90,000) *paksu*—not a small number—are actively engaged in *musok*, contrary to Kendall's suggestion that male shamans are rare. I have met many *paksu* who successfully hide their *musok* related activities from outsiders while working as hoteliers, reporters, restaurateurs, pharmacists, businessmen, and office workers.

During my fieldwork in Korea, I observed many people seeking advice from male shamans as well as sponsoring *kut* (rituals) by male shamans. Pak Paksu, a male shaman in Seoul, has a reputation for catering to men exclusively, because his clients are mostly (about 95%) men engaged in politics or business. More than twenty *paksu* that I met in the Seoul area have told me that the majority of their clients are also male.

The ritual garments used by *kangshinmu* are not all "women's clothing" as implied by Kendall (1987:27). Many are male garments modeled after historic generals' and government officials' attire of the Chosŏn Dynasty. *Kangshinmu* honor spirits during the ritual by wearing the ritual garment exclusively

---

[41] Laurel Kendall, *The Life and Hard Times of a Korean Shaman* (Honolulu: University of Hawaii Press, 1988). I have not come across any iron ornaments used in the Hanyang *kut* tradition.

[42] There are about 90,000 *kangshinmu* registered with three officially recognized societies of shamans—Taehan Sŭnggong Kyŏngshin Yŏnhaphoe, Han'guk Musok Ch'ong Yŏnhaphoe, and Taehan Pulgyo (Hogarth 1995:183).

associated with them. It is important to note that the majority of the spirits invited during a ritual are male spirits.

Male shamans (*paksu*) always wear ordinary men's *hanbok* (traditional clothing) while performing the first and last *kŏri* (sections) of Seoul *kut* (see plate 3).

Since most of the spirits summoned by shamans during the rituals are male, the shaman puts on ritual garments designed to represent these male spirits during the subsequent *kŏri* (see plates 4 and 5). However, when the *paksu* calls a specific female spirit, he adds women's attire appropriate for the specific role, always retaining his own male clothing underneath the ritual garments. For example, to guide the souls of the departed when possessed by the spirit of Pari Kongju (Princess Pari), the *paksu* adds the formal dress of a princess over his male clothing (see plate 6).

It is incorrect to state that the *paksu* (male shaman) is wearing "women's clothing, down to the pantaloons that hide beneath his billowing skirt and slip" (Kendall 1987:27). The *paksu* wears *paji* (men's trousers) underneath the ritual outfit, not women's pantaloons as suggested by Kendall. If I may understand the pantaloons to be *sokkot*, it is the long baggy underwear that women wear underneath the slip and skirt as part of traditional dress. In fact, Korean men, including *paksu*, never wear *sokkot*, in either sacred or secular contexts.[43]

It is interesting to note that when Yi Sang-Sun, a female *kangshinmu*, is possessed by the spirit of General Chakdu,[44] she puts on men's black trousers underneath the ritual skirts before climbing up barefoot on to the sharp edges of the *chakdu* knives.

Pseudonyms for *Kangshinmu*

For centuries, *mudang* (ritual specialists) have been considered lower class citizens and strong prejudice still remains. Consequently most *kangshinmu* (spirit-possessed shamans) do not reveal their legal names to their clients or to the general public. Most *kangshinmu* prefer to be known by pseudonyms that reflect their features, lifestyles, personalities, relationships with spirits, or areas of residence. Many well known *kangshinmu* in the Seoul area are identified by nicknames. For example, one is known as *Koch'ugaru mudang* (Red Pepper Powder *mudang*) because she used to sell red peppers in the market before she became a shaman. *Kombo mudang* (Pockmarked Face *mudang*) is nicknamed

---

[43] There may be a few *paksu* who are cross-dressers, as in any population, but we are not discussing here the personal habits of a few exceptions to the rule.

[44] *Chakdu* are twin ritual blades. A shaman who is possessed by the spirit of General Chakdu will stand on the sharpened edges of the *chakdu* in his or her bare feet as a symbolic sacrifice in order to get rid of malevolent spirits causing misfortunes.

for her smallpox scars. *Ot'obai mudang* (Autobike *mudang*) once owned a motorcycle shop and *Tokkaebi mudang* is known for his goblin spirit. *Komoknamu mudang* (Old Tree *mudang*) has an unusually old tree in her yard. Namdaemun *mudang* (South Gate *mudang*) lives near Namdaemun (South Gate) in downtown Seoul.

Since Koreans consider it extremely impolite to address or refer to adults by their personal given names, they use both teknonymy and geononymy extensively. In the anthropological literature, teknonymy refers to "the practice of addressing an adult not by his or her own name, but by the name of a child, adding the relationship between the child and the adult," while geononymy refers to "the practice of using place names as qualifiers for kinship terms" (Lee K.K. and Harvey 1973:38, 41). For example, if a couple has a child named Mi-Ja, they will be referred to as "Mi-Ja's father" and "Mi-Ja's mother," rather than their own given names. People may identify themselves by the names of their residence. For example, one often hears on the telephone, "This is Yongsan," or "This is Pusan," referring to an area in Seoul or a city located in the southern part of the country, respectively, where the speaker lives. Some shamans simply identify themselves by their legal names. Throughout this work, I refer to shamans by their legal names, pseudonyms, or nicknames, respecting their personal preferences. For those who wished to remain anonymous, I use aliases as I did for Mrs. A, the first shaman I met in 1991.

Sŏnsaengnim

"*Sŏnsaengnim*" (literally, "teacher")[45] is used to respectfully address a person in everyday life. The term *sŏnsaengnim* is widely used for shamans since some of them have been officially honored by the government as traditional artists since the 1980s. For example, a well known shaman, once known simply as "Yugaemi," has been referred to as "Kim Sŏnsaengnim" since she was designated as the *poyuja* (designated performer) of Important Intangible Cultural Property number 104, Seoul *Saenam Kut*, in 1996.[46]

In recent years, well known *kangshinmu* (spirit-possessed shamans) and *haksŭpmu* (apprenticed *mudang*) have been called "*myŏngmu*" (famous ritual specialists) in public performances, much like the term "*myŏngch'ang*" (famous singer) is used for great *p'ansori* (epic song) or *minyo* (folk song) singers while "*myŏngin*" (famous person) is used for famous artists and artisans in various genres.

---

[45] *Sŏnsaeng* means teacher, but one calls a teacher "*sŏnsaengnim*," adding the honorific *nim* after *sŏnsaeng* to show respect.

[46] "Yugaemi" comes from her given name, "Yugam."

Among the *kangshinmu* in the Hanyang *kut* (rituals) tradition, the most respected performers/*kangshinmu* are referred to as *k'ŭn mudang* (great *mudang*), *kudae manshin* (older-generation *manshin*), or *saenam manshin* (specialist in *saenam kut*, a large-scale ritual for the departed). To be respected as a great *mudang*, one is expected to know two epic songs, "*Hwangje P'uri*" and "*Pari Kongju*," which are sung during the Hanyang *kut* (rituals) held for the living and departed, respectively. In Seoul, there are about half a dozen great *kangshinmu* remaining at the present time.

Musokin

Nowadays the term *musokin* (巫俗人)[47] is generally accepted by the public for the spirit-possessed shamans. Shamans also call themselves *musokin*. The term *musokin* is reserved for the *kangshinmu* (spirit-possessed shamans), the ritual specialists.

It is important to note that within the communitas[48] of *musok*, *kangshinmu* (spirit-possessed shamans) are respectfully referred to as *kija-nim* (祈者, literally, one who prays),[49] *kyeja-nim* (係者 or 繼者, literally, one who continues the tradition), *cheja-nim* (祭者, literally, one who offers rituals), or *cheja-nim* (弟子, one who learns from the spirits).

Personally, I use the terms "*kijanim*" or "*sŏnsaengnim*" to address *kangshinmu*. Both terms are acceptable and appreciated by the *kangshinmu*. I call them *kijanim* when I am alone with the *kangshinmu* or surrounded by *musok* insiders. The neutral term *sŏnsaengnim* works well in various situations.

When discussing Korean *musok* and *mudang*, I reserve the term "shaman" exclusively for the male or female *kangshinmu* (spirit-possessed *mudang*).

---

[47] Also romanized as *musogin*. The term *ch'ŏnjugyoin* refers to Korean Catholics (*Ch'ŏnjugyo* being Catholicism and *in* meaning person), but the term *musokin* does not refer to general *musok* believers.

[48] "Communitas," a Latin term, is used here to distinguish the "modality of social relationship" from the community, an area of common living (Turner 1969:96). For Turner, the term is dynamic, transient, anti-structural and ritually induced.

[49] *Nim* is an honorific. *Kija* is made up of two words—*ki* (prayer) and *ja* (person)—and is interpreted as a person who prays, but Soon-Hwa Sun defines *kija* as "one who makes wishes" (Sun 1992:101). Alexandre Guillemoz uses different Sino-Korean characters for *kija* (祈子) and defines this term as "the person who prays" (1998:88), but *kija* (祈子) is generally understood among Koreans as the specific act of praying for a child, preferably a son (子), to be born.

6. Various Diviners

It is important to note also that there are many divination (*chŏmbok*) specialists in Korea beside *kangshinmu, sesŭpmu* and *haksŭpmu*. Many of these divination specialists acquire their expertise by mastering the esoteric knowledge of manuals such as *Yŏk Hak* (*Chu Yŏk* or Chinese *I Ching*),[50] *Yukkap* (Sexagenary cycle) also known as *Kanji, T'ojŏng Pigyŏl* (Secret of T'ojŏng),[51] *Chŏnggamrok*,[52] and so on. Others specialize in divination by methods such as *kwansang* (reading facial structure), *susang* (palm reading), *kolsang* (reading bone structure), *saju* (horoscope based on birth information),[53] *chŏmsŏng* (astrology), *p'ungsu* (geomancy),[54] and so on. They provide such services as *chakmyŏng* or *sŏngmyŏng* (creating auspicious names) and *t'aegil* (choosing auspicious dates), having attained insight into *ŭm/yang* (Chinese *yin/yang*) and *ohaeng* (five elements) principles. They also examine *kunghap* (compatibility between two people) based on the couple's *saju* (birth information).

I once observed a friend asking a *yŏksulga*, a person who had mastered the *Yŏk Hak*, about her son and his potential bride. My friend and her son did not know the girl personally, but they had obtained the girl's birth information through their matchmaker. She gave Mr. Chin, the *yŏksulga*, the *saju* of her son and of the girl to check their *kunghap* (compatibility). Mr. Chin said "No," advising my friend not to pursue the matter. But when my friend asked Mr. Chin again a few months later with another girl's *saju*, he was enthusiastic about that

---

[50] *I Ching* or *Yi Jing* (易經) is the ancient Chinese divination manual also known as *The Book of Changes*. *The Book of Changes* was compiled during the Zhou Dynasty (1122–255 B.C.E.) (Wu J.N. 1991). *The Book of Changes* is known as *Chu Yŏk* in Korea. *Chu* refers to the Chinese Zhou Dynasty and *yŏk* is the Korean pronunciation of the first Chinese ideograph in the title, 易. *Chuyŏk* was also known as *Chŏmch'algyŏng* in *Samguk Yusa* [Memorabilia of the Three Kingdoms of Ancient Korea] (Pak Y.S. 1988:335).

[51] *T'ojŏng Pigyŏl* is the divination manual written by T'ojŏng (birth name, Yi Chi-Ham) during the reign of King Myŏngjong (r. 1545–1567), the 13th king of the Chosŏn Dynasty. It is used to divine one's annual fortune according to one's time, date, month, and year of birth, usually at the beginning of the year.

[52] *Chŏnggamrok* is a compendium in which all the books of prophecy since the Age of the Three Kingdoms were collected together. The core of this book is filled with prophecies by the fictitious characters Chŏng Kam and Yi Shim, proclaiming the coming of an ideal society (Kim N.P. 1993:130).

[53] *Saju* (literally, "four columns") refers to one's time, date, month, and year of birth.

[54] *P'ungsu*, literally meaning "wind and water," is *feng shui* in Chinese. *P'ungsu* geomancy is an art of reading forces of *ŭm* and *yang* (Chinese, *yin* and *yang*) to determine the most beneficial locations for houses and gravesites.

relationship. Shortly after the second divination, the couple married and they now have a seven-year-old son.

People in general prefer to consult reputable *yŏksulga* rather than *kangshinmu* (spirit-possessed *mudang*) for divination. Despite the fact that *kangshinmu* may be revered for their divining power, many people are reluctant to consult with them, for fear of being forced to sponsor an expensive *kut* (ritual) that *kangshinmu* are known to solicit. There is a saying in Korean: "*Mudang chip e chŏmborŏ karyŏmyŏn, ssal damgŭgo gagŏra* (Before going to see a *mudang* for divination, soak rice in water)." It can be interpreted as: "Since you are going to be roped into sponsoring a ritual anyway, you might as well prepare to make the rice cake (which will be used in a ritual) before going to see a *mudang*." The saying suggests how people feel. In addition, people hesitate to contact *kangshinmu* for fear of being identified as *musok* practitioners and looked down on by the community.

The *yŏksulga* specialists do not perform any rituals for their clients but often write amulets to prevent misfortune. They do not wish to be mistaken for *musok* practitioners. In reality, however, because many *kangshinmu* and *haksŭpmu* also learn to divine with the various methods mentioned above, it is difficult to distinguish *yŏksulga* from *mudang*.

CHAPTER 3

Musok in View of Classic Shamanism

1. *Musok* and Shamanism

Mircea Eliade defines shamanism as a "technique of ecstasy," because he considers the shaman's magical flight to other worlds an important element, believing that the shaman's soul would "leave his body and ascend to the sky or descend to the underworld" (1964:5). In stressing the "ascent-to-the-sky" and "descent-to-the-underworld" elements of shamanism, Eliade concludes that possession, the entering of a spirit into the shaman's body, is a non-shamanic feature. Johan Reinhard suggests that this is due to Eliade's "historical" interpretation, which is supposed to show that the soul journey aspect in prior times was of primary importance among the Tungus and spirit possession was a later development (1976:140).

Reinhard argues that spirit possession is also a form of shamanism (1976). Soul journey, spirit possession, and trance are ways that shamans interact with their spirit helpers of the supranormal world. Trance, according to I.M. Lewis, is either due to the temporary absence of the subject's soul ("soul-loss"), or it represents possession by a supernatural power. The first interpretation stresses a loss of personal vital force, a "de-possession," while the second emphasizes the intrusion of an external power. In some cultures both these views are entertained simultaneously, so that the "de-possessed" person is "possessed" by a spirit or power (Lewis 1989:25).

Although "soul journey" and "spirit possession" describe the means of communication between shamans and their spirit-helpers of the supranormal world, the shamans' techniques and the expected outcomes reflect the socio-cultural background of each shamanic tradition.

While "classic" Inner Asian shamanism involves the soul journey as a means of communication with the other world, Korean *kangshinmu* (spirit-possessed *mudang*) communicate with the spirits (*shin*) through spirit possession (*kangshin*), seeking help to avoid or to get rid of malevolent spirits (*kwi* or *kwishin*) that cause people ill fortune.

Korean *musok* deals with both spirit possession by *shin* (spirits) and spirit intrusion by *kwi* (malevolent spirits). The difference between spirit possession and spirit intrusion is explained by Forrest Clements:

> *Spirit intrusion* includes all cases of disease ascribed to the presence in the body of a supernatural being. *Possession* is restricted to cases in which the supernatural being speaks through his host. Generally, the only form of sickness it includes is insanity, although this may have other causes, such as the loss of the soul. The criterion of true possession is the belief that the voice of the possessed person is really that of the supernatural intruder. (Clements [1932] 1965:189–190)

Although in Eliade's view the term "shamanism" in the strict sense refers to a religious phenomenon of Siberia and Inner Asia (1987:202), Eliade recognizes that the use of the term "shamanism" may be extended to include other parts of the world where similar kinds of practices occur (ibid.: passim). In this broader sense, in addition to Inner Asia, Northern Siberia and other Arctic regions, shamanism can be found in Africa, in North and South America, and in other parts of Asia, including Japan and South Korea.

2. *Kangshinmu* and Shaman

In Northeast and Inner Asia, according to Eliade, "the chief methods of recruiting shamans are (1) hereditary transmission of the shamanic profession and (2) spontaneous vocation ('call' or 'election')" (Eliade 1987:202). In Korea, however, if a *mudang* is recruited from her hereditary family tradition, she is referred to as *sesŭpmu* (hereditary *mudang*), but if a man or woman is elected by the spirits, he or she is referred to as *kangshinmu* (spirit-possessed *mudang*).

To consider the Korean *kangshinmu* (spirit-possessed *mudang*) as shamans, I would like to employ the term "shaman" as defined by Reinhard:

> A shaman is a person who at his will can enter into a non-ordinary psychic state (in which he either has his soul undertake a journey to the spirit world or he becomes possessed by a spirit) in order to make contact with the spirit world on behalf of members of his community. (Reinhard 1976:16)

For the etymology of the word "shaman," Vilmos Dioszegi suggests that the term may have been derived from the Evenk word *saman*, originating from the Tunguso-Manchurian verb *ša* meaning "to know" (Dioszegi 1947:211, cited in

Siikala 1987:14). Bing-an Wu postulates that the term "shaman" was originally a Jurchen word denoting female shamans only (Wu B.A. 1989:263).

The role of the "shaman" (both male and female), on the other hand, is described by S.M. Shirokogoroff:

> In all Tungus languages this term refers to persons of both sexes who have mastered spirits, who at their will can introduce these spirits into themselves and use their power over the spirits in their own interests, particularly helping other people, who suffer from the spirits. (Shirokogoroff [1935] 1980:269)

Among Korean *mudang* (ritual specialists), the term "shaman," as defined above, may be applied only to *kangshinmu* (spirit-possessed *mudang*), because only they communicate with spirits and spirit-helpers of the supranormal world through spirit possession or by calling spirits into their bodies at will. By this same definition, the *sesŭpmu* (hereditary *mudang*) or *haksŭpmu* (apprenticed *mudang*) are not to be considered shamans. To clarify the distinction, I will refer to the *kangshinmu* as spirit-possessed shaman, while continuing to refer to others as *mudang,* including both *sesŭpmu* and *haksŭpmu.*

When most *musok* practitioners are translated as "shamans," it becomes difficult for readers to learn about the differences in Korean ritual specialists. For example, as Howard explains:

> In Chindo, *"mudang"* broadly specified any shaman, *"munyŏ"* only female shaman, and *"tan'gol"* a hereditary shaman. For convenience, I translate all three terms as "shaman" or practitioners and, in keeping with local use, reserve *"chŏmjangi"* for fortune-tellers. (Howard 1990:161)

Kangshinmu (spirit-possessed shamans), once elected by the spirits, must undergo a transition, which is found in many forms of spirit possession, "beginning with involuntary affliction interpreted as divine calling and ending with the routine practice of ecstasy by the established shaman" (Lewis 1989:8). Victor Turner's concept of "liminality" suggests a framework for understanding the liminal experience whereby an ordinary person is transformed into a *kangshinmu,* a spirit-possessed shaman. Liminality, from the Latin word *limen* (meaning threshold), suggests the great importance of real or symbolic thresholds. Turner explains *limen* thusly:

> [A] threshold, but at least in the case of protracted initiation rites or major seasonal festivals it is a very long threshold, a corridor almost, or a tunnel which may become a pilgrim's road, or, passing from dynamics to statics, may cease to be a mere transition and become a set way of life, a state, that of the anchorite or monk. (Turner 1992:49)

Turner refers to those undergoing the liminal experience as "liminaries" who are betwixt and between established states, considering that "they evade ordinary cognitive classification, too, for they are not this or that, here or there, one thing or the other" (Turner 1992:49).

Turner bases his theory of liminality on Arnold van Gennep's *schéma* of *rites de passage* which includes three phases: separation (*séparation*), transition (*marge*), and incorporation (*agrégation*) in serial terms, and *preliminal, liminal,* and *postliminal* in temporal terms, accompanying changes of age and status in many cultures (Gennep 1960:11). Thus we may interpret Gennep's complete schema of rites of passage as including preliminal rites (rites of separation), liminal rites (rites of transition), and postliminal rites (rites of incorporation).

Korean *kangshinmu* (spirit-possessed shamans) commonly suffer from *shinbyŏng* (spirit sickness)[1] in the preliminal period, learn esoteric knowledge and ritual techniques as liminaries in the liminal period, and are transformed into *kangshinmu* through a "sacramental ritual," as Raymond Firth puts it, to serve the community in the postliminal period (1958:126).

The Pre-liminal Period for the Korean Shaman

If someone is ill, Koreans generally seek help from neighborhood pharmacists, medical doctors, herbal specialists, and so on. If no cure can be found among community resources, the sick person may seek the help of a *mudang*.

Kangshinmu may determine causes for the patient's suffering and heal through "divine prescriptions" or suggest rituals. For example, a patient who bled continuously for two days after her visit to a dentist was cured by *kangshinmu* Yi Myŏng-Suk in Seoul who communicated with spirits and relayed the "divine prescription." The patient was to drink a glass of water mixed with a few spinach leaves. When the patient did this, "the bleeding stopped immediately," as I have described elsewhere (Seo 1997:76). Despite the fact that Yi delivers the messages from the spirits, she does not know how such ingredients and methods actually heal. Through many years of curing experiences, Yi is convinced that it is the will of the spirits and the patient's faith in the spirits' power that heals (personal communication 1993).

In *musok*, physical illness is often interpreted as temporary spirit intrusions of *kwi* (malevolent spirits) or *shin* (spirits), as mentioned earlier. Spirit intrusion is a disease that is "ascribed to the presence in the body of a supernatural being" (Clements [1932] 1965:189). At that point many people will turn to a *kangshinmu* (spirit-possessed shaman) for consultation and diagnosis. If a person is believed to be sick because of the instrusion of *kwi* (malevolent spirits),

---

[1] *Shinbyŏng* (spirit sickness) is also referred to as *mubyŏng* (sickness related to *musok*).

a healing ritual (*pyŏng kut* or *uhwan kut*) is suggested; however, if a person is sick due to spirit possession by *shin* (spirits), the path to becoming a shaman is recommended.

If afflicted by *shinbyŏng*, a person may have difficulty carrying on his or her daily routine or maintaining an occupation. The symptoms of *shinbyŏng* can be divided generally into somatic, mental, and behavioral categories. Youngsook Kim Harvey explains:

> Somatic symptoms include anorexia, circulatory distresses such as extreme coldness and/or numbness of hands and feet, diarrhea, arrested peristaltic movement, feeling faint or dizzy, headaches, aches in joints, insomnia, malaise, nausea, palpitation of the heart, respiratory congestion which is experienced as "heaviness of the heart" and sometimes acutely painful ringing in the ear, sudden elevations in body temperature, weight loss, and others. Mental symptoms generally include auditory and/or visual hallucinations and strange dreams which later prove to have been symbolically prophetic. Behavioral symptoms include a variety of actions that are clearly inappropriate, such as bathing in mid-winter with cold water in an open courtyard, or traveling in the cheapest public conveyances dressed in extravagantly luxurious winter clothes in warm weather, or stopping strangers on the streets and telling them their fortunes. (Harvey 1984:437–8)

In addition to physical pain, the afflicted may experience financial difficulties, often ending in bankruptcy, or facing the death of family members through *indari*.[2] These demoralizing trials known as *shin'gamul*, of which *shinbyŏng* is one type, can be expected to persist until the elected yields to the will of the spirits and becomes a *kangshinmu*, a spirit-possessed shaman.

Sometimes a person finds a sacred object such as a *myŏngdo* (brass mirror), *shinryŏng* (ritual bell), or *shink'al* (ritual knife) hidden in the ground or under stones. These sacred objects, known as *kuaebi*,[3] may have been hidden by *kangshinmu* who had no spirit child[4] to bestow them on during their lifetimes, or who were forced to hide them from the authorities attempting to eradicate *musok*

---

[2] The literal meaning of *indari* is "human bridge." In the context of *musok*, *indari* is understood as multiple deaths or injuries occurring within one family before the afflicted accepts the fate of being a shaman.

[3] *Kuaebi* is also known as *kuŏp* or *kuŏbi* (Yi W.S. 1999:146).

[4] I translate the terms *shin chason, shin pumo, shin ŏmŏni* and *shin abŏji* as spirit child, spirit parents, spirit mother and spirit father, respectively. Relationships between spirit children and spirit parents are established when a new shaman is initiated and are like the relationships between godparents and godchildren created when a child is baptized in the Christian church. An additional responsibility is given to spirit parents to teach ritual knowledge and techniques to the spirit children.

throughout Korean history. The person who finds these hidden sacred objects, *kuaebi*, interprets this experience as a divine omen and often accepts the fate of becoming a *kangshinmu* (see plate 7).

Once called by spirits, the path as a shaman becomes an obligation for the afflicted, not a choice. Those who refuse to accept their fate, it is believed, will continue to suffer from *shin'gamul* physically or financially. Once the decision to yield to the spirits is reached, family and friends begin to look for an established *kangshinmu* to officiate at the *kangshin kut* or *naerim kut* (initiation ritual).[5] Their search is often guided by dreams or the recommendation of others. The *kangshinmu* who officiates at the initiation ritual becomes the neophyte's teacher, as *shin ŏmŏni* (spirit mother) or *shin abŏji* (spirit father).[6] The neophyte, male or female, may choose either a spirit mother or spirit father.

As preparation for the *naerim kut*, the afflicted goes through a ritual called *hŏju kut* with the *shin ŏmŏni* (spirit mother-to-be) or *shin abŏji* (spirit father-to-be) in order to separate the good spirits (*shin*) from the malevolent ones (*kwi shin*). In addition to the *hŏju kut*, the *shin'gamul* and finding *kuaebi* are part of the preliminary process that the afflicted must experience as a chosen one.

The Liminal Period for the Korean Shaman

Initiation Ritual, Naerim Kut

Shamans of Inner Asia and Korea initially suffer symptoms of spirit sickness as a necessary transition into shamanhood. Mastering esoteric knowledge is considered important in Inner Asia as Eliade explains:

> However selected, a shaman is not recognized as such until after he has received two kinds of teaching: (1) ecstatic (dreams, trances, etc.) and (2) traditional (shamanic techniques, names and functions of the spirits, mythology and genealogy of the clan, secret language, etc.). This twofold course of instruction, given by the spirits and the old master shamans, is equivalent to an initiation. Sometimes initiation is public and constitutes an autonomous ritual in itself. But absence of this kind of ritual in no sense implies absence of an

---

[5] *Kangshin* means spirit possession. *Naerim* means descent, referring to the descent of spirits into the shaman.

[6] Although Harvey asserts that "[i]t is the custom among Korean shamans to address and refer to the shaman who officiates at one's initiation *kut* by the fictive kinship term of *suyŏng-ŏmŏni* [adopted mother]," I have not observed the term *suyŏng-ŏmŏni* being used among shamans during my fieldwork (Harvey 1984:238). The officiating shaman is referred to as *shin ŏmŏni* (spirit mother) or *shin abŏji* (spirit father).

initiation; the latter can perfectly well occur in dream or in the neophyte's ecstatic experience. (Eliade 1964:13)

In Korea, however, the initiation ritual is a requisite for a shaman to be accepted and respected by the *musok* community. During a *naerim kut* (initiation ritual), a crucial transformation takes place when spirits begin to inhabit the body of the initiand and to speak through him. This is understood as the opening of the initiand's *malmun* (literally, "gate of words"), and he or she is then considered transformed into a neophyte shaman. The first moment of spirit possession (*kangshin*) is thought to be the pivotal point for the candidate, transforming an afflicted person into a neophyte shaman and marking the beginning of his liminal period.

The criterion of the spirits talking through the Korean shaman recalls Clement's definition of spirit possession as a distinct type of spirit intrusion:

Possession is restricted to cases in which the supernatural being speaks through his host. . . . The criterion of true possession is the belief that the voice of the possessed person is really that of the supernatural intruder. (Clements [1932] 1965:189–190)

A neophyte shaman may be possessed by several spirits. The first spirit to possess the afflicted, transforming him into a neophyte shaman, becomes the *momju* (literally, "body-governing spirit"), the most intimate and important spirit throughout his or her shamanic career. The order in which various spirits descend to the neophyte differs greatly from one individual to another. Some initiands remember exactly which spirits possessed them and in what order, while others recall the event only vaguely. Some spirits announce their identities as they enter the body while others have to be coaxed to introduce themselves by the experienced *kangshinmu* (spirit-possessed shamans) at hand. A neophyte may be able to identify some of his or her ancestor spirits but not all of them. At times I have observed that the neophyte identifies a spirit by pointing to one of the spirits represented in the wall paintings in the ritual hall. Usually at least three shamans are present during the initiation ritual guiding the initiand, encouraging him or her to describe the spirits in detail, or suggesting what to ask the spirits. Often one *kangshinmu* writes down the names of the spirits in order to keep a record of the spirit possessions for the initiand.[7]

Until the spirit descends and possession takes place, the afflicted does not know if they will actually become a shaman. It is only when possession by the spirits (*kangshin*) occurs during the initiation ritual that one is declared a

---

[7] Nowadays a professional videographer is often hired to record the entire initiation ritual to keep a record. I was also asked to record several initiation rituals by spirit parents-to-be.

kangshinmu. Once *kangshin* takes place, the formal rite of installing the neophyte shaman continues and completes the *naerim kut*.[8]

In order to see the future of the neophyte, a divination is held during the *naerim kut* (initiation ritual). Seven covered bowls, known as *naeryŏk pongji*, are laid out for the neophyte to select three and uncover them. Depending on which bowls they choose, their future career as a *kangshinmu* is foretold, because the contents of each bowl have esoteric meaning.

In the Seoul area, *naeryŏk pongji* as a rule contain water, millet, straw, bean, salt, ashes, and uncooked rice. *Naeryŏk pongji*, however, vary in number and contents. For example, Akamatsu and Akiba noted that there were twelve dishes filled with unhusked rice, unhusked glutinous rice, straw, ashes, small beans, soy beans, mung beans, millet, chestnuts, salt, water, and cow dung ([1938] 1991, 2:66).

It is understood that if a neophyte chooses dishes filled with water or rice, one will become a great shaman (Akamatsu and Akiba [1938] 1991, 2:66). It is considered unlucky if a neophyte chooses ashes, straws, millets, or salt (Yi Sang-Sun, personal communication, October 1998). According to Kim T'aegon, grains are associated with particular spirits; for example, red beans with Sŏnang, yellow beans with Kunung, rice with Chesŏk, sesame seeds with Sanshin, buckwheat with T'ŏ Hŏju, water with Yongshin, hay with Hŏju, and ashes with Pujŏngshin (Kim T.G. 1991:360).

Although the *naerim kut* begins in anticipation of producing a shaman, this does not always happen, because sometimes the spirits do not possess a candidate during the *naerim kut*. This uncertainty produces anxiety among the attendees, but when it is declared that no shaman will be created during that ritual, people rejoice in tremendous relief. A person afflicted with spirit sickness for several years, ironically, may be freed at last from the fear of becoming a shaman.

When *kangshin* (spirit possession) does not take place during the attempted *naerim kut*, either they give up entirely or try again at a later date, following the decision made by the spirit parent-to-be.

During my fieldwork, I witnessed several *naerim kut* (initiation rituals) where *kangshin* did not take place. People prepare for the initiation ritual, but the creation of a shaman is entirely up to the spirits and unknown powers. Initially I was disappointed and frustrated when I could not capture the moment of *kangshin* (spirit possession) after holding my video camera and recording, often for more than ten hours before they reached the decision to halt the ritual. It was important, however, to learn that not every *naerim kut* produces a *kangshinmu* (spirit-possessed shaman). I was happy to see the afflicted released

---

[8] In earlier days, the *chipshin kut* was held following the *naerim kut* (initiation ritual) in order to foster harmony among one's possessing spirits and others (Akamatsu and Akiba [1938] 1991, 2:66), but the *chipshin kut* is no longer held in the Seoul area.

from the fate of becoming a *kangshinmu*, for no Korean wishes to be spirit-possessed. One of the worst curses is, *"Nŏŭi chibe mudang nawara!"* (Let there be a *mudang* in your family!) Perhaps the sentiment reflected in this statement expresses how much people dread becoming a *mudang*.

Liminality is understood by Colin Turnbull as "a subjective experience in which 'thisness' becomes 'thatness'" (Turnbull 1990:77). This liminality may be experienced unexpectedly by some people, because *kangshin* (spirit possession) may take place without any initiatory sickness or warning. For instance, Mr. Kim's liminal experience of *kangshin* occurred when he went to the mountains with his friends. He suddenly began to tell the fortunes of people around him. He knew he was controlled by an unknown power, for he realized he was saying things he did not know. He decided immediately to accept the fate of being a *kangshinmu* and had been specializing in divination for nearly a decade when I met him (personal communication 1994).

Mrs. Yi's first *kangshin* and transformation also took place unexpectedly. She was attending someone else's *naerim kut* (initiation ritual) where the initiand was having a great deal of difficulty receiving the spirits. Mrs. Yi suddenly began to speak of things she had no knowledge of, while clapping both hands and feeling elated. She knew that spirits had descended upon her unexpectedly and she, too, accepted the fate of becoming a *kangshinmu*. Unlike Mr. Kim, Mrs. Yi acquired musical skills, learning to present a *kut* (ritual) in the Hanyang style although she was born in Kyŏngsang Province in the south (personal communication 1994).

Cases like that of Mrs. Yi clearly generate considerable fear of attending *musok*-related activities among lay people, knowing that the spirits sometimes possess bystanders. The apprehension is so strongly ingrained that many Koreans are too terrified to get to know about *musok*. I was no exception to this rule. I myself was scared nine years ago when I began my fieldwork among *kangshinmu*, especially after learning that the wife of a colleague, an ethnomusicology graduate from the University of Washington, had been spirit-possessed while she was in Korea doing research in traditional dance for her MA degree.[9]

Learning as Part of Liminal Experience

After the *naerim kut* (initiation ritual), the neophyte shaman gradually begins to regain their health and to learn the esoteric knowledge necessary for a

---

[9] Park Hŭi-A (née Ch'ae), a Korean American, became a *kangshinmu* involuntarily in 1981 (Kim I.H. 1983:75). Since her initiation (June 23, 1981) she has traveled extensively, performing shamanic ritual dance, trance dance, and traditional Korean dance throughout the United States, Europe, and Korea (Haft 1992: passim).

shamanic career from their *shin ŏmŏni* (spirit mother) or *shin abŏji* (spirit father). Sacred objects, metaphors, codes, and myths are explained in visual, auditory, and kinesthetic ways, while the neophyte acquires the techniques of calling and controlling the spirits.

Traditionally, the neophyte studied under their *shin ŏmŏni* or *shin abŏji* for about three years as a participant/observer. In earlier times the neophyte moved in with the *shin ŏmŏni* or *shin abŏji* and was intimately involved in the spirit parent's daily routine. The neophyte usually began by doing menial chores like cleaning, carrying things, and so on, and through *nunch'i* (social sense)[10] they learned a great deal while living under the spirit parent's roof. Nowadays, however, most neophytes and spirit parents keep separate residences but attempt to work closely together.

If other shamans are studying under the same *shin ŏmŏni* or *shin abŏji*, the newest neophyte becomes the "baby" in the "family," regardless of age. The hierarchy within this "family" is quite rigid and sometimes difficulties arise as the "siblings" compete for attention and recognition from the *shin ŏmŏni* or *shin abŏji*. Absolute obedience to the *shin pumo* (spirit parents), as well as to older "siblings," is expected of a neophyte during this apprenticeship period. Ideally the relationship between a neophyte and *shin ŏmŏni* (spirit mother) or *shin abŏji* (spirit father) lasts beyond the instructional years for their lifetimes. In real life, however, the ties are often severed due to personal conflicts or separation caused by the relocation of one or the other.

For those who are lost without a spirit parent's help, instruction is available at the schools established for spirit-possessed shamans as discussed in chapter 4. One may also purchase ritual song texts, manuals for rituals, videotapes and audio recordings (CD or cassette) of the ritual songs at specialty shops. The shop owner may refuse a lay person wishing to purchase these materials, because they are considered sacred. Several well known Seoul area *paksu* (male shamans)—Kim Chong-Tŏk (1989), Chang Sŏng-Man (1988), Pak In-O (1990), and Ha Man-Su (1992)—have all published books on the Hanyang *kut* suitable for instructional purposes. Pak In-O, for example, uses his book in his classroom instruction.

Musical Training

Since music plays an important role for shamans in both Inner Asia and Korea, it is an essential part of the instruction given to a neophyte during the

---

[10] *Nunch'i* is defined by Choi as "social sensitivity—one's ability to understand a social situation, to make quick judgments about it and respond appropriately" (Choi C. 1989a:236). Others define it as "social perceptiveness" (Kim U.C. and Choi S.C. 1995:247–8) and "savoir faire" (Harvey 1984:288).

liminal period. Inner Asian shamans learn songs from experienced shamans or in their dreams. They must master songs and dances, as well as learn to accompany themselves on drums before they are permitted to conduct a ritual. The importance of drum and drumstick is shared by most shamans of Inner Asia, even though the shapes, sizes, and symbolism of the drums and drumsticks may differ from one ethnic group to another. Drums are often created according to instructions received in the shaman's dreams or community members may make them as an offering to the new shaman (Dioszegi 1968; Potapov 1968). For the Korean neophyte shamans, an hourglass-shaped drum (*changgu*) must be purchased unless their spirit parents (*shin pumo*) give them a new drum. Sometimes a shaman may inherit their spirit parent's drum, which may have been handed down for several generations, as in the cases of Kim and Yi discussed in chapter 6.

In Korea, the first moment of *kangshin* (spirit possession) marks the beginning of the musical training required of a neophyte *kangshinmu* (spirit-possessed shaman) to become a ritual specialist. They learn songs from the vast repertoires of *mugyŏng* (incantations) and *muga* (ritual songs), which may last several hours each. Musical competence determines what type of *kangshinmu* one will become. Some *kangshinmu*, due to limited vocal skills, decline to perform songs but specialize in small-scale rituals, prayers, divination, and writing amulets or talismans.

Musicianship divides Seoul area shamans into two large groups: *chŏnnae* and *ch'ŏngsŭng mudang*. *Chŏnnae* are those who devote themselves to divination and small-scale rituals where no songs and dances are required, while *ch'ŏngsŭng mudang* are musically talented performers who officiate at large-scale rituals by singing and dancing. When a *chŏnnae mudang* is asked by a client to officiate at a large-scale *kut*, they hire musically talented *ch'ŏngsŭng mudang* and *chaebi* (professional musicians) to carry out the ritual. Despite the fact that no *kangshinmu* or musicians could explain the word *"ch'ŏngsŭng"* to me, by observing their musical practices, I have surmised that the term originates from *ch'ŏngsong* (請訟), Sino-Korean words expressing "an invitation to sing or recite" but mispronounced colloquially as *ch'ŏngsŭng*.

Musically talented *kangshinmu* are in great demand. They may specialize in two styles of rituals: *anjŭn kŏri* (literally, seated ritual) or *sŏn kŏri* (literally, standing ritual). In both styles, recitation and solo songs are performed. In the latter style, dance and duet songs are also performed. *Kangshinmu* must also learn to play percussion instruments such as the *ching* (gong) or *chegŭm* (cymbals). Musical instruments, musicians, and ritual music are discussed further in chapters 6, 7, and 8, respectively.

The Post-liminal Period for the Korean Shaman

Status of the Korean Shaman

Of the three phases of transformation—separation, transition, and incorporation—Turner says, "the first and last speak for themselves; they detach ritual subjects from their old places in society and return them, inwardly transformed and outwardly changed, to new places" (Turner 1992:48–49). The liminal process is characterized by "a ritual of status elevation" (Turner 1969:167). In Korea, the afflicted initiand becomes a *kangshinmu* through a liminal process in which the novice is transformed irreversibly from a lower to a higher position in the community of *musok* believers and begins to participate in ritual interactions regulated by the belief system of *musok*.

The duties of the *kangshinmu* include helping people by healing, prophesying, and officiating at rituals as required by crises or as part of calendrical events. It is important to note that not all initiated *kangshinmu* are actively involved in *musok* practices. Some *kangshinmu* have *shindang* (shrine rooms) for their private offerings of *oksu* (sacred water) and prayers, but no outsiders know about their secrets. Some ostensibly convert to other religions such as Buddhism, Catholicism, or Christianity.[11] I know two Seoul-area *paksu* (male shamans) who practice *musok* but present themselves as Buddhist monks.[12] Most *kangshinmu* practice *musok* within a tightly guarded group of people.

---

[11] In Korea, "Christianity" refers to the Protestant faith, excluding Catholicism.

[12] These two *paksu* (male shamans) hold their annual *chinjŏk kut* (rituals to celebrate their initiation dates) quietly with family members. Each shaman hires the same shamans and musicians over the years to ensure the secrecy. They used to officiate at rituals for clients but engage nowadays mainly in fortune-telling.

CHAPTER 4

Korean Shamans

1. Shamans and Their Shrines

The neophyte *kangshinmu* (spirit-possessed shaman) must prepare a place in their home for a *shindang* (shrine),[1] a sacred room where no one is allowed without the *kangshinmu*'s invitation. If they cannot afford a separate room in a house, a small area is reserved for an altar in a clean, quiet corner of a room. *Shindang* are also known as *chŏnan*, especially among older *kangshinmu* in Seoul.

After the *naerim kut* (initiation ritual), the *shin pumo* (spirit parents) show the neophyte *kangshinmu* how to set up the *shindang*. A small private ritual called *t'apsang* is performed for the occasion. The walls are washed and pictures of the spirits are either hung or attached to the walls. When all the pictures have been hung on the walls, they are completely covered with *paekji* (white mulberry paper) while prayers are said and *p'at* (red beans)[2] are thrown at the papers to cast out all evil spirits. As the papers are taken away, the *aedong kija* (neophyte)[3] lights candles and incense, and offers *oksu* (sacred water) to every spirit installed. Goblets filled with wine are also offered underneath all the images, except for two—those of Sambul Chesŏk and Ch'ilsŏng, who are known not to enjoy wine.[4]

---

[1] A *shindang* is a room where an altar for the spirits is placed. At times a large building like a *kuttang* (ritual hall) is also referred to as *shindang*.
[2] *P'at* (red bean) is used because the color red is thought to have the power to repel evil forces.
[3] *Aedong kija*, literally meaning a "baby shaman," is used as a term of endearment for the neophyte.
[4] Sambul Chesŏk are three Buddhist spirits—Amit'abul (Sakyamuni, the historical Buddha), Kwanseŭm Posal (Avalokitesvara Bodhisattva), and Taeseji Posal (Mahastha-

Most *kangshinmu* display paintings or statues of spirits in their *shindang*, but others hang paper banners with names of spirits and decorate altars with only brass bells and mirrors known as *myŏngdo*. *Myŏngdo*, a round convex brass mirror, is considered the most important sacred object for *kangshinmu*, along with the *pangul* (bell tree) and *puch'ae* (fan). *Myŏngdo* also referred to as *myŏngdu*, come in various sizes. Shapes of the sun, moon, or seven stars are sometimes engraved on the *myŏngdo*, but often they are simply represented by Sino-Korean characters corresponding to the sun (日, *il*), the moon (月, *wŏl*), and the seven stars (七星, *ch'ilsŏng*, or 北斗七星, *pukdu ch'ilsŏng*).

Like Korean *kangshinmu*, Inner Asian shamans set up altars in their homes. Nadyezhda Duvan, a Siberian shaman from Bulava,[5] told me that in her tradition the altar is always placed toward the south (personal communication 1997), but Korean *kangshinmu* favor south or east.

Korean *sesŭpmu* (hereditary *mudang*) and *haksŭpmu* (apprenticed *mudang*), on the other hand, do not have their own shrines. As the need arises, both *mudang*—*sesŭpmu* and *haksŭpmu*—set up temporary altars to pray and to perform rituals at clients' request. *Kangshinmu*, *sesŭpmu*, and *haksŭpmu* all have places in their homes reserved for their ritual garments, drums, and ritual objects.

The images and *kimul* (ritual receptacles)[6] may initially be purchased or handed down from the spirit parents to the neophyte, and many more may be added later on. In one *t'apsang* ceremony I attended, most of the ritual receptacles had been handed down from the spirit mother, while a few new ones had been presented by the spirit siblings, spirit aunts, and spirit uncles. The neophyte served a red bean porridge[7] to the guests—five *kangshinmu* and me—after the small ritual (November 1998).

---

maprata Bodhisattva)—worshiped by *musok* believers and they are usually represented in monks' attire. Ch'ilsŏng (literally, seven stars) refers to the Seven Star Spirits who look after humans from birth to death. They are considered Taoist spirits and are often represented in paintings as seven sages.

[5] Nadyezhda Duvan was born in the village of Bulava, Ulchi region, in the territory of Khabarovsk in Eastern Siberia. Bulava is located in the northern section of the Amur River region of Siberia. The Ulchis are the descendants of the Tungus tribes of Ilou, Mohe, and Pohai, a southern speaking Manchu-Tungus language group (Duvan 1998:91).

[6] *Kimul* are also called *shin'gi*. They are usually made of brass or porcelain. The size and shape of *kimul* vary greatly. *Kimul* include dishes and bowls for water and food offerings, wine jugs and cups, incense burners, and candle holders. When the ritual receptacle is used for Bodhisattva, it is called *pulgi* by *kangshinmu* as well as by Buddhist monks. They are cleaned periodically and always prior to rituals.

[7] A porridge made of red beans (*p'at*) is served to cast out misfortune, because the color red is thought to have the power to repel evil forces. In secular context, people serve red

In the *shindang* (shrine room), candles are always lit and incense continually burns on the altar.[8] Several images of deified humans like Tan'gun, Buddha, and historic generals are set on the altar, and offerings such as rice, wine, candy, fruits, and money are placed in front of them. Ritual objects, books, garments, and musical instruments are usually kept under the altar or in one corner of the *shindang*. A *chŏmsang* (divination table) is also placed in the *shindang* (see plate 2). *Yŏpchŏn* (old brass coins), a pile of rice, or *sant'ong* (literally, counting box) filled with sticks that the *kangshinmu* uses for divination are placed on the *chŏmsang*.

The *kangshinmu* (spirit-possessed shaman) regards the *shindang* as a sacred place where they pray and worship the spirits privately. The *kangshinmu* always enters the room properly dressed, never in bare feet or casual attire, to pay obeisance to the spirits who reside in the *shindang*. The *kangshinmu* invites clients into their *shindang* to confer, to divine, to pray, or to write amulets.

Kneeling in front of the altar, the *kangshinmu* begins the day with prayers and by offering a bowl of *oksu* (sacred water)[9] to the spirits. The water offered is usually not from the tap but fetched by the *kangshinmu* from streams or springs when they go to a mountain to pray and meditate. If they cannot go far, they may get water from a nearby well. This practice is intended to show *chŏngsŏng* (earnest devotion)[10] to the spirits. The need to fetch sacred water relates to the epic song "*Pari Kongju*" (Princess Pari) where the seventh princess finds *yaksu* (literally, medicinal water)[11] and brings her parents back from the dead with the power of water.

I have met few Korean *mudang* living in the Seattle area in northwestern America, and eventually I found one *kangshinmu* (spirit-possessed shaman), a woman in her early seventies. I was given her phone number by a Korean friend who was one of her many satisfied clients. When I visited this *kangshinmu*, she welcomed my friend and me into her home. While her husband watched a video of a Korean soap opera in one corner of the living room, we sat around the kitchen table and chatted. It was difficult to converse for the husband did not offer to turn down the volume of the television although he was dozing off and on. The home appeared to be a modest apartment. In the kitchen, living room, and dining area, there was no visible sign that she was a *kangshinmu*.

---

bean porridge (*p'atjuk*) on Tongji day, the longest night of the year, in the 11th month of the lunar calendar.

[8] I once heard a *paksu* shaman advising a neophyte who lives alone to extinguish candles and incense whenever she has to leave the apartment for a long period of time for fear of fire (November 1998).

[9] *Oksu* is also referred to as *chŏnghwasu*.

[10] *Chŏngsŏng* may be translated as devotion, genuineness, sincerity, or earnestness.

[11] *Yaksu* is also referred to as *yakryŏngsu* (Ryu T.S. 1989:340).

Her nickname was "Alaska *halmŏni*" (Grandma from Alaska). Since Koreans often refer to relatives by associating them with places, like "Texas aunt," or "Seoul uncle," the nickname "Alaska *halmŏni*" does not draw any undue attention in the Korean American community. She told me that she became spirit-possessed in her forties and practiced *musok* in Korea for about two decades. When her two daughters reached marriageable age, the couple decided to immigrate to the United States to improve their daughters' chances of marriage, hiding the fact that their mother was a *kangshinmu*. The family moved to Alaska where no one knew her background. Except for secretly keeping a *shindang*, she did not engage in any *musok* related activities during that time.

After both of her daughters had married and moved to other parts of America, she began to tell fortunes and do small rituals for her clients. As her reputation spread, many Koreans living in different American cities would make long distance telephone calls to Alaska *halmŏni* for consultation. Realizing the possibility of practicing *musok* in America, the couple decided to move to Washington State, settling on the outskirts of Tacoma where a large number of Korean Americans reside. She told me that the mountains in Washington State are filled with such great powers and good spirits that she goes there often to pray for her clients.

To my amazement, she was a good diviner. She began to summarize my past and current interests without asking my *saju* (hour, date, month, and year of birth). Most *kangshinmu* ask clients for their *saju* before divining, as Mrs. A had done in 1991. Other *kangshinmu* do not ask any questions but proceed immediately to look into the client's past, present, and future. Despite the lack of physical evidence that *musok* was being practiced in the apartment, I was convinced that she was a *kangshinmu*. When I asked if she had a *shindang* (shrine room), her eyes lighted up and she smiled broadly. She seemed pleased that I had asked. She opened her bedroom door to show my friend and me into her *shindang* where offerings were laid for the spirits, candles were lit, and incense was burning. The *shindang* was spotlessly clean and the fruits on the altar were fresh. She told me that only a few people had seen her *shindang* for she is reluctant to invite casual clients into her sacred room. There are so many Korean Christians in America who oppose *musok* practice that she keeps her *shindang* secret to avoid criticism. I truly appreciated her showing the *shindang* to my friend and me.

Several *shindang* I have visited in Seoul, Suwŏn, and Inch'ŏn are large enough to hold a *kut*. These *shindang* often take up one entire floor of a two- or three-story building owned by well-established *kangshinmu* (spirit-possessed shamans). I know one *kangshinmu* in Seoul who rents three floors of a six-story building for a monthly rent of about $2,000 in US funds.[12] She uses one floor for a *shindang*, one for quiet prayers, and the other for her family's living quarters.

Mrs. G, reputedly one of the best *kangshinmu* in the Seoul area, performs several small rituals a day or officiates at *kut* (large-scale rituals) once or twice a week. In order to facilitate her activities, she has acquired a two-story building in a residential neighborhood separate from her own residence.[13] Her *shindang* is located on the top floor while her staff prepares offerings on the premises using a kitchen and other rooms on the ground floor.

Sacred Paintings

Shinryŏng hwabon (or *hwabon* for short) are sacred paintings of spirits. They are hung on the walls of the *shindang* (shrine room). The *manshin* (spirit-possessed shamans) from Hwanghae Province of North Korea not only display *hwabon* on their *shindang* walls, but they also transport selected ones to ritual sites in order to create temporary sacred areas for their *kut* (rituals). *Kangshinmu* (spirit-possessed shamans) or *haksŭpmu* (apprenticed *mudang*) in the Seoul area also decorate the back of the stage with *hwabon* if they present Hanyang *kut* as performances in secular context. In the sacred context, *hwabon* for the *kangshinmu* of Hanyang *kut* remain in their *shindang* (shrine) or *kuttang* (ritual halls).

The subjects of *hwabon* (sacred paintings) are often deities and spirits that have appeared in the *kangshinmu*'s dreams. The *hwabon* in a *kangshinmu*'s shrine are often commissioned works since a painter must create the *hwabon* following the *kangshinmu*'s descriptions.

For those who cannot afford to commission paintings, it is acceptable to purchase and hang mass-produced paintings of deities—such as Tan'gun, Buddha, and historic generals. Since the *hwabon* are the visualization of deities and their symbolic powers, the main subjects appear in the foreground of the painting. *Hwabon* are painted in vibrant colors—red, blue, black, white, and yellow (Pak Y.S. 1993:61).

Shinryŏng hwabon (sacred paintings) are known as *muhwa* (*musok* paintings), *mushindo* (paintings of *musok* spirits), or *musokdo* (*musok* paintings)

---

[12] Unaksa Posal told me that her rent was 1,580,000 *wŏn* per month, approximately $2,000 in US funds (personal communication, November 1993).

[13] The fact that this *kangshinmu* has a separate family residence is unknown even to her clients. When my son and I were invited to the home in the spring of 1999, we appreciated her hospitality. The house is located in a residential area in the northwestern section of Seoul about half an hour's drive from her *shindang*. It has three bedrooms with modern conveniences, a large garden with a picnic table, and space for two cars to park inside the electronically controlled gate.

among scholars and the general public. The paintings are also referred to as *maji* if they are painted on *maji*, a paper made of hemp. They may be referred to as *t'aenghwa* (Buddhist paintings) if the subjects of the paintings are associated with Buddhism or if the paintings are created by *kŭmŏ* (Buddhist monks). *Hwabon* painted by *kŭmŏ* are often in scroll form. *Shinryŏng hwabon* are painted on silk, cotton, or paper of various shapes and sizes. Most *hwabon* are about 60 centimeters wide and 110 centimeters long (Kim T.G. 1993:12). Very few old *hwabon* remain because as a rule *hwabon* are destroyed along with ritual clothing at the death of the *kangshinmu* (Yun Y.S. 1994:22). The most popular subjects of *hwabon* are figures of Obang Shinjang (Spirit protecting the five directions—center, east, west, south, and north), Ch'ilsŏng (Seven Star Spirits), and Sanshin (Mountain Spirit) with his tiger.

Amulets and Talismans

Kangshinmu (spirit-possessed shamans) generally create amulets to ward off evil spirits that may cause misfortune, as well as talismans to invite good spirits who bring much luck, health, and happiness to their clients. All *mudang* including *sesŭpmu* (hereditary *mudang*), *haksŭpmu* (apprenticed *mudang*), and *kangshinmu* (spirit-possessed *mudang*) produce amulets or talismans.[14]

As Theodor Gaster explains in the "Amulets and Talismans" entry in *The Encyclopedia of Religion*,

> An amulet is an object, supposedly charged with magical power, that is carried on the person or displayed in a house, barn, or place of business in order to ward off misadventure, disease, or the assaults of malign beings, demonic or human. A talisman is an object similarly used to enhance a person's potentialities and fortune. Amulets and talismans are two sides of the same coin. The former are designed to repel what is baneful; the latter, to impel what is beneficial. (Gaster 1987:243)

Amulets and talismans created by *mudang* may be grouped into two types: *pujak* and *pujŏk*. *Pujak* are made of natural objects such as shells, eggs, mugwort, tiger's claws, rooster's feathers, and so on, and are believed to have esoteric powers furnished by the *mudang*. *Pujak* may also be carved of stone, metal, or wood.

Pujŏk are two-dimensional forms. According to Sang-Sook Lee and G.D. Sibley, *pujŏk* as a rule are drawn on 4 x 6 inch rectangles of yellow or white mulberry paper (1981:30). *Pujŏk* may also be created on leaves, bark, bamboo, leather, or cloth (Kim M.G. 1987:85). Symbols, figures, and characters

---

[14] Buddhist monks and *yŏksulga* (diviners) also make amulets and talismans.

embodying esoteric powers are drawn or written on the *pujŏk*. Sanskrit, Chinese, and Korean words are often transformed into artistic renditions.

The *mudang* decides on the color of mulberry paper according to the needs of the clients. In addition to white and yellow colored *pujŏk* paper, red or blue ones may be used. The most commonly used yellow papers are referred to as *koehwangji*. If a person is about to become a shaman, yellow paper is used to solicit spiritual power from their ancestors. Blue serves to prevent any harm or business problems by asking the spirits of powerful generals to intervene. Red and white papers are used to seek help from Sanshinryŏngnim (Mountain Spirit) and Pulsanim (Buddha), respectively (Mun K.P. 1997a:361).

The *pujŏk* is painted with a brush dipped into a solution of powdered red cinnabar pigment (*kyŏngmyŏngjusa*) mixed with sesame oil, sugar, and water. Papers and manuals are available at *manmulsang* (literally, shops that sell ten thousand items), which retail *musok*-related goods.

Mudang create *pujŏk* by choosing appropriate symbols and characters from the manuals while empowering them with prayers. The efficacy of the amulet or talisman, however, is believed to emerge solely from the prayers and magical powers of the *kangshinmu*. Prior to creating an amulet or talisman, the *kangshinmu* cleanses, prays, meditates, and selects the appropriate hour to create the *pujŏk* (Ryu S.C. 1992:153). He also observes taboos, for example, abstaining from sex and not attending funerals. Prices of *pujŏk* vary greatly because people are willing to pay high prices for the ones created by *kangshinmu* (spirit-possessed shamans) whose efficacy on amulets or talismans is well known and trusted.

When a *pujŏk* is made for personal use, its content is usually not revealed to the client. It is presented sealed in a small bag or an envelope. Since the *pujŏk* is usually folded and put into a small container,[15] the client may carry it in their pocket, purse, or wallet. If a person resists carrying the *pujŏk* openly, a family member will sometimes attach it to the loved one's clothing. One can attach the *pujŏk* inside the lining of a jacket or a dress without its being noticed by the wearer.

Ready-made generic *pujŏk* may be purchased through *mudang* or at specialty shops. They are usually drawn or printed in red ink on yellow paper or embroidered with red thread on yellow cloth, because both red and yellow are considered powerful colors for repelling malevolent spirits. Some Koreans display these *pujŏk* on the wall as decorations, but most do this in order to repel evil spirits or usher in good spirits, not only in their own homes but also in their modern offices and stores. One may also buy key chains with amulet designs at souvenir shops. These amulets are thought to bestow health, wealth, employment, fulfilled wishes, good relationships, academic achievements, and to prevent traffic accidents. It is interesting to note that each gift box containing

---

[15] They are often folded and sealed in a 1 inch x 2 inch envelope or a miniature purse.

an amulet key chain has a warning label, saying that the less one believes in its power, the less the effect.

In Korea, amulets are created not only for the living but also for the departed. In *musok*, the concept of the other world is rather vague, presuming that the resting-place for the departed is located somewhere beyond the western horizon. Borrowing from the Buddhist tradition, Buddhist scriptures *(dhâranî)* are written on yellow paper with red ink and placed on top of the corpse before burial in order to insure a safe journey for the departed to the other world (Yi Sang-Sun, personal communication, February 1999).

Ritual Garments

For a ritual officiated by *kangshinmu* (spirit-possessed shamans), a number of spirits are chosen to be invited and entertained throughout the various *kŏri* (sections). Prior to the *kut* all the ritual garments are selected and hung along a wall in a pre-determined order in preparation for receiving the spirits.[16] In addition to the ritual garments, the *kangshinmu* wear hats, crowns, or wigs to indicate the corresponding spirits' appearance. Accessories like the *yŏmju* (Buddhist prayer beads), *kasa* (sashes), or belts may be added to enhance the outfit.

Kangshinmu need to acquire *shinbok* (literally, "spirit clothing," that is, ritual garments), also referred to as *mubok* or *shinjang*,[17] as well as *shin'gu* (ritual objects), and musical instruments like drums and cymbals. Some *kangshinmu* special order unique ritual garments, but most *kangshinmu* nowadays purchase them ready-made, since these are readily available at specialty shops or directly from *shinbok* garment factories.

While in earlier days garments were made of cotton, hemp, or silk, nowadays they are often made of washable silk or synthetic fibers. The cost of each garment varies widely depending on the type of material used. Garments tailor-made from silk are the most expensive. Some neophyte shamans may receive their first set of ritual garments as a gift from the *shin pumo* (spirit parents), but often they must purchase these themselves. Later, *kangshinmu* may receive garments from clients who offer them as gifts. Some *kangshinmu* order the *shinbok* to be made by a tailor in order to produce unique garments, giving specific instructions to duplicate the spirit clothing they saw in their dreams.[18]

---

[16] Some *kangshinmu* leave the collection of ritual garments in a suitcase and take out the appropriate garments as needed during the ritual.

[17] *Shinjang* here means ritual garments. *Shinjang* has homophones, but the different meanings become clear by the Sino-Korean characters assigned to them (see glossary).

[18] I once observed a meeting held between a *paksu* (male shaman) and a tailor. The male shaman described the attire of the spirit who had appeared in his dream. He made specific

Generally, *manmulsang* (specialty store) owners or wholesale dealers will deliver a variety of ready-made *shinbok* to the door within an hour if a rush order is placed by telephone.

Prior to the ritual, new *hanbok* (traditional clothing) for departed relatives are purchased in anticipation of calling their spirits during *chosang* (ancestor) *kŏri*. One day I observed an unusual happening at a *kut*. This *kut* had begun at seven in the morning and had continued well into the evening when the *kangshinmu* was possessed by the unexpected spirit of a dead relative. She was scolding everyone, saying that she was hurt because no one had cared enough to prepare new clothing for her. No amount of pleading and apology from all four *kangshinmu* in the ritual hall did any good. The spirit was so demanding that the *kangshinmu* could not continue the ritual. The only thing to do then was to call a specialty shop so that the appropriate garment for this spirit could be delivered as soon as possible. This happened about eight in the evening and the *kangshinmu* had difficulty locating the shop owner who had already left the shop for the night. Within the hour the store owner, who had been reached by cellular phone,[19] brought the garment to the ritual hall located in a remote area. Once the *kangshinmu* put on the garment, the spirit was content and the *kut* was underway again, continuing until dawn.[20]

During a *chinjŏk kut*—a ritual sponsored by a shaman for their own spirit helpers as a personal celebration—the entire personal collection of the garments of spirits dear to the *kangshinmu* are displayed in addition to the standard garments required for the ritual. The *kangshinmu* dances wearing garments from the personal collection during the *chinjŏk kut*. Sometimes they dance briefly, holding each set of garments in their arms to entertain the various spirits, taking into consideration the limited time frame of the *kut*.[21] Even those *kangshinmu* (spirit-possessed shamans) who do not usually sing or dance will dance for the occasion with the clothing of their personal spirits.

As discussed above, both male and female *kangshinmu* wear the same ritual garments to honor the spirits whom they call to descend during the *kut*. If the possessing spirits are male generals, both male and female *kangshinmu* wear the same symbolic male generals' outfits and hats regardless of the sex of the *kangshinmu*.[22] Garments such as the *ch'ŏnik* (outer garment with long and wide

---

requests to the tailor for colors, textures, and styles of clothing in order to duplicate the garment (January 1998).

[19] Cellular phones are referred to as "hand phones" in Korea.

[20] This *kut* was held on November 20, 1998 at Sŏnhakdang in Inch'ŏn.

[21] Some dance all day long to entertain the spirits, as Mrs. Kang did in March 1994 (see chapter 1).

[22] In earlier writings, some authors seem to have misunderstood certain aspects of *musok* practice. Clark, for example, states that "[w]hile the Paksoo wears the outer dress of a woman while Shamanizing, the Mootang, on the other hand, always wears the outer dress

sleeves), *k'waeja* (long tunic), and *kugunbok* (coat-like garment with narrow sleeves) are fashioned after Chosŏn Dynasty military costumes.

The *ch'ŏnik* (outer garment with wide sleeves), also known as *ch'ŏllyuk* or *ch'ŏllik*, is fashioned after the Chosŏn Dynasty military officers' uniforms. The sleeves have wide white trim and extend to the floor. The garment is created in three colors—blue (*nam*), gold (*hwang*), and red (*hong*)—and worn for specific spirits during the rituals. The dark blue *ch'ŏnik* is worn for the spirits associated with war, victory, and courage, while the red one is for the spirits promoting peace and harmony.[23] During the Chŏnan *kŏri*(section), the gold *ch'ŏnik* is worn for the spirit of Kwan-Un-Jang.

The *k'waeja* (a long tunic),[24] also known as *chŏnbok*, for Hanyang *kut* comes in two colors: blue and black. Blue is worn for Shinjang and Taegam spirits and black is for Pyŏlsang and T'ŏ Taegam spirits. Black is often replaced by dark brown nowadays.

The *kugunbok*, a coat with red sleeves and red lining, is often called *sŏpsu* by the *kangshinmu* who perform the Hanyang *kut*. The bodice of the *kugunbok* is red, black, or dark brown. I think the term *sŏpsu* comes from *hyŏpsu*, a Chosŏn Dynasty military officer's outer garment with red narrow sleeves and red lining, which is also known as *tongdari*.

In addition to the *ch'ŏnik*, *k'waeja*, and *kugunbok*, the officiating *kangshinmu* wears the *changsam*, a long outer garment fashioned after Buddhist monks' robes.

Similarly, an ornate dress of a princess is worn by both male and female *kangshinmu* when possessed by the spirit of Pari Kongju (Princess Pari) for the recitation of the epic song "*Pari Kongju*" and for the dance of *toryŏng dolgi* (ritual circumambulation) during the Saenam *kut*, a large-scale Hanyang *kut* for the departed.

The *ch'ima*, a traditional woman's pleated skirt in floor length, is used as a ritual garment in *musok*. *Ch'ima* comes in two colors: red (*hong ch'ima*) and indigo blue (*nam ch'ima*). The *nam ch'ima* (indigo blue skirt) is considered the most essential piece of ritual clothing for the *kangshinmu* because it was the only ritual garment used during the periods when *musok* had to be practiced secretly from government authorities who confiscated ritual objects, ritual garments, and musical instruments. The sacred meaning of the *nam ch'ima* was

---

of a man" (Clark [1932] 1961:183). Paksoo (*paksu*) here refers to male shamans. Clark uses Mootang (*mudang*), on the other hand, to refer to female shamans.

[23] The dark blue *ch'ŏnik* is fashioned after the uniforms of *tangsanggwan* and the red one after *tanghagwan* of the Chŏson Dynasty. Both *tangsanggwan* and *tanghagwan* were military officers, *tangsanggwan* being the higher rank (Cho H.Y. 1997:160).

[24] The *k'waeja* is worn by *mudang* throughout country, including *sesŭpmu* (hereditary *mudang*).

concealed from outsiders because the skirt was made in the same style as everyday women's clothing.

The *paksu* (male shaman) puts on *nam ch'ima* before adding other ritual garments. For the Hanyang *kut*, the *nam ch'ima* is worn for the spirits associated with ancestors, courage, and war, while the *hong ch'ima* (red skirt) is worn for the spirits promoting peace and harmony or is used as a veil. The *nam ch'ima* is worn in the Hanyang *kut* during *chosang*, Sangsan, Pyŏlsang, Shinjang, and Taegam *kŏri* (sections).

In addition to the *kut*—rituals which include dance and musical offerings—small-scale rituals are also held by *kangshinmu*. The purpose and the funds available determine the size and type of ritual. The small-scale rituals called *pison* or *ch'isŏng* are generally performed by *kangshinmu* in plain *hanbok* (traditional clothing); in other words, male *kangshinmu* wear *paji chŏgori* (pants and top) and female *kangshinmu* wear *ch'ima chŏgori* (skirt and top).[25]

In the *sesŭpmu* (hereditary *mudang*) tradition, female *mudang* and *shimbang* (male *mudang* on Cheju island) wear ordinary Korean traditional clothing (*hanbok*) for their *kut*, except that occasionally they may add hats, colored vests, or other outer garments. Since no spirit possession takes place during the *sesŭpmu kut*, the diverse garments of the spirits are unnecessary for their ritual practice. During the Namhaean *Pyŏlshin Kut* held along the southern coast of South Kyŏngsang Province, colorful tunics and outer garments are used during the ritual. Sometimes elaborate headgear, red skirt, *k'waeja* (tunic), or *sŏpsu* (long outer garment) with multi-colored sleeves and black satin sash are used (Kungnip Munhwajae Yŏn'guso 1998: passim).

In the *haksŭpmu* (apprenticed *mudang*) tradition, the *kut* is not a sacred ritual but a public performance in secular context. The *haksŭpmu*, including actors and folk singers, will dress according to the repertoire they choose to perform. If they perform the Seoul or Hwanghae Province style *kut* on the concert stage, *haksŭpmu* wear costumes fashioned after the *shinbok* (ritual clothing) used by *kangshinmu* (spirit-possessed shamans) of those areas. Despite the fact that the *haksŭpmu* are dressed in costumes similar to the *kangshinmu*'s ritual garments, *haksŭpmu* are not possessed by spirits during their *kut* performance. When *haksŭpmu* perform repertoires from the *sesŭpmu kut* (hereditary *mudang* ritual), they usually wear white *hanbok* (traditional clothing) following the *sesŭpmu* tradition.

---

[25] Small-scale rituals like *p'udak-kŏri* or *yŏngjangch'igi* for the sick, and *yŏt'am* for a couple before their wedding, may be performed by *kangshinmu* in plain or ritual clothing.

2. Shamans and Their Clients

When people hear of the initiation of a neophyte shaman, they may attend the initiation ritual (*naerim kut*) and ask for divination after the neophyte is transformed into a *kangshinmu* (spirit-possessed shaman), because it is commonly believed that a new shaman is particularly accurate in fortune telling. Those who attend the initiation ritual often become *tan'gol* (regular clients). In sacred contexts, once the *tan'gol* relationship is established, the *kangshinmu* may refer to their regular followers as *tan'gol shindo* or *tan'gol* for short.

Tan'gol refers to a continuing relationship between two parties either in sacred or secular contexts in Korean social life. In secular contexts, *tan'gol* relationships may exist, for example, with people who favor a specific store. The shop owner may consider their regular customers as *tan'gol sonnim* (regular visitors) or *tan'gol* for short, while the customers may refer to the store as their *tan'gol kagae* (regular store).

Later on, the number of clients increases through the recommendations of the shaman's satisfied clients. The favorable reputation of a *kangshinmu* (spirit-possessed shaman) is usually based on the accuracy of divination and the efficacy of rituals performed for clients.

In the *sesŭpmu* (hereditary *mudang*) tradition, close relationships between client and *mudang* may continue through several generations within designated areas or neighborhoods known as *tanggolp'an*. *Sesŭpmu* are responsible for the welfare of people within the designated territory as a religious leader, while villagers reciprocate by offering grain to the *sesŭpmu* twice a year in the spring and fall.[26] *Sesŭpmu* may inherit the *tanggolp'an* or purchase it from another *sesŭpmu*. Nowadays, however, the number of regular clients for *sesŭpmu* is diminishing as many people from rural areas leave their towns seeking jobs in the cities. In other words, the size of *tanggolp'an* has been shrinking and the mutually dependent relationship between the *tan'gol mudang* and villagers of the *tanggolp'an* has been deteriorating.

Kangshinmu, too, used to have many regular family clients in their own neighborhoods. For *kangshinmu*, regular clients are becoming scarce nowadays because people wander from one *kangshinmu* to another, comparing predictions made by different *kangshinmu* like those who seek a second or third medical opinion from a physician. As a rule, it appears that family members who believe they have received immeasurable help from *kangshinmu* remain faithful to their *kangshinmu* in appreciation. I know several *kangshinmu* who have kept continuous relationships with a number of clients for several decades. Some

---

[26] In Honam area, *sesŭpmu* received "one or two *mal* (one *mal* is about half a bushel) of polished grain" from every household in the *tanggolp'an* in the spring and autumn (Kim T.G. 1983a:4). One *mal* is about 4.76 gallons or 18 liters.

inherit clients from their spirit parents or other *kangshinmu*. I observed one *kangshinmu* who had three altars in her *shindang*: one for her own spirits and two for the spirits of two other shamans who had passed away. The clients of the latter two *kangshinmu* have continued their relationship with the new one for several years. It was evident how much these *kangshinmu* care about their clients. They are familiar with the intimate histories of clients, they pray for them continuously, and forewarn their clients if the need arises.

In earlier days, the homes of *sesŭpmu* or *kangshinmu* were known in the neighborhoods because of the reverberant sounds of percussion instruments played during rituals. In contemporary Seoul, however, *kangshinmu* (spirit-possessed shamans) often reside in high-rise apartment buildings, practicing *musok* in other locations. Since the *kut* (ritual) is rarely held at the *kangshinmu*'s or clients' houses nowadays, *kangshinmu* can live among others completely unnoticed.

The ideal way to meet *kangshinmu* is through their clients' introductions, but this assistance is seldom available since most *musok* believers keep their relationship with the *kangshinmu* secret. Kangshinmu H, who resides in Washington State, told me that her practice is flourishing as clients increase due to satisfied customers' recommendations, although her reputation is not widespread in the Korean American community[27] because clients do not openly discuss their association with her. She told me that she arranges meetings with clients, allowing ample time between appointments so that clients leaving will not be seen by the incoming ones, to insure the privacy of both parties (personal communication, December 1995).

In Seattle where I live, two daily and two weekly Korean language newspapers often carry advertisements for divination by local *kangshinmu* or those in other areas of the United States who offer toll-free telephone numbers. In the local telephone directories published annually for the Korean American community, one can find several names and contact numbers of *kangshinmu* or *haksŭpmu* (apprenticed *mudang*).[28]

In contemporary Korea, one may also select a *kangshinmu* from magazine articles or books.[29] Yi Wŏn-Sŏp, for example, introduces forty-four *kangshinmu*

---

[27] The majority of Korean Americans are closely involved with Christian (Protestant) communities (Kim H.C. 1977: passim).

[28] Eight names are published in the *Korean Business Directory* under the heading of *yŏksul/unmyŏngch'ŏlhak* (divination based on *I Ching*) (The Central Daily 1998–99:171), and three in the *Korean Business Directory of Washington* under the heading *unmyŏngch'ŏlhak* (Korea Times 1998–99:147).

[29] Monthly magazines like *Queen* or *Yŏsŏng Tonga* feature articles about shamans based on interviews. Books published introducing shamans include:
Han'guk Minjok Hakhoe, ed. 1997. *Han'guk ŭi Myŏngmu* [Famous shamans of Korea]. Seoul: Mundŏksa.

in his book *Shinjŏm ŭi Myŏngin* [Well known *kangshinmu* diviners], published in 1996. He provides biographical information, describing the unique capability of each *kangshinmu* based on his interviews with them. The book contains photos, addresses, and phone numbers of the *kangshinmu* so that readers may contact them directly.

Since 1999, one may find information on *kangshinmu* on the World Wide Web.[30] Websites provide names, photos, and biographical information of *kangshinmu*. The address, map, telephone number, and e-mail address of each shaman are also included so that viewers may contact the *kangshinmu* directly.

When signs for *musok* practice are placed in front of houses or office buildings, people may drop in spontaneously for consultation, not knowing whether the diviner is an "analytical" *haksŭpmu* or "mediumistic" *kangshinmu* (Young 1980:56). As mentioned earlier, *haksŭpmu* acquire the technique of divination through books, while *kangshinmu* communicate spontaneously with the spirits.

Having observed a great number of *kangshinmu* over the last four decades, Sŏ Chŏng-Bŏm learned to classify *kangshinmu* into four types based on how they communicate with the spirits: some *kangshinmu* hear directly from spirits (radio type), while others see visual signs from spirits (slide type) or are guided to write down the messages (writing type). Some *kangshinmu* receive auditory as well as visual insights from spirits (television type) (personal communication 1993).

Divination is called *mukkuri*, *chŏmbok*, or *chŏmsa*. A white flag placed above the roof or near the window of a house indicates that the diviner is a *kangshinmu*. If the *kangshinmu* is musically trained and can officiate at a *kut* (large-scale ritual), a red flag is flown in addition to the white one, indicating that the *kangshinmu* is able to offer both divination and ritual services. One can see many red and white flags flying in Seoul, but it is important to keep in mind that most shamans still hide their *musok* practice from their neighbors.

Several shamans have told me about unfortunate experiences in dealing with strangers who walked in and insulted them for practicing "superstition." Some try to convert the shamans to other religions, usually to Protestantism. Perhaps this is a good place to recall an experience of mine in the field. One day I had an appointment to see a *paksu* (male shaman) and I arrived on time. When I rang the bell of the *paksu*'s house, a woman asked "Who is there?" over the

---

Mun Kyu-P'il, ed. 1997. *Hanŭn P'ulgo Tŏk ŭn Ssak'o* [Vent grudges and accumulate virtue]. Seoul: People Bank.

———. 1997. *Han'guk ŭi Musokin* [*Musok* practitioners in Korea]. Seoul: People Bank.

Yi Wŏn-Sŏp. 1996. *Shinjom ŭi Myŏngin* [Well known *kangshinmu* diviners]. Seoul: Pitsaem.

———. 1999. *Han'guk ŭi Mudang* [Korean *mudang*]. Seoul: Blue Family.

[30] For example, http://shamanism.view.co.kr.

intercom. I answered, "It's Maria Seo." Instead of buzzing to open the door for me, she said "We are Buddhists," and hung up. I was startled, but I soon realized that my name, "Maria," was the problem.[31] "Maria" is the Catholic name I received when I was baptized in Korea in my early teens. While living in North America for nearly four decades, I have used the name "Maria" instead of my Korean name, "Kong-Ju,"[32] which is sometimes difficult for English speakers to remember. I am so used to calling myself "Maria" that I did so without anticipating such a reaction.

I suppose the woman did not see the point of letting a Catholic person into a shaman's home. But why did she say they were Buddhists? Remembering that many shamans call themselves *posal* to outsiders, I concluded that she was hiding *musok* practice behind Buddhism. I buzzed again. "Who is there?" asked the woman. I gave her my Korean name, quickly adding that I had an appointment to see Mr. J. A young man rushed to the door and welcomed me. When I visited Mr. J again, I was invited to join the family for a meal and met Mrs. J, the woman who had answered the door. She was embarrassed and wanted to explain. As she was about to speak, Mr. J interrupted her, saying "Maria understands," and all of us around the dining table laughed knowingly, including family members and Mr. Kim, Mr. J's spirit son.

Clients of shamans may be *shindo* (*musok* believers) or outsiders who come for the first time to get help in a time of crisis. It is a challenge to the *kangshinmu* to convince the newcomer so that he will return for more consultations. I met one woman who visited *kangshinmu* Sut'ak (literally, rooster) twice in one day. She told me that she had met Sut'ak about a year earlier when she tagged along with her friend who came for consultation. At that meeting Sut'ak told her that her teenage daughter would leave home unexpectedly. In order to prevent this from happening, Sut'ak suggested that she sponsor a *ch'isŏng*, a small-scale ritual. She and her friend did not pay much attention to the warning for the daughter was doing well at school and appeared happy. About nine months later, when the daughter left home abruptly, the family was terribly worried, not knowing the girl's whereabouts for a few months. Regretting that she did not listen to Sut'ak earlier, she came to ask what could be done.

---

[31] Some *kangshinmu* tell me to use my Korean given name instead of "Maria," others encourage me to use "Maria" because they feel good to know that a Catholic is interested in learning more about *musok*. I heard many times that *kangshinmu* experience much difficulty in calling the spirits during a ritual if any Christians are present, therefore, sometimes Christians are asked to leave. I sometimes detected *kangshinmu* feeling uneasy when they first heard my Christian name. After the initial hesitation, however, all of the shamans I met have extended invitations for me to attend their *kut*.

[32] My Korean name, Kong-Ju (公珠), literally means precious pearl.

Sut'ak suggested to her that she sponsor a *kut*, a large-scale ritual, assuring her that if they agreed on the date of the *kut*, she would hear from her daughter within two hours. Having decided on the ritual date, she returned home. It took about an hour for her to get back home. As she entered the house the phone rang, and it was her daughter. Sut'ak and I were still visiting when the woman called. She was so excited to hear from her daughter that she wanted to come back immediately to bring money for the *kut*. She brought the agreed amount of 7,000,000 *wŏn* (about $6,000 in US funds) in cash in a large envelope and her husband joined later to discuss details about the *kut*. It was an amazing experience for me to observe these two meetings in one day. A few days later, I was able to record the ritual held for the young girl's safe homecoming.[33]

In order to maintain lasting relationships with *tan'gol* (regular clients) the *kangshinmu* must continue to pray and care for the members of their families. The first day of every lunar month, clients visit their *tan'gol kangshinmu* with offerings[34] and pray together in front of the altar in the *shindang* (shrine room).

Clients are advised by the *kangshinmu* to sponsor *kut* periodically or whenever the need arises. Since it costs so much to sponsor a *kut*, casual clients often hesitate to do so, but regular clients follow the *kangshinmu*'s suggestions implicitly, believing in the power of their *kangshinmu* and the efficacy of the *kut*.

It may be easy to assume that *musok* is practiced primarily by females, but if one gets to know more about the *chegajip* (sponsors), it becomes clear that men are often involved behind the scenes. Many men pay for expensive large-scale *kut*, but they often choose not to attend the rituals themselves to avoid any undue attention. Sometimes I have witnessed *kut* (rituals) attended by a lone male client without any of his female family members present. Some of these men were businessmen close to bankruptcy who wanted help but did not want their families to know. A family who sponsors a *kut* is referred to as *chegajip*, the male head of the family as *taeju*, and the wife or female head as *kiju*.

Pak Paksu and Ham Paksu, both male shamans in Seoul, have reputations for catering to men exclusively, because their clients are mostly (about 95%) male politicians or businessmen. Ms. Kim, a Seoul area shaman in her late thirties, told me that over 80% of her clients are male. She feels deep sympathy for men clients because she believes that they usually have more serious problems to worry about than women. According to her, women clients are concerned mostly with their family members' health, wealth, relationships, children's education and marriage, or the husband's extramarital affairs, but most men are concerned with making the right decisions for their careers and livelihood. She, too, finds that the majority of her male clients tend to be

---

[33] This *kut* was held on November 18, 1998, at Pohyŏnsanshin'gak in Seoul, attended by the girl's mother as the father was busy at work.

[34] *Tan'gol* bring cash, candles, boxes of incense, or bags of rice for their monthly offering.

politicians, businessmen, or office workers (personal communication, April 1999).

In general, social grace and diplomacy are essential to retain clients for long periods of time. Sometimes clients will overlook the capricious or unusual behavior of the *kangshinmu* if they believe that they have exceptional *shint'ongryŏk* (power to communicate with spirits) or the ability to perform the *kut* with successful results. It is a challenge for the *kangshinmu* to maintain good relationships with their clients, their own family, other *mudang*, musicians, helpers, merchants, and business associates. *Shint'ongryŏk* and social skills are the *sine qua non* for *kangshinmu* to prosper and expand their *musok* practices.

3. Shaman Associations

The National Association for Shamans, Kyŏngshin Yŏnhaphoe

While the core relationship between the client and the shaman remains personal and private, their relationship expands temporarily during rituals to include family members, friends, performers (invited shamans, musicians, and helpers), and onlookers. As the number of practicing shamans in Korea increases, networks have been established among the shamans to support each other. Some belong to large organizations while others prefer to work with small alliances.

Kyŏngshin Yŏnhaphoe, one of the associations for *kangshinmu* (spirit-possessed shamans), was founded by Ch'oe Nam-Ŏk in 1971. Its full name, Taehan Sŭnggong Kyŏngshin Yŏnhaphoe, has been translated into English as "The Korean Anti-Communist Spirit-Worshippers' Association" (Sun 1992:86) or "The Korean Shaman Association for Victory over Communism" by Kim T'aegon (1983b:289).[35]

Although members of the association are mostly spirit-possessed shamans, Ch'oe, the founder and director, is not spirit-possessed. His interest in *musok* began when he and his wife were healed by *kangshinmu* through *kut* (rituals) in the late 1960s. He told me that in his early forties he was completely paralyzed. He consulted several excellent doctors, but no physician or medication could cure him. A desperate man, he reached out for the *kangshinmu*, feeling like "a drowning man clutching at a bit of straw," as the Korean proverb has it. After the *kut*, he miraculously recovered in less than 24 hours. He was truly amazed

---

[35] Guillemoz translates Taehan Sŭnggong Kyŏngshin Yŏnhaphoe as "The Korean Federation of Associations for Victory over Communism and Respect of Beliefs" (1998:74). Hogarth translates it as "The Korean Spirit Worshippers' Association for Victory Over Communism" (1995:25).

and grateful. Later he witnessed his wife's healing during a *kut* (personal communication, November 1993).

Ch'oe wished to do something for the *kangshinmu* since he felt personally indebted to them. Realizing that *kangshinmu* are generally ostracized by the community, he volunteered to be their spokesman. He wanted to improve the image and status of *kangshinmu*. Believing in the strength of a nationwide organization, he talked with many *kangshinmu*, and within six months he was able to create an organization in South Korea with more than one hundred branches. The membership directory published in 1991 lists 1,557 *kangshinmu*—923 women and 634 men—belonging to 190 branches.[36]

Ch'oe was born into a Christian family in Sinŭiju, North P'yŏngan Province, North Korea, in 1925. His wife is Roman Catholic, his son is Buddhist, his daughter-in-law is Christian, and Ch'oe himself is now a *musok* believer. Ch'oe's business office and the office of Taehan Sŭnggong Kyŏngshin Yŏnhaphoe are located in the same office building in Seoul.

As the name of the association implies, members have helped to capture North Korean agents involved in espionage in South Korea. The law requires any Korean citizen who encounters strangers or suspicious incidents to report them to government authorities in order to reduce espionage activities from North Korea. Members of the association report their findings to government agencies for further investigation. When *kangshinmu* make pilgrimages to sacred places deep in the mountains, they sometimes notice unusual activities or encounter North Koreans in hiding. At times, when North Koreans come disguised to consult *kangshinmu* as clients, their true identities may be detected by the *kangshinmu* who alert the police. Between 1971 and 1991, members of the association reported to the police more than 68 times and assisted directly in capturing thirty North Korean spies.[37] Members have semi-annual *myŏlgong* (elimination of communism) training sessions at various branches of the association.

Since November 12, 1991, the association has published *Han'guk Minsok Shinmun* [Korean folk newspaper], a bi-weekly publication. Board members of the newspaper and the association are *kangshinmu*, but the staff members are not. The association has close relationships with numerous established *kuttang* (ritual halls) throughout the nation, in cities, on the outskirts of cities, and in remote mountain areas.

---

[36] *Kyŏngshin 20 Nyŏnsa Hwabo* [Twenty-year photo history of Kyŏngshin Association] published in 1991, includes names and photos of Taehan Sŭnggong Kyŏngshin Yŏnhaphoe members, as well as members' activities over the past twenty years.

[37] In 1972 members of Taehan Sŭnggong Kyŏngshin Yŏnhaphoe assisted in capturing 8 spies in Ch'ŏngwŏn, Northern Ch'ungch'ŏng Province, and Yi Ch'ung-Ho in the Seoul area, as well as 21 spies in Samch'ŏk, Kangwŏn Province in 1979 (Taehan Sŭnggong Kyŏngshin Yŏnhaphoe 1991).

The administrators of the association also attempt to eliminate fake *kangshinmu* and to control those who ask exorbitant fees from their clients, hoping to protect the shamans' reputation. Shaman members of the association pay annual membership fees, often donating additional gifts of money and offering assistance according to their individual abilities. A source of criticism about this association stems from *kangshinmu* who do not want to contribute for the benefit of the association. Some do not feel the need to belong to the organization, while others support it wholeheartedly. There are now two main organizations—Taehan Sŭnggong Kyŏngshin Yŏnhaphoe and Taehan Chŏngdohoe—established for *kangshinmu*, but some *kangshinmu* do not belong to either of them. Chŏngdohoe, formerly known as Taehan Chŏngshin Kyŏdohoe, has about sixty thousand members (*Han'guk Minsok Tae Sajŏn P'yŏnch'an Wiwŏnhoe* 1991:382).

Through the years, many scholars have studied *musok* working with several shamans in one area or in different regions, while others have focused on a single informant.[38] I have worked in depth with one shaman and one musician, but I have also worked with the members of several groups of shamans and musicians in the Seoul area. I learned valuable lessons by working with members of the large organizations, gaining varied perspectives. I had assumed from earlier readings that *musok* practitioners were limited to housewives or small groups of women. I was surprised to find these large associations of male and female shamans and to discover how widely *musok* is practiced in contemporary Korea.

The Taehan Sŭnggong Kyŏngshin Yŏnhaphoe is not a "secret organization" as defined by Georg Simmel. According to Simmel, a secret organization is an organization whose existence is concealed completely and the membership, purpose, and specific rules of the association remain secret to outsiders (Simmel 1950:346). Members of the Taehan Sŭnggong Kyŏngshin Yŏnhaphoe, in general, practice their religion privately but not secretly. This privacy is found in many societies as a strategy "to escape being stigmatized" by society (Warren and Laslett 1980:26).

Annual activities of Taehan Sŭnggong Kyŏngshin Yŏnhaphoe include divination for the nation held at the beginning of each lunar year, *Nara kut* (ritual for the nation) in June, Tan'gun *Che* (Ritual for Tan'gun) on October 3 at

---

[38] Laurel Kendall, for example, focused on Yongsu's mother in the 1970s, while Cho Hŭng-Yun focused on Yi Chi-San (a male shaman) in the 1980s and Kim Yu-Gam (a female shaman) in the 1990s. Halla Pai Huhm also worked with Yi Chi-San. Youngsook Kim Harvey, like many other scholars, studied several individual shamans. Alexandre Guillemoz, Hyun-key Kim Hogarth, and Barbara Elizabeth Young, on the other hand, worked with individual shamans as well as members of the organization Taehan Sŭnggong Kyŏngshin Yŏnhaphoe.

Manisan (Mt. Mani), *P'aldo Kut Taehoe* (Festival of Rituals from the Eight Provinces)[39] in the fall, and an annual meeting and luncheon in the winter.

The Annual Meeting and Luncheon of the Association

Kangshinmu members of the Taehan Sŭnggong Kyŏngshin Yŏnhaphoe have many official gatherings. In 1993 I was invited to attend their annual meeting and luncheon. When I arrived at the meeting hall on December 21st, there were about ten *paksu* (male *kangshinmu*) in the receiving line, all dressed in Western business suits and ties, greeting members and guests. A couple of *paksu* I knew came rushing toward me from the receiving line. They took me aside and told me that I should not be there in an exclusive *kangshinmu* gathering. Since this was the first official meeting to which I had been invited, I did not know what to expect or how to conduct myself. Suddenly someone came out from the hall to welcome me, thanking me for taking time to come. The *paksu* who were concerned about my presence looked pleased to learn that I was an invited guest. On this occasion five guests—two politicians, two well known scholars, and myself—had been invited. The guests were ushered in, seated in the front of the hall facing the room full of *kangshinmu*, and introduced. One politician and one scholar delivered encouraging speeches to about two hundred and fifty *kangshinmu* who had gathered from the various regions of Korea. After the speeches, the guests were led to another room to wait while the *kangshinmu* finished the business meeting. I learned that these four guests had been invited regularly for several years. I felt fortunate to be included. About half an hour later, the guests were brought to the luncheon in the adjoining restaurant where I was seated among the most powerful shamans. The exciting experience of being in the same room with so many *kangshinmu* shall remain with me for a long time. Among the members, I recognized several *kangshinmu* I had met before, but I certainly did not know them all. Since that time I have been approached by several *kangshinmu* on subways, at markets, or at concerts. They usually refer to the annual luncheon where they saw me. Among the many *kangshinmu* I have

---

[39] *P'aldo* (eight provinces) refers to the entire peninsula of Korea which once was divided into eight provinces—Hamgyŏngdo, Pyŏngando, Hwanghaedo, Kyŏnggido, Kangwŏndo, Kyŏngsangdo, Ch'ungch'ŏngdo, and Chŏllado. Contemporary Korea (North and South) has eighteen provinces. Nine provinces—Chagando, Hamgyŏng Namdo, Hamgyŏng Pukdo (*nam* means south and *puk* means north), Hwanghae Namdo, Hwanghae Pukdo, Kangwŏndo, P'yŏngan Namdo, P'yŏngan Pukdo, and Yanggangdo—are situated in North Korea. The other nine provinces—Chejudo, Chŏlla Namdo, Chŏlla Pukdo, Ch'ungch'ŏng Namdo, Ch'ungch'ŏng Pukdo, Kangwŏndo, Kyŏnggido, Kyŏngsang Namdo, and Kyŏngsang Pukdo—are located in South Korea.

met during the last nine years, I keep in touch personally with about two dozen members of this association.

The Annual P'aldo Kut

The annual *P'aldo Kut Taehoe* (Festival of Rituals from the Eight Provinces) is held by the members of the Taehan Sŭnggong Kyŏngshin Yŏnhaphoe. The eighth annual gathering of the *P'aldo Kut Taehoe* was held on September 23, 1998, at Changch'ung Stadium in Seoul. Earlier in June 1998, I was officially invited by President Ch'oe of Taehan Sŭnggong Kyŏngshin Yŏnhaphoe via an international telephone call between Seoul and Seattle. Since I had not received an invitation in the mail before I left Seattle to attend this gathering, I assumed that President Ch'oe had sent it to my Seoul address. But when I arrived in Seoul the evening before the event, I realized that none had been delivered to the house.

I did not call the office about the invitation but went to the stadium at about a quarter to eleven in the morning, expecting to be admitted. Cars and buses filled the entire parking lot, as well as the nearby streets, which were temporarily blocked for this event. Realizing that it would be nearly impossible to find anyone I might know in the crowd, I looked for the ticket booth, but it was closed. Noticing a few people with extra tickets in their hands, I approached them, asking if they would sell me a ticket. They told me in no uncertain terms that this was a closed affair. If I did not have a ticket or an invitation, I was definitely not welcome. I tried to explain my circumstances, but no one paid any attention to me.

Finally I saw Mr. K, a well known shaman, who had just arrived with his entourage and was being escorted toward the VIP room. Since I knew Mr. K, I decided to follow this group of people, and I was able to enter the stadium unnoticed. I waited outside of the VIP room while greetings were exchanged among Mr. K and the officials of Taehan Sŭnggong Kyŏngshin Yŏnhaphoe. Then I poked my face into the room. Many officers including President Ch'oe were happy that I had come from so far away and welcomed me warmly. President Ch'oe asked someone to show me the way to the VIP section reserved for special guests. I slipped away from the VIP seats to set up my video camera in the audience for I had permission to photograph and videotape the entire event.

The gathering began with the formal ceremonial entry of each group of shamans with their own musicians and banners, just like athletes making grand entrances prior to a game (see plate 8). When all the participants (approximately three hundred shamans and musicians) were gathered in the center area, the ceremony began with the saluting of the South Korean national flag and the singing of the national anthem. President Ch'oe and a few invited guests addressed encouraging remarks to the participants and the audience. Then began the performances of seven *kut*—two from the Seoul area and five from various provinces. The five provinces represented were Kyŏnggi Province, Kangwŏn Province, North P'yŏngan Province, South Chŏlla Province, and South Kyŏngsang Province.

Since these events were taking place in a much larger space than the usual ritual halls, all the performances were modified and choreographed to be visually appealing to the audience (see plate 9). The music was greatly amplified. The audience appeared to be more than three thousand people. Although I had watched videotaped recordings of all the previous annual gatherings beforehand, I was truly impressed by the actual event. It is difficult to imagine how much effort is invested in producing such a large-scale event. Realizing that all the participants are spirit-possessed shamans (except for a few hereditary *mudang*), I was thrilled to spend the day among so many ritual specialists. The audience consisted mostly of fellow shamans, families, and relatives. I felt very fortunate to be part of the audience and to observe how contemporary shamans strive to foster friendship and to continue their ritual traditions together on such a grand scale, filling more than one third the capacity of the 10,000-seat Changch'ung Stadium.

The 9th annual gathering of the *P'aldo Kut Taehoe* (Festival of Rituals from the Eight Provinces) was held on October 13, 1999, at the same stadium in Seoul. The rituals presented during the 9th annual gathering differed from those of the 8th annual *P'aldo Kut Taehoe*, but the whole day proceeded with the same atmosphere and enthusiasm.

Thirty Shamans Featured on a TV Talk Show

Several programs about *musok* (Korean indigenous religion) and *musok* practitioners have been produced for television. Topics include divination, initiation experience, regional varieties of *kut* (ritual), personal interviews, and exposés of fake *mudang*. On April 13, 1994, thirty *kangshinmu* (spirit-possessed shaman) members of the Taehan Sŭnggong Kyŏngshin Yŏnhaphoe were invited to be guests on a television program called *"Musokin Samship In gwa Hamkke"* [With thirty shamans] on KBS (Korean Broadcasting System). Ten *paksu* (male shamans) and twenty female shamans were seated in several rows. Near each *kangshinmu*, an individual sign was placed indicating his or her assigned seat number, name, and the name of the shaman's principal spirit, for example, number 8, Pang Ch'ang-Hwan, General Ch'oe Yŏng, and number 24, Kim Hye-Jŏng, Taeshin Halmŏni. The *kangshinmu* wore Korean traditional clothing except for two: one female *kangshinmu* wore a Western-style dress and one *paksu* wore a Western suit and tie.

The two talk show hosts asked interesting questions to be answered with yes or no. As each question was asked, each of the thirty *kangshinmu* answered yes or no by pressing a buzzer provided at their seats. After the answers had been tabulated electronically, a number indicating how many shamans agreed on a given question appeared in a large screen. Following each tabulation, short conversations on the same topic took place between the hosts and the *kangshinmu*. When one of the hosts asked the question, "Can *mudang* sense what other *mudang* feel without any direct communication, like through telepathy?" all thirty *kangshinmu* buzzed "yes" in total agreement, and the score board displayed "30." One *kangshinmu* who lives in Pusan said that although her *shin ŏmŏni* (spirit mother) resides in Seoul about 300 miles away, she knows how her *shin ŏmŏni* feels without even speaking with her on the phone.

When they were asked, "Can you make correct divination for foreigners?" twenty-eight said, "Yes." Lacking language skills, they divine through interpreters. Pang, a *paksu* who resided in Los Angeles and New York for about two years in the 1980s, said that most foreigners were skeptical and often tested *kangshinmu* to see if they knew small details about the inside of their residences which the *kangshinmu* had never visited. When every detail of their questions had been answered to their satisfaction, foreigners generally began to discuss personal problems.

Another question concerned the *kangshinmu* and their family life: "Do you think *kangshinmu* tend to neglect their marital relationships?" Twenty *kangshinmu* replied in the affirmative. Later on two *paksu*, Cho Cha-Ryong and Pak In-O, explained that no *kangshinmu* would intentionally ignore his or her spouse, but because the *kangshinmu* must spend much of their waking hours praying for clients as well as for themselves, spouses may feel neglected. Cho also added that *kangshinmu* abstain from sex for three days prior to a *kut* (ritual), especially if they plan to "ride the *chakdu*" (*chakdu t'anda*). Riding the *chakdu* refers to a shaman's act of standing barefoot on the sacred twin blades (*chakdu*) during the ritual.

When asked, "Can *mudang* decide the fee of a ritual on their own?" ten said "yes." Cho Cha-Ryong, who said "no," explained that if spirits wish to receive 1,000,000 *wŏn* for a *kut*, the *mudang* relays the message to the clients. If the clients want to pay only 800,000 *wŏn*, the *mudang* has to appeal to the spirits on behalf of the clients, but the spirits have the final say in this matter. There were a few more questions and the program ended with the question, "Are you happy being a *mudang*?" Twenty-nine buzzed, "Yes."

After the taping of this show in the KBS studio, the participants gathered to talk about their experiences. Several *kangshinmu* were unhappy because their answers were cut short or re-directed, not allowing them enough time to explain in depth. Most *kangshinmu* were frustrated because they did not have the chance to express their views since questions were directed to only a few during the program. I thought it quite remarkable that thirty *kangshinmu* had been invited by KBS. Since it is generally perceived that *musok* is no longer practiced in contemporary Korea, it provided a rare opportunity for viewers to see thirty *kangshinmu* on television for half an hour. Several viewers told me that they were surprised to realize that the *kangshinmu* on television did not look at all "weird" (*yisang haji ant'a*) but appeared as ordinary as any other Korean. Others commented that they were shocked to learn that *musok* is a living tradition.

The Association of Male Shamans, Hyangp'unghoe

Under the organizational skills of Yi Chae-Hŭng,[40] in 1995 a dozen *paksu* (male shamans) in the greater Seoul area created an exclusively male shaman group, known as Hyangp'unghoe (see plate 10). According to Yi, all the *paksu*, in their thirties to early fifties, are "elite" practicing shamans (personal communication, 1998). Members regularly socialize in their monthly meetings. Whenever a guest is to be invited, all members must unanimously agree beforehand. When I was invited in 1999, I was the third guest to attend their exclusive meeting in four years. Since 1997, they have been performing large-scale *kut* for the public in which all members of the association participate. Most Hanyang *kut* are carried out by three shamans, but for their *kut* performances, Hyangp'unghoe members rotate roles[41] since every member is a competent shaman who can perform any role.

The current president of Hyangp'unghoe is Yi Kil-Su; the general secretary, Ma Tu-Sŏn. Yim Ki-Uk plays an important role in leading the group, having specialized in the Hanyang *kut* for over three decades since his first spirit-possession at the age of seven.

Ham Kwang-P'il (b. 1936), a *paksu*, advises the Hyangp'unghoe members, offering his expertise in the Hanyang *kut*. The association's videographer, Yi

---

[40] Yi Chae-Hŭng is interested in promoting awareness of Korean traditional culture. He is the leading member of Seoul Minsok Hakhoe (Seoul Folklore Society).

[41] For instance, for the *chinogwi kut* (ritual for the dead) held for the "Unknown heroes of Korea" on June 14, 1997, Yi Kil-Su did *pujong kŏri, kamang ch'ongbae, kamang* and *chungdi noraekarak, ttŭn taewang* and *malmi kŏri*; Ko Sŏng-Ju did the *pulsa kŏri*; Cho Sŏng-Bong did *todang kŏri* and *twitchŏn kŏri*; Kim Tong-Ho did the *ponhyang* and *taeshin kŏri*; Yim Ki-Uk did *sangsan, pyŏlsang, shinjang* and *toryŏng kŏri*, as well as *pe karŭgi*; Ma Tu-Sŏn did *sŏngju kŏri*; and Pak Ŭi-Shik did *ch'angbu kŏri*. The other members participated by playing drums or cymbals, acting as *chegajip* (sponsors), and looking after details behind the scenes. To illustrate the rotating roles, I will provide one example here. The *pulsa kŏri* was performed by Ko Sŏng-Ju on June 14, 1997, as mentioned above, but for the *ch'ŏnshin kut* held on January 10, 1999, *pulsa kŏri* was performed by Yim Ki-Uk.

Hŭng-Dŏk (b. 1951), has been involved in Seoul area *musok* for more than two decades.

The founding members are listed in table 1 in alphabetical order followed by their year of birth and the names of their *shindang* (shrine room). The *shindang* is a sacred area usually in a shaman's home. If a *kangshinmu* is well established, he or she may create a name for the *shindang* and place a sign displaying the *shindang*'s name in front of the home. If the *shindang* is located away from the residence, the sign is placed there, not at the shaman's private home. The fact that all Hyangp'unghoe members have named their *shindang* suggests that they have many clients and are successful in their practices. In table 1, the last three names (Ch'oe Chong-In, Chŏng Sŏng-Jae, Chŏng Tong-Su) represent the new members who joined Hyang'unghoe in the spring of 1999.

Table 1
Hyangp'unghoe Members and Their *Shindang* (Shrine Room) Names

	member	year of birth	*shindang*
1.	Cho Sŏng-Bong	1951	Okch'ŏnbang
2.	Kim Tu-Nam	1959	Sŏngdaeam
3.	Kim Tong-Ho	1957	Samildang
4.	Kim Yŏng-Il	1956	Kukshindang
5.	Ko Sŏng-Ju	1954	Koryŏam
6.	Ma Tu-Sŏn	1953	Unhyŏn'gung
7.	O Chin-U	1956	Ilsŏngdang
8.	Pak Ŭi-Shik	1949	Sŏngjosa
9.	Pak Yŏng-Hun	1969	Oktoryŏng
10.	Yim Ki-Uk	1958	Ch'ilsŏngam
11.	Yi Kil-Su	1946	Yonghaeam
12.	Yi Sŏng-Jae	1952	Ch'ŏnjishinmyŏng
13.	Ch'oe Chong-In	1951	Ch'ŏngsach'orong
14.	Chŏng Sŏng-Jae	1962	Ch'ŏnjiindang
15.	Chŏng Tong-Su	1967	Yongmunjŏngsa

4. Shaman School, Musok Pojonhoe

Many neophyte shamans study privately with a *shin ŏmŏni* (spirit mother) or a *shin abŏji* (spirit father), but others are left alone when their ties with the spirit mother or spirit father are severed. For those without *shin pumo* (spirit parents), classroom instruction is available in Seoul for the contemporary neophyte *kangshinmu* (spirit-possessed shaman). Since established *kangshinmu* strive to maintain high standards in ritual performances, the teacher-shaman's role—either in private or in the classroom setting—becomes significant.

The first school for *kangshinmu* was established in Seoul in 1988, offering a six-month course with four-hour lessons seven days a week. The monthly fee for the school was in the range of $60 to $75 in US funds (1992–1994).[42] Many *kangshinmu* gather every night in the basement of the building where the Taehan Sŭnggong Kyŏngshin Yŏnhaphoe is located in order to attend classes designed exclusively for them by the Musok Pojonhoe (*Musok* Preservation Association).[43]

This school is run by Pak In-O (b. 1936), one of the vice-presidents of the Taehan Sŭnggong Kyŏngshin Yŏnhaphoe association. The school was founded in November, 1988, by Pak who began teaching two *kangshinmu* students in a small office located on the third floor of the building. The class was soon moved to a spacious, fairly soundproof basement room where students may play drums and gongs without concern for neighbors. The current classroom is about 50 *p'yŏng* (165 square meters)[44] in size. Classes are held nightly except when Pak and his students attend *kut* (rituals) together or go for *yonggung kido* or *san kido*—to pray by the ocean or deep in the mountains, respectively.

Pak In-O is a *paksu* (spirit-possessed male shaman) who became spirit-possessed at the age of eighteen. The genealogy of his *shin pumo* (spirit parents) can be traced up to the third ascending generation. His *shin ŏmŏni* (spirit mother) was Han Chŏng-Suk while Han's spirit mother was Yangssi Halmŏni (Grandma Yang), also known as Yang Kwangdae (musician Yang). Yang's spirit mother was Kang Yŏng-Ran who used to be one of the best known *kangshinmu* in the Hanyang *kut*.

Since both Kang Yŏng-Ran and Yangssi Halmŏni are known to have been employed at the inner court of the Chosŏn Dynasty, it is understood that Pak In-O performs *kut* following the *munsŏ* (correct rules)[45] of the court tradition of the Hanyang *kut* as transmitted by Kang Yŏng-Ran (Yang 1995:80). Under the guidance of Pak In-O at the Musok Pojonhoe, nearly eight hundred students have learned the *munsŏ* of the Hanyang *kut* since 1988.

The six-month intensive training program provides the basic skills to carry on as a shaman, but many students return to the school for further training to

---

[42] Mr. Pak waived my tuition and welcomed me to the classes as an observer. During my stays in Seoul between 1992 and 1994, I attended more than sixty classes, sometimes sporadically, at other times every night for periods of two to three weeks.

[43] Musok Pojonhoe is translated as "The Association for the Preservation of Shamanism" by Guillemoz (1998:75).

[44] One *p'yŏng*, a unit of area, is equivalent to approximately 3.3 square meters or 35.58 square feet.

[45] *Munsŏ* (literally, a document) refers to ritual knowledge including correct rules for rituals, songs, dances, instrumental music, garments, and table offerings.

improve their skills and expand their knowledge. Some leave school without completing the course when they become anxious to make more money rather than taking time to study, because they earn a lot of money even without going through the training experience. About 85% of the students earn a living as *kangshinmu* outside the school (Pak, personal communication, October 1993). A few of the students are *shin chason* (spirit children) of Pak In-O, but the majority of the students are those who do not have their own *shin pumo* (spirit parents) or those who are encouraged by their own spirit parents to study under Pak. The school provides ritual music and dance lessons, but perhaps its most valuable role is that of instilling pride and confidence in being a shaman, as well as in providing esoteric knowledge to neophyte students.

In one corner of the room, an altar is set up where offerings, candles, and incense burners are placed. When students enter or leave the room, they prostrate themselves before the altar to show respect to the spirits who reside there. The spirits are represented both in images and in calligraphy. At the left of the altar are seen images of the Three Buddhas (Sambul Chesŏk) and the Seven Star Spirits (Big Dipper or Ch'ilsŏng); calligraphic characters representing the Water Spirit (Yongshin), Hwan In, T'angun, Hwan Ung, the Mountain Spirit (Sanshin); and images of the Five Generals guarding the Five Directions (Obang Shinjang), and General Ch'oe Yŏng (see plate 11).

Students begin to gather about six o'clock. After paying their respects to the spirits at the altar, they usually pick up drums (*changgu*) to practice on their own. Pak, the only instructor in the school, arrives about seven. The class begins with ritual music lessons, progresses to ritual dance lessons, and ends with half-hour lectures on *musok*. Before the class is dismissed, Mr. Pak welcomes questions from the students.

At the school, I met students ranging in age from fourteen to early sixties. Some commute long distances from Inch'ŏn, P'yŏngt'aek, and Suwŏn in adjoining Kyŏnggi Province, all about an hour's train ride from Seoul. Students from other provinces move temporarily to Seoul for instruction, living in rented rooms away from their families. In the southern parts of Korea where the hereditary *musok* tradition is strong, guidance for those who become spirit-possessed is nearly impossible to find. Consequently, spirit-possessed neophytes seek instruction in the Seoul area, either at this school or privately with a spirit mother or spirit father. Most male students live alone during the course, away from their families, but some have wives staying with them who travel back and forth from Seoul to their hometowns to look after their households and children.

Beginners learn ritual songs from the textbook, *Chŏnt'ong Hanyang Kut Kŏri*, published by Pak (1990). The book contains no musical notation, only the ritual song texts. When a student has memorized the words of a ritual song and feels fairly comfortable singing without the book, he learns to drum to accompany himself. They often leave their books open on the floor beside their drums for occasional reference until they completely memorize the verses.

Because the texts are printed in large type, students can read the verses while drumming.

Since drumming patterns are not notated in the book, students must learn aurally to drum, listening to others. Students observe how others play until they are ready to try on their own. The *changgu* is played with two sticks, a *yŏlch'ae* (bamboo stick) held in the right hand and a *kunggul ch'ae* (wooden stick) in the left. Pak, who sits in front of the class facing the students, uses the *yŏlch'ae* (bamboo stick) in his left hand since he is left-handed and a *kunggul ch'ae* (wooden stick) in his right. This mirror image instruction apparently helps students to follow the drumming patterns more easily. If a student has difficulty following the *changgu* pattern, Pak or a senior student will give individual attention. As a rule, lessons on the *changgu* rhythmic patterns begin with simple patterns and progress to more complex ones. The pace of progress, however, is determined by individual ability. The student may join in as much as he or she is able.

Although during the *kut* (ritual), shamans usually stand and move about while singing, students in the classroom are encouraged to sit while learning ritual songs. This measure had to be enforced in the class because of some unusual episodes that happened in earlier days. Still inexperienced in controlling the spirits, neophyte students often become possessed by spirits while they are practicing ritual songs and dances because some songs are sung to call the spirits to descend. In order to avoid confusion in the class, the students now are seated while learning ritual songs.

To learn ritual dances, one must stand up. The students learn various steps, holding ritual objects like the bell tree (*pangul*), fan (*puch'ae*), cymbals (*chegŭm*) or the five directional flags (*obang shinjanggi*) (see plate 12). They learn the esoteric meanings of the dance, including the symbolic meanings of steps, turns, arm movements, and directions of the dance. If spirit possession takes place while students are learning to dance, others pause and listen to what the possessing spirit has to say, then continue the lesson.

When Pak notices that a student is ready for a solo song or dance performance, he invites the *kangshinmu* student to stand up and sing while fellow students provide the drum accompaniment together. These rehearsals enable students to gain the self-confidence needed to participate in the *kut* (rituals). When a student becomes competent, he learns to sing and dance fully clothed in ritual garments. This teaches students how to put on the ritual clothing and accessories, as well as how to handle the floor-length garments gracefully while singing and dancing. Students must learn to sing and dance holding ritual instruments such as fan, bell tree, pair of ritual knives, set of ritual flags, and cymbals.

Students learn stylized speech patterns used in rituals. They learn how to deliver messages (*kongsu*) and convey blessings (*tŏkdam*) from the spirits. The subject matter may differ from one spirit to another, but a stylized pattern of speech is sustained with some variation. While possessed by a spirit, *kangshinmu* may speak to clients concerning private or specific matters (*kongsu*), and the flow of speech should be rendered in the style of the benediction (*tŏkdam*). Students also learn how to ad-lib witty phrases (*chaedam*).

Several experienced shaman students have told me that they attend the school in order to learn *para ch'um*, a Buddhist spirit dance, which is Pak's specialty. Holding two large cymbals (*para*), Pak dances wearing a monk's robe and cowl. His dance steps are part of his prayer and his body movements become offerings to the spirits. He discreetly forms the Sino-Korean characters symbolizing the Sun (日), unit (目), and seven (七) with his dance steps. Even for advanced students, learning this dance is a challenge.

For "riding on *chakdu*" (*chakdu t'ada*), Pak stands barefoot on the sharp edges of two knives, carrying on his shoulders a whole pig (*t'ong sasil*), cleaned and purified as an offering (see plate 13). Two of his students—a male and a female student—have learned this tradition and they, too, climb on the *chakdu* carrying a whole pig as an offering to the spirits.

Several *kut p'ae* (ritual groups) have been formed by students from this school after training. I keep in close contact with a few of these groups. Many times I have observed how students are transformed into highly competent ritual specialists over the years. Occasionally I meet former students from this school in unexpected places. Although we recognize each other, I have learned not to say hello first. Every student I meet always finds a way to greet me discreetly, often apologizing for not acknowledging me openly. When other people sense that the shaman knows me somehow and ask if we know each other, the shamans are quick to say that they met me somewhere, never mentioning the school. Some students prefer to conceal the fact that they learned their skills and knowledge from any teacher, claiming that the spirits bestowed all their skills upon them. I have learned to keep silent in these situations.

One evening in 1992, I arrived at the school a little after seven to find that the class had already begun. Since the entrance is located at the back of the classroom, students pay little attention to who enters or leaves during their lessons. As I sat at the back of the classroom, I was surprised to see Mrs. A in the first row, singing and accompanying herself on the drum (*changgu*). As mentioned earlier, Mrs. A was the first *kangshinmu* (spirit-possessed shaman) I met in my fieldwork. When the singing session was over, students got up to put away the drums in one corner of the room and begin their ritual dance lesson. As Mrs. A stood up, she noticed me. I smiled, but she did not. She seemed ill at ease.

After the class, Mrs. A and I went to a nearby teahouse (*tabang*) to talk. At first she was angry. Apparently this was the school that Mr. A had told me that Mrs. A attended daily to pursue her new interest in Korean music back in 1991. It soon became clear why they did not tell me about the school or the repertoire Mrs. A was learning. I have attended several *kut* that Mrs. A performed with others and was amazed how well she sings. Whenever I praised her for her singing, Mrs. A used to tell me that she receives all her instruction, including ritual singing, from the spirits in her dreams, since her relationship with her spirit mother was severed. Toward the end of the conversation that evening, she pleaded with me not to tell anyone that she was learning ritual songs at the school. Since we know people in the same neighborhood, she was extremely concerned about her reputation. I promised her that I would not mention that she was a student at Musok Pojonhoe (*Musok* Preservation Association) to any neighbors. She was appreciative when I said that I would not use her legal name if I were to discuss her or her family in my work.

I have also met other shamans who claim that they have been taught exclusively by the spirits, while others are proud to tell me about their teachers. Since a few aged *kangshinmu* are known to have the correct *munsŏ* (ritual knowledge) for the Hanyang *kut*, many young shamans are eager to study under them. Among the Seoul area *kangshinmu*, this saying is considered well founded: *"Yŏnggŏm ŭn shinryŏngnimi chudoe, chaejunŭn paewŏra"* (The spirits may bestow supernatural power on you, but you have to learn the skills and artistry).

CHAPTER 5

Kut in Sacred and Secular Contexts

Kut are usually performed in a sacred context, but in recent years many *kut* have been presented on concert stages for the general public in a secular context. The main difference between secular and sacred contexts is the purpose or intent of the ritual. Rituals in sacred context are performed for ritual "efficacy" while rituals in secular context are performed for "entertainment" (Schechner 1988:120).

In the following sections, I will examine the etymology of the term *"kut"* and explain various types of *kut* in diverse performance contexts: *kut* by *kangshinmu* (spirit-possessed shamans) and *sesŭpmu* (hereditary *mudang*) in sacred context and *"kut"* presented by folk singers in secular context. I will also discuss how ritual music from the northwestern provinces is used for *"Paebaengi Kut,"* one of the *sŏdo sori* (folksong) repertoires, and ritual music from the Hanyang *kut* is adapted to theater productions. In addition, I will introduce several *kut* recognized by the government as Important Intangible Cultural Properties and discuss the changes taking place in rituals presented for the public in sacred context by *kangshinmu* and *sesŭpmu*.

Etymology of *"Kut"*

Considering the etymology of the word *"kut,"* Yi Nŭng-Hwa has postulated that its meaning is embedded in *"kujŭn nal"* (foul weather day) or *"kujŭn il"* (euphemism for a funeral) in view of the fact that some rituals are held for the deceased or to alleviate illness or misfortune ([1927] 1991:176). On the other hand, G.J. Ramstedt (1949) traces its origin in North Asian terms—the Tugusian *"kutu,"* the Mongolian *"qutug,"* and the Turkish *"qut"*—all of which mean "happiness" or "fortune" (Ramstedt 1949:132). It is interesting to note that Yi and Ramstedt each focused on one type of ritual, namely for the deceased and for the living, respectively.

According to Pak, a *sesŭpmu* (hereditary *mudang*), the term *"kut"* comes from *"kushi,"* an old term for a large container for cooked rice prepared at rituals or celebrations for many participants (personal communication, 2000). In *musok*, people believe that the ancestor spirits look after the health and prosperity of the living. One of the basic necessities for health is sustenance. In Korea, this means rice. If the ancestor spirits are pleased, there will be many healthy babies born to the family, providing valuable labor for the plentiful harvest to keep the living well. Rice produced with the blessing of the ancestor spirits is prepared and offered to them at rituals. On the offering table, a bowl of cooked rice for each ancestor is laid out, as well as a variety of cakes made from rice. A bowl of uncooked rice is also placed in anticipation of plentiful blessings from the spirits.

"Kut" may be associated with the Yakut word *"kut"* (soul). The Korean language is said to be a branch of the Altaic language family to which the Yakut language also belongs (Lee, P. 1993:4). Some *kut* (rituals) are held to lead the soul of the departed safely to another world or to marry two souls to ensure peace and harmony for them as well as for the living members of their families. During the *kut*, *kangshinmu* (spirit-possessed shamans) may call for the souls of ancestors to communicate with the living relatives and to comfort one another. The Yakut people believe that at death both the good and the evil go up to the sky where the soul (*kut*) takes the form of a bird (Eliade 1974:206). In Korean *musok*, some souls are also believed to be transformed into birds after death.

Variety of *Kut*

As mentioned earlier, *kut* is commonly understood as a large-scale ritual performance with music and dance, but small-scale seasonal offerings for one's family ancestors without any music may also be referred to as *kut*. Large-scale *kut* with music and dance may be led by musically trained ritual specialists—*kangshinmu* (spirit-possessed shamans), *sesŭpmu* (hereditary *mudang*), or *haksŭpmu* (apprenticed *mudang*).

Some large-scale *kut* may be performed without a *mudang* (ritual specialist), as in the Hahoe *pyŏlshin kut*, Sudong *pyŏlshin kut*, and *ture kut*. *P'ungmul kut* are led by musicians who play percussion instruments and *hojŏk* (conical oboe). *P'ungmul p'ae* (groups of village musicians) may perform *kut* without any *mudang* as in the Ŏmmiri *Changsŭngje* in Kwangju and P'ilbong *Tangsanje* in Yimshilgun, both in Chŏlla Province (Lim J.H. 1999:104).

Some *maŭl kut* (literally, village *kut*) are led by musicians, while some are led by *mudang*, as in the Changmal *Todang kut* of Kyŏnggi Province, *Taedong kut* of Hwanghae Province, Wido *Ttibae Nori* of North Chŏlla Province, and *Yŏngdŭng kut* of Cheju Island.

Mudang kut are led by musically trained *mudang* (ritual specialists) who are accompanied by *chaebi* (ritual musicians). Both *kangshinmu* (spirit-possessed shamans) and *sesŭpmu* (hereditary *mudang*) officiate at various rituals for individual clients and their families, for neighborhoods, and for the nation. In addition, the *kangshinmu* hold rituals for *momju*, their personal spirits.

Kut by Spirit-Possessed Shamans

There are many types of *kut* performed by *kangshinmu* (spirit-possessed shamans). In addition to various life cycle rituals, *kut* may be held for other reasons—the *chaesu kut* to usher in good fortune (*chaesu*),[1] *pyŏng kut* to heal the sick, *chinogwi kut* for the dead,[2] *honryŏng kut* to marry two souls so that they may rest in peace (see plate 14),[3] *maŭl kut* for the welfare of a neighborhood, *nara kut* for the nation, and so on. See chapters 9 and 10 for more detailed descriptions of *chaesu kut* (also known as *ch'ŏnshin kut*) and Seoul *Saenam Kut* (a type of *chinogwi kut*).

Sacred rituals for the departed are important to the surviving family members, because the relationships between the living and the dead are considered mutually dependent.

---

[1] The *kut* held to usher in good fortune is generally called *chaesu kut* but is referred to as *ch'ŏlmul kut* in Hwanghae Province and *toshin* in Chŏlla Provinces (Hwang L.S. 1990:103).

[2] The *kut* held for the benefit of a departed soul is called *chinogwi kut* in Seoul, *suwang kut* in Hwanghae Province, *tari kut* in North and South P'yŏngan Provinces, *mangmuk kut* in North and South Hamgyŏng Provinces, *ogu kut* in *tonghaean* (northeastern coastal region), *ogusaenam kut* in the southeastern coastal region, *ssikkim kut* in North and South Chŏlla Provinces, *Siwang maji* in Cheju Province, and *kil karŭm* in North and South Ch'ungch'ŏng Province (Hwang L.S. 1998:42).

[3] *Honryŏng* [*honnyŏng*] *kut* is a posthumous wedding ritual. It is also referred to as *mangja honsa kut* or *chŏsŭng kut*. The souls of two unmarried people are united in the ritual sponsored by the families after the deaths. Since people believe that dead souls do not age, the marriage might take place later when the family can find a suitable spouse for their loved one and is ready to sponsor a *kut*. As Roger Janelli and Dawnhee Yim Janelli explain, "[d]ead children never become adults, as they do in China (Jordan 1972:140-55; Wolf, A. 1974b:148). Posthumous marriages, for example, are performed only for those who died at a marriageable age, never for those who died as children, regardless of how many years have passed since their deaths" (Janelli and Janelli 1982:160).

Rituals for neighborhoods are held in Korea under various names.[4] They are group-oriented, recurrent, and anticipated. Despite the fact that neighborhood rituals give rhythm to social life and strengthen the established values of the community, the number of neighborhood *kut* is declining. In the Seoul area about one hundred *todang kut* for neighborhoods are performed during the first and tenth months of the lunar calendar. The seasonal rituals—*kkotmaji kut* in spring, *ipmaji kut* in summer, *sin'gokmaji kut* in fall, and *sibaesari kut*[5] in winter—were performed until recently (Huhm 1980:12).

At the present time, many *kut* are sponsored by individual families to heal sickness or to overcome economic crises. When a family moves into a new home, they hold Sŏngju *kut,* also known as *ant'aek kut,* for peace and prosperity. Some families sponsor periodic or calendric rituals in the privacy of their homes to avoid criticism from outsiders. Many socially prominent families have sponsored *kut* two or three times a year for several generations. The *kangshinmu* and musicians are selected carefully in order to keep their *musok* related activities secret.[6] Since most of these sponsors' houses are surrounded by enormous gardens, the rituals are scarcely noticed by the neighbors.

The most important audience for the *kut* are spirits, gods, and the souls of departed family members. At times, no *chegajip* (sponsor) is present at the *kut* performed by *kangshinmu* if the ritual is sponsored by those who reside overseas or by families who wish to remain anonymous. With or without sponsors present, the *kangshinmu* and the musicians go through the ritual with the same sincerity.

Ritual offerings of food, music, and dance for the spirits may also be enjoyed by the people who attend the *kut.* During the *kut,* offerings of food and drink placed on the altar may be distributed to the people in the audience by the *kangshinmu* as symbolic blessings from the spirits. At the end of the *kut,* ritual offerings of fresh fruits, meats, candies, and various types of *ttŏk* (rice cakes) are given to friends to take home at the discretion of the sponsors. The food

---

[4] The neighborhood *kut* held in the Seoul area is called *todang pugun kut*. It is called *taedong kut* or *todang kut* in Kyŏnggi Province. It is referred to as *tangsan kut* in North and South Chŏlla Provinces, *pyŏlshin kut* or *sŏnang kut* in the eastern coastal region, and *taedong kut* in Hwanghae Province (Hwang L.S. 1998:39). In Cheju Island, it is known as *shin'gwase kut, yŏngdŭng kut, mabullim kut,* or *shinman'guk taeje* depending on the season when the *kut* is held for the neighborhood (Hwang L.S. 1990:103).

[5] *Sibaesari kut* mentioned by Huhm refers to the *sebaesari kut* held in the first month of the lunar calendar (Chang S.M. 1992:221).

[6] I cannot divulge information about these sponsors or their ritual practices, for they are families of well known politicians, medical doctors, scholars, businessmen, and deans of colleges. Whenever I attended rituals held at their residences, I did not photograph or videotape the sponsors, respecting the hosts' wishes to remain anonymous.

prepared for those attending the *kut* is arranged by the *tangju*,[7] the *kangshinmu* responsible for the entire ritual. Sometimes the *tangju* may request the owners of the *kuttang* (ritual hall) to provide food (*tangshim*) for a fee, but usually the *tangju* prepares the food offerings at home to reduce the cost. The hospitality and generosity shown to guests are overwhelming. For instance, I have attended several *kut* held for large audiences—some with over four hundred people—and boxed lunches, *ttŏk* (rice cake), and canned soft drinks were offered to all. If the *kut* is performed in a secular context on a concert stage, the practice of sharing food and drink is often limited or dispensed with.

Once the clients agree to sponsor a *kut*, they offer a deposit for the cost of the ritual to the *tangju kangshinmu* who looks after the event from beginning to end, including the *sarye ch'isŏng*, a small ritual that takes place on the third day after the *kut*. The *kangshinmu* selects an auspicious date for the *kut*. The most popular dates for *kut* are those that contains the number nine, that is, the 9th, 19th, and 29th days of the month (according to the lunar calendar) or days with the signs of the pig or horse from the twelve zodiac signs.[8]

Kuttang (ritual halls) are overbooked on popular dates.[9] For example, six *kut* may be held at the same time in the three adjoining rooms at Kuksadang, which is about 9 meters by 20 meters.[10] There is scarcely space for anyone to move when multiple *kut* are in progress. A cacophony inevitably results as each *kut* proceeds at its own pace. The sixth and twelfth lunar months, however, are considered *ssŏgŭn dal* (literally, rotten months), and no ritual is held during these two months as a rule unless it is an emergency.

When the date of the *kut* has been chosen, the *tangju* (the hired *kangshinmu*) calls his or her in-group members[11] and a *chaebi* (musician) for

---

[7] *Tangju* is also known as *chumu* (literally, the principal *mudang*) in the Seoul and Kyŏnggi areas. They are referred to as *kyŏnggwan* in Hwanghae Province, and *kŭmjul* in Kyŏngsang and Kangwŏn Provinces (Yi W.S. 1999:30).

[8] The twelve zodiac signs used by Koreans for the 12-day cycle are mouse, cow, tiger, rabbit, dragon, snake, horse, sheep, monkey, chicken, dog, and pig.

[9] Numerous *kuttang* (ritual halls) are located in mountains throughout Korea. For example, *kuttang* nestled in the mountains surrounding Seoul include Chŏnssi Kuttang on Tobong Mountain; Pŏmbawi Kuttang on Surak Mountain; Pohyŏn Sanshin'gak, Samgoksa Kuttang, and Hayanjip (literally, white house) Kuttang on Samgak Mountain; Kuksadang on Inwang Mountain; Namsan Kuttang on Nam Mountain; and Ch'ŏnshindang on Kwanak Mountain. Each *kuttang* has three to fifteen ritual halls. *Kangshinmu* from the Seoul area also use *kuttang* located in other provinces.

[10] The two smaller rooms, one on each side of the building, are about nine meters by three meters; the largest room in the center is about nine meters by fourteen meters.

[11] The group members who perform *kut* together are referred to as *kutp'ae* by outsiders but *kangshinmu* do not use the term among themselves. It is important to realize that

assistance. If more than one musician is required for the *kut*, the first musician recruits his in-group of musicians for the occasion. The musician responsible for hiring other musicians is often the *p'iri* player, referred to as the *chaebi tangju*. He has complete freedom to select musicians for the upcoming *kut*. Some *kangshinmu* will not decide on the date of a *kut* until their favorite musicians have agreed to work at the ritual, especially for Hanyang *kut* where the ensemble music plays an essential part.

The *tangju*'s responsibilities begin prior to the *kut* and extend beyond the ritual date. When assisting *kangshinmu* and *chaebi* have performed their roles during the *kut*, they may leave, but the *tangju* must remain to look after the details. On the third day after the *kut*, the clients gather at the *tangju*'s shrine, and together they offer a small-scale ritual, *sarye ch'isŏng*, to thank the spirits.[12]

Kangshinmu in Seoul perform small and private rituals as well as large-scale *kut* incorporating *muak*—songs and instrumental music. The small-scale rituals are generally called *pison* or *sonbibim*, both referring to the act of praying by rubbing one's palms together in a circular or vertical motion. Small-scale rituals may or may not include music. Among the *pison, aekmaegi* is a ritual that seeks to prevent misfortune, while *kosa* is a ritual held for a family's peace, health, and safety. For the sick, *pison, p'udak-kŏri*, or *yŏngjangch'igi* is held. *Pison* is accomplished through prayer, while *p'udak kŏri* involves *taesu daemyŏng* where one's misfortune is transferred to another object. For example, a chicken is presented as a sacrificial offering in place of the sick person. It is believed that a patient will regain health if a chicken is sacrificed for him. A chicken's feet and wings are tied during the *p'udak kŏri* ritual and a paper containing the information of the patient—name and *saju* (information about the time and date of birth)—is slipped underneath the tied chicken wings. For the same effect, an egg may replace a chicken for *taesudaemyŏng*. The sacrificial chicken or egg is buried after the ritual.

Yŏngjangch'igi, on the other hand, is a ritual carried out as if the patient were already dead, going through a mock burial. The patient lies down and is covered by a cloth, prayers are said, and grains are thrown over the body to dispel bad spirits, thereby restoring the patient's health. Once I witnessed a *yŏngjangch'igi* held for a patient who had been temporarily discharged from a Western style hospital to undergo the ritual. The patient was still wearing a hospital bracelet. After the *yŏngjangch'igi*, the patient immediately resumed her hospital stay, waiting for the ritual to take effect.

If a person dies, a small-scale ritual called *chipkashim* may be held privately at the home of the dead after the burial to cleanse and purify the residence. If

---

group members change frequently, often due to personal conflicts. While working together, however, they refer to each other as *sikku* (family member).

[12] This small-scale ritual is also referred to as *samil ch'isŏng* (literally, the third day offering).

chinogwi kut, a large-scale ritual for the dead, is held at the home of the dead, a small-scale ritual called *chari kŏji* is held prior to the formal *chinogwi kut* to purify the place where the person died. Clean clothing is laid out where the person died and seven coins are placed on top symbolizing Ch'ilsŏng (Seven Star Spirits) who is known to look after the dead as well as the living, while the *kangshinmu* prays for the dead, punctuating phrases with cymbals.

If a person died by accident, the *kangshinmu* goes to the scene of the death to pick up the soul prior to performing *chinogwi kut*. Once I observed *kilje* (literally, street ritual) performed by three *kangshinmu*—Yi Yŏng-Hŭi, a male shaman, and his two spirit daughters. Several members of the grieving family attended the *kilje* while their friends also mourned for the dead. Mr. Kim was killed by a car as he walked along the side of the road. The ritual for Mr. Kim began about six in the evening by the roadside in the outskirts of Seoul and continued at a *kuttang* (ritual hall) until the next morning (March 2000).

Ch'isŏng, a small-scale ritual offering, may be held any time of the year. *Hongsu maegi*, a type of *ch'isŏng*, is held during the first month of the lunar calendar to prevent unforeseen disasters in the coming year, while *pangsaengje*, held in the spring, is for freeing turtles and fish, sending them back to the river and ocean.[13] This compassionate action is also practiced in Buddhism. In present-day Seoul, a floating Buddhist temple on the Han River has an extra room reserved for *musok* practitioners in order to hold *pangsaengje* throughout the year.[14]

Kangshinmu may perform *yŏt'am*, a ritual before a wedding to let the ancestors of both the bride's and groom's families know about the happy occasion and to ask for their blessings. *Hwan'gap yŏt'am* is held for a person who becomes sixty years old. *Kangshinmu* also perform *kemshimbach'im*, a ritual to pray for a son to be born or wishing for the health of a new baby and his mother after the son is born (Kim T.G. 1983b:278).

Pison or *ch'isŏng* are usually offered by one *kangshinmu* who prays and sings while accompanying himself on either *koritchak* or *ching*. Dance is omitted in these small-scale rituals. The size of *pison* or *ch'isŏng* may be enlarged to a mid-size ritual employing additional *kangshinmu* and musicians.

In addition to holding rituals for clients, a few rituals are held exclusively for the shamans. For example, *hŏju kut* and *naerim kut* are held for the neophyte shamans and *chinjŏk kut* for established ones. The *hŏju kut* takes place prior to the *naerim kut* (initiation ritual) to separate good spirits (*shin*) from malevolent ones (*kwi shin*). The *naerim kut*, also known as *kangshin kut* or *shin kut*, is held to initiate a *kangshinmu* (spirit-possessed shaman).

---

[13] As a symbolic gesture, people go to markets to buy turtles and fish to free them back to the river. Street vendors also sell live turtles and fish at parking areas along the rivers.

[14] Beginning on the 14th of the first lunar month, *pansaengje* may be offered throughout the year. Some make *pansaengje* offerings each month.

Shamans generally celebrate the anniversary of their *naerim kut* (initiation ritual) by officiating at a ritual known as *chinjŏk kut*. The first two *chinjŏk kut* held by a neophyte *kangshinmu* are usually referred to as *kari kut* and *sosŭl kut*.[15] For the *chinjŏk kut*, the *kangshinmu* invites his or her colleagues, regular clients, family, and friends, and offers thanks to the spirits and ancestors. Some shamans hold the *chinjŏk kut* twice a year, in the spring and fall, while others do it only once every other year or occasionally, whenever funds are available. When Yim Ki-Uk, a Seoul area *paksu* (male shaman), held four *chinjŏk kut* in the year of the tiger (February 1998–February 1999), it was mainly due to personal reasons.

Invited *kangshinmu* attend their friends' *chinjŏk kut* to observe, to celebrate, and to show their respect. Since most of the shamans are busy with their own activities, they seldom have time to observe others' rituals except at someone else's *chinjŏk kut*.

The Annual *P'aldo Kut* sponsored by the Taehan Sŭnggong Kyŏngshin Yŏnhaphoe provides an opportunity for *kangshinmu* to socialize and to support each other for a whole day once a year. Many *kangshinmu* participate and enjoy watching others perform at this annual gathering (see chapter 4 and plates 8 & 9).

Kut by Hereditary *Mudang*

Korean *sesŭpmu* (hereditary *mudang*) are usually female. The musical training of *sesŭpmu*, in contrast to that of *kangshinmu* (spirit-possessed shamans), begins within the family at an early age. Since hereditary *mudang* families generally practice virilocal endogamy,[16] a woman usually continues her musical training under her mother-in-law after marriage and emerges as a *tanggol mudang* (vernacular term for hereditary *mudang*),[17] carrying on the tradition of her husband's family. Male members of *sesŭpmu* families assist the female *mudang* in various ways according to their abilities. If musically talented, husbands and male relatives of the *sesŭpmu* will provide music for the rituals by singing or playing instruments for song and dance accompaniment. They are known as *koin, hwarang,* or *yŏmjang*. If additional musicians are needed, musicians from outside the extended family of the *sesŭpmu* may be invited to perform. They are professional instrumentalists, known as *pigabi*. Other male family members engage in various tasks such as making *chohwa* (paper flowers), purchasing and arranging offerings on the altar, and assisting clients at rituals.

---

[15] *Sosŭl kut* is sometimes referred to as *pullil kut*.

[16] Hereditary *mudang* nearly always marry within the *mudang* community. The wife lives in the home of her husband and in-laws after the wedding ceremony.

[17] *Tanggol mudang* are also known as *tan'gol mudang*.

Since the *kut* in *sesŭpmu* tradition is performed without *kongsu* where the spirits speak through the ritual specialists, the quality of musical performance and dramatic presentation of the joys and sorrows of life have been highly developed to attract and sustain the interest of audiences.

Kut by *sesŭpmu* in a sacred context is now a dying tradition in many parts of contemporary Korea as people have migrated to the cities since the 1960s, reducing the rural population and the funding sources for *kut* within small communities. Many *sesŭpmu* who were also farmers moved away from the countryside to the cities for better job opportunities, adapting to new situations and breaking away from the practice of performing *kut* for life cycle rituals and seasonal celebrations. In coastal regions of the peninsula, though, *musok* practice still thrives. On the eastern coast, for example, two groups of *sesŭpmu* are still actively engaged in *musok,* led by Song Tong-Suk[18] and Kim Sŏk-Ch'ul[19] (Chŏng P.H. 1992:38). Despite the fact that the need for hereditary *mudang kut* in a sacred context has decreased in farming communities and in the countryside, their *kut* has sustained its popularity by being presented in a secular context as part of the traditional performance of music, dance, and drama.

The music, speech, dance, and symbolism of *sesŭpmu* rituals have influenced the development of various secular genres of Korean folk music, dance, and theater. Many of the present-day folk music genres in Korea—both vocal and instrumental—have developed largely from the *kut* music of the hereditary *mudang* tradition. Vocal genres like *p'ansori* (solo epic singing with *puk* accompaniment),[20] *pyŏngch'ang* (solo singing accompanying oneself on a string instrument),[21] *ch'anggŭk* (opera),[22] and *Namdo minyo* (regional folk songs of southwestern provinces) reflect the melodic and rhythmic formulae of the

---

[18] Song Tong-Suk's group consists of about ten members, including Pyŏn Nan-Ho, Song's former wife, and their daughter Song Myŏng-Hŭi and her husband Kim Chang-Gil. Song's current wife, Kim Mi-Hyang, works with the group as well for the annual Tano festival held each May in Kangrŭng [Kangnŭng] City, Kangwŏn Province.

[19] Kim Sŏk-Ch'ul belongs to the 4th generation of a *sesŭpmu* family. Kim Sŏk-Ch'ul and his two brothers and sisters-in-law—elder brother, Kim Ho-Ch'ul, and his wife, Yi Kŭm-Ok, and younger brother, Kim Ch'ae-Ch'ul, and his wife, Chŏng Ch'ae Ran—lead the largest group of *sesŭpmu* nowadays. Kim's group has about thirty members including Kim Sŏk-Ch'ul's three daughters and their spouses.

[20] *P'ansori* is often described as a "one-person opera." The singer sings, acts, and tells stories, accompanied by a *puk* (double-headed barrel drum) played by another musician.

[21] *Pyŏngch'ang* began with *kayagŭm* (twelve-string zither) and *kŏmun'go* (six-string zither) accompaniment but nowadays *pyŏngch'ang* with *haegŭm* (two-string fiddle) and *ajaeng* (bowed zither) are also performed.

[22] *Ch'anggŭk* is a musical drama sung in *p'ansori* style, but with several singers, accompanied by string and wind instrumental ensembles, and drums—*puk* (double-headed barrel drum) and *changgu* (hourglass-shaped drum).

sesŭpmu kut music in both North and South Chŏlla provinces. Instrumental music genres like *sanjo* (instrumental solo accompanied by *changgu* or *puk*),[23] *shinawi* (instrumental ensemble),[24] and *samulnori* (ensemble of four percussion instruments)[25] have also developed from the *sesŭpmu* music tradition. The intricate compound rhythms of the southeastern *kut* music provide the basis for *samulnori* and the mournful melodic lines of the southwestern *kut* music echo in *p'ansori, sanjo,* and *shinawi*. As the demand for *kut* as sacred ritual diminishes, many hereditary *mudang* and their musicians become *minsok ŭmak* (folk music) performers in present-day Korea since they are considered the best singers and instrumentalists trained in these musical genres.

"*Kut*" by Secular Musicians and Actors

"*Kut*" by Folk Singers

Musically talented people who learn to perform songs from the *kut* (ritual) repertoire are referred to as *haksŭpmu* (literally, apprenticed *mudang*). Although they are called "apprenticed *mudang*" (*haksŭpmu*), they are not actually *mudang* (ritual specialists). In recent years, *haksŭpmu* have begun to include *kut* songs in their performances and have even claimed to present the *kut* of the *kangshinmu* tradition on the concert stage. Despite the fact that these professional singers sing the same songs as the *kangshinmu,* performances are carried out for "entertainment," not for ritual "efficacy" (Schechner 1988:120).

I would like to discuss two "*kut*" performed by *haksŭpmu* in secular contexts—one by Kim Hye-Ran and one by Pak Chŏng-Uk. Both Kim and Pak are well known professional folk singers. They learned ritual songs from *kangshinmu* teachers in order to perform properly according to the ritual

---

[23] *Sanjo* is a solo instrumental genre developed in the late 19th century. *Sanjo* may be performed on such instruments as *kayagŭm, kŏmun'go, haegŭm, ajaeng, taegŭm* (transverse flute), *hojŏk* (conical oboe), and *p'iri* (cylindrical oboe).

[24] *Shinawi* is an instrumental ensemble where all the musicians improvise based on music derived from the *sesŭpmu* (hereditary *mudang*) *kut* in southwestern Chŏlla Provinces.

[25] *Samulnori* literally means "four things to play." The *samulnori* ensemble plays four percussion instruments: *changgu* (hourglass-shaped drum), *ching* (large gong), *kkwaenggwari* (small gong), and *puk* (double-headed barrel drum). The group Samulnori was formed in 1978 by four young male musicians. The founding members—Kim Duk-Soo [Kim Tŏk-Su], Ch'oe Chong-Sil, Lee Kwang-Su, and Kim Yong-Bae—were born into the hereditary *namsadang* (itinerant entertainers) tradition. The members of *namsadang* perform masked drama, acrobatics, and *p'ungmul nori* (playing folk musical instruments) for village gatherings, celebrations, and life cycle rituals.

tradition. The first *"kut"* was performed at Yesul ŭi Chŏndang in Seoul[26] by Kim Hye-Ran (b. 1951),[27] and the other was performed by Pak Chŏng-Uk (b. 1964) at the Sejong Cultural Center, also in Seoul.[28]

Kim Hye-Ran is a professional singer designated by the government as *isuja* (master artist) of Important Intangible Cultural Property number 57, Kyŏnggi Province *minyo* (folk songs).[29]

The *kut* concert by Kim Hye-Ran was so popular that the entire performance had to be repeated immediately following the scheduled one in order to accommodate the overflow of invited guests and ticket holders. In general, Korean traditional music concerts are not as well attended as Western classical music performances in Korea. Kim Hye-Ran, although known as one of the top *minyo* singers, would probably have had difficulty drawing a full house had she given a traditional *minyo* recital. She was able to draw such a large crowd to this concert because it was announced as "The Seoul *Kut*"—part of the celebration of Seoul's 600-year anniversary as the capital of Korea. The *kut* by Kim Hye-Ran was a ticketed event with each ticket costing 10,000 *wŏn* (about $12 in US funds, 1993), but the majority of the audience consisted of invited guests.

A great number of cultural and sports activities are regularly scheduled in Korea, giving the public a wide variety of events to choose from. Organizers of these events usually send out many invitations, anticipating that only a fraction of the invited guests will actually attend the event. Consequently, it has become common practice in Korea for a person receiving an invitation to arrive at the box office about an hour before the scheduled event to exchange the invitation for a complimentary ticket with an assigned seat number. When I arrived at the Yesul ŭi Chŏndang on November 27, 1993, about one hour before the performance, I found the ticket office closed and the entire foyer so crowded that there was no room to move. I was pushed by waves of people from the foyer to the auditorium, and I entered with the invitation still in my hand. The ushers gave up checking tickets, and the performance, scheduled for 5:30 p.m., finally began about half an hour late.

---

[26] The *"kut"* was performed on November 7, 1993, in Yesul ŭi Chŏndang's T'owŏl Theater, which seats 667.

[27] Kim Hye-Ran's legal name is Kim Suk-Gŭn.

[28] The concert, Pak Chong-Uk's *Shinmyŏng P'uri*, was held in the Small Theater of Sejong Cultural Center, January 11–13, 1998.

[29] The term *minyo* "was borrowed from Japan since *'min'yo'* is generally accepted to have been introduced by the novelist Mori Ogai (1862–1922) as a loan-word based on the German *Volkslied*. As a combination of two common Sino-Korean characters, *'min'* [民] for 'people' or 'folk' and *'yo'* [謠] for 'songs,' it may nonetheless have been used sporadically before then" (Howard 1990:100).

Audience members filled all the aisles and were even seated on the stage, but still it was impossible to accommodate all who had come to see the performance. I later learned that people who could not be accommodated at the first concert waited about two hours because the organizers had announced that an encore performance would immediately follow the first.

Posters for this recital showed the singer Kim dressed in the ritual attire of a *kangshinmu* (spirit-possessed shaman) as in a Hanyang *kut*. The first paragraph of the program notes,[30] however, attempted to clarify the fact that Kim Hye-Ran was not really a *kangshinmu*, but rather a professional singer who had studied under An Pi-Ch'wi,[31] a famous Kyŏnggi Province *minyo* singer.

For Kim Hye-Ran's recital, two shamans were on stage—Chang Chŏng-Suk, who played cymbals, and Kim Ch'un-Gang, who played the *changgu* (hourglass-shaped drum) and supervised the entire *kut*. In addition, a *samjaebi* (trio ensemble) of *chaebi* (professional ritual musicians) playing *p'iri* (cylindrical oboe), *haegŭm* (2-string fiddle), and *taegŭm* (flute) had been hired for the occasion.[32]

The center of the stage was decorated with a table of offerings and Kim Hye-Ran was assisted by twelve professional Kyŏnggi *minyo* (folk song) singers who acted as *chomu* (assisting shamans) and *chegajip* (clients) during the performance. Many details appeared similar to the Hanyang *kut* held by a shaman, but the performance differed from the conventional *kut* in many respects. For example, in place of *kongsu*—where the possessing spirit speaks through a shaman—Kim Hye-Ran and other singers, pretending to be possessed by the spirits, recited dialogues they had learned from the *kangshinmu* teachers. Also, eight Kyŏnggi *minyo* singers sang *Hoeshimgok*, a well known folk song, which is not a ritual song of the Hanyang *kut* repertoire.

Older audience members who came expecting to see a real *kut* for sentimental reasons were disappointed, but younger members were excited, because Kim's performance provided a glimpse of the Hanyang *kut* that many people in contemporary Korea presumed had completely vanished.

Kim Hye-Ran's concert made a significant contribution toward making the music of Hanyang *kut* more accessible to the general public and minimizing the unfounded fear of becoming a shaman if one—especially a musically gifted person—participated or attended in a *musok* related activity. With a polished concert-style performance, Kim succeeded in showing that songs from the Hanyang *kut* are musically appealing. A few weeks later, the entire event was

---

[30] Yi Chi-San, a *paksu* (male shaman), wrote part of the program notes.

[31] An Pi-Ch'wi (1926–1997) was the *poyuja* (bearer) of Intangible Cultural Property no. 57 for Kyŏnggi Province *minyo* (folk songs), designated by the government in 1975.

[32] The musicians were Kim Ch'an-Sŏp (*p'iri*), Kim Han-Guk (*haegŭm*), and Pak Mun-Ung (*taegŭm*).

televised nationwide as "The Seoul *Kut*" by the Korean Broadcasting System, vastly increasing the audience beyond the original performances.

As a Kyŏnggi *minyo* (folk song) singer, Kim Hye-Ran had been learning songs of Hanyang *kut* repertoire for several years from *kangshinmu*. Her *kangshinmu* teachers were Kim Yu-Gam, a female shaman, and Yi Chi-San, a *paksu* (male shaman), who are both well known for their performance skills in the Hanyang *kut*. Kim Hye-Ran, being a native of Seoul, was able to master both sacred and secular genres of songs from Seoul and the adjoining Kyŏnggi Province because she has the "insider's" inherent knowledge of speech patterns, musical concepts, and aesthetics of the area.

The standard Korean language taught in schools and used in national broadcasting follows rules set by the government. But *sat'uri*—dialects with unique accents and particular expressions—exist in the vernacular language in all parts of the country. Similar to the *sat'uri* in spoken language, *t'ori* (musical dialects) likewise exist in the various regions of Korea. Musical *t'ori* are expressed in their distinctive melodic lines, vocal timbres, ornamentation, and rhythmic patterns, particularly in folk songs. Musical *t'ori* may be broadly divided into four groups: *kyŏng t'ori* in Seoul and nearby Kyŏnggi Province, *menari t'ori* in the eastern provinces, *yukjabaeki t'ori* in the southwestern provinces, and *sushimga t'ori* in the northwestern provinces (Yi P.H. 1982b:173–186).

One must be aware that music is never permanent, never confined to one area, often extending beyond geographical boundaries, and constantly changing. Many musicians attempt and achieve "bi-musicality" or multi-musicality by learning the music of other areas in addition to their own (Hood 1960:55–59). But within Korea, few *minyo* singers gain mastery of the musical *t'ori* of other regions because it is difficult to assimilate flawlessly the inherent aesthetics of other styles. Consequently, many professional singers specialize in secular and sacred song repertoires from one geographical area of the same musical *t'ori*.[33]

The famous late *p'ansori* singer Kim So-Hŭi, for example, a native of Chŏlla Province, sang hereditary *mudang* songs at a *ssikkim kut*[34] held for two of her students who died in 1984. The hereditary *mudang* officiating at the *ssikkim kut* in Chŏlla style invited Kim So-Hŭi to sing several songs for her deceased students, knowing that Kim, a native of Chŏlla province, could sing in the musical *t'ori* of that province. Ch'ae Su-Jŏng, a young *p'ansori* singer, also was able to assist in the *ssikkim kut* held for Kim Ch'ang-Jo and Kim Chuk-P'a (this

---

[33] An exception to this, for example, is Yu Chi-Suk who was born in Kanghwa, Inch'ŏn, but studied in Seoul under Oh Pok-Nyŏ, *poyuja* for Important Intangible Cultural Property no. 29 *Sŏdo Sori*, the folk song tradition of the northwestern provinces. In 1995, Yu was designated as *chŏnsu kyoyuk pojoja*, an assistant teacher responsible for *Sŏdo Sori*, Important Intangible Cultural Property no. 29.

[34] A ritual for the dead is called *ssikkim kut* in both North and South Chŏlla Provinces.

ritual will be discussed below). Similarly, Pak Chŏng-Uk, who specializes in folk songs from the northwestern provinces, performs a *ch'ŏlmul kut*[35] from the same area in *sushimga t'ori*.

The second concert-stage "*kut*," by folk singer Pak Chŏng-Uk, was performed on January 13, 1998. At first people with tickets were ushered into the theater, filling it to about one third capacity. When the performance was about to start, a large number of people rushed into the theater and filled the remaining seats. They packed all the aisles, leaving no room to move. I learned later that many people had been waiting in line to purchase tickets. In an effort to begin the concert on time, people were asked to enter the theater without tickets, and the concert eventually started about half an hour later.

The first part of the program was performed by Pak, his students, and guest artists who sang folk songs of Hwanghae Province. Following the intermission, the second half of the evening concert consisted of the *ch'ŏlmul kut*. An altar filled with offerings was placed on the stage, and *kangshinmu* Yi Sŏn-Bi (b. 1934), Pak's teacher, was invited to perform the *pisu kŏri*.[36] Many singers—more than a dozen—sang together the ritual songs of Hwanghae Province *kangshinmu*, wearing vibrantly colored costumes and hats fashioned after the *kangshinmu* ritual clothing of that province. The variety of costumes worn by the choir disregarded the sacred symbolic relationship of each garment to the particular *kŏri* (section) of the *kut*. Although the concert had been announced as a *ch'ŏlmul kut*, Pak and the entire company sang only a few selected songs from the *ch'ŏlmul kut* repertoire for the occasion.

Throughout several curtain calls, Pak and the other singers showered the audience with candies, the symbolic sharing of food, throwing them from the stage. People seemed to enjoy catching them in midair and sharing with those who could not catch them directly. Since I was holding a video camera, people sitting nearby offered me candy after the curtain finally came down.

During the *ch'ŏlmul kut* Pak held on February 4, 2000, for the millennium, music accompaniment was provided by a percussion ensemble made up of *samulnori* musicians who played *changgu*, *ching*, *kkwaenggwari*, and *puk*, and a *hojŏk* (conical oboe) player.

The reactions of *kangshinmu* (spirit-possessed shamans) to the "*kut*" performances by *haksŭpmu* (apprenticed *mudang*) were not favorable. The *kangshinmu* were mainly concerned that the modified concert in a secular context might give a wrong impression of their ritual practices to general audiences.

---

[35] *Ch'ŏlmul kut* is a ritual held in the northwestern Hwanghae Province to usher in good fortune. It takes two to three days to perform the entire ritual in sacred context. *Ch'ŏlmul kut* is usually held in the first lunar month or in the fall.

[36] *Pisu kŏri* in the northwestern tradition is the same as *chakdu kŏri* in the Hanyang *kut*.

Kim Hye-Ran's concert provided a pivotal point for many *kangshinmu* of Hanyang *kut*, for they felt challenged to present the authentic *kut*—the ritual of *musok* in a sacred context—to the public. Following the concert, several *kangshinmu*, including Kim Ch'un-Gang, who had directed Kim Hye-Ran's "*kut*" on stage, decided to produce compact discs of their own singing in order to share genuine shaman music. Three well known *kangshinmu* in Seoul—Kim Yu-Gam, Yi Sang-Sun, and Kisaeng Paksu (nickname)—produced a series of three audio cassette tapes of Hanyang *kut* music. These tapes are not for sale to the public but circulate in the *kangshinmu* world, where they serve as reference tools for neophyte shamans, even though the recorded songs represent only a small portion of Hanyang *kut* music. Two other rare, noncommercial recordings feature Yi Sang-Sun, a *kangshinmu*, singing "*Hwangje P'uri*" (1995) and "*Pari Kongju*" (1999) epic songs, accompanying herself on the *changgu*.

Seoul area *kangshinmu* (spirit-possessed shamans) also began to participate in public performances, presenting a few *kŏri* (sections) in condensed versions of the Hanyang *kut* on the concert stage.

"*Kut*" as Theater Production

Sŏnt'aek (The Choice): Kut-nori Theatre was performed February 5–21, 1999, at the Munite Theater (Munye Hoegwan), a small hall in Seoul. The play was produced by the Hyun-Bin [Hyŏn-Bin] Theatre Company under the direction of Kim Il-U, with music supervised by folk singer Yi Kŭm-Mi.

The play was adapted from the novel *Sŏnt'aek (The Choice)* by Yi Mun-Yŏl and presented a combination of western-style theatre with the traditional *kangshinmu kut*. The play selects five *kŏri* (sections) from the Seoul *Saenam Kut*, a ritual for the departed, which normally includes more than two dozen *kŏri* when performed in a sacred context.

Unlike other plays that include some elements of *musok* rituals, *Sŏnt'aek* is performed entirely as a ritual for Lady Chang of Andong (1598–1681). Lady Chang was given the title *chŏngbuin* by the government in recognition of her role as a wise mother and fine wife (*hyŏnmo yangch'ŏ*) of the Yi family during the Chosŏn Dynasty.[37] She grew up as an only child and was taught to read at an early age by her father. She began to write poems at age fifteen and produced several books and essays during her lifetime. For example, *Kyugonshiŭibang*, a cookbook written by Lady Chang, has been handed down within her family for generations, but it became known to the public only about three decades ago.

---

[37] Lady Chang married into the Yi family at the age of nineteen, but she is referred to by her maiden name Chang since a Korean woman does not change her family name to that of her husband after marriage.

The book was recently translated into modern Korean by Hwang Hye-Sŏng. Several books about Lady Chang have been published by her descendants.

The play *Sŏnt'aek* (*The Choice*) progresses in the following order:

1. *Pujong Kŏri*

The play begins as Yi Yong-Yi, the principal "spirit-possessed shaman," recites prayers to purify the ritual area.

2. *Chosang Kŏri, Ch'o Yŏngshil*[38]

During the *chosang kŏri*, the principal "shaman" invites the ancestors, assisted by a "shaman" playing an hourglass-shaped drum (*changgu*). The soul of Lady Chang is invited, and she speaks through the "shaman" about her life. The uninvited soul of Hwang Chin-I,[39] a well known female entertainer (*kisaeng*), arrives, and she, too, speaks her mind.

3. *Shinjang Kŏri, Taegam Kŏri, Mugam Kŏri*

"Shaman" Yi Wŏn-Jong performs *shinjang kŏri*, divining with the five directional flags. He explains the meaning of the colors—white, yellow, red, green, or black—associated with each of the five directions, asking several audience members to choose one of the flags for divination.

Kim Yŏn-Jae performs *taegam kŏri*, offering blessings to the audience and selling rice cakes as a means of fund-raising to benefit starving children in North Korea.

During the *mugam kŏri*, the audience is invited to come to the center of the stage to participate. Several members of the audience join in the dancing while music is provided by two professional female musicians, Yun Hŭi-Jŏng and Chŏng Yu-Jin playing *haegŭm* (two-string fiddle) and *p'iri* (bamboo oboe),

---

[38] *Ch'o yŏngshil* consists of three words: *ch'o* (first), *yŏng* (spirits, souls), and *shil* (place). During the *Saenam kut*, the souls are invited three times: during *ch'o* (first) *yŏngshil*, *wŏn* (main) *yŏngshil*, and *twi* (last) *yŏngshil*. Each time, the invited souls speak to the surviving relatives through *kangshinmu*.

[39] Hwang Chin-I (c.1506–1544) is generally regarded as Korea's greatest female poet. According to Peter Lee, her works on the mutability of love are acclaimed for their depth of feeling, meditative rhythms, and rich symbolism (Lee, P. 1981:92).

respectively, assisted by the "shamans" playing *changgu* (drum) and *chegŭm* (cymbals).

4. Saenam Kŏri, Wŏn Yŏngshil

During this *kŏri*, a short version of *"Pari Kongju"* (Princess Pari) epic song is recited and Lady Chang's soul "appears" through the "shaman" Yi during *wŏn yŏngshil*. Lady Chang speaks about her life and ideals. She bids farewell, speaking her last words to audience members who play the part of surviving relatives.

5. Toryŏng Tolgi, Pe Karŭgi

As the last rite, "family members" led by a "shaman" walk together, guiding the departed soul to the other world during the *toryŏng tolgi* (ritual circumambulation). The play ends with the *pe karŭgi*, where the "shaman" tears two long pieces of cloth made of cotton and hemp, symbolizing this world and the next, in order to send Lady Chang in peace to the other world.

Several scholars and *kangshinmu* (spirit-possessed shamans) were in the audience at the performance I attended on February 6, 1999. The play was well received by *kangshinmu*, scholars, and the general public.

Sim Woo-sung [Shim Wu-Sŏng] (b. 1934), a well known actor and folklorist, has created a number of monodramas incorporating traditional *pallim* (mime), puppetry, and Korean masked dance. He performs his works without speech. Several of his works are influenced greatly by *musok* rituals—*P'anmunjŏm Pyŏlshin-kut*, *Kŏch'ang Pyŏlshin-kut*, and *Kyŏlhon-kut* to name a few. The *Kyŏlhon-kut* (wedding of souls) derives from the *Chŏsŭng honsa kut*, a sacred ritual to unite two souls who died unmarried. In his drama *Kyŏlhon-kut*, however, Sim attempts to transcend the political ideologies of the divided Korea through this symbolic "marriage" of North and South Korea.

Paebaengi Kut—A Parody of *Kut*

Paebaengi Kut is a secular epic song performance from the northwestern provinces, now part of North Korea. Like the *p'ansori* (epic song) from the southern part of the peninsula, the *Paebaengi Kut* is performed by a solo singer with a drum accompaniment provided by an instrumentalist. Both *Paebaengi Kut* and *p'ansori* singers sing (*ch'ang*), narrate (*aniri*), act (*nŏrŭmsae*), and dance (*pallim*), with minimal props—a fan, a stick, and a kerchief. The drummer shouts encouragement (*ch'uimsae*) while providing musical accompaniment. *Paebaengi Kut* is accompanied by the hourglass-shaped drum (*changgu*), unlike *p'ansori*, which is accompanied by the double-headed barrel drum known as *sori puk* or *kojang puk*.

Well known *Paebaengi Kut* singers include Chang Su-Gil, Ch'oe Sun-Gyŏng, Kim Ch'il-Sŏng, Kim Chong-Jo, Kim Kwan-Jun, Kim Sŏng-Min, Kim Yong-Hun, Mun Ch'ang-Gyu, Paek Shin-Haeng, Yang So-Un, Yi Ŭn-Gwan, and Yi Yin-Su (Sŏng K.R. and Yi P.H. 1992:582). Since the division of the country in 1945, a few musicians who moved to South Korea from the north have continued this genre of singing. Among the singers who specialize in *Paebaengi Kut*, Yi Ŭn-Gwan (b. 1917) studied *Paebaengi Kut* with Yi Yin-Su, a student of Kim Kwan-Jun. In 1969, the government designated *Paebaengi Kut* as part of Important Intangible Cultural Property number 29, *Sŏdo Sori* (folk songs from the northwestern provinces), and Yi Ŭn-Gwan as its *poyuja* (holder).

Although the original composer of *Paebaengi Kut* is unknown, Kim Kwan-Jun, a well known *sŏdo sori* (northwest regional folk song) singer, is acknowledged as the first singer to perform *Paebaengi Kut*. Some say that Kim added music to a text written by An Ch'ang-Ho, a respected patriot[40] who is said to have created the play in order to reduce superstition among the people (Sŏng K.R. and Yi P.H. 1992:583). *Paebaengi Kut* is a parody of *musok* practice, making fun of fake *mudang* as well as corrupt Buddhist monks.

Since 1934, about a dozen transcribed texts of *Paebaengi Kut* have been collected and published by several scholars. The transcriptions were based on performances by Kim Kyŏng-Bok, Kim Sŏng-Min, Yi Ŭn-Gwan, Kim Yong-Hun, and Yang So-Un. The most recently published text is that of a performance by Kim Kyŏng-Bok (b. 1915) transcribed by Yang Jongsung [Yang Chong-Sŭng] in 1998.

The story of *Paebaengi Kut* takes place in Seoul about 360 years ago during the 23rd year of King Sukjong of the Chosŏn Dynasty (Sim U.S. 1988:170). There were three friends—Yi, Kim, and Ch'oe—who were all civil servants titled *chŏngsŭng*. Wishing to have heirs, their three wives went to several temples to pray for sons. After many months of praying, the three wives became pregnant and all three produced girls. As expectant mothers, Mrs. Yi dreamed of catching three falling moons (*se wŏl*), Mrs. Kim dreamed of catching four moons (*ne wŏl*), and Mrs. Ch'oe dreamed of tightly braiding a *talbi* (hairpiece,

---

[40] An Ch'ang-Ho (1878–1938), also known as Tosan, was a towering historic figure who contributed greatly toward Korea's independence from Japan through his organizational skills, strong personal character, and intellectual leadership among Korean nationalists, particularly among those living abroad (Kim H.C. 1996:xv).

described coloquially as *paebae*).⁴¹ So the three families named their girls according to their dreams—Yi Sewŏlne, Kim Newŏlne, and Ch'oe Paebaengi.

The three families lived as neighbors, the Ch'oes in the middle, facing the Yis in the front and the Kims behind. Later, two of the girls—Sewŏlne and Newŏlne—got married, but not Paebaengi. One day a young monk came to Paebaengi's house asking for alms for the temple. Since her parents were away, Paebaengi opened the door. The young people fell in love at first sight. When the monk returned to his temple, he began to suffer from love sickness. The monks at the temple decided to help him. They put the young monk in a basket and brought it to Paebaengi's house, asking her father to keep it for them in a clean corner of the house for it was filled with offerings for the temple. They told Mr. Ch'oe that they would return to fetch the basket one day. Paebaengi's father placed the basket in a clean corner of his house inside Paebaengi's room.

One day Paebaengi, suffering from love sickness, began to lament, expressing her wish to see the young monk again. Realizing their feelings were mutual, the young monk hidden in the basket began to sing in response to Paebaengi. For months, they shared the nights, but the monk remained in the basket during the day. One day the monk decided to go away to earn money, promising Paebaengi that he would come back to fetch her within a few months. He never returned, and Paebaengi died waiting for him.

The Ch'oes were so shocked by the sudden death of their only child that they advertised throughout the nation that if any *mudang* could bring back Paebaengi's soul so that they could speak with her, they would give half of their belongings. "Five thousand seven hundred and seventy-two" *mudang* from every corner of the peninsula came to try calling back Paebaengi's soul, but none succeeded. To describe the *mudang* coming from different regions, the singer uses appropriate musical *t'ori* (regional musical dialects) to sing their dialogues.

One day a fellow traveling from another town was having a drink at a tavern. Hearing *kut* music, he asked the tavern owner what was happening. Feeling sorry for Paebaengi, the woman told him all about Paebaengi. She not only described how many bolts of silk and the exact amount of money Paebaengi had left behind, but also where she had hidden it. Since the fellow did not even have any money to pay for his drinks, he decided to take a chance at fooling the Ch'oes by using the knowledge acquired from the tavern owner.

Pretending to be a *paksu* (male spirit-possessed shaman), he asked for the chance to call back Paebaengi's soul for the family. The story is woven with many twists and turns, describing how slyly the fake shaman escaped from being caught in his lies. The text is filled with wit and innuendo and sung with humor. Since he was able to describe all the worldly possessions that Paebaengi

---

⁴¹ A *talbi* is a braided hairpiece, over which a woman's hair is arranged in order to appear more voluminous.

left behind, Paebaengi's parents, as well as the neighbors and friends, Sewŏlne and Newŏlne, were all convinced that the fake *paksu* was possessed by the spirit of Paebaengi and that she was with them in person. Paebaengi's parents willingly offered whatever the "*paksu*" demanded, assuming that he was communicating the wishes of Paebaengi.

Having duped the family, the young fellow walked away with a great fortune. After sharing a generous portion of his newfound wealth with the owner of the tavern, he was on his merry way.

Despite the fact that the entire *Paebaengi Kut* is performed only occasionally nowadays, "Paebaengi" lives in everyday language. People often say "*Paebaengi ga watkuna!*" (Paebaengi, you really came!) when they greet someone they have not seen for a long time and have missed a great deal. Sometimes people will express their joy in seeing someone by saying, "*Ige nugunya? Paebaengi ga aninya?*" (Who could this be? Aren't you Paebaengi?), and so on. In the *kangshinmu* world, however, "Paebaengi" is used as a euphemism for fake or untrained shamans.

Kut as Intangible Cultural Properties

In 1962, the Korean government established the *munhwajae pohobŏp* (law protecting cultural properties) to designate and protect cultural properties in four categories—*yuhyŏng munhwajae* (tangible cultural properties), *muhyŏng munhwajae* (intangible cultural properties), *kinyŏmmul* (monuments), and *minsok charyo* (folk materials).

Government-appointed officials and consultants—*munhwajae wiwŏn* and *munhwajae chŏnmun wiwŏn*—investigate, select, and recommend cultural properties. Then the Munhwajaech'ŏng (Bureau of Cultural Properties) [42] deliberates and designates the important cultural properties, judging their value from artistic, academic, and historic perspectives, as well as evaluating the distinct regional characteristics of the proposed cultural properties. Selections may be made, for example, from buildings, books, sculptures, or paintings for tangible cultural properties; from drama, music, dance, or rituals for intangible cultural properties; from historical places, tombs, or natural phenomena for the monuments; and from clothing and implements used for daily life or calendrical events for folk materials. Keith Howard presents the following information on the designated cultural properties:

> By the end of 1991, there were 2,342 national and 2,642 provincial Tangible Assets, comprising buildings, classical books, calligraphy, documents,

---

[42] Munhwajaech'ŏng was formerly known as Munhwajae Kwanriguk [Kwalliguk].

pictures, sculpture, and craftwork of high historic or artistic value. 224 Folk Assets encompassed public morals and customs relating to food, clothing, housing, occupation, religion, or annual customs and objects "indispensable to the understanding of changes and progress of national life." In practice, this category included 134 houses and three complete folk villages. The Monument category conserved shell-mounds, ancient tombs, castle and palace sites, pottery remains, strata containing remains, scenic places, animals, plants, minerals and caves of "high scientific value."

By 1991, 93 Intangible Cultural Assets were appointed (numbered from 1 to 98, allowing for deletions). These comprised 17 music genres, 7 dances, 14 dramas, 33 plays and rituals, 30 manufactures, and 3 additional Assets concerned with food preparation and martial arts. (Howard 1996:93–94)

As of 1999, one hundred and ten Important Intangible Cultural Properties had been designated (Munhwajaech'ŏng 1999). In the case of intangible cultural properties, their presentations are temporal, variable and not fixed. The transmission of the artistry of the intangible cultural property focuses on inherent knowledge of a given genre handed down aurally for generations. Therefore, once Important Intangible Cultural Properties are designated, the government officials must find and recognize a qualified individual or group of people who may carry on the designated cultural properties in their *wŏnhyŏng* (original form). If it is an individual, he or she is officially recognized as *poyuja* (literally, retainer or holder) of the cultural property and becomes responsible for preserving, presenting, and educating others to carry on the cultural tradition in the original form. If it is a group, the group is designated as *poyu tanch'e* (literally, designated group).

Government-designated cultural properties are managed by the Munhwajaech'ŏng and known as "Important Intangible Cultural Properties" (*Chungyo Muhyŏng Munhwajae*). Cultural properties of outstanding value may also be designated as "Intangible Cultural Properties" by the mayor of a city or the governor of a province (Office of Cultural Properties 1995). To give examples from the rituals discussed in this work, the Seoul *Saenam Kut* is designated by the national government's Munhwajaech'ŏng as Important Intangible Cultural Property number 104, whereas the ritual for General Nam Yi is designated by the mayor of Seoul as Intangible Cultural Property number 20.

Once the cultural property and *poyuja* (holder) are designated, the entire responsibility of transmission is left to the *poyuja*. An individual or a group with artistic skills believed to be equal or even better than those of the *poyuja* recognized by the government must go through training under the current *poyuja* if they wish to become the next *poyuja*.

Among the students learning from the *poyuja*, a hierarchy exists, challenging students to excel in their training. In earlier days, a few talented students were selected from the numerous *ilban chŏnsusaeng* (regular students) as *chŏnsusaeng* or *chŏnsuja* (disciple). A few *chŏnsuja* were then chosen to become *isuja* (master artists)[43] after about five years of rigorous training. A single *isuja* was then selected as *chŏnsukyoyuk chogyo* (teaching assistant for transmission and education). It was considered the highest honor for a student to be the *poyuja hubo* (candidate to be the next *poyuja*). Nowadays students under the guidance of *poyuja* are divided into three groups: *chŏnsuja* (official trainees), *isuja* (artists who have mastered the tradition), and *chŏnsukyoyuk pojoja* (assistants responsible for transmission and education) who are also considered *poyuja hubo* (next in line to become the designated performer).

The recommended minimum age for a qualified person to be recognized as *poyuja* was fifty years, with a few possible exceptions. Since 1995 a forty-year-old qualified person may be appointed as *poyuja* if the need arises. Among the current 181 *poyuja*, 94 are in their seventies or older, the average age of all *poyuja* being 69.5 years.

The honor of being recognized as *poyuja* lasts a lifetime unless the honoree becomes physically or mentally incapacitated or emigrates to another country. But as Lee Yong-Hak notes, old age sometimes causes the gradual deterioration of the performance skills needed to present the *wŏnhyŏng* (original form) of their designated cultural properties (Lee Y.H. 1999:44). In some cases the *poyuja* cannot carry out the performance as well as before but may be unwilling to let anyone else stand in, causing much difficulty in sustaining the tradition.

There are nine *kut* by *kangshinmu* designated as Important Intangible Cultural Properties (IICP) and two as Intangible Cultural Properties (ICP).

Table 2
Kut (by *Kangshinmu*) Designated as Important Intangible Cultural Properties

	Number	Title	Year
1.	9	Ŭnsan *Pyŏlshinje*	1966
2.	71	Cheju Ch'ilmŏri *Tang Kut*	1980
3.	82 *ka* [a]	Tonghaean *Pyŏlshin Kut*	1985
4.	82 *na* [b]	Sŏhaean *Paeyŏnshin Kut mit Taedong Kut*	1985
5.	82 *ta* [c]	Wido *Ttibaet Nori*	1985
6.	82 *ra* [d]	Namhaean *Pyŏlshin Kut*	1987
7.	90	Hwanghaedo *P'yŏngsan Sonorŭm Kut*	1988
8.	98	Kyŏnggi *Todang Kut*	1990
9.	104	Seoul *Saenam Kut*	1996

---

[43] Yang Jongsung translates *isuja* as "the master artists" (1994:61–64).

Kut designated as Intangible Cultural Properties are Kuri Kalmae *Todang Kut* (ICP no. 15, 1995) and Nam Yi *Changgun Che* (ICP no. 20, 1999), designated by Kyŏnggi Province and the City of Seoul, respectively.

The people who are recognized as *poyuja* (holders) of the Important Intangible Cultural Properties had an obligation to present the designated performance genres to the public in their *wŏnhyŏng* (original forms) annually.[44] The government provides funds partially to defray the cost of these events, encouraging the artists and ritual specialists to disseminate indigenous culture among Koreans. In order to present the Important Intangible Cultural Properties to the public, *kangshinmu poyuja* began to conduct their sacred rituals on secular concert stages in condensed form, making adjustments to complete the performance within the allotted time. The rituals designated as Important Intangible Cultural Properties are enjoyed by the public as performance of the archetypes of Korean arts incorporating drama, dance, and music.

One such performance I attended was that of Kim Kŭm-Hwa and her group who presented their *taedong kut* at Hoam Arts Hall in Seoul on December 4, 1993. Kim Kŭm-Hwa (b. 1931), a *manshin* (spirit-possessed shaman from Hwanghae Province) was recognized as the *poyuja* (literally, retainer or holder), the designated performer of Important Intangible Cultural Property number 82 *na* [b], *Sŏhaean Paeyŏnshin Kut* and *Taedong Kut*, in 1985. Kim Kŭm-Hwa is one of many *manshin* who fled from North Korea to South Korea during the Korean War (1950–1953). Residing in Seoul, she continues to perform the northern style *kut*. The *taedong kut* performed by Kim Kŭm-Hwa at the Hoam Arts Hall was a ticketed event and the tickets were completely sold out two months prior to the performance date.[45]

By performing the *taedong kut* in a well-respected theater rather than at a shrine, Kim Kŭm-Hwa reduced the apprehension the general public might feel about attending a *kut*. This *kut* was shortened from a two-day ritual to a three-hour version, and a scholar[46] on stage explained the *kut*. The ritual included *kongsu* (a possessing spirit speaking through a shaman) and *pisu*—the unique central feature of a shaman *kut*, where the shaman possessed by a spirit stands barefoot on the sharp edges of knives to pray and dance.[47] Audience members for this *kut* participated by donating *pyŏlbi* (monetary contributions) during the *kut* in addition to the ticket price, which ranged from $12 to $40 in US funds, and by joining in *ŭmbok* (sharing food and drink) inside the theater after the *kut*.

---

[44] In January 1999, the government eliminated the responsibility of the *poyuja* to have the annual performance by Law Number 5,719. The law went into effect as of July 1 (Lee Y.H. 1999:107).

[45] Hoam Arts Hall in Seoul has 866 seats.

[46] Dr. Hwang Lu-si.

[47] *Pisu* in Hwanghae Province is known as *chakdu* in the Hanyang *kut*.

Public Performance of *Kut* in Sacred Contexts

Other *kangshinmu*, who had not been recognized by the government for their artistry, also began to present their sacred rituals on concert stages. For example, Shin Myŏng-Gi (b. 1955), a *kangshinmu*, presented a *kut* at Unhyŏn'gung,[48] an old palace in Seoul, as her seventh annual offering to Queen Myŏngsŏng who was known to have patronized *musok* in the late Chosŏn Dynasty. At this *kut*, Shin was assisted by several *manshin* (spirit-possessed shamans from Hwanghae Province). Pang Ch'ang-Hwan (b. 1943), a *paksu* (male shaman) in Seoul, has performed Chesŏk *kut* on the concert stages of Yŏn'gang Hall (1997), Hoam Art Hall (1998), and the Large Hall of Sejong Cultural Center (1999).[49] Both Shin Myŏng-Gi and Pang Ch'ang-Hwan performed *kut* in the northwestern Hwanghae province styles.

Another *kangshinmu*, Kim Chae-Yŏn, officiated at the "Mokmyŏk San Tae Ch'ŏnje" [Ritual for Heaven on Mokmyŏk Mountain], the seventh annual offering to the spirits of Nam San (South Mountain),[50] in Seoul on October 17, 1999.

Several other *kangshinmu* occasionally perform Hanyang *kut* on public stages. For example, Yi Sŏng-Jae (b. 1955), a male shaman, held a *kut* on top of Nam San, and Yi Ŭn-Suk (b. 1960) performed at an outdoor concert stage located on Nam San, both in 1999.

Kut on concert stages are usually performed in an abridged version lasting two to four hours, allowing only a few *kŏri* (sections) from the *kut* to be sampled by the audience. The Korean Broadcasting System (television company) often sponsors *kut* performances from various regions. Seoul Nori Madang, an open-air theater, also presents various *kut*, as well as other genres of traditional performing arts, including puppet shows, and folk music concerts. The Seoul Nori Madang program runs every weekend from April to October, and *kut*—including Seoul *Saenam Kut*, Chindo *kut*, and Hwanghae Province *kut*—have been performed there on several occasions.

In addition to Seoul Nori Madang, Korea House, Namsan'gol Hanok Maŭl (Village of Traditional Houses in Namsan Valley), Unhyŏn'gung (literally, Cloud Hill Palace), and Seoul Chungyo Muhyŏng Munhwajae Chŏnsu Hoegwan (Seoul Training Center for Important Intangible Cultural Properties) present parts of *kut* from various regions as public performances, sponsored by the Korean government.

---

[48] This event was held outdoors on November 8, 1998, with about five hundred people attending. During the lunch hour, boxed lunches were offered to the audience. Percussion music was performed by the Chaengi P'ungmul Kutp'ae musicians.

[49] The Sejong Cultural Center in Seoul has 3,895 seats.

[50] Nam San (South Mountain) was known as Mokmyŏk San during the Chosŏn Dynasty.

Most of the *kut* mentioned above are held to wish for the wealth, health, and happiness of the general public. The *kut* for the departed, however, cannot satisfactorily be performed when it is done merely for the sake of an artistic presentation. Since 1998, several attempts have been made to hold *kut* for the departed as a sacred ritual despite the fact that they are held on a public stage. I would like to mention three styles of *kut* held for the departed—Seoul *Saenam Kut*, *ssikkim kut* of Chŏlla Province, and *suwang kut* of Hwanghae Province.

The third annual presentation of Seoul *Saenam Kut*, Important Intangible Cultural Property number 104, was held on October 31, 1998, at Kyŏngbok Palace in Seoul. The ritual might have appeared to be just a performance to the general public, like the first two annual Seoul *Saenam Kut* presented previously, but this ritual was held for the soul of the late Mrs. Han.

This was unlike any other performance-oriented Seoul *Saenam Kut* where the mourners would be *kangshinmu* dressed in mourning costume. Mrs. Han's husband and daughter-in-law were actually present during the entire ritual on and off the stage (see plate 40).

The family had hired shamans to pray and lead Mrs. Han safely to the other world. The *tangju* (the shaman hired for the ritual) was Yi Sŏng-Jae, a male shaman, and the fee for the ritual received from Mrs. Han's family was 6,000,000 *wŏn* (about $5,000 in US funds).

During the First Chŏnju *Sanjo* Festival (October 8–10, 1999), Chindo *ssikkim kut* (ritual for departed in Chŏlla Provinces) was held by Ch'ae Chŏng-Rye, a hereditary *mudang*, from Chindo, South Chŏlla Province. Ch'ae Chŏng-Rye was assisted by her student, Ch'ae Su-Jŏng (not related), a young professional *p'ansori* singer. The *changgu* (drum) and *ching* (gong) accompaniment were provided by Kang Chŏng-T'ae and Ham In-Ch'ŏn, respectively. This *ssikkim kut* was for the souls of Kim Ch'ang-Jo (1865–1920), the creator of the *sanjo* genre, and Kim Chuk-P'a (1911–1989),[51] a well-known *kayagŭm* player who was a granddaughter of Kim Ch'ang-Jo. Most people who attended this ritual truly mourned, wishing for both artists to rest in peace (see plate 15).

On November 5, 1999, a sacred ritual was held to comfort the souls of the prisoners who died at the Sŏdaemun Hyŏngmuso (literally, West Gate Prison) in Seoul. Since the prison was built in 1908, many patriots and freedom fighters had been imprisoned and tortured to death. Despite the fact that the structures no longer function as a prison, the buildings, as well as the execution site, remain as a reminder of the recent tragic history of Korea. Kim Mae-Mul (b. 1939), a *manshin* (shaman from Hwanghae Province), and Pak In-Gyŏm (b. 1946), a *paksu* (male shaman), officiated at the *Suwang Kut*[52] for the souls of ninety

---

[51] Kim Chuk-P'a's legal name was Kim Nan-Ch'o.

[52] *Suwang Kut* is a Hwanghae Province style ritual for the dead, held for those who passed away at least three years prior to the ritual date.

prisoners who were put to death at the Sŏdaemun Hyŏngmuso. The souls of the ninety prisoners were selected because their sacrifices during the Japanese occupation era had been acknowledged by the government (see plate 16).

To comfort the souls of the unknown patriots and freedom fighters, numerous blank *wip'ae* (tablets) were symbolically placed at the entrance to the execution building (see plate 17).

CHAPTER 6

Musical Instruments Used in Hanyang *Kut*

In this chapter, I will discuss musical instruments that are played by *kangshinmu* (spirit-possessed shamans) and *chaebi* (ritual musicians), and the various instrumental ensembles used in Hanyang *kut* (rituals). Instruments played by *kangshinmu* in Hanyang *kut* include *changgu* (hourglass-shaped drum), *chegŭm* (brass cymbals), *pangul* (bell tree), and *koritchak* (willow basket). *Kangshinmu* in Hanyang *kut* also occasionally play *ching* (large gong), *kkwaenggwari* (small gong), and *puk* (barrel drum). Large-scale rituals may have an instrumental ensemble known as *samhyŏn yukkak*, which consists of six *chaebi* playing two *p'iri* (cylindrical oboe), *haegŭm* (two-string fiddle), *taegŭm* (flute), *changgu*, and *puk*. Other instruments occasionally played by *chaebi* in Hanyang *kut* in recent years include *t'aep'yŏngso* (conical oboe) and *ajaeng* (bowed zither).

1. Traditional Instruments Played by Shamans

1.1 *Changgu*, Hourglass-Shaped Drum

"*Changgu*" has been the standardized name for the hourglass-shaped double-headed drum since 1996 (see plate 18). It is also known as *changgo* or *seyogo*. The word *changgo* (杖鼓) is made up of two Sino-Korean words, *chang* (杖 stick) and *go* (鼓 drum), or *chang* (長 long) and *go* (鼓 drum). The term *seyogo* describes the shape of the body—*seyo* (細腰 slender-waisted) and *go* (鼓 drum). The body of the *changgu* is hollow and made of paulownia wood (*odong*). The *changgu* is a lashed drum with sliding belts (*choimjul* or *ch'uksu*) that regulate the tension and pitch of the drum heads.

Changgu are made in various sizes for different genres of music. The *chŏngak changgu* used for court music and for the upper class chamber ensemble is larger in size and consequently has a richer sound than the *minsok changgu* used for *p'ungmul* (outdoor music), folk music, and most ritual music. *Changgu* are also made in various sizes to suit the players—from children to adults. For comfort in playing, the *changgu* heads may be switched for left handed players like Kim Duk Soo (Kim Tŏk-Su), the founder and leader of Hanullim Samulnori.

The *changgu* player normally uses the left palm to strike the left head (*kung p'yŏn*), playing the other head (*ch'ae p'yŏn*) with a bamboo stick (*yŏl ch'ae*) held in the right hand. For *p'ungmul kut* or dance accompaniment at the *kut*, the *changgu* player uses two sticks to play—*yŏl ch'ae* and *kunggul ch'ae*. Naturally the *kunggul ch'ae*, made of wood and held in the player's left hand, can produce a much louder bass sound than the bare palm. For *p'ungmul kut* the player uses the *kunggul ch'ae* to play on both heads of the drum, but shamans play only the left head of the drum with *kunggul ch'ae*, striking always the center of the head. When the *changgu* player uses the *yŏl ch'ae* (bamboo stick), they strike the right head mainly in the center but produce varied sounds by occasionally playing on the rim of the drum.

In *musok*, the two sides of the *changgu* have symbolic meaning: the right head (*ch'ae p'yŏn*) for the gate of this world, the left head (*kung p'yŏn*)[1] for the gate of the other world (Cho H.Y. 1990a:74).

Traditionally, the *changgu* used in Hanyang *kut* is a court style drum (*chŏngak changgu*). The *changgu* is often handed down within a family or through spirit parent/spirit child relationships. Kim Yu-Gam, a shaman, for example, received her *chŏngak changgu* from her mother, Pan Sŭng-Ŏp, a shaman of the Chosŏn Dynasty court who told her that the instrument was about three hundred years old.

The *chŏngak changgu* that shaman Yi Sang-Sun owns is said to be about one hundred years old. Yi received the *changgu* from Yi Pong-Sun who had inherited it from her spirit mother, Yi Ŭn-Sun, also known as Tosŏbang of the Tonamdong area of Seoul. Nowadays most shamans use the folk style drum (*minsok changgu*), which is smaller and less expensive than the court style *chŏngak changgu*.

The body of the *changgu* used for court music is painted red, but the *changgu* used for *p'ungmul* (outdoor folk music) is unpainted. Despite the fact that *changgu* heads are reported to be made from cow hide (left) and horse hide (right) in the literature, many musicians prefer the sounds produced by drum heads made of dog hide for the left and *noru* (roe deer hide) for the right. The

---

[1] The left head of the drum is referred to as "*puk p'yŏn*" by Cho Hung-youn [Hŭng-Yun] (1990:74) and Keith Howard (1998b:68), but I have used the term *kung p'yŏn* because it is the standard term used among Korean traditional musicians.

late Kim Myŏng-Sŏn claimed that "the word *changgu* is made of two words: *chang* (獐 roe deer) and *gu* (狗 dog)" (Chin K.S. 1993:19).[2]

1.2 *Chegŭm*, Brass Cymbals

The *chegŭm* (pair of brass cymbals) used in *musok* rituals are thin and circular in shape (see plate 19 and CD tracks 1–2, 4, 10, 19–20, 22, 24, 26–27). The size of the *chegŭm* varies greatly, averaging about 50 cm in diameter. The player holds a cymbal in each hand by means of cloth handles attached to the center of the *chegŭm*, striking them together to produce sound. Shamans usually play the *chegŭm* while seated to provide accompaniment for dance, but they sometimes dance with the *chegŭm*, singing a song.

For example, the *kangshinmu* sings "*Para T'aryŏng*" while dancing, accompanying himself or herself on *chegŭm* during the *Pulsa kŏri* in the Hanyang *kut* (see CD track 22). The pair of *chegŭm* is believed to symbolize the sun and moon (Cho H.Y. 1997:162).

The *chegŭm* used in *musok* are, as a rule, smaller in size than the *para* (cymbals) used for Buddhist rituals. If the cymbals are used for singing or dancing for Buddhist spirits during the *musok* ritual, they are referred to as *para* or *chabara*.

1.3 *Pangul*, Bell Tree

The *pangul* is a bell or a small bell tree made of brass (see plate 20 and CD tracks 19, 33–35). A single bell *(pangul)* is sometimes referred to as *chong*. The *pangul* (bell tree) is often used by *mudang* while singing and dancing and sometimes during divination.

Pangul, also known as *shinryŏng* (ritual bells) or *muryŏng* (bells used in *musok*), are clapperless brass bell trees. The *kangshinmu* shakes this bell tree to invoke the spirits, believing that the spirits are fond of the *soe sori* (metal sound) made by the bells. The *kangshinmu* dance with the *pangul* also using it as a musical instrument to accompany songs and incantations.

Shapes and sizes vary, but the *pangul* generally used in Hanyang *kut* are made up of seven or twelve small bells. The bells are attached to the sides of a U-shaped piece of metal, and the *kangshinmu* holds a handle attached to the bottom part of the U-shaped piece. Some *pangul* have three bells dangling from one side and four from the other, symbolizing man and woman, respectively (Cho H.Y. 1990a:80). *Ch'ilsoe pangul* (seven bells) symbolize the power of

---

[2] Kim Myŏng-Sŏn (1924–1994), known as Kim O-Ch'ae, was a well known *changgu* player.

Ch'ilsŏng (Seven Stars of the Big Dipper) and the bell tree is also referred to as Ch'ilsŏng *ryŏng* or Ch'ilsŏng *pangul* (both meaning bell for the Seven Stars). During Hanyang *kut* the *kangshinmu* holds the *pangul* in the left hand with the *puch'ae* (fan) in the right while dancing.

The bell tree of twelve small bells is known as the *yŏldu pangul* (twelve bells) or the Taeshin *pangul* (bell for the Taeshin spirit) and it is used for *kut* and divination. Taeshin is believed to be a powerful helping spirit for shamans, especially in divination.

The bell trees used in rituals from Hwanghae Province include *kunung pangul*, 7 *pangul*, 12 *pangul*, and 99 *pangul*. *Kunung pangul*, also known as *mae pangul*, is made of two or three bells usually larger than those mentioned above (Yang J.S. 1998:123).

The 99 *pangul* is also known as 99 *sangsoe pangul* (99 metal bell tree) (Choi C.M. 1983:97). The 99 bells are attached to one handle but organized into several units (see plate 21). The ninety-nine bells are first grouped into thirty-three units of three bells each. The thirty-three units are then arranged in eleven larger units, each with three small units. Each set of eleven units is then tied with leather strips to hold them together. The *manshin* (spirit-possessed shaman of Hwanghae Province) usually holds 99 *sangsoe pangul* from the top, letting the weight fall, except when the *kut* is held to honor a departed *manshin* (Yang J.S. 1998:125). Unlike the Hanyang *kut*, the *manshin* in the Hwanghae Province tradition holds the bells in the right hand and the fan in the left.

1.4 *Koritchak*, Willow Basket

The *koritchak*, a clothesbasket woven from willow branches, is used in *musok* as a musical instrument (see plate 22 and CD track 28). Shamans scratch it with a stick made of paulownia wood to accompany their songs or recitations. It is believed that *kangshinmu* began to use the *koritchak* as a rhythm instrument while performing rituals or saying prayers in secret during the years when *musok* survived underground and musical instruments were destroyed or confiscated by the authorities. Only a few older *kangshinmu* know how to play the *koritchak* properly nowadays, using it for small-scale rituals like the *ch'isŏng*. When *koritchak* is not used as musical instrument, ritual clothing is stored in it.

1.5 *Ching*, Large Gong

The *ching*, also known as *taegŭm*,[3] is a large flat gong. It is usually about 40 cm in diameter with a rim lip of about 8–10 cm. The player holds the instrument in the left hand by a cloth handle looped through two holes in the rim. With the right hand, he or she strikes the *ching* with a large cloth-wrapped wooden mallet. For a long invocation song, the *ching* is placed on the floor and played with the cloth-wrapped wooden mallet.

1.6 *Kkwaenggwari*, Small Gong

The *kkwaenggwari* is a small, lipped, flat bronze gong, also known as *sogŭm* (small gong), *soe* (metal), *kwangsoe* (large metal), or the onomatopoeic *kkaengmaegi* (*kkaeng* for an open sound and *maek* for a dampened one). The musician holds the *kkwaenggwari* with the left hand, supporting the instrument with the left thumb through a loop in the lip, while the left thumb and fingers release or hold the resonating surface to produce either open or dampened sound. Although its size is not standardized, the average *kkwaenggwari* is about 20 cm in diameter with a 5cm lip. The musician strikes the instrument with a wooden mallet or a bamboo mallet with a wooden tip.

1.7 *Puk*, Double-Headed Barrel Drum

The *puk* is a shallow double-headed barrel drum that is struck with a *puk pangmangi* (wooden stick) (see plate 27 and CD tracks 6–9, 26–27). *Puk* is often transliterated as *buk* in English. *Puk* is sometimes played by shamans during *anjŭn kŏri* (seated sections) of small-scale rituals.

2. Traditional Instruments Played by Ritual Musicians

2.1 *P'iri*, Cylindrical Oboe

The *p'iri* is a small cylindrical double-reed aerophone made of bamboo (see plate 23 and CD tracks 5–9, 11–20, 22, 24–25, 30–32, 34–38). There are three types of *p'iri* in Korea—the Tang *p'iri* (*p'iri* from China), *hyang p'iri* (Korean

---

[3] The *taegŭm* (大金) here means a large flat gong. Although *taegŭm* is a homophone of another instrument, the transverse bamboo flute (*taegŭm*, 大笒), the Sino-Korean characters indicate the difference in meanings.

p'iri), and *se p'iri* (slender *p'iri*). The Tang *p'iri* (*p'iri* from China) is used for Confucian ritual music, *hyang p'iri* (Korean *p'iri*) for *musok* ritual music and folk music, and *se p'iri* (slender *p'iri*) for court music.

The *p'iri* emits a strong, expressive, reedy sound. The *hyang p'iri* (native Korean *p'iri*) is the lead instrument of the *muak* ensemble. Its bamboo tube (*kwandae*) is about 10 inches long and half an inch in diameter. The *hyang p'iri* has eight finger holes about an inch apart, seven in front and one in back. It is played through the *sŏ*, a double-reed mouthpiece about three inches long.

The *p'iri* is also known as *pil-yul* or *pillyul*. In *musok*, the sound of the *p'iri* signifies the opening of the gate of the other world (Cho H.Y. 1997:163).

2.2 *Haegŭm*, Two-String Spiked Fiddle

The *haegŭm*, also known by the onomatopoeic *kkaengkkaengi*, is a two-string spiked fiddle with a range of three octaves (see plate 24 and CD tracks 5, 10–20, 22, 24–25, 30–32, 34–38). The silk strings are tuned a 5th apart. The player, sitting cross-legged, places the instrument on top of the left knee and holds it with the left hand while bowing with the right. In *musok*, the *haegŭm* sound is believed to symbolize the presence of spirits.

2.3 *Taegŭm*, Bamboo Flute

The *taegŭm* is one of the three bamboo flutes known as *samjuk*—*taegŭm* (large flute), *chunggŭm* (medium flute), and *sogŭm* (small flute) from the Shilla period (57 B.C.E.–935). The *taegŭm*, a large transverse bamboo flute, originally named *taeham*, is also commonly known as *chŏ* or *chŏttae* (see plate 25 and CD tracks 5–16, 19–20, 22, 30–32, 34–38). The *taegŭm* has a *ch'wigong* (mouth hole), a *ch'ŏnggong* (hole covered with a thin membrane called *ch'ŏng* or *kalch'ŏng*), six *chigong* (finger holes), and a *ch'ilsŏnggong* (hole to tune the instrument). *Ssanggoljuk*, a thick bamboo tube with joints shaped with grooves on both sides, can produce a firm and rich sound and is thought to be the best material for *taegŭm*.

There are two types of *taegŭm*: *chŏngak taegŭm* and *sanjo taegŭm*. The *chŏngak taegŭm* is used for court or upper class music, while the *sanjo taegŭm* is used for folk music in the central and southern provinces. Contemporary composers employ both types of *taegŭm* in their works, choosing the appropriate one to suit the genre of composition they wish to create.

The *chŏngak taegŭm* and *sanjo taegŭm* are about 80 cm and 70 cm in length, respectively. The lowest pitch produced on the *chŏngak taegŭm* is close to B flat and C on the *sanjo taegŭm*.

About 80 cm long with a hole covered by a thin membrane called *kalch'ŏng*, the *taegŭm* produces the buzzing sound favored by Korean aesthetics. It has a range of over two octaves (b flat to e" flat). Korean string and wind ensembles tune to the b flat produced by the *taegŭm*.

The *sanjo taegŭm* is usually used for folk music and *musok* ritual music, except for the Hanyang *kut* where musicians use the *chŏngak taegŭm*. This musical practice of performance on the *chŏngak taegŭm* for Hanyang *kut* suggests that *musok* was accepted by the court and the upper classes in the capital city during the Chosŏn Dynasty. In *musok*, the sound of the *taegŭm* is understood to represent lightning (Cho H.Y. 1997:163). The *taegŭm* is referred to as *chŏ, chŏttae,* or *kalttae* among the Seoul area *chaebi* musicians.

2.4 *Changgu*, Hourglass-Shaped Drum

The *changgu* was discussed earlier in this chapter. Despite the fact that the *changgu* is always played by the *kangshinmu* (spirit-possessed shamans) during rituals, an exception is made when the *samhyŏn yukkak* ensemble of six musicians is hired for a large-scale *kut* (see plate 27 and CD tracks 6–9). Since the repertoire of the *samhyŏn yukkak* includes pieces such as "Chajin Hwanip" framed in the complicated sixteen-beat *changdan* (rhythmic cycle), great skill and musicianship are required of the *changgu* player (see CD track 6). A *chaebi* (ritual musician) performs *changgu* only as part of the *samhyŏn yukkak* ensemble. A *chaebi* playing *changgu* in the Hanyang *kut* never sings during the ritual.

2.5 *Puk*, Barrel Drum

The *puk* is a shallow double-headed barrel drum, struck with a *puk pangmangi* (wooden stick). *Puk* is often transliterated as *buk* in English. The *puk*, like the *changgu*, is played by a *chaebi* (ritual musician) in the *samhyŏn yukkak* ensemble (see plate 27 and CD tracks 6–9).

2.6 *T'aep'yŏngso*, Conical Oboe

The *t'aep'yŏngso* is a conical wooden oboe made of citron wood (*yuja*) or yellow mulberry (*whangsang*) (see plate 30). Its brass bell is called *tong p'allang*. Also called *hojŏk, hoga, saenap,* or the onomatopoeic *nallari*, the *t'aep'yŏngso* is about 47 cm long with eight finger holes. The instrument produces a strong, piercing sound, perhaps the loudest sound among the traditional instruments used for outdoor music. This instrument has been in use for the Hanyang *kut* during the *chakdu kŏri* only in recent years. The instrument is often played when several *kut* are in progress simultaneously. The *p'iri* player often switches to *t'aep'yŏngso*, producing a louder sound so that his own group of ritual specialists can follow the music better.

For the Hanyang *kut, ssang hojŏk* (literally, twin *hojŏk*, that is, a pair of *hojŏk*) are performed by two professional musicians (see CD tracks 26–27). *Ssang hojŏk* are performed only on rare occasions, mainly because there are only three or four musicians who can play the repertoire in present-day Seoul.

2.7 *Ajaeng*, Bowed Zither

The body of the *ajaeng,* a bowed zither, is made of *odong* (paulownia) wood. The traditional *ajaeng* has seven silk strings supported by movable wooden bridges, its sound being produced by bowing with a rosined forsythia branch. For ritual music the *sanjo ajaeng,* smaller and shorter than the traditional one, is used. The *sanjo ajaeng,* developed in the 1960s for folk music genres, has eight strings, also supported by moveable wooden bridges. The bow for the *sanjo ajaeng*, however, is often replaced by one similar to the Western cello bow. For ritual music the *ajaeng* may be played by bowing or by plucking with the fingers of the right hand. The *ajaeng* is a new addition to the Hanyang *kut* music and is sometimes used instead of *haegŭm* (see CD tracks 6–9), but it has long been an important melodic instrument in the *sesŭpmu* (hereditary *mudang*) rituals in North and South Chŏlla Provinces.

3. Ensembles Hired for Hanyang *Kut*

Since the fee for a musician ranges from $100 to $1,000 for one *kut*, the number of musicians to hire is up to the sponsors and the principal *kangshinmu* (*tangju*). If the sponsor's resources are very limited, the *kangshinmu* may elect to hold the *kut* without hiring any musicians in order to minimize costs. In that case, the ritual music is provided solely by the *kangshinmu* who play percussion instruments like *changgu* (hourglass-shaped drum), *chegŭm* (cymbals), *chong* (bell), *pangul* (bell tree), *ching* (large gong), *kkwaenggwari* (small gong), *koritchak* (basket), and *puk* (barrel drum). Since many *kut* and small-scale rituals are held without hired musicians, the general public is left with the impression that the *kangshinmu* ritual is carried out with only percussion instruments such as *changgu* (hourglass-shaped drum) and *chegŭm* (cymbals).

When funds are available, the musicians for the Hanyang *kut* are hired in the following order: the first instrument to be hired is the *p'iri* (cylindrical oboe); second, *haegŭm* (two-string fiddle); third, *taegŭm* (transverse flute); then a second *p'iri*. If five instrumentalists are hired, a second *taegŭm* is hired. If six are to be hired, then *puk* (double-headed barrel drum) and *changgu* (hourglass-shaped drum) are added.

The various ensembles have different names. *Oe chaebi* literally means a single musician while *yang chaebi* means two musicians (see plates 3 and 19). *Sam chaebi*, *sa chaebi*, and *o chaebi* literally refer to the number of musicians involved, because *sam*, *sa*, and *o* mean three, four, and five in Korean. The various ensembles for *muak* (ritual music) are discussed in the following table.

Table 3
Instrumental Ensembles for Hanyang *Kut*

oe chaebi	one *p'iri* is the only melodic instrument
yang chaebi	one *p'iri* and one *haegŭm* are played together
sam chaebi (also known as *sejaebi*)	trio of *p'iri*, *haegŭm*, and *taegŭm* are played
sa chaebi	two *p'iri*, one *haegŭm*, and one *taegŭm* are played
o chaebi[4]	two *p'iri*, two *taegŭm*, and one *haegŭm* are played
samhyŏn yukkak	two *p'iri* (*mok p'iri* and *kyŏt p'iri*),[5] one *haegŭm*, one *taegŭm*, one *puk*, and one *changgu*[6] are played

As mentioned earlier, if a single musician is to be hired for the *kut*, it is always a *p'iri* player. Most *kangshinmu* have a favorite *p'iri* player with whom they work closely. I have observed, for example, that Yi Sang-Sun, a *kangshinmu*, has worked well with Kim Chŏm-Sŏk, a *chaebi* musician, for several years. Other pairs include Kim Min-Jŏng (*kangshinmu*) with Hŏ Yong-Ŏp (*chaebi*); Pak In-O (*kangshinmu*) with Yang Hwa-Yŏng (*chaebi*); Chang Sŏng-Man (*kangshinmu*) with Yi Han-Bok (*chaebi*); Yim Ki-Uk (*kangshinmu*)

---

[4] I have not attended any ritual where *o chaebi* ensemble was hired.

[5] *Mok p'iri* (literally, head or leading *p'iri*) refers to the principal player and *kyŏt p'iri* (literally, side *p'iri*) refers to the second player.

[6] An extra *chaebi* (ritual musician) is hired as the drummer (*changgu*) for *samhyŏn yukkak* because the ensemble uses such complicated rhythmic patterns that a professional musician is required. In order to reduce the cost of hiring another drummer for the ritual, Yi Sang-Sun, a *kangshinmu*, learned to play the 16-beat *chajin hwanip* rhythmic cycle on the *changgu* in 1996.

with Han Yŏng-Sŏ (*chaebi*); Shin Hyŏn-Ju (*kangshinmu*) with Ch'oe Hyŏng-Gŭn (*chaebi*); and Sohn I-Hwa (*kangshinmu*) with Yi Sŏn-Ho (*chaebi*).

The ideal instrumental ensemble for Hanyang *kut* accompaniment is the *sam chaebi* (trio of *p'iri*, *haegŭm*, and *taegŭm*), also referred to as *han t'ŭl* (one set) (see plate 26). I know only one *paksu* (male shaman) in the Seoul area who was able to maintain his own *han t'ŭl* ensemble made up of excellent musicians from 1989.[7] His *kut* were so much in demand that he was able to keep these musicians busy nearly every day except the first and the fifteenth day of each lunar month when he went to the mountains to pray to the Sanshin (mountain spirit) for his *tan'gol* (regular clients). Other than the two dates mentioned, the musicians seldom had holidays except when the *paksu* traveled to other countries to divine for Koreans living overseas.

Within the *sam chaebi* ensemble, the *haegŭm* player is usually the oldest member and is considered the leader of the ensemble, while the youngest member plays *p'iri*. The hierarchy of Paksu Pak's *sam chaebi*, however, is an exception to this rule. In this group, the youngest musician plays *haegŭm*. From the two woodwind players in his *sam chaebi*, Paksu Pak requested that the younger musician play *taegŭm*, the older one *p'iri*. Both musicians are equally fine *taegŭm* players, but he made the decision based on his personal preference for the sound of *taegŭm* produced by the younger musician.

Except for Paksu Pak's *sam chaebi* (trio), musicians for the *kut* are usually organized on a temporary basis. When the *kangshinmu* contacts the first musician, they discuss the size of the ensemble for the upcoming *kut*. When the type of ensemble has been determined, the musician will seek others who are available for the occasion. The musician responsible for organizing the ensemble members is known as *chaebi tangju*, and is usually a *p'iri* player, as mentioned earlier.

Each individual musician is expected to know the entire repertoire used in the ritual and to be able to play for the Hanyang *kut* without rehearsal. There are usually networks of musicians who work together, but sometimes it is necessary to hire a new person. Musicians usually gather shortly before the *kut*. If necessary, a new musician is introduced to others then. Because musicians do not rehearse together before the *kut*, adding a new person is often a trying experience for the musicians, as well as for the shamans.

Some musicians are in such demand that they may play for two *kut* in one day. In order to arrive in time for the next *kut*, they will leave the first *kut* before the concluding *kŏri* (act) where instrumental music is not needed.

I have had the privilege of being invited to many *kut* in the Seoul area where the *sa chaebi* (four musicians hired for *haegŭm*, *taegŭm*, and two *p'iri*) or

---

[7] Because of a stroke, this *paksu* (male shaman) has not performed *kut* for his clients since 1998, but he continues to hire the three musicians for his personal *chinjŏk kut* held yearly.

samhyŏn yukkak—an ensemble of *haegŭm, taegŭm, changgu, puk*, and two *p'iri*—played.[8]

I have observed that a *kut* with *samhyŏn yukkak* is usually sponsored by a *kangshinmu* for the *chinjŏk kut* celebrating the anniversary of his or her initiation. Once initiated, *kangshinmu* celebrate the day of their initiation annually, giving thanks to the spirits, families, friends, and clients, as discussed earlier. *Kangshinmu* spare no expense for the *chinjŏk kut* held for this occasion. They prepare the feast with great care and devotion and hire the best musicians they can afford. One can get a sense of how well a *kangshinmu* is doing financially by attending his or her *chinjŏk kut*, because the ritual usually begins at the *shindang* (shrine) established as part of his or her residence and continues to a larger scale *kut* in a *kuttang* (ritual hall).

Samhyŏn yukkak refers to an instrumental ensemble developed in the Hanyang area in the latter part of the Chosŏn Dynasty, and it also refers to the music that is played by such an ensemble (see plate 27). The *samhyŏn yukkak* ensemble consists of six musicians playing Korean traditional instruments—two *hyang p'iri* (bamboo cylindrical oboes), *taegŭm* (transverse bamboo flute), *haegŭm* (2-string fiddle), *changgu* (hourglass-shaped drum), and *puk* (barrel drum).

According to Kim Chŏm-Sŏk,[9] the complete Hanyang *Samhyŏn Yukkak* suite consists of twelve pieces: (1) "*Chajin Hwanip*," (2) "*Yŏmbul T'aryŏng*," (3) "*Pan Yŏmbul*," (4) "*Samhyŏn Todŭri*," (5) "*Yŏmbul Todŭri*," (6) "*T'aryŏng*," (7) "*Pyŏlgok T'aryŏng*," (8) "*Nŭjŭn Hŏt'ŭn T'aryŏng*," (9) "*Chajin Hŏt'ŭn T'aryŏng*," (10) "*Kutkŏri*," (11) "*Chajin Kutkŏri*," and (12) "*Tangak*." The Hanyang *Samhyŏn Yukkak* suite is rarely performed in its entirety since musicians usually play only certain selections according to the various performance contexts. For more information about the various pieces, see chapter 8.

The music of Hanyang *Samhyŏn yukkak* was performed at banquets for courtiers and processions for the elite, as well as at weddings or wealthy family members' *hwan'gap chanch'i* (60th birthday celebrations). *Samhyŏn yukkak* ensembles also played to accompany traditional dances and masked dance dramas, and during folk activities such as archery competitions or performances

---

[8] *Samhyŏn yukkak* originally referred to an ensemble of *samhyŏn* (literally, three strings)—*kayagŭm* (12-string zither), *kŏmun'go* (6-string zither), and *hyang pip'a* (plucked lute)—and *yukkak* (six aerophones)—two *hojŏk* (conical oboes), two *p'iri* (cylindrical oboes), and two *nabal* (long trumpets) (Chang S.H. 1991:573). The present-day *samhyŏn yukkak* ensemble, however, consists of different instruments than in earlier days. *Samhyŏn yukkak* nowadays is played with six instruments— two *p'iri*, *haegŭm* (2-string fiddle), *taegŭm* (flute), *changgu* (hourglass-shaped drum), and *puk* (barrel drum).

[9] Kim Chŏm-Sŏk is appointed by the government as *chŏnsu kyoyuk pojoja*, musician responsible for the education and transmission of the Seoul *Saenam Kut*.

of tightrope walking. In addition, *Samhyŏn yukkak* has been a quintessential part of ritual musical offerings in *kut* (Korean indigenous religious rituals), especially in Seoul and Kyŏnggi Province, as well as in large-scale rituals held at Buddhist temples. *Samhyŏn yukkak* musicians from Hanyang traveled and performed throughout the Korean peninsula, and several regional variations of *Samhyŏn yukkak* have developed, integrating the local aesthetics, and have been enjoyed by people as secular instrumental music.

CHAPTER 7

The Musicians of Hanyang *Kut*

In this chapter, I will discuss *kangshinmu* (spirit-possessed shamans) who perform music at rituals, and I will introduce several *chaebi* (ritual musicians) who perform at Hanyang *kut*.

1. The Musician-Shaman

The musical practices of shamans around the world are diverse. Inner Asian and circumpolar shamans, for example, use frame drums during their rituals to accompany themselves while singing and dancing. A shaman symbolically mounts his or her drum to fly either to heaven or to the underworld or to call the spirits from there to come to him (Ellingson 1974:8). In Malawi, healers work closely with musicians who provide the drumming to produce trance states (Friedson 1996: passim). During possession rituals, Haitian healers dance to music provided by an ensemble of drums, gourd rattle, and an *ogan*, a resonant iron percussion instrument (Bourguignon 1976:19).

Observing differences in musical practices, Gilbert Rouget coins the term "musicant" for the shaman who is actively involved in music making for his or her shamanic journey. He terms, on the other hand, the possessee in possession rituals as "musicated," because music is made *for* the one undergoing possession (1985:132).

If one looks into the musical practices of the *kangshinmu*, these Korean spirit-possessed ritual specialists are both "musicant" and "musicated," to borrow Rouget's terms. The *kangshinmu* sometimes sings songs as offerings to the spirits, accompanying himself or herself on the *changgu*, an hourglass-shaped drum, but he or she also sometimes sings and dances, accompanied by music of other instrumentalists. In other words, the *kangshinmu* is "musicated" by an instrumental ensemble made up of other *kangshinmu* and hired professional musicians. The drums and cymbals are played by *kangshinmu* during the *kut* (ritual), while other instruments—aerophones or chordophones—are played by *chaebi*, hired professional musicians, who are not spirit-possessed. The number of *chegŭm* (cymbal) players varies because *kangshinmu* attending a *kut* as visitors often join in playing *chegŭm* as a courtesy, creating an extremely loud percussion ensemble (sometimes as many as a dozen or more *kangshinmu* play cymbals), all of which adds to the "musicating" of the officiating *kangshinmu*.

A seated *kangshinmu* who plays *changgu* (hourglass-shaped drum) is the leader of the percussion ensemble in the Hanyang *kut*. As the spirit descends to the dancing *kangshinmu*, he or she begins *tomu*, hopping up and down in one spot balancing himself or herself on the balls of the feet until fully possessed by the spirit, slowing down only when the spirit is ready to speak through his or her voice. The exact moment of spirit possession of the dancing *kangshinmu* is felt simultaneously by the *kangshinmu* who plays the *changgu*, who then signals the musicians (who are not *kangshinmu*) to stop or fade out their melodic instrumental playing while the percussion ensemble continues to provide an accompaniment, accelerating or slowing down to match the pace set by the dancing *kangshinmu*. It is crucial for the *kangshinmu* to catch the moment of *kangshin* (spirit possession) to synchronize all of their musical offerings. Although I have played *changgu* and *chegŭm* (cymbals) to accompany songs and dances for *kangshinmu* during rehearsals or informal gatherings, for the reason stated above I was never invited to play *changgu* at a *kut* but was often asked by the *kangshinmu* to play the *chegŭm*.

Unlike the Hanyang *kut*, in the Hwanghae province style *kangshinmu kut* traditions, the principal drummer (*changgu*) and large gong (*ching*)[1] player are not spirit-possessed shamans but trained musicians, usually women. In Hwanghae Province style *kut*, the musicians who play *changgu* and *ching* are known as *sangjanggu halmŏni*, or *k'ŭn halmŏni* and *chagŭn halmŏni*, respectively.[2] In the North and South P'yŏngan Provinces style *kut*, two

---

[1] In the Hwanghae Province style ritual, *changgu* (drum) and *ching* (large gong) are the most important percussion instruments, unlike Seoul *kut* where *changgu* and *chegŭm* (cymbals) are considered essential.

[2] *Halmŏni* literally means "grandmother." Since the average age of most of the active women musicians nowadays ranges from fifty to eighty, they are referred to as *halmŏni* to show respect. I noticed that within a group of *manshin* from Hwanghae Province, the musicians who play drum and gong were referred to as *k'ŭn imo* and *chagŭn imo*, respectively. *Imo* literally means a "mother's sister." In this group, the *manshin* Kim (b. 1939) and the musicians were about the same age. Since they have worked together more than three decades, the musicians were called "aunts" to express the affection felt in the group. In secular context *k'ŭn imo* and *chagŭn imo* refers to an older and younger aunt, respectively, but it seems to me that the adjectives (*k'ŭn* [big] and *chagŭn* [little]) are

changgu, known as *ssang changgu* (literally, twin *changgu*), are played by musicians. The principal drummer is known as *sulmaji halmŏni* (Hwang L.S. 1992:202).

The first musical instrument a neophyte *kangshinmu* learns is usually *chegŭm* (cymbals). It may appear to be simple to play *chegŭm* well or in unison, but that, too, requires many hours of practice and a knowledge of the ritual. Let me share with you the experience of two scholars—Dr. Hyun-key Kim Hogarth (social anthropologist) and Prof. Sŏ Chŏng-bŏm (linguist)—described by Hogarth.

> In fact, I was allowed to play the cymbals, together with Prof. Sŏ Chŏng-bŏm at Mr. Cho Cha-ryŏng's *chinjŏk kut*. However, the discord that we created was such that Mr. Cho could not achieve his trance/ecstasy state, necessary for spirit possession. (Hogarth 1995:43)

The Hanyang *kut* is composed of songs, dances and *kongsu*, also known as *shint'ak*, where possessing spirits speak through the *kangshinmu*. As mentioned earlier, ritual songs may be sung as solos or duets by shamans. For *mansubaji* (call-and-response style duet songs), the seated *kidae* (the assisting *kangshinmu* who plays *changgu*, an hourglass-shaped drum) sings in response to the principal *kangshinmu* while providing the *changgu* accompaniment for both singers.

Although Halla Pai Huhm observes that "[k]*idae* are mostly those in whom the spirits have not appeared," the *kidae* I have met in various Hanyang *kut* were all spirit-possessed *kangshinmu* (Huhm 1980:10). The practice of hiring *haksŭpmu* (apprenticed *mudang*) as *kidae* singers appears to have stopped since so many musically trained *kangshinmu* are readily available for *kut* nowadays (personal communication with Mr. L, a ritual musician, October 1998). According to two musicians, Kim and Hŏ, the last well known *kidae* in the Hanyang *kut* who was not spirit-possessed was the late Pak Ŏ-Jin (1923–1989), known as Wangshipri Ot'obai,[3] who was highly respected by many *kangshinmu* (personal communication, March and October 1999, respectively). Several *kangshinmu*—"Pak Chong-Bok, Sun's Mother in Sangbongdong, Ch'angsu's Mother in Yit'aewŏn, and Yi Sang-Sun"—studied the music and ritual skills of the Hanyang *kut* with her (Yi K.W. 1997:505).

---

used in the ritual tradition in order to reflect the importance of the role of drummer, because the drummer is referred to as *k'ŭn halmŏni* or *k'ŭn imo*, even though she may be younger than the gong player.

[3] The nickname of Wangshipri Ot'obai came about when Pak Ŏ-Jin and her husband lived in the Wangshipri area and "owned two motorcycles [autobike or *ot'obai*] and a truck for their business" (Yi K.W. 1997:503).

As mentioned earlier, *ch'ŏngsong mudang* (musically talented *kangshinmu* singers) are in great demand. *Ch'ŏngsong mudang* are also known as *ch'ŏngsŭng mudang*. They are envied by many.[4] Sometimes I come across a *ch'ŏngsong mudang* secretly working away from his or her usual *kut p'ae* (group). When the shaman notices my presence, they will invariably find ways to urge me to keep the fact secret. The fear that the shaman feels appears to be so real that I usually have to promise I will not mention the fact to other shamans. I have learned not to say hello to any *kangshinmu* first in unfamiliar situations but to wait to be acknowledged. I have been careful not to discuss anything about shamans with other shamans or musicians, knowing how their world is so intricately interwoven. I learned a lot about the politics among the shamans and musicians through my years of observation. Knowledge of their world beneath the surface sometimes helps me to handle myself in difficult situations.

2. *Chaebi*, Ritual Musicians

Musicians hired for the Hanyang *kut* by the *kangshinmu* are all male instrumentalists referred to as *chaebi, aksa,* or *chŏnak*.[5] They are sometimes called *kkaengkkaengi* or *kkingkkingi,* employing onomatopoeic words for the sound of the *haegŭm* (two-stringed fiddle), but the term most frequently used for musicians in the *musok* world is *chaebi*.

The *chaebi* are hired to enhance the music for the shaman's songs and dances. Unlike the musical practice of musicians in the *sesŭpmu* traditions, *chaebi* never sing in the Hanyang *kut* but only provide instrumental music for songs and dances. In order to play the shaman's songs, *chaebi* musicians follow the melodic lines on their instruments in heterophony (*susŏng karak*).

---

[4] Many *kangshinmu* wish to be *"ch'ŏngsŭng mudang,"* Harvey asserted, noting "she [Suwŏn *manshin*] enjoyed performing in large *kut*; she hoped that her fellow shamans would make her a *ch'ŏngsŏng-mansin* (expert shamans who do consulting)" (Harvey 1984:308). In the world of *kangshinmu*, when one is invited to perform *muga* (ritual songs or recitations) in a few *kŏri* (sections) in other *kangshinmu*'s *kut*, they say *"ch'ŏngsŭng kanda"* ([I am or we are] going *ch'ŏngsŭng*). The *ch'ŏngsŭng mudang* do not offer consultation, but follow the wishes of the *tangju kangshinmu* who organizes the *kut*. The role of *ch'ŏngsŭng mudang* is limited to performing songs and dances during the assigned *kŏri* for the Hanyang *kut*.

[5] Musicians are known as *"koin"* in the southwestern provinces, *"aengjung"* or *"hwaraengi"* in eastern provinces, *"sani"* or *"hwaraengi"* in Kyŏnggi Province. They are also generally referred to as *"chaein, kongin, hwarang, kwangdae"* (Akamatsu and Akiba [1938] 1992, 2:255) or *akgong* (Yim T.G. 1986:76).

The *kangshinmu* singer may begin a song on any note or in any key according to his or her vocal range, expecting musicians to follow his or her lead without hesitation. Instrumentalists must have a good ear as well as the musical skills necessary to perform well in heterophony at rituals without any rehearsal.

The *chaebi* musicians also provide music for the *chegajip* (sponsors of the ritual) as they prostrate themselves in front of the altar for the spirits, and during *mugam*, an impromptu dance by sponsors and other participants. The *chaebi* are not only expected to be skilled on their instruments, but they must also know the ritual since they must often adjust and improvise music during the *kut*. In reality, individual musicianship and knowledge of the ritual vary greatly among the *chaebi*.

Among the *chaebi* musicians, a delicate boundary exists between *sani* and *ssoeni*. *Sani* musicians are men born into the families of either *kangshinmu* or *chaebi*. If a *sani* musician's family has been involved in *musok* continually for several generations, the musician is referred to as *ch'al sani*,[6] a musician holding firmly to the *musok* tradition. *Ssoeni* are male musicians who learned to play instruments in order to be hired for the *kut*. Despite the fact that a few *ssoeni* musicians are known to be great *chaebi*, they are usually considered outsiders and looked down upon by *sani* musicians. *Ssoeni* musicians are also referred to as *ch'ŏngsolgaebi*,[7] presupposing a lack of experience and knowledge of *musok* (Hŏ, personal communication, October 1998).

Since musicians involved in *musok* are generally ostracized by the outside community, they usually do not want their *musok* related activities known to the outside world. I refer to musicians by their legal names if they permit me to do so. I choose not to identify musicians as *sani*, *ch'al sani* or *ssoeni* in this work. Exceptions are made for musicians who are proud to be known as *sani*.

Many *sani* musicians begin their musical training at an early age because they love the ritual music they heard growing up. Some wish to avoid the fate of becoming *kangshinmu*,[8] while others simply want to make a living. Individual stories of musicians are often as compelling as those of *kangshinmu*.

Let me recount here the story of one musician as an example. For more than two decades, Mr. M, a ritual musician, has helped scholars to learn about *musok*. During my fieldwork, he often invited me to attend the *kut* where he was planning to work after getting permission from the officiating *kangshinmu*. He

---

[6] *Ch'al sani* refers to the musicians who are sticking to the tradition tenaciously. *Ch'al* is an adjective meaning tenacious, adhesive, and persevering.

[7] *Ch'ŏngsolgaebi* literally means a "green stick." It comes from *ch'ŏngsol kaji*, meaning a "freshly cut (tree) branch, still green."

[8] In order to avoid the fate of becoming a spirit-possessed shaman, some members of *sani* families become musicians, while others become photographers or visual artists, specializing in *musok* related works. Others become involved in the *musok* world as chauffeurs, shopkeepers, helpers for rituals, and so on.

introduced me to other musicians with great enthusiasm, asserting that I was interested in ritual music and musicians, unlike some researchers who were interested only in the *kangshinmu* or the *kut*. Mr. M is a musician in his early forties with such a vast knowledge of ritual that he has earned the respect of *kangshinmu* who work with him. Many times I have observed the *kangshinmu* turning to him for guidance as to the correct procedure during the *kut*. His main instrument is *p'iri* (oboe), but he also plays *haegŭm* (fiddle) and *taegŭm* (flute) quite well.

One day when Mr. M gave me a ride to downtown Seoul from a *kuttang* (ritual hall) nestled on a mountainside, he told me how he became involved in *kut* music. When he was about three or four years old, he used to notice golden rays surrounding the *yogang* (chamber pot) whenever he urinated into it. A very mischievous child, he would occasionally climb up to the *maru* (raised wooden floor bridging two rooms in a Korean style house)[9] and stand on the edge of it to urinate towards the garden. Whenever he did this, his family could hear bells and the loud sounds of drums although no one was actually playing. The young boy used to simply collapse with fright. One day his aunt, a well known *kangshinmu*, came for a visit and heard the drums and the bells ringing. Wishing to help her nephew, she encouraged him to become a *chaebi* musician as soon as he was old enough to handle an instrument. He began to learn to play *p'iri*. She knew that her nephew's fate was to be involved in *musok*, but she wanted to prevent him from becoming a *kangshinmu*. She knew that the life of a musician would be easier than that of a *kangshinmu* like herself. And that is how Mr. M became a *chaebi*, grateful for his aunt's guidance. Just about a year before I met him, he had learned a family secret—that his paternal grandmother and great-great-grandmother were also *kangshinmu* (personal communication, Dec. 1993).

In recent years, many musicians have become involved in *muak* (ritual music) for economic reasons, because musicians hired for *kut* are paid much more than for other performance jobs. Several musicians with university degrees discreetly play for *kut* in order to generate extra income while keeping other socially acceptable jobs such as teacher or orchestra musician.

The genealogy of musicians in the *sesŭpmu* tradition is well known because many are also involved as instrumentalists in the folk music genre (Pak C.J. 1993: passim). Program notes of folk musicians' concerts or liner notes on recordings report who the musicians' teachers are. But the genealogy of musicians working for the *kangshinmu* is intentionally kept vague by those

---

[9] *Maru*, a raised wooden floor in a Korean house, is used traditionally for a ritual area if a *kut* is held in a private home. Yi Chŏng-yŏng suggests that the term *maru* came from an Oronchun word as "[t]he Oronchun people used to have a place of *maru* as the most sacred place in the tents and no females were allowed to be there. The Tungus people seemed to have the same idea that the women were not allowed to be next to the *maru*, which became the symbol of divine presence" (Yi C.Y. 1983:199).

involved. *Sani* musicians belong to a lineage of musician families that has been involved in *musok* or *muak* (ritual music of *musok*) for several generations, but their reluctance to reveal information makes it difficult to construct a clear genealogy of musician families or teacher/student lineage. Many musicians, for example, recognize the late Mr. Yi Yun-Sŏng as their teacher of *muak*, but his son, a *chaebi* in his early forties, initially appeared to be uncomfortable talking with me about his father in 1993.

Ritual musicians (*chaebi*), as a rule, learn to play *p'iri* first because the *p'iri* is the essential melodic instrument in *kut* music, and *p'iri* players are in great demand. If a single *chaebi* musician is to be hired for a *kut*, it is always a *p'iri* player. When a *chaebi* musician is hired for a *kut*, he usually does not know with whom he will be playing for the occasion. Sometimes he may be able to play his main instrument throughout the entire *kut*, but he must be flexible and play other instruments if necessary. For example, if one musician finds that he is in the company of a better-known musician specializing in the same instrument, the less experienced musician must offer to play another instrument to be polite. I can recall meeting musicians who specialized in one instrument exclusively, but they were usually beginners in the trade who had been called in to replace someone at the last moment. The marketability of a musician limited to one instrument is considered poor. Most *chaebi* (ritual musicians) I have met who play for the Hanyang *kut* are skilled on several instruments. For example, Kim Chŏng-Gil, who is known mainly as a *haegŭm* player, occasionally plays *taegŭm* and *t'aep'yŏngso* during a ritual if the need arises. Both Hŏ Yong-Ŏp and Kim Chŏm-Sŏk play *p'iri, haegŭm, taegŭm,* and *t'aep'yŏngso*.

In order to become *chaebi*, one must not only learn how to play several instruments but also acquire various *muak* repertoires. It is a common practice in Korea for a student to switch teachers according to his or her level of progress while learning secular music or *muak* just as one may begin to learn piano under a neighborhood teacher but move on to an established piano professor as an advanced student. One may choose to stay with one master later on with the hope of following in his or her footsteps, especially if the teacher is a *poyuja* (holder) or has a chance of being designated the next *poyuja* of an Important Intangible Cultural Property by the government.

Among the *chaebi* I have met, some were willing to talk about their learning experiences, but others declined. Unfortunately, not many musicians know or remember their teachers' ages, and there are now few written sources that refer to *musok* musicians unless the musicians are known to have been involved in secular music as well. I would first like to mention four *chaebi*—Kim Sun-Bong, Kim Chŏm-Sŏk, Kim Chŏng-Gil, and Hŏ Yong-Ŏp—who are perhaps the most sought after musicians for the Hanyang *kut* rituals in contemporary Seoul. Since 1993, I have attended various *kut* where these musicians performed as solo or ensemble musicians with each other or with other musicians whom I will discuss later.

I will also present diagrams showing the genealogies of *chaebi* of Hanyang *kut*, indicating the musicians' family ties as well as the lineage of their teachers and students.

While learning about musicians and their families, I realized how perplexing it is to work with people's memories. In many cases, people could not recall the names of family musicians or the year of their birth and death. Most musicians would say something like, "My grandfather would be about one hundred this year if he had lived but he died when he was seventy two." Making such comments, musicians usually offer to come up with approximate years of their birth and death.[10] In cases where the dates were unclear, I decided not to provide any inaccurate dates or information in this work.

Some musicians told me that it is unclear for them whom they should consider to be their real teachers. They certainly can name their first teachers who taught them the basic techniques of playing the instruments. They also tell me that they learned new repertoires, musical skills and aesthetics, ritual procedures, and so on from several teachers later in their careers and that they find it difficult to credit one or two. Musicians were reluctant to talk about other musicians' teachers mainly because they were unsure how another musician regards his own teachers.

Kim Sun-Bong (b. 1931)

Kim Sun-Bong was born in Kwangju, Kyŏnggi province, and studied *p'iri* and *taegŭm* with his grandfather, Kim In-Hak, a well known *shinawi*[11] *p'iri* musician of Kyŏnggi area. Kim Sun-Bong's father, Kim Sŏk-Kŭn, was also a musician but not as well known as his father. Having settled in Seoul in his thirties, Kim Sun-Bong played for the Hanyang *kut* for many years.

Since the early 1980s, Kim Sun-Bong was a core member of the *sam chaebi* (trio musicians) working for Pak Sŏng-Ki, a *paksu*. The *sam chaebi*—Kim Sun-Bong (*p'iri*), Kim Chŏm-Sŏk (*taegŭm*), and Hŏ Yong-Ŏp (*haegŭm*)—ceased to work together regularly after *paksu* Pak suffered a stroke in the late 1990s. Since then Kim Sun-Bong has been working with a group of musicians consolidated by Ch'oe Hyŏng-Gŭn. In 1999, Kim Sun-Bong was recognized by the City of

---

[10] Koreans use two systems for calculating age. In one system, one starts counting age by starting with one year at birth (to include the time in the womb). Koreans then become a year older on New Year's Day. For example, a baby born in Korea on December 31, 1999 becomes two years old on January 1, 2000. The other system, called *man*, is similar to the Western system of counting according to birthdays. Thus the baby in our example would turn two years old on December 31, 2001.

[11] *Shinawi* is a genre of instrumental ensemble music.

Seoul as the *poyuja* (designated performer) for Intangible Cultural Property number 20, Nam Yi *Changgun Che* (Ritual for General Nam Yi).[12]

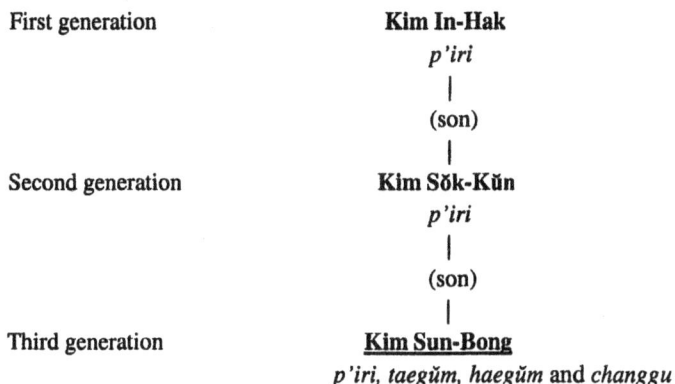

Figure 2. Kim Sun-Bong and His Family Musicians

Kim Chŏm-Sŏk (b. 1939)

Kim Chŏm-Sŏk is designated by the government as *chŏnsu kyoyuk pojoja*, musician responsible for the education and transmission of Important Intangible Cultural Property no. 104, Seoul *Saenam Kut*. Kim Chŏm-Sŏk was born in Seoul, the second son of Kim Chin-Yong (1904–1969), a renowned *musok* ritual musician. Kim Chin-Yong's mother, who was suddenly possessed by spirits at the age of forty, was thrown out of the upper class Kim clan household with her youngest child, four-year-old Chin-Yong, and had to raise her son alone. She later became a famous *kangshinmu*, known as "Shindangdong Pulsabang" or "Kŭpsalbang" in the Seoul area. As a young man, Kim Chin-Yong grew up observing his mother officiate at Hanyang *kut* and began to learn to play ritual music on several instruments. He studied *p'iri* with Kim Hwa-Ch'un, *taegŭm* with Kim Kye-Sŏn, and *haegŭm* with Cho Wŏn-Sun.

Kim Chin-Yong, having lived the life of a shaman's son and a *chaebi* (ritual musician), had experienced so much hardship that he tried to dissuade his second son, Chŏm-Sŏk, from pursuing his interest in ritual music. Kim, however, finally gave in and decided to teach his son properly, recognizing the earnest desire and talent in his son. When Chŏm-Sŏk was eighteen years old, the father and son team was ready to perform together at rituals, playing *taegŭm* and *p'iri*, respectively.

---

[12] General Nam Yi (1444–1468) died young while imprisoned under a false accusation.

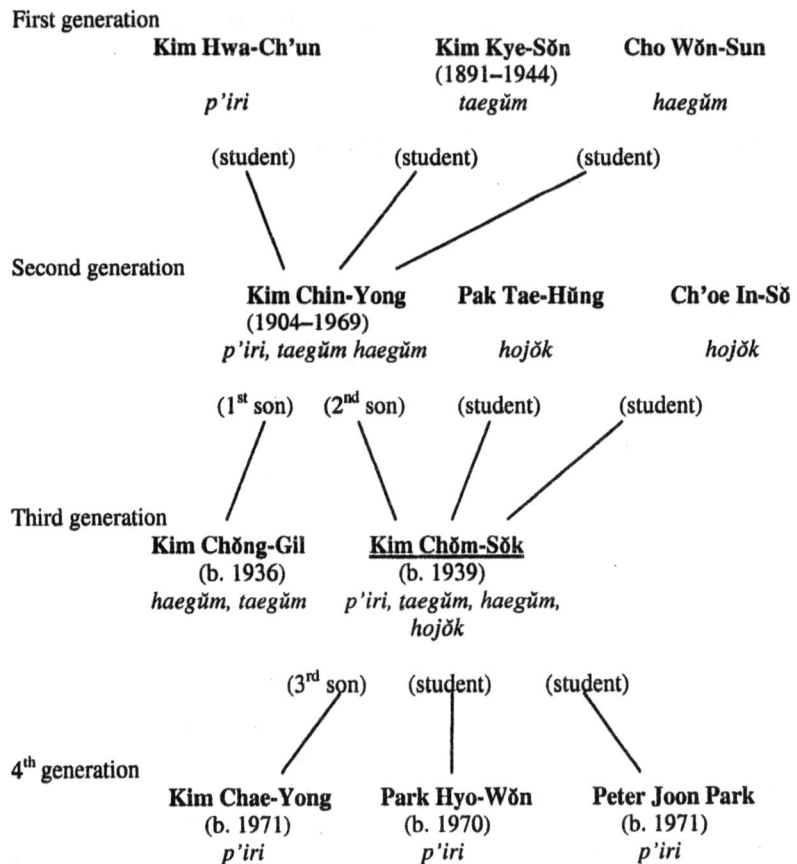

Figure 3. Lineage of Teachers, Students and Family Musicians of Kim Chŏm-Sŏk

For Seoul area ritual music, instrumentalists are hired according to the purpose of the ritual and funds available. If a single musician is to be hired, it is a *p'iri* player, adding the *haegŭm* player if a second musician is used. If a trio is required, *p'iri*, *haegŭm*, and *taegŭm* players are hired. First class musicians like Kim Chin-Yong and Kim Chŏm-Sŏk, who are capable of playing several instruments, are greatly admired and frequently hired by Hanyang *kut* shamans. Kim Chŏm-Sŏk had the special experience of performing with many great musicians who were contemporary with his father.

Kim began to play *p'iri* under his father's guidance and studied *t'aep'yŏngso* with Ch'oe In-Sŏ and Pak Tae-Hŭng. Kim Chŏm-Sŏk's legal name is Kim Chŏng-Ch'i, but he is more widely known by his alias, Kim Chŏm-Sŏk.

His wife, Shin Chŏng-Ae, is a folk singer specializing in *sŏdo sori*, northwestern province style songs. The couple has three sons and three grandsons.

Kim Chae-Yong (b. 1971), the third son of Kim Chŏm-Sŏk, is a *p'iri* player and is designated by the government as an *isuja* (master artist) for Seoul *Saenam Kut*, Important Intangible Cultural Property no. 104.

One of Kim Chŏm-Sŏk's five brothers, Kim Chŏng-Gil (b. 1936), has been performing *haegŭm* at Hanyang *kut* together with Chŏm-Sŏk for many years. Kim Chŏng-Gil was a guitar player in his youth but began in his thirties to study *haegŭm* with his father, Kim Chin-Yong, and later with Kim Chong-Hŭi. In 1996, Kim Chŏng-Gil was designated as an *isuja* for Seoul *Saenam Kut*, Important Intangible Cultural Property no. 104, but he declined the honor for personal reasons.

Hŏ Yong-Ŏp (b. 1947)

Hŏ Yong-Ŏp was born in Sut'aek ri, Kuri myŏn, Yangju kun, Kyŏnggi province, the second son of Hŏ Sang-Chŏn (1921–1963), a great *p'iri* musician. Hŏ Yong-Ŏp learned to play *p'iri* imitating his father behind the father's back from an early age. His father tried very hard to dissuade Yong-Ŏp from becoming a musician because he had experienced a difficult life as a ritual musician, being looked down upon as a lower class citizen. Finding out one day that his eleven-year-old son had been playing *p'iri*, Hŏ Sang-Chŏn was so upset that he gave Yong-Ŏp a severe beating in order to discourage him from ever playing *p'iri* again.

When Yong-Ŏp was fifteen, his father passed away. Unlike his father, his uncle Hŏ Sang-Bok (1912–1984) encouraged both Yong-Ŏp and his [Hŏ Sang-Bok's] own son, Hŏ Mu-Gil (b. 1953), to learn to play various instruments. Being a fine musician himself, Hŏ Sang-Bok began to teach his nephew, Yong-Ŏp, both *taegŭm* and *haegŭm*. He also encouraged Yong-Ŏp to study with another great musician, Yi Ch'ung-Sŏn. Later Yong-Ŏp continued his studies with Kang Hak-Su, the disciple of Kim Yŏ-Gwan, a court musician of the latter part of the Chosŏn Dynasty. Hŏ Yong-Ŏp is a versatile *chaebi* who is in great demand in contemporary Seoul as a *p'iri, taegŭm, haegŭm, t'aep'yŏngso*, and *changgu* player. Hŏ Yong-Ŏp is designated by the government as an *isuja* (master artist) for Seoul *Saenam Kut*, Important Intangible Cultural Property no. 104.

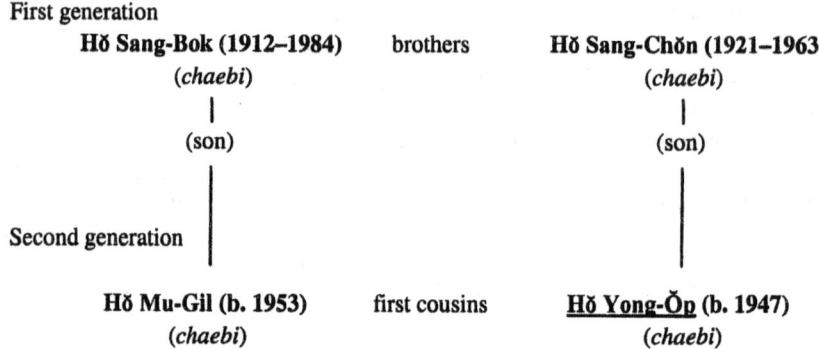

Figure 4. Hŏ Yong-Ŏp and his Family Musicians

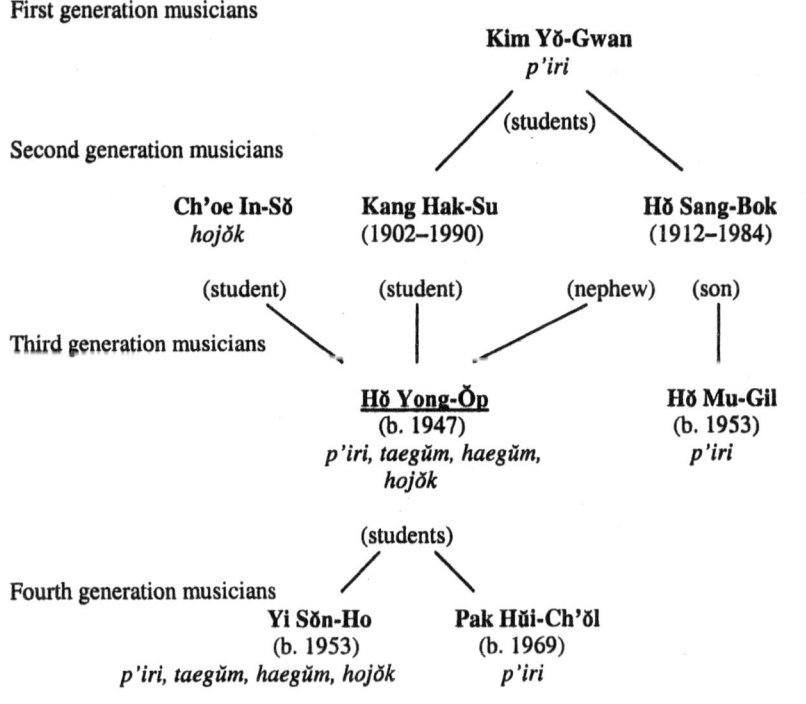

Figure 5. Hŏ Yong-Ŏp's Teachers and Various Instruments He Has Learned

Table 4
Hŏ Yong-Ŏp's Teachers on Various Instruments

Chi Kap-Sŏng	changgu
Chi Yŏng-Hŭi (1909–1980)[13]	p'iri, haegŭm
Ch'oe In-Sŏ	t'aep'yŏngso
Chŏng Kyu-Nam	t'aep'yŏngso
Han Pŏm-Su	taegŭm
Hŏ Sang-Bok (1912–1984)	taegŭm, haegŭm
Kang Hak-Su (1902-1990)	p'iri
Yi Chŏng-Ŏp	changgu
Yi Ch'ung-Sŏn (1901–1989)	p'iri, taegŭm
Yi Yil-Sŏn	p'iri

Han Yŏng-Sŏ (b. 1947)

In the beginning, Han learned the basic playing techniques of *p'iri* and *haegŭm* from Yi Ch'ung-Sŏn (1901–1989) and *p'iri* repertoire for Hanyang *kut* music from the late Chi Kap-Sŏng, a well known *sani* musician. Han Yŏng-Sŏ was adopted by Chi Kap-Sŏng and studied *p'iri* and drums (*changgu* and *puk*) with him. Han later studied *taegŭm* with Han Pŏm-Su.

In recent years, Han Yŏng-Sŏ has studied with Kim Chŏm-Sŏk the *p'iri* and *taegŭm* repertoire required to take part in the Seoul *Saenam Kut* rituals. He has been a member of the folk instrumental ensemble of KBS (Korean Broadcasting System) in Seoul.

Kim Ch'an-Sŏp (b. 1947)

Kim Ch'an-Sŏp is a *chaebi* (ritual musician) and a member of the folk instrumental ensemble of KBS (Korean Broadcasting System) in Seoul. He studied music with his stepfather Yi Ch'ung-Sŏn, the second son of Yi Tŏk-Jae, a well known *p'iri* player. Three sons of Yi Tŏk-Jae—Yi Il-Sŏn, Yi Ch'ung-Sŏn, and Yi Tal-Sŏn—were *p'iri* players.

---

[13] Chi Yŏng-Hŭi's legal name was Chi Ch'ŏn-Man.

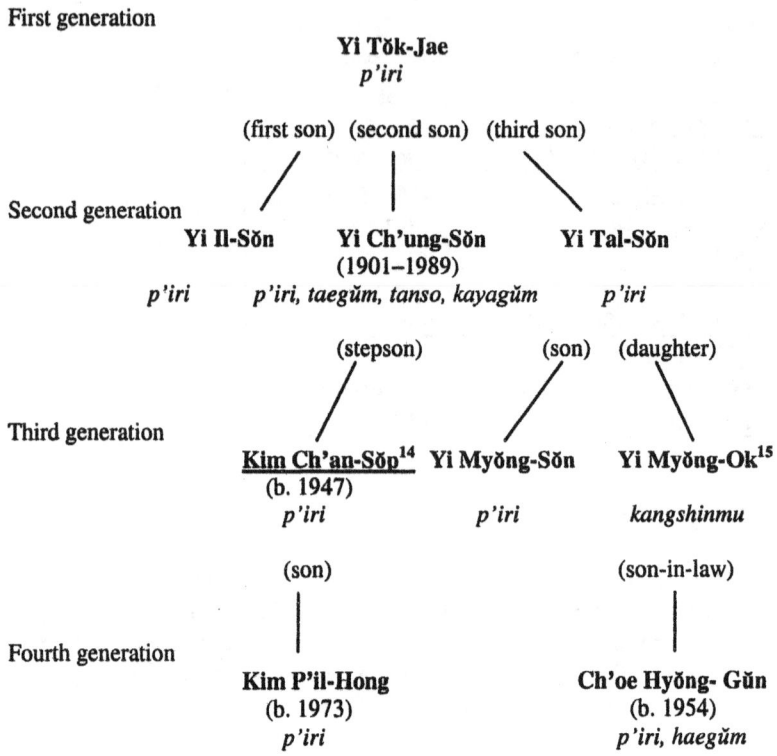

Figure 6. Kim Ch'an-Sŏp and His Family Musicians

---

[14] Kim Ch'an-Sŏp's elder sister, a stepdaughter of Yi Ch'ung-Sŏn, is Kim Ch'un-Gang, a well known *kangshinmu* in Seoul and Kyŏnggi area. She is also known as Ŭnju's mother. Kim Ch'un-Gang is the shaman who supervised Kim Hye-Ran's "*kut*" performance (see chapter 5).

[15] Yi Myŏng-Ok (b. 1937) was recognized as the *poyuja* (designated performer) for Intangible Cultural Property no. 20 of Seoul City, Nam Yi *Changgun Che* (Ritual for General Nam Yi) in 1999.

Yang Hwa-Yŏng (b. 1952)

Yang Hwa-Yŏng is a *p'iri* musician who usually works with Pak In-O, a male *kangshinmu*. He learned to play *p'iri* from his uncle, Yang Kwang-San, who taught techniques as well as the repertoire used in Hanyang *kut* music.

Yang Hwa-Yŏng's great-grandfather, Yang Kyŏng-Wŏn, taught many students who produced a number of fine *chaebi* in the Hanyang *kut*. The following two diagrams show the genealogy of Yang Hwa-Yŏng and the lineage of Yang Kyŏng-Wŏn's students, attesting to Yang Kyŏng-Wŏn's influence on the musicians of today.

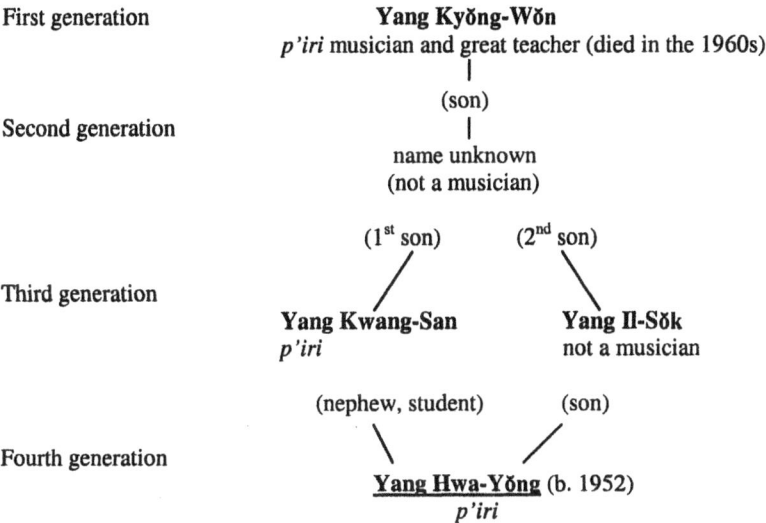

Figure 7. Yang Hwa-Yŏng and His Family Musicians

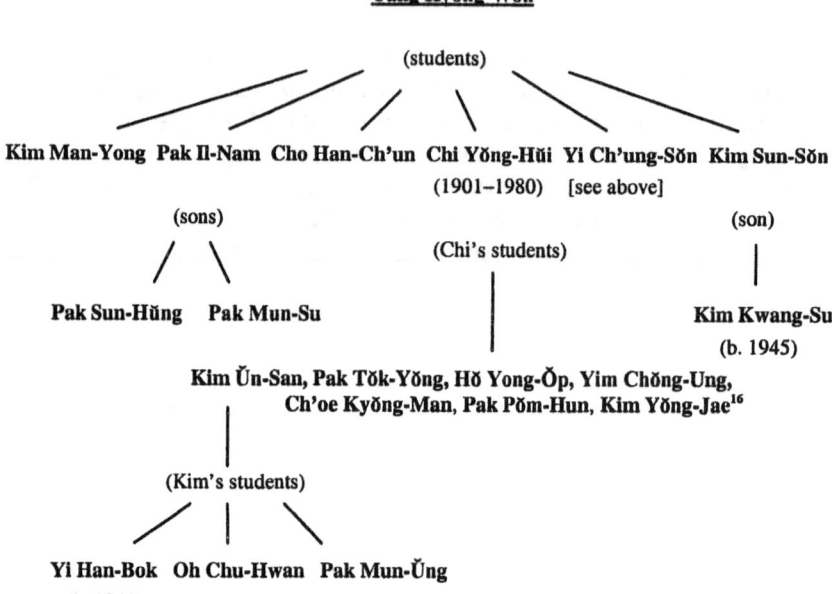

Figure 8. Yang Kyŏng-Wŏn and His Students

Yi Ki-Jŏng (b. 1955)

Yi Ki-Jŏng, a *p'iri* and *haegŭm chaebi,* is a son of the well known *muak* teacher Yi Yun-Sŏng. Yi Yun-Sŏng, a student of Yi Ch'ung-Sŏn, taught *p'iri* to many students including Yi Ki-Jŏng (son), Ch'oe Hyŏng-Gŭn (adopted son), Chi Kap-P'al, Hobakjip Adŭl, Kim Ch'ang-Ho, Kim Chong-Hŭi, Pak Yŏng-Bong, Shin Hak-Sa, and Yi Sŏn-Ho!

---

[16] Ch'oe Kyŏng-Man is a world renowned *p'iri* performer and a member of the KBS folk music ensemble. Pak Pŏm-Hun is the conductor of the Chungang Korean Traditional Orchestra. Not involved in making ritual music in a sacred context, Pak has been teaching *p'iri* at Chungang University in Seoul. Kim Yŏng-Jae is a well known *haegŭm* and *kŏmun'go* performer in secular folk music genres. Kim studied *haegŭm* with Chi Yŏng-Hŭi and *kŏmun'go* with Shin K'wae-Dong (1910–1977). He is also a composer and teaches at Han'guk Yesul Chonghap Hakkyo (The Korean National University of Arts, School of Korean Traditional Arts).

The Musicians of Hanyang Kut

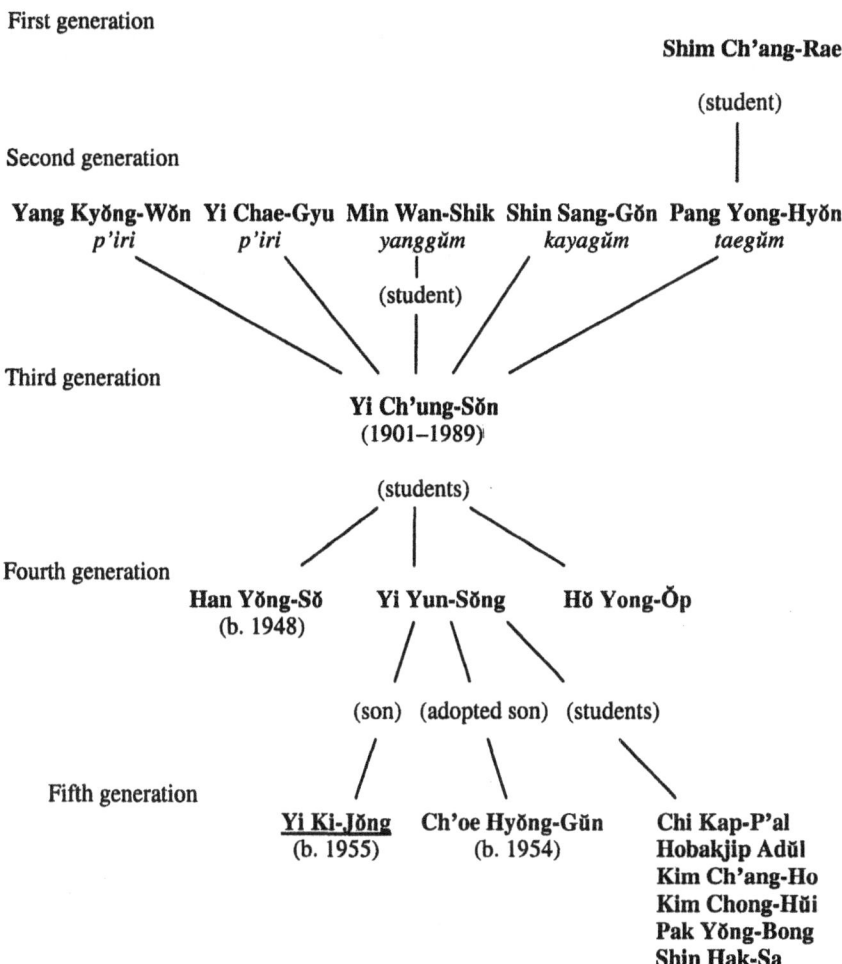

Figure 9. Yi Ki-Jŏng's Teachers

Yi Sŏn-Ho (b. 1953)

Yi Sŏn-Ho is a musician who learned *p'iri* from Yi Yun-Sŏng and *haegŭm*, *hojŏk*, and *taegŭm* from Hŏ Yong-Ŏp. He is a versatile musician and often takes part in the *sam chaebi* ensemble playing *taegŭm* with Kim Chŏm-Sŏk and Kim Chŏng-Gil playing *p'iri* and *haegŭm*, respectively.

Yi is an *isuja* (master artist) designated by the government as an instrumentalist for Seoul *Saenam Kut*, Important Intangible Cultural Property no. 104. He has taught several musicians but he considers one student in particular, Kim Chong-Yŏp (b. 1971), to be his successor.

In addition to the musicians discussed above, I would like to mention the names of other musicians who have been actively involved in Hanyang *kut* music (listed alphabetically in the table below).

Table 5
Other Musicians Involved in Hanyang *Kut* Ritual Music

Name	Specialty
Chang Yŏng-Gŭn	*haegŭm*
Ch'oe Sŭng-Hun (b. 1961)	*p'iri* and *taegŭm*
Ch'oe Yŏng-Sam	*taegŭm*
Hwang Ho-Gyun	*changgu*
Kim Hyŏng-P'yo (b. 1952)	*p'iri, haegŭm,* and *ajaeng*
Kim Kwang-Su (b. 1945)	*p'iri*
Kim Sang-Bong	*haegŭm*
Mun Chong-Ho (b. 1942)	*p'iri*
Mun Yŏng-Hŭi (b. 1939)	*p'iri*
Oh Chae-Hwan	*p'iri*
Oh Ki-Hwan	*p'iri*
Pak Mun-Ung	*taegŭm*
Pak Yŏng-Bong	*p'iri*
Pak Tŏk-Yŏng	*p'iri, taegŭm,* and *hojŏk*
Pang In-Gŭn (b. 1940)[17]	*changgu, p'iri, hojŏk,* and *haegŭm*
Shin Chae-Dong	*p'iri, taegŭm,* and *ajaeng*
Yi Pyŏng-Guk (b. 1961)	*p'iri*
Yi Sang-Gŭn (b. 1968)	*taegŭm*
Yi Sŏng-Il	*p'iri* and *hojŏk*
Yim Ki-T'aek (b. 1963),	*taegŭm*
Yun Pyŏng-O	*p'iri*

Several musicians have not been mentioned here due to their wish to remain anonymous. Musicians who play at *kangshinmu* (spirit-possessed shaman) or *sesŭpmu* (hereditary *mudang*) rituals of various regional styles in Seoul are not

---

[17] Pang In-Gŭn is also known as Pang Tol-Gŭn.

included here because the focus of this work is the Hanyang *kut* and its musical practitioners. According to several musicians and *kangshinmu*, there are about sixty musicians currently specializing in Hanyang *kut*.

CHAPTER 8

Music in Hanyang *Kut*

Muak refers to ritual songs and instrumental music used in *musok* rituals. Ritual music is also known as *kut ŭmak* (literally, ritual music) and *kuttang ŭmak* (literally, ritual hall music) or *tangak* for short.

Rituals were held on a grand scale in the political centers of different kingdoms and dynasties throughout Korean history. One may detect historical ties and musical influences remaining in the regional variations of present-day *muak*. The musical influences from Koguryŏ period (37 B.C.E.–668) court music remain in the *muak* of Hwanghae Province and North and South P'yŏngan Provinces, from Paekche Kingdom (18 B.C.E.–660) in the *muak* of North and South Chŏlla Provinces, from Shilla Kingdom (57 B.C.E.–935) in the *muak* of North and South Kyŏngsang Provinces, and from Koryŏ Dynasty (918–1392) in the *muak* of Kyŏnggi Province (Kim K.S. 1972:128). *Muak* of Hanyang *kut* reflects the court music of the Chosŏn Dynasty (1392–1910) whose capital was Hanyang, present-day Seoul.

Seoul has been the capital of Korea for over six centuries. *Kangshinmu* of Hanyang *kut* often allude to their ties with the Chosŏn Dynasty court by distinguishing *kungan kut* (rituals held in the court) from *kungbak kut* (rituals held outside the court) in order to suggest authenticity and to invoke a long line of tradition.

In earlier days, the boundary of Hanyang was marked by a wall with four gates—East, West, South, and North—surrounding the capital. Within the four gates, four styles of the Hanyang *kut* are known to have existed. Three of these were performed outside the court—*kaksimjŏlbon* in the eastern part of the city, *nodŭlbon* in the Usuhyŏn area of the southern part, and *kup'abalbon* in the western part—and one inside the court (Cho H.Y. 1997:135).[1]

---

[1] *Kakshimjŏlbon* refers to the Changwidong and Wangshipri areas in the east part of modern metropolitan Seoul, *nodŭlbon* refers to the Noryangjin area in the south, and *kup'abalbon* refers to the Ilsan area in the west.

155

Muga, Ritual Songs

Ritual songs are called *muga* or *shin'ga*[2] and are sung as solos or duets, accompanied by the *changgu* (hourglass-shaped drum). Solo songs include short songs, stylized recitations, and long epic songs. The melodic contours of Korean music are generally expressed in pentatonic modes, emphasizing the principal notes in each mode with ornamentation. In Hanyang *kut*, melodies of ritual songs are basically in Kyŏngsŏ *t'ori*, the musical dialect of Seoul, Kyŏnggi, and the northwestern Provinces, which is a *sol* pentatonic scale—*sol, la, do, re,* and *mi* (Ch'oi H. 1996:31). The main tones of the *sol* pentatonic scale are *sol, do,* and *mi*. The distinctive melodic patterns of Kyŏngsŏ *t'ori* stems from the intervals of the perfect fourth between *sol* and *do* and the major third between *do* and *mi. Sol* pentatonic scale songs usually end on either *sol* or *do.*

In Hanyang *kut*, *kangshinmu* sing incantations, epic songs, strophic songs, duet songs, and vocal parts of musical offerings with an instrumental ensemble. The Hanyang *kut* songs may be grouped into two types: solo and duet songs. Solo songs are sung either seated or while dancing. Incantation songs—like *Kamang Ch'ŏngbae* and *Chungdi Patsan*—or epic songs like *Hwangje P'uri* are sung by one *kangshinmu*, accompanying himself or herself on the *changgu* (hourglass-shaped drum). For the epic song *Pari Kongju*, the *kangshinmu* sings alone accompanying himself or herself on two instruments—*pangul* (bell tree) and *changgu* (drum). He or she shakes the *pangul* and plays just one head of the *changgu*. For epic songs and incantations, the *kangshinmu* sings stock melodies (several short melodies), alternating and creating variations.

T'aryŏng (solo strophic songs)[3] are sung by a principal *kangshinmu* while the *changgu* accompaniment is provided by an assisting *kangshinmu* (see CD track 25). The principal *kangshinmu* sings *t'aryŏng* songs while dancing, holding various ritual objects in both hands, except when he or she sings *"Para T'aryŏng"* accompanying himself or herself on *para,* a pair of cymbals (see CD track 22).

---

[2] *Shin'ga* may also be romanized as *sin'ga*. Boudewijn Walraven informs us that "[t]he term *muga* is of rather recent origin and probably was first used by Akamatsu. Son Chint'ae, the first systematic collector, used *sin'ga*, 'songs of the gods.' In North Korea, Hong Kimun uses *mudang sori*, which is equivalent to *muga,* but puristically avoids Sino-Korean" (Walraven 1985:12). I have chosen to use the term *muga* for shaman songs, having observed that *muga* is the term most commonly used by Seoul area *kangshinmu* and musicians.

[3] Yi Nŭng Hwa postulated that the term *t'aryŏng* (打令), referring to a song, came from its homophone *t'aryŏng* (妥靈), which has referred to the ritual offering of song and dance since the Koryŏ period (918–1392) (Yi N.H. [1927] 1991:180).

Noraekarak are strophic solo or duet songs. "*Noraekarak*," literally meaning "songs," consists of two words: *norae* (song) and *karak* (also meaning song or melody). Korean traditional songs are usually divided into two groups: *sori* and *norae*. *Sori* refers to folk songs like *minyo* and *p'ansori* while *norae* refers to songs like *kagok*, *kasa*, and *shijo*[4] sung by the upper classes.

During the *anjŭn kŏri* (seated sections) of a *kut*, a *kangshinmu* sings *noraekarak* alone, accompanying himself or herself on *changgu* (see CD tracks 5, 18, and 32). But whenever *noraekarak* are sung in duet, the principal *kangshinmu* stands and sings while the assisting *kangshinmu* sits at the *changgu*, singing and providing *changgu* accompaniment for both singers. These *noraekarak* duets are sung in unison (see CD track 34). *Noraekarak* songs are sung to entertain *chŏngshin* (literally, correct or true spirits), that is, those spirits officially invited during the *kut*.

Mansubaji (duet songs)[5] are sung by two *kangshinmu*. As with *noraekarak* duets, the principal *kangshinmu* sings standing while the assisting one is seated at the *changgu*, singing and providing a *changgu* accompaniment for both singers. The principal *kangshinmu* adds bell sounds by shaking the *pangul* (bell tree) held in the left hand. *Mansubaji* are sung in each *kŏri* (section) except *pujŏng kŏri*, the first section performed during the Hanyang *kut*. When *mansubaji* is sung for *chŏngshin* (invited spirits), the principal *kangshinmu* plays the bell tree (see CD track 35). But when *mansubaji* is sung for miscellaneous spirits during *twitchŏn kŏri* at the end of the ritual, the *pangul* (bell tree) is not used. Thus *twitchŏn mansubaji* duet is sung with *changgu* accompaniment alone (see CD track 29).

During the ritual performance, the singer shaman uses the *nogaba* method to call and praise spirits while singing songs like *t'aryŏng*, *noraekarak*, or *mansubaji*. *Nogaba* is an abbreviation for *Norae gasa bakkwŏburŭgi*, which refers to the practice of providing different lyrics for a given melody (Noh 1995:365).[6] Shamans choose appropriate texts for the given *kŏri* (section). For instance, shamans will sing "Shinjang *T'aryŏng*" during the Shinjang *kŏri* and

---

[4] *Shijo* is often transliterated as *sijo*.

[5] *Mansubaji* duet songs are also referred to as *paraji* (literally, support). The term *paraji* also refers to a person who assists a monk in various ways, including responding in songs. *Mansubaji* is also known as *tapch'ang* (literally, responding song), indicating the call and response style of singing (Lee H.K. 1957:171), or *taech'ang* (also meaning responding song) (Kim K.S. 1972:129).

[6] The term *nogaba* originally referred to a tradition that began in the late 18th century as Korean Catholic priests taught didactic songs to their congregations using Korean folk song melodies. Since few Koreans knew any Western languages, missionaries encouraged them to sing hymns with Korean words set to Western melodies or Korean folk song melodies (Noh 1995:365).

"Taegam *T'aryŏng*" during the Taegam *kŏri* to honor the respective spirits of the given *kŏri* (sections).

Some of the *noraekarak* song texts are from *shijo*, the classic three-line poem of the Chosŏn Dynasty.[7] Boudewijn Walraven notes the relationship between *noraekarak* and *shijo*:

> Sometimes complete *sijo* are inserted in the song, sometimes *sijo* lines or half-lines are used. A *muga* with a remarkable number of *sijo* is *Sanmanura noraekkarak* (AA I, 78-86). It contains no less than six complete *sijo*. Then there are several lines which incorporate parts of *sijo*. All these *sijo* are of well-known types, with such subjects as the task of a real man, life in seclusion, the joys of wine etc., subjects which have not much to do with shamanism. There are quite a few lines which celebrate the king and wish for his longevity and health (such as are often found in *sijo*), which makes it plausible that this kind of *noraekkarak* developed among the *mudang* of the capital who frequented the royal palace. (Walraven 1994:116)

Noraekarak are sung with similar *changdan* (rhythmic cycles) as the *shijo*, suggesting the close ties between court music and the ritual music of Hanyang *kut*.

The *noraekarak* song text consists of stanzas of three lines each. At the end of each first and second line of a stanza, the melody extends a few extra beats beyond the last syllables. This extension is called *yŏŭm* (literally, lingering note) or *yŏm* for short. Some *kangshinmu* play three-beat *yŏm*, some play five-beat *yŏm*. Some don't play *yŏm*, focusing on the song text and not realizing that the accompanying instrumental melodies are a bit longer than the vocal melodies. The aesthetics created by *yŏm* enhance the stable and refined quality of *noraekarak*.

Most contemporary *kangshinmu* do not use *yŏm* except those who are known as "*ch'ae majŭn mudang*." The term *ch'ae majŭn* (literally, whipped) *mudang* alludes to the rigorous training process one had to endure to master the musical skills under the strict supervision of teachers. I heard Yi Sang-Sun encouraging students to learn properly, telling them that if a *kangshinmu* provides *yŏm* on the drum, instrumentalists immediately recognize the shaman as a well-trained musician and show respect (April 2000).

As several *kangshinmu* have put it, the number of *kut* is on the rise, but clients' level of knowledge of *kut* is diminishing. In earlier days, if a *kangshinmu* skipped a song or switched the order of *kŏri*, clients were quick to point out that the shaman was untrained. If a shaman was ridiculed by clients, it was difficult for him or her to be hired again in the same neighborhood. People

---

[7] *Shijo* were orally transmitted until the texts began to be written down from the eighteenth century onward (Lee, P. 1981:xxii).

knew how to enjoy *kut* because they had many opportunities to attend *kut* sponsored by their families or neighbors. People learned what to look for in rituals, comparing one ritual with another. In contemporary Korea, people sponsoring *kut* often have very limited experience and may not know what to expect. Consequently, some *kangshinmu* feel they can get away with minimal training for they are often more eager to make money than to invest the time to learn things properly. Untrained *kangshinmu* often demand a great deal of money for *kut*, suggesting to their clients that the more the *kut* costs, the better the result will be.

Unlike *noraekarak*, the *t'aryŏng* and *mansubaji* songs are sung in *kutkŏri changdan*, a twelve-beat rhythmic cycle. Many *kangshinmu* in Hanyang *kut* nowadays can sing *t'aryŏng* and *mansubaji*, but only a few have mastered *noraekarak* with its complicated rhythmic pattern.

When *t'aryŏng* and *noraekarak* are sung with an instrumental ensemble as musical offerings to the spirits, the aesthetics of these musical offerings are found in the performance of heterophony[8] in the vocal and instrument parts. The vocal melodies become part of the music and blend into the instrumental ensemble music. For these musical offerings, the instrumental ensemble does not provide an accompaniment (*panju*) to the singer, but rather they perform together with the singer (*yŏnju* or *hapju*). The lyrics of songs are often overshadowed by instrumental sounds when the music is performed as an offering in ritual context. It is also interesting to note that no vocables are used in the ritual songs for the Hanyang *kut*. Vocables are often used in the ritual songs of *kut* in Chŏlla and Kyŏngsang Provinces.

When an instrumental ensemble performs during a ritual, each melodic instrument plays *susŏng karak* (variations of a main melody). Each instrument has its own *susŏng karak* (melodic lines) to accompany songs. These *susŏng karak* are handed down aurally over generations. The individual musician has to learn the melodies on his particular instrument for each song. When musicians and singer perform together, the sounds blend to create a rich and heterophonic texture.

Epic Songs in Sacred Context

Korean epic songs exist in both sacred and secular contexts. The secular epic songs, *p'ansori*, are performed for entertainment, while the sacred epic songs of the *kangshinmu* (spirit-possessed shamans) and *sesŭpmu* (hereditary *mudang*) remain part of the rituals and are not readily accessible to the general public.

---

[8] Heterophony is a term used to describe simultaneous variation of a single melody (Cooke 1980:537).

Epic songs are found in many parts of the world, but not everywhere. As Ruth Finnegan writes about epics and oral poetry, "Its absence in some cultures disappoints the expectation that 'epic' is a universal poetic stage in the development of society" (1977:10). Well known epic songs include the Sumerian *Gilgamesh*, the Greek Homeric *Iliad* and *Odyssey*, the Indian *Mahabharata* and *Ramayana*, the medieval European *Song of Roland*, the Finnish *Kalevala*, the Kirghiz *Mana*, and the Tibetan *Ge-sar sgrungs*, known in its many versions throughout Tibet, Mongolia, China, Buryats, Siberia, and other neighboring areas.

The original composers of epic songs are unknown because of the nature of aural transmission. The epic singers disseminated information through songs or retold histories from the vast number of verses in their memories when there was no means of rapid communication in the vast lands, using epic songs as a repository of knowledge. They improvised during the performance, creating new dialogues to make the stories more interesting to the audience.

The epic singer is musician, poet, composer, and performer all wrapped up in one. Epic singers present much of their poetry in the first person as if they were themselves the hero of the story, while narrating the hero's actions in the third person. The singer may use alternate modes, as in Tungus epic, in which direct speech is sung in the first person with the connecting third person narrative merely spoken. Kindaichi Kyosuke, who has connected the oral beginnings of Japanese literature with the literature of the preliterate peoples of northern Asia, in particular the Ainu, was convinced that "the origins of oral literature could be found in the archaic north Asian practice of shamanism, and he pointed to the Ainu epics with their ubiquitous use of the first-person diction as clear evidence of this idea" (Philippi 1982:xiii).

Some scholars have suggested that one of the main historical origins of epic poetry in central Asia is in shamanism, based on the hero's journey to the other world and narration in a dream-like first person style (Eliade 1964:213, 1987:207; Reichl 1970:3). Albert Lord assumes that the poet was sorcerer and seer before he became "artist," suggesting that the numerous repetitions in epic songs were there, not for the sake of meter, nor for the sake of convenience in building a line, but rather for the sake of redoubled prayer in hope of surer fulfillment. He also postulates that "the metrical convenience, or even better, the metrical necessity, is probably a late phenomenon, indispensable for the growth of epic from what must have been comparatively simple narrative incantations to more complex tales intended more and more for entertainment" (1965:66–67).

The epics among Altai Urianhai "begin with an account of the origin of the earth and the creation of people" (Pegg n.d.:93), much like the Korean epic songs which tell of the creation of the world and of the origin of peoples. Several scholars studying *musok* have begun to examine the myths and the history of the nation contained in the epic songs of the *mudang*. From the 1960s Kim T'aegon, a folklorist, collected and published texts of *muga* (*musok* songs)

(1976, 1978, 1979, 1992). Sŏ Tae-Sŏk compared the texts for different regional variants of the epic songs *Chesŏk Ponp'uri* and *Pari Kongju* (1992). A few scholars have translated some song texts into English (Lee J.Y. 1980; Heyman 1983; Walraven 1985). In recent years *muga* texts have been published by shamans themselves in Korea. Kim Kŭm-Hwa, a *manshin*, published *Kim Kŭm-Hwa Mugajip* [Kim Kŭm-Hwa's collection of *muga*] (1995); the song texts for the Seoul *Saenam Kut* were edited and published by the government under the supervision of Kim Yu-Gam, a *kangshinmu* (1998).

Most epic singers of the world perform to the accompaniment of drums or stringed instruments.[9] Some epics, for example, the Kirghiz epic *Manas* or the Tibetan *Ge-sar sgrungs*, are unaccompanied. In Korea, epic songs in sacred contexts are always accompanied by a single *changgu* (double-headed hourglass-shaped drum).

The Korean *mudang*—*sesŭpmu* (hereditary *mudang*) or *kangshinmu* (spirit-possessed shaman)—sings and dances to the accompaniment of *changgu* played by a male musician in the *sesŭpmu* ritual or by a male or female *kangshinmu* in the *kangshinmu* ritual. The *changgu* is essential while other instruments are optional and may be added depending on funds available.

For most ritual songs and dances, the *changgu* is played using both drum heads—*ch'ae p'yŏn* (right head) with *yŏl ch'ae* (thin bamboo stick) and *kung p'yŏn* (left head) with *kung ch'ae* (wooden mallet). But for some epic songs in the *sesŭpmu* and *kangshinmu* rituals, such as *Pari Kongju*, only one head (*kung p'yŏn*) of the *changgu* is played with a drum stick (*kung ch'ae*). In the "classic" shamanism of North and Inner Asia, shamans use a shallow frame drum that usually has a circular or ellipsoidal wooden body with one skinhead and is played with a stick (Ellingson 1987:498). The use of only one head of the *changgu* for certain Korean ritual epic songs suggests to me a similarity of musical practice with the shamans' single-headed frame drums of "classic" shamanism.

Despite the fact that the *sesŭpmu* (hereditary *mudang*) herself does not generally play drum during the ritual, she accompanies herself on *changgu* for the *ch'ŏ olligi* section during the *son kut* of the *sikkim kut*. While reciting *ch'ŏ olligi*, which lasts about half an hour, the *sesŭpmu* stands up and plays *changgu*, holding it with the left hand and striking the *kung p'yŏn* (left head) with the *ching ch'ae* (wooden mallet covered with cloth usually used for *ching* [gong]) in the right hand (Park M.K. 1996:60).

In the northeastern region of North and South Hamgyŏng Provinces in North Korea, the *mudang* also strikes only one side of the *changgu* during

---

[9] "Kazakh shaman *baqsis* use the *qobyz* (a two-stringed bowed lute) for their ritual songs, while Afghani shamans play the *qobuz*, a two-stringed horsehair fiddle. For Afghani ritual music, shamans often adorn their *qobyz* with bells and pieces of metal for a jingling effect, as Inner Asian shamans adorn their drums in a similar manner" (Slobin 1976:280).

ch'ŏnsu or *ch'ŏngbae kŏri*, using a wooden stick wrapped at the end with cloth and held in the right hand (Yi P.H. 1985:105).

Throughout the peninsula, *mudang* who specialize in *tokkyŏng* (recitation of sutras) and prayers use *changgu* or *puk* (double-headed barrel drum). They usually place the *ching* (large gong) or *kkwaenggwari* (small gong) on the floor beside the drum. They play the drum (*changgu* or *puk*) with the right hand using only the right head of the drum while playing *ching* with the left hand to accompany their own songs.

"*Pari Kongju*" and "*Hwangje P'uri*" are epic songs sung by Seoul area *kangshinmu* (spirit-possessed shamans) during certain Hanyang *kut* (rituals). "*Pari Kongju*," also known as "*Malmi*," is sung during *chinogwi kut* and *saenam kut* (rituals held for the departed) (see CD track 33). "*Hwangje P'uri*" is sung during Sŏngju *kut*, a ritual held to usher in good fortune at a new home for the ritual's sponsor.

In a small-scale *chinogwi kut*, the *changgu* is placed in front of the presiding shaman who sits on the floor to sing. The shaman will play only one head (*kung p'yŏn*) of the *changgu* using a wooden stick (*kung ch'ae*) with the right hand while shaking the *pangul* (bell tree) intermittently with the left hand. The *kung p'yŏn* is usually on the left side, but in this case the *changgu* is turned around so that it is on the right.

In the large-scale Seoul *Saenam kut*, however, the shaman sits on a chair fully dressed in the formal attire of Princess Pari to recite the epic song "*Pari Kongju*." For "*Pari Kongju*," the *kangshinmu* places a *ching* (large gong) on the floor first, leans the *changgu* on its *ch'ae p'yon* (right head) against the *ching*, and secures the *kung p'yŏn* (left head) with his or her knees. Seated on a chair, the *kangshinmu* shakes the *pangul* (bell tree) with the left hand and plays the *changgu* (drum) on the *kung p'yŏn* with a *kunggul ch'ae* held in the right hand (see plate 20).

Inner Asian shamans mount small bells or jingling pieces of metal either on or inside their drums or separately on their costumes (Ellingson 1987:498). In some areas, jingling metal pieces are not attached to their ritual costumes but to a belt to be worn over the shoulder or about the waist (see plate 28).

Nadyezhda Duvan (b. 1950), a Siberian shaman whom I met in Seattle in 1998, does not have any jingling pieces attached to her drum or ritual clothing, but wears a *yampa*, a belt to which metal objects of various shapes are attached (see plate 29). She told me that individual shamans select the shapes and sizes of the metal pieces. Some pieces are inspired by dreams, others are chosen because the shaman likes them. Duvan makes the metal pieces sound by moving her hips from side to side while dancing with a drum.

The Korean shaman's belt, ritual clothing, and drums do not have any metal attachments. In order to create metallic sounds, the Korean shaman holds a *pangul* (bell tree) in the left hand and shakes it intermittently.

The Korean shamans' musical practice of using a single head of *changgu* or *puk* (drums) and jingling *pangul* (bell trees) while singing epic songs prompts me to hypothesize historical ties between the Korean and Inner Asian shamans.

Epic Songs in Secular Context

Korean epic songs in secular context are known as *p'ansori*. *P'ansori* singers used to be known as *kwangdae*.[10] The word *kwangdae* existed as early as the Koryŏ period (918–1392), when it appears to have designated a masked performer. Later, as its meaning broadened, it came to refer to any type of entertainer, but by the late eighteenth century it was applied narrowly and specifically to male singers of *p'ansori* (Pihl 1994:7). The *kwangdae* (male *p'ansori* singers) are usually related to the female *sesŭpmu* (hereditary *mudang*) in Chŏlla provinces. Marshall Pihl explains the relationship of the *kwangdae* and the hereditary *mudang* as follows:

> The men had several specialties and were grouped into three classifications: instrumentalists, called *agin* or *kongin*, who played flute and drum; physical performers, called *chaein*, who did tumbling, rope-walking, and acrobatics; and singers, called *kwangdae*. All three were commonly lumped together as *chaein* or *kwangdae*. As a matter of natural evolution, the husband of a shaman,[11] who had served as accompanist and assistant to his wife, eventually emerged as a professional actor or singer on his own. The set of skills he already possessed were easily transferred to a secular context. (Pihl 1994:20)

The Korean *p'ansori* singer stands and sings accompanied by the *puk* (double-headed barrel drum) player who is seated to the left of the singer. Both artists perform on a straw mat called the *sori-p'an* (literally, singing place) provided for the performance on a stage or on the ground (Heyman 1993:210). The *p'ansori* singer narrates (*aniri*), sings (*ch'ang*), explains,[12] dances (*pallim*), or acts with gestures (*nŏrŭmsae*) while the drummer (*kosu*) plays the rhythmic cycles (*changdan*) and occasionally shouts cheers (*ch'uimsae*) to encourage the singer. The *p'ansori* singer uses a fan or a long scarf for added dramatic effect. A simple scarf may be used to express emotions while the folded fan is symbolically used variously as a weapon, as a saw to cut open gourds, or whatever the story requires.

---

[10] *P'ansori* singers are no longer referred to as *kwangdae*, but occasionally as *sori kkun*.
[11] "Shaman" here refers to female *sesŭpmu* (hereditary *mudang*).
[12] The act of explaining events or situations is referred to as "*toch'ang*" in *ch'anggŭk* (Killick 1998:556).

In contemporary Korea, five *p'ansori* works—*Ch'unhyangjŏn, Shimch'ŏngjŏn, Hŭngbojŏn, Chŏkbyŏkka,* and *Sugungga*—survive from the twelve *p'ansori* of earlier days.[13] In oral narrative performance, passages both sung and spoken can contribute to drama and characterization. Pihl explains further that in Korean *p'ansori*:

> The spoken *aniri* passages are often loosely structured and serve as bridges between songs, scenes, and juxtapose the events. They are also a means of delivering dialogues in which the characters exchange numerous short lines. The sung *ch'ang* passages are built around single themes involving little action or dialogue and stand out as well-formed structures with their own internal integrity. When used as the vehicle for a monologue, a *ch'ang* is sung in the first person of the character involved. As a descriptive passage, it becomes an objective, third-person account of people, actions, places, goods, and so forth. (Pihl 1994:86)

P'ansori singers were exclusively men until the 1920s when four women *p'ansori* singers appeared.[14] In contemporary Korea, there are several female *p'ansori* singers known as *myŏngch'ang* (well known singers), including An Suk-Sŏn, Oh Chŏng-Suk, and Sŏng Ch'ang-Sun. *P'ansori* singers are no longer associated exclusively with *sesŭpmu* (hereditary *mudang*). Since 1959 when the department of Korean traditional music was established in the School of Music at Seoul National University, male and female musicians have studied *p'ansori* as well as other genres of vocal and instrumental music at twenty-two universities throughout the nation (NCKTPA 1999:487).

Changdan, Rhythmic Cycles in Ritual Music

Considering melody, harmony, and rhythm as important elements of music, one may find that rhythm plays a more substantial role in Korean ritual music and traditional folk music than melody or harmony. All traditional Korean music is framed in rhythmic cycles known as *changdan*. *Changdan* literally means "long and short"—*chang* (長, long) and *dan* (短, short). Each *changdan*

---

[13] Seven *p'ansori* works—*Pyŏn'gangsoe T'aryŏng, Onggojip T'aryŏng, Paebijang T'aryŏng, Kangnŭng Maehwa T'aryŏng, Changki T'aryŏng, Musugi T'aryŏng,* and *Kashinsŏn T'aryŏng*—are no longer performed except for occasional performances of *Pyŏngangsoe T'aryŏng* and *Paebijang T'aryŏng* (Ch'oe T.H. 1994:27).

[14] The first four female *p'ansori* singers of the 1920s were Pae Sŏl-Hyang (1895–1938), Yi Hwajungsŏn (1898–1943), Kim Ch'o-Hyang (1900–unknown), and Kim Rok-Ju (1896–1923) (Pak H. 1994:195–201).

(rhythmic cycle) is formed by combining four elements—meter (*pakcha*), tempo (*pparŭgi*), dynamics (*kangyak*), and phrasing (*hanbae*).

The ritual songs and instrumental pieces of Hanyang *kut* are framed within distinctive *changdan* (rhythmic cycles). For dance accompaniment, musicians play instrumental pieces named after the rhythmic cycles used in the ritual music—*yŏmbul, kutkŏri, tangak,* and so on. For *Pyŏlsang kŏri*, the ensemble provides music beginning with *Pyŏlsang changdan*. For *subi* (miscellaneous spirits), *hwimori changdan* is used.

If the *kut* is performed by two *kangshinmu*, one *kangshinmu* sings or dances, while the other provides *changgu* (hourglass-shaped drum) accompaniment appropriate to each section of the ritual. The *chegŭm* (cymbals) are used only in dance accompaniment music, but they are not as essential as the drum because they are used merely to accentuate certain beats in the *changdan* (rhythmic cycle).

Having observed a *kangshinmu* providing instrumental music using only a single *changgu* for an entire ritual of Hanyang *kut*, I am convinced that the most important instrument for the shaman ritual is the *changgu*. This musical practice of the spirit-possessed shamans in the Seoul area suggests to me that the drum is the basic ritual musical instrument, as it is for Inner Asian shamans, leading me to presume that melodic instruments (such as *p'iri* [double-reed oboe], *taegŭm* [bamboo flute], and *haegŭm* [two-stringed fiddle]) were added later to the shaman's songs, the *muga*.

Korean songs and instrumental pieces in secular contexts usually have titles, but the instrumental music used in rituals—both the *kangshinmu* and *sesŭpmu* traditions—are usually referred to only by the name of the *changdan* employed. Even though there are distinctive melodic lines framed in the rhythmic cycles, the name of the *changdan* alone will suffice as the title of the piece. Secular instrumental music derived from *sesŭpmu* ritual music such as *sanjo, shinawi*, and *samulnori* also refers to musical sections by the name of the *changdan* used. For example, *sanjo*, a solo instrumental genre of music, consists of several sections named *chinyang, chungmori, hwimori*, and so on, all names being the names of the *changdan* used.

The importance of *changdan* (rhythmic cycles) becomes evident in Hanyang *kut* as the percussion ensemble made up of drum and cymbals provides music framed in various *changdan* for specific purposes. For dance accompaniment, *kutkŏri* and *tangak changdan* are most frequently used (see CD tracks 19–20). But when the *kangshinmu* dances during *Sangsan kŏri*, the percussion ensemble provides *ch'wit'ae* (see CD track 24), *yŏmbul*, and *pan yŏmbul changdan* (see CD tracks 11–12) in addition to *kutkŏri* and *tangak*.

For most chamber music, the right head of the *changgu* (drum) is struck with a thin bamboo stick called *ch'ae* or *yŏl ch'ae*; the left head is struck with the bare palm. When the *changgu* is played for *kut* or for outdoor ensemble music (*p'ungmul*), the left head of the *changgu* is struck with a wooden mallet (*kunggul ch'ae*) rather than with the palm. Notation for the left hand is the same regardless of how it is played.

In *chŏngganbo*, traditional Korean music notation, a column of squares is used to represent *changdan* (rhythmic cycles), each square representing one beat. Various symbols are written in the squares to indicate basic drum strokes for the *changgu* (see table below). Rests are indicated by blank spaces in the notation. Rests do not mean stopping the sound, but rather letting it continue to ring and fade naturally. Other symbols may be used for other instruments to indicate pitch.

Traditional Korean drum notation merely indicates the basic strokes. It does not provide any information regarding tempo, dynamics, timbre, or variation. Concepts and aesthetics underlying the musical sound and performance practices are acquired by aural transmission.

While discussing musical notations in aural traditions, Mantle Hood notes that:

> The correct translation of the symbols into musical sounds depends on a familiarity with the oral tradition that supports them. A knowledge of the oral tradition is necessary because: (1) certain symbols may be ambiguous, that is, they may not fulfill our basic requirement for clarity of representation in an efficient system of notation; (2) in the course of development, each tradition has emphasized certain aspects of musical expression, and reflecting this emphasis, its notation may have become too rigid to accommodate a variety of other practices known in actual performance. (Hood 1971:71–76)

Changgu players initially learn the basic patterns and rhythmic cycles by *kuŭm* (literally, mouth sounds), onomatopoeic words indicating the different strokes used for producing the various *changgu* sounds. Each drum stroke has its own name, comparable to the *bol* used for the *tala* in Indian music (Kaufmann 1967) and other *kuŭm* used for different Korean instruments.[15]

---

[15] Korean *kuŭm* used for string instruments to indicate various pitches include *tŏng, tung, tŭng, tang, tong,* and *ching,* and *kuŭm* for wind instruments include *na, nu, nŏ, no,* and *nŭ* (Kim K.S. 1972:21).

Music in Hanyang Kut

Table 6
The Basic Drum Strokes on *Changgu*

Changgu notation	Western notation	*kuŭm* (name)	Performance technique
⊕	R / L	*ttŏng* or *hap*	Right and left heads are struck at same time.
○	♩	*k'ung* or *kung*	Left head is struck.
o	✗	*ku* or *chipgo*	Damped or light stroke on left head.
⊙	♪♩	*ku k'ung*	Double stroke on left head (quick stroke followed by main beat).
|	♩	*ttak*	Right head is struck with *yŏlch'ae* (bamboo stick).
.	✗	*tak*	Damped or light stroke on right head.
⋮	♪♩	*kittak*	Right head is struck like *ttak*, preceded by a soft and quick stroke with the tip of *yŏlch'ae*.
⋮	♩	*ttarŭrŭrŭ*	Right head is struck several times in an accelerating pattern.

Traditional Korean notation is read vertically from top to bottom. An example of traditional notation is presented, but I will also introduce the notation horizontally, to be read from left to right. Additional short lines that extend above the notation indicate the groupings of the beats. I have also included modified Western staff notation. Notes above the percussion staff indicate drum strokes on the right head of the *changgu*, while notes below the staff indicate strokes on the left head. Examples of the *changdan* may be heard on the accompanying compact disc.

Figure 10. Column of Korean Notation Read from Top to Bottom and Modified Form of Korean Notation (above) Read from Left to Right

The most important beat in any rhythmic cycle is the *hap changdan*, the first beat. The aesthetics of Korean music is expressed in the energy flowing through tension and release. The four main strokes in the *changdan* are "*chip* (集), *hae* (解), *kyŏl* (結), and *t'al* (脫)" (Yun S.U. 1978:40). *Chip* (literally, gathering) refers to a point where energy (*ki*, Chinese *chi*) of *ŭm* and *yang* (Chinese *yin* and *yang*) meet. In music, this is expressed as *hap* (or *ttŏng*), playing left and right heads of the *changgu* together (*hap* means together). On *changgu*, *ŭm* is expressed on the left head and *yang* on the right, symbolizing earth and heaven, respectively. When both heads produce sound together, energy is gathered as *hap*. Once energy is born, it becomes alive and moves forward, creating tension of *kiun* (flow of energy) to reach the highest or most important point, expressed in music as *kyŏl* (or *ttak*), and then the energy is released through *hae* (or *k'ung*) or *t'al* (or *ttarŭrŭrŭ*) on *changgu*.

A portion of *changdan* (rhythmic cycle) used for creating tension of energy is referred to as *ollim ch'ae* (literally, rising beats), while the portion of *changdan* releasing energy is called *naerim ch'ae* (literally, lowering beats). For example, within a three-beat *changdan*, the rhythmic cycle could begin with *hap* on the first beat, then develop and reach *ttak* on the second beat, and release on the third beat as *k'ung*.

Most *changdan* (rhythmic cycles) in Korean music, including court, folk, and *musok* ritual music, focus on the three beats expressed as *hap*, *k'ung*, and

Music in Hanyang Kut

ttak and their variations on the *changgu*. Within each beat there are usually three *tchok* (sections), producing triplets and triple meters, a predominant feature in indigenous folk, ritual, and court music in Korea. The triple *tchok* constantly move forward, changing and balancing the flow of energy.

If a beat is divided into three *tchok* (sections), three symbols may be written in one square of the Korean *chŏngganbo* notation, each symbol representing one third of the beat. Sometimes a drum stroke may occur on the last third of a beat. This is indicated by two horizontal dashes to represent rests for the first two thirds of the beat and then a vertical line to represent the drum stroke.

1. *Kutkŏri Changdan*

As its name implies, *kutkŏri changdan* is one of the most frequently used rhythmic cycles in *kut* (rituals). There are various versions of *kutkŏri changdan* used in other regional styles of *kut* and also in secular music. Here I will focus on the version used in Hanyang *kut*. *Kutkŏri changdan* is a twelve-beat rhythmic cycle (see figures 11–13 and CD track 1). *Kutkŏri changdan* is used for *t'aryŏng* songs (CD tracks 22, 25, 28) and various instrumental pieces, including "*Kutkŏri*" (CD tracks 19 and 26) and "*Kkot Banga T'aryŏng*" (CD track 26).

Figure 11. *Kutkŏri Changdan* in Korean Notation

Figure 12. *Kutkŏri Changdan* in Western Notation

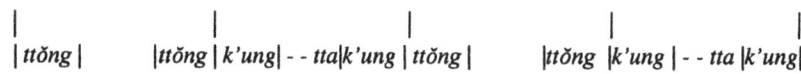

Figure 13. *Kutkŏri Changdan* in *Kuŭm* (Onomatopoeic Words)

Chegŭm (cymbals) are often played in accompaniment with the *changgu* and melodic instruments. The *chegŭm* accent certain beats of each *changdan*.

Figure 14. *Chegŭm* (Cymbals) Pattern for *Kutkŏri Changdan* in Korean Notation

Figure 15. *Chegŭm* (Cymbals) Pattern for *Kutkŏri Changdan* in Western Notation

2. *Pyŏlsang Changdan*

Pyŏlsang changdan is another twelve-beat rhythmic cycle used in Hanyang *kut*. *Pyŏlsang changdan* is also known as *t'aryŏng changdan*. It is used for various pieces, including instrumental pieces also called *t'aryŏng* (see CD tracks 9 and 10), but it is not used for *t'aryŏng* songs.[16] Most *kangshinmu* and *chaebi* refer to it as *pyŏlsang changdan* and I will follow their practice.

Pyŏlsang changdan is used in three *samhyŏn yukkak* pieces: "*T'aryŏng*," "*Pyŏlgok T'aryŏng*," and "*Nŭjŭn Hŏt'ŭn T'aryŏng*." Two pieces, "*T'aryŏng*" and "*Pyŏlgok T'aryŏng*," are also part of the *Yŏngsan Hoesang* suite, which is performed by various types of instrumental ensembles. "*Pyŏlgok T'aryŏng*" is known as "*Kunak*" in the *Yŏngsan Hoesang* suite.

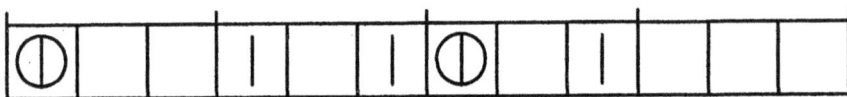

Figure 16. *Pyŏlsang Changdan* in Korean Notation

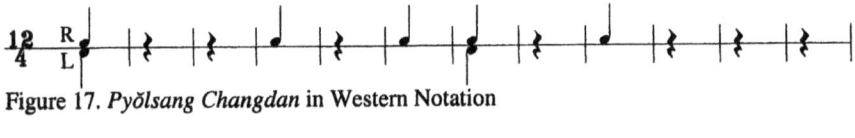

Figure 17. *Pyŏlsang Changdan* in Western Notation

|ttŏng| |ttak| |ttak|ttŏng| |ttak| | |

Figure 18. *Pyŏlsang Changdan* in *Kuŭm* (Onomatopoeic Words)

---

[16] The *changdan* used for *t'aryŏng* songs is *kutkŏri*.

Music in Hanyang Kut

Figure 19. *Chegŭm* (Cymbals) Pattern for *Pyŏlsang Changdan* in Korean Notation

Figure 20. *Chegŭm* (Cymbals) Pattern for *Pyŏlsang Changdan* in Western Notation

Kutkŏri and *pyŏlsang changdan* are both twelve-beat rhythmic cycles. In both cases, the twelve beats may be heard as four main phrases, each phrase consisting of three beats, thus producing a triple meter. But they are different from each other because each *changdan* has a distinct flow of energy, shifting the points of *chip* (集), *hae* (解), *kyŏl* (結), and *t'al* (脫) within the twelve beats. Each *changdan* is distinguished by different drum strokes and accentuation on the *changgu* and *chegŭm*.

3. *Tangak Changdan*

Another frequently used *changdan* in Hanyang *kut* is *tangak changdan*. *Tangak changdan* is a 12-beat rhythmic cycle with a quick tempo so that it feels more like four beats with triplet subdivisions (see CD track 2). *Tangak changdan* is also onomatopoeically called *Tŏng-tŏk-kungi*.

This *changdan* is used in various pieces, including *"Chajin Hŏt'ŭn T'aryŏng"* (CD track 15), *"Tangak"* (CD track 20), *"Chajin T'aryŏng"* (CD track 27), and *"Chajin Kutkŏri"* (CD track 38).

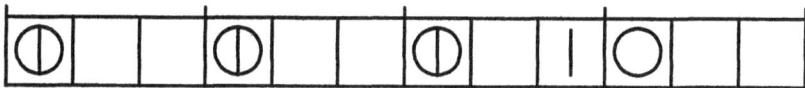

Figure 21. *Tangak Changdan* in Korean Notation

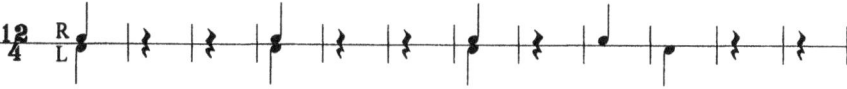

Figure 22. *Tangak Changdan* in Western Notation

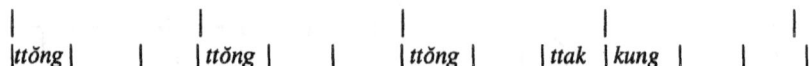

Figure 23. *Tangak Changdan* in *Kuŭm* (Onomatopoeic Words)

The *chegŭm* (cymbals) play on each of the four main beats of *tangak changdan*.

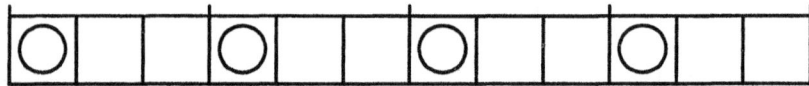

Figure 24. *Chegŭm* (Cymbals) Pattern for *Tangak Changdan* in Korean Notation

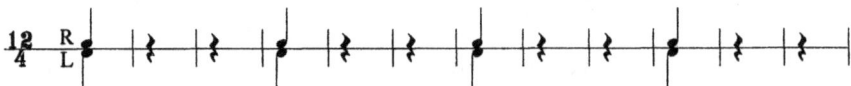

Figure 25. *Chegŭm* (Cymbals) Pattern for *Tangak Changdan* in Western Notation

4. Ŏtmori Changdan

For incantation songs, *kangshinmu* use several short melodies, adding subtle variations. Recitations and epic songs are text oriented and usually rendered in *ŏtmori changdan*, a rhythmic cycle made up of five-beat patterns, either 3 + 2 or 2 + 3 (see CD tracks 3 and 30). To accompany the recitation, two sets of five-beat patterns are often combined. The most common patterns are (3 + 2) + (3 + 2), with such variations as (3 + 2) + (2 + 3) or (2 + 3) + (3 + 2).

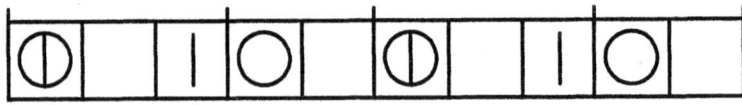

Figure 26. *Ŏtmori Changdan* in Korean Notation

Figure 27. *Ŏtmori Changdan* in Western Notation

5. Hwimori Changdan

Hwimori changdan is a fast 4-beat rhythmic cycle (see CD track 4 and end of track 29). It is played like a fast version of *Tangak changdan* (see above).

6. Shijo Changdan

In Hanyang *kut*, the *noraekarak* songs are sung by *kangshinmu* with a rhythmic cycle that is related to *shijo changdan*. When *shijo* (poems) are sung in *chŏngak* (court music),[17] the accompanying drum combines five-beat and eight-beat patterns in *shijo changdan* to suit the text of the 3-line stanzas.

First line   5 + 8 + 8 + 5 + 8
Second line 5 + 8 + 8 + 5 + 8
Third line   5 + 8 + 5 + 8

Figure 28. Combination of 5-Beat and 8-Beat Patterns in *Shijo Changdan*

The five-beat and eight-beat patterns of *shijo* are played on the *changgu* as follows:

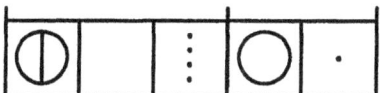

Figure 29. Five-Beat Pattern of *Shijo Changdan* in Korean Notation

Figure 30. Five-Beat Pattern of *Shijo Changdan* in Western Notation

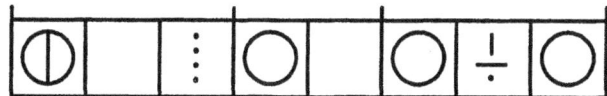

Figure 31. Eight-Beat Pattern of *Shijo Changdan* in Korean Notation

---

[17] *Chŏngak* refers to a genre of music enjoyed by the court and the upper classes (*yangban*).

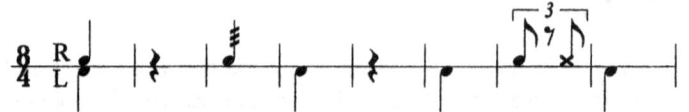
Figure 32. Eight-Beat Pattern of *Shijo Changdan* in Western Notation

When the shaman sings *noraekarak*, the drum accompaniment is provided in five-beat and eight-beat patterns, but not in the same sequence as in the traditional *chŏngak shijo* (see CD tracks 5, 18, 32, and 34).

A few *kangshinmu* have told me that they conceptualize the *noraekarak* rhythm as basically in triple meter, with occasional additional beats. They think of the rhythm as having two different *changdan*, one short (3 beats) and one long (3 + 2 beats). They view the additional two beats in the long *changdan* as not very important, suggesting that the two extra beats were used to complete the phrases. I have observed that most *kangshinmu* nowadays play the *changgu* expressing the five-beat pattern as one long (3 + 2) *changdan*, with the eight-beat pattern ([3 + 2] + 3) as one long (3 + 2) plus one short (3) or one short plus one long (3 + [3 + 2]), similar to the traditional *chŏngak shijo changdan* mentioned earlier.

7. *Chajin Hwanip*

Chajin Hwanip is the first piece in the Hanyang *Samhyŏn Yukkak* suite. It is also known as "*Chajin Hanip*," "*Chajinnani*," "*Kŏsangak*," and "*Yŏmyangch'un*." It is based on the music of *kagok* (lyric songs). This piece uses a slow 16-beat cycle, which consists of two phrases: 11 beats and 5 beats (see CD track 6).

Figure 33. *Chajin Hwanip* in Korean Notation

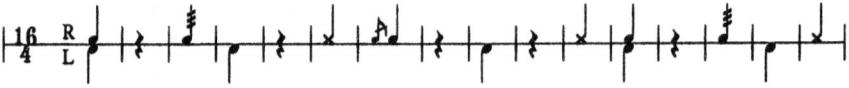
Figure 34. *Chajin Hwanip* in Western Notation

8. Seryŏngsan

Seryŏngsan is the third piece of the *Yŏngsan Hoesang* suite. It uses a 10-beat rhythmic cycle, consisting of 4 phrases: 3 + 2 + 2 + 3 (see CD track 7).

Figure 35. *Seryŏngsan* in Korean Notation

Figure 36. *Seryŏngsan* in Western Notation

9. Yŏmbul Changdan

Yŏmbul changdan is a six-beat cycle used in the instrumental piece "*Yŏmbul T'aryŏng*" (see CD track 11). This piece is also known as "*Yŏmbul*" or "*Kin Yŏmbul*." It is the second piece in the suite of Hanyang *Samhyŏn Yukkak* music.

Figure 37. *Yŏmbul Changdan* in Korean Notation

Figure 38. *Yŏmbul Changdan* in Western Notation

Yŏmbul changdan can also be played as a 12-beat rhythmic cycle, but it is usually performed as a 6-beat cycle.

10. *Pan Yŏmbul*

Pan yŏmbul (also known as *chajin yŏmbul* and *todŭri changdan*) is a 6-beat rhythmic cycle that is played in a faster tempo than *yŏmbul changdan*. *Pan* means half, suggesting that *pan yŏmbul* is half the length of the 12-beat *yŏmbul changdan*. *Pan yŏmbul* can be played like *yŏmbul* in the figure above or it can be played in a modified form during Hanyang *kut* as notated in the figure below.

Pan yŏmbul is used in various instrumental pieces, including *"Samhyŏn todŭri"* (CD track 8) and *"Pan yŏmbul"* (CD track 12). These pieces are also part of the Hanyang *Samhyŏn Yukkak* suite.

Figure 39. *Pan Yŏmbul Changdan* in Korean Notation

Figure 40. *Pan Yŏmbul Changdan* in Western Notation

The *chegŭm* (cymbals) play the following pattern for *pan yŏmbul*.

Figure 41. *Chegŭm* (Cymbals) Pattern for *Pan Yŏmbul* in Korean Notation

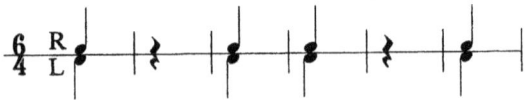

Figure 42. *Chegŭm* (Cymbals) Pattern for *Pan Yŏmbul* in Western Notation

11. *Ch'wit'ae*

"*Ch'wit'ae*" is also known as "*Manp'a Chŏngshik Jigok*." It uses a 12-beat rhythmic cycle.

Figure 43. *Ch'wit'ae* in Korean Notation

Figure 44. *Ch'wit'ae* in Western Notation

Each beat has three *tchok* (sections), giving a sense of triplets and compound meter. Instead of *ch'wit'ae changdan*, many musicians play *pyŏlsang changdan* to accompany the instrumental piece "*Ch'wit'ae*" (CD track 24). *Pyŏlsang changdan* is also a 12-beat rhythmic cycle, but played in a quicker tempo. The quick 12-beat *pyŏlsang changdan* can be played in the same duration as 4 beats of the slower *ch'wit'ae changdan*. In other words, one cycle of *ch'wit'ae changdan* can be replaced by playing the faster paced *pyŏlsang changdan* three times.

12. *Kil Kunak*

Kil kunak is an 8-beat rhythmic cycle.

Figure 45. *Kil Kunak* in Korean Notation

Figure 46. *Kil Kunak* in Western Notation

Instead of *kil kunak changdan*, many musicians play *pyŏlsang changdan* to accompany the instrumental piece "*Kil kunak*" (see CD track 37). The twelve beats of *Pyŏlsang changdan* can be played in the same duration as four beats of *kil kunak changdan*. During one cycle of *kil kunak changdan*, *pyŏlsang changdan* is played twice.

The *changdan* (rhythmic cycles) discussed above are some of the main ones used in the ritual music of Hanyang *kut*. I will now discuss some changes in performance practice. Then in the following chapters I will show during which parts of *ch'ŏnshin kut* and *saenam kut* (rituals) the music is used (chapters 9 and 10).

Changes in Performance Practice

Nowadays one can observe instruments like the *t'aepyŏngso* (conical oboe) and *ajaeng* (bowed zither) being played at the Hanyang *kut*. While neither instrument is considered a traditional instrument in the Hanyang *kut*, they have become part of the musical practice of the contemporary Hanyang *kut*, influenced by the *sesŭpmu* (hereditary *mudang*) ritual music tradition where the two instruments (*t'aepyŏngso* and *ajaeng*) are considered essential melodic instruments. As Yang Jongsung observed, *yang chaebi* (duo musicians) may choose to play *p'iri* and *taegŭm* instead of *p'iri* and *haegŭm*, the two instruments traditionally assigned for this type of ensemble (1999a:29). As I understand it, this new performance practice sometimes happens at the request of the officiating shaman or may be due to the limited musicianship of the *chaebi* hired for the occasion. Sometimes the *samhyŏn yukkak* ensemble is played by two *p'iri*, *taegŭm*, *puk*, *changgu*, and *ajaeng* (bowed zither), which replaces *haegŭm* (two-string fiddle).

At times an ensemble larger than the traditional *samhyŏn yukkak* is used to increase the volume of certain instruments. Adding extra instruments or experimenting with new instrumentation for the ensemble in the Hanyang *kut* results in the "invention" of new "traditions" (Hobsbawm 1983:1).[18] In January 1998, I attended a *chinjŏk kut* where eleven *chaebi* (musicians) had been hired. The *kuttang* where this *kut* was held had three adjoining rooms. An altar was set up in one room where the *kangshinmu* officiated the *kut*, the middle room was reserved for the musicians and me, while the third room was packed with family

---

[18] 'Invented tradition' is taken to mean a set of practices, normally governed by overtly or tacitly accepted rules and of a ritual or symbolic nature, which seek to inculcate certain values and norms of behavior by repetition, which automatically implies continuity with the past (Hobsbawm 1983:1).

members, relatives, regular clients, guests, a videographer, and several reporters. The side panels of the rooms were removed to open up a large space for this ritual. This was a *chinjŏk kut* for Yi Chun-Yŏng (b. 1967), a young male *kangshinmu*, assisted by his mother and older sister who are both also *kangshinmu*. Yi Chun-Yŏng is also known as Ch'onggak Tosa (literally, enlightened bachelor). It was an exceptional experience for me to attend this *kut* where offerings included music by eleven *chaebi* and an astonishing amount of food, including six large pigs set aside as an offering.

When Yi performed a *kut* on October 13, 1999, nine musicians were hired. Most of the time, the musicians played instruments like *ajaeng, changgu, haegŭm, taegŭm,* and *p'iri* during the Pulsa *kŏri*.

But while Yi was "riding" *chakdu* (sharp blades), standing barefoot on the blades, one musician played *ajaeng,* another one *changgu,* and the other seven all played *t'aepyŏngso* (conical oboes) in unison (see plate 30). When I asked him later why he had hired so many musicians, Yi Chun-Yŏng simply smiled and said it was because he likes the boisterous musical sound when he is possessed by the Spirit of General Chakdu.

Musicians for both of these rituals (1998 and 1999) were wearing garments and hats fashioned after the Chosŏn Dynasty court musicians' attire (see plate 30). Since the fall of the Chosŏn Dynasty in 1910, such garments in red, green, or gold colors have been worn only by musicians who perform the court genres of music on the concert stage. Musicians performing folk genres of music in sacred and secular contexts have always worn white *hanbok* with white or pale blue *turumagi*, an outer garment. When I asked musicians how they felt about wearing the court costumes during a *musok* ritual, most of them said it was all right with them because they were simply following the wishes of the shaman Yi who had hired them for the occasion.[19]

As mentioned earlier, for *mansubaji* (call-and-response style duet songs), the assisting *kangshinmu* plays the *changgu*, an hourglass-shaped drum, while singing in response to the principal *kangshinmu*, as well as providing the drum accompaniment for both singers. During a ritual held on October 7, 1999, a *chaebi* (ritual musician) was hired as a *changgu* player. During *mansubaji*, the officiating shaman began to sing the leading phrases but the *chaebi* drummer did not know how to respond; therefore, the shaman ended up singing one part of *mansubaji,* the duet song, alone and the drum was played for the response part with no responding verses. I do not know quite what prompted the new experiment for that occasion, but having a musician replace the shaman at the drum for *mansubaji* obviously did not work. As mentioned earlier, in Hanyang *kut* the *chaebi* do not sing during any ritual. This is why in the Hanyang *kut*, the

---

[19] The ritual was held as a part of the ninth annual gathering of spirit-possessed shamans at the Changch'ung Gymnasium in Seoul (October 1999).

changgu is played not by a *chaebi*, a hired musician, but always by a shaman (male or female) who can sing the ritual duet songs.

Another change in the Hanyang *kut* is the addition of *tokkyŏng kŏri*, a *kŏri* (section) where a hired male *pŏpsa* sings and recites Buddhist sutras. He accompanies himself with *changgu* (hourglass-shaped drum) and *ching* (large gong) or *kkwaenggwari* (small gong). He uses the right hand to play one head of the drum and the left hand to play either *ching*, which is placed to the left of the drum, or *kkwaenggwari*, which is placed in the center of the drum. This style of *kŏri* (section) is imported from the regional *kut* called *anjŭn kut* (literally, seated ritual), which is generally practiced in the southern provinces by *sesŭpmu* (hereditary *mudang*) and *haksŭpmu* (apprenticed *mudang*). Nowadays female *kangshinmu* as well as *posal* are occasionally hired to perform *tokkyŏng kŏri* during the Hanyang *kut*.

Twip'uri and Karaoke Singing

After an event, performers usually gather for *twip'uri* to eat, drink, sing, or dance to relax. I noticed one day that a disc jockey had been hired to bring in a *karaoke* machine at the end of a *chinjŏk kut*. After the formal *kut* was completed, several spirit daughters and guests sang with the accompaniment provided by the machine in the *kuttang* (ritual hall), Pohyŏn Sanshin'gak.[20] The repertoire consisted mostly of popular and folk songs in secular genres.

Singing songs to a pre-recorded musical accompaniment supplied by a *karaoke* machine has been popular at wedding receptions, celebrations of a child's *tol* (first birthday), and *hwan'gap chanch'i* (sixtieth birthday parties).[21] Koreans have been also enjoying *noraebang* (literally, singing room) where one can rent a room by the hour to sing songs in privacy.[22]

Several older *kangshinmu* and *chaebi* told me that they used to have *twip'uri* after their work had finished. It is rare nowadays to have *twip'uri* because people tend to rush to other commitments as soon as the *kut* is over. During the fall of 1998, I was invited several times by a few groups of *kangshinmu* for their *twip'uri*. The *twip'uri* were always filled with much fun and genuine fellowship. Their *twip'uri* are held in private homes, restaurants, and *noraebang*, but not at the *kuttang*.

---

[20] It was at the end of a two-day *chinjŏk kut* by Yi Chŏng-Yŏn (February 11–12, 1994).

[21] "In Korea, it is traditional to observe the rite of passage into old age, the *hwan'gap janch'i*, on the sixtieth birthday. In pre-industrial Korea, this was a particularly auspicious marker as it is to indicate the end of the fifth cycle of life (one lunar cycle is made up of twelve years)" (Chin S.Y. 1989:130–131).

[22] *Noraebang* is similar to the Japanese *karaoke* room. It is said that the first *noraebang* appeared in the Pusan area in 1990 (Song D.Y. 1998:103).

CHAPTER 9

Ch'ŏnshin Kut and Music

The *chaesu kut* (ritual held to usher in good fortune) in the Seoul area is also called *ch'ŏnshin kut*.[1] Since Hanyang *kut* shamans prefer the term *ch'ŏnshin kut* for the rituals they perform for the health, wealth, and peace of their clients, I will follow that practice here.

The *ch'ŏnshin kut* is a large-scale Hanyang *kut* usually carried out in a sequence of twelve *kŏri* (sections),[2] which are not always performed the same way or in the same sequence.

In order to identify some of these differences, Lee Jung-Young created a chart comparing five Hanyang *chaesu kut* observed by scholars—Chijo Akamatsu and Takashi Akiba (1938), Kim T'aegon (1972), Ryu Tong Sik [Yu Tong-Shik] ([1975] 1989), Chang Pyung Kil [Chang Pyŏng-Gil] (1970), and Lee Jung Young—all on separate occasions (Lee J.Y. 1981:37). In fact, the *kut* observed by Ryu Tong Sik included in Lee's comparison chart for Seoul *chaesu kut* was not actually from the Hanyang *kut* tradition but rather from the Hwanghae Province tradition.[3] This is a common type of confusion.

---

[1] *Ch'ŏnshin kut* were originally held to offer fresh fruits and grains to the spirits, but now *ch'ŏnshin kut* refers to the *chaesu kut* held throughout the year.

[2] The number of *kŏri* (sections) in the *kut* varies greatly. In the Seoul area, twelve *kŏri* are usually performed during the *chaesu kut* for good luck, but twenty-four are performed for the Seoul *Saenam kut*, a large-scale ritual for the departed (see chapter 10). In Hwanghae province, *man'gu taet'ak kut* is performed with twenty-four *kŏri*, while "some elaborate village ceremonies on the east coast may have as many as twenty or thirty *kŏri*" (Ch'oe K.S. 1989:132).

[3] It was a *sangsan pugun kut* performed by Kim Kŭm-Hwa (Ryu T.S. 1989:317). On the very next page of Ryu's work, Ryu discusses a Hanyang *kut*, which progresses in the following order: *pujŏng kŏri, kamang kŏri, sanmanura, pyŏlsŏng kŏri, taegam kŏri, chesŏk kŏri, sŏngju kŏri, hogu kŏri, kunŭng kŏri, ch'angbu kŏri, malmyŏng kŏri,* and *twitjŏn p'uri* (Ryu T.S. 1989:318).

A great deal of variation exists in the *ch'ŏnshin kut*, not only from one *kangshinmu* to another, but also among the various *kut* performed by the same *kangshinmu*, reflecting the budget, allotted time, and individual circumstances of the sponsoring family. The order of ritual sequence as well as the musical competence of shamans and musicians produce a unique performance at each *kut*.

In table 7, I have outlined two *ch'ŏnshin kut* I observed in Seoul to indicate the different sequences of *kŏri* (sections) used in the same type of *kut*. They were performed by Hyangp'unghoe members (1998) and Yi Sang Sun (1999). For comparison, I have also included the *kut* described in two earlier works: *Mudang Naeryŏk* (History of *mudang*) by Nan-Gok (1885) and *Chosŏn Musok ŭi Yŏn'gu* (Research on Korean *musok*) by Akamatsu and Akiba ([1938] 1991).

Table 7
The Twelve *Kŏri* (Sections) of Hanyang *Ch'ŏnshin Kut*

	Mudang Naeryŏk ([1885] 1969)	*Chosŏn Musok ŭi Yŏn'gu* ([1938] 1991)	Hyangp'unghoe (1998)	Yi Sang-Sun (1999)
1.	kamŭng ch'ŏngbae[4]	pujŏng kŏri	pujŏng kŏri	pujŏng kŏri
2.	Chesŏk kŏri	kamang kŏri	ponhyang kŏri	ch'ŏngung maji kŏri
3.	Pyŏlsang kŏri	san manura kŏri	taeshin kŏri	todang kŏri
4.	tae kŏri	pyŏlsŏng kŏri	Sangsan kŏri	ponhyang kŏri
5.	hogu kŏri	Taegam kŏri	Pyŏlsang kŏri	chosang kŏri
6.	chosang kŏri	Chesŏk kŏri	Shinjang kŏri	Sangsan kŏri
7.	manshin malmyŏng	ch'ŏnwang kŏri	Taegam kŏri	Pyŏlsang kŏri
8.	Shinjang	hogwi kŏri	todang kŏri	Shinjang kŏri
9.	Ch'angbu kŏri	kunung kŏri	Sŏngju kŏri	Taegam kŏri
10.	Sŏngju kŏri	Ch'angbu kŏri	kunung kŏri	Sŏngju kŏri
11.	kurŭng	malmyŏng kŏri	Ch'angbu kŏri	Ch'angbu kŏri
12.	twitchŏn	twitchŏn kŏri	twitchŏn kŏri	twitchŏn kŏri

Mudang Naeryŏk is a manuscript by Nan-Gok published in 1885 (Izumi 1969:59).[5] Observing the scenes from the twelve *kŏri* drawn in this manuscript,

---

[4] Nan-Gok called the first *kŏri* in the Hanyang *kut* "*kamŭng ch'ŏngbae*," which is actually a part of *pujŏng kŏri*.

one can note a few changes made in contemporary ritual practices. For example, the *kangshinmu* is shown in a drawing holding a ritual fan and bell tree tied with one yellow cloth during *hogu*, *chosang*, *manshin malmyŏng*, and *ch'angbu kŏri*. Some contemporary *kangshinmu* tie the cymbals with a long white cloth but the ritual fan and bell tree are no longer tied together. Unlike the illustrations, *kangshinmu* nowadays do not hold *wŏldo* during Pyŏlsang *kŏri*, and they wear red garments for Sŏngju *kŏri* instead of light blue ones. The black flag of *obang shinjanggi* (five-directional flags) shown in the drawing has been replaced by a green flag, and instead of holding black and white flags in the left hand and blue, yellow, and red flags in the right, nowadays Hanyang *kangshinmu* hold green and blue flags in the left hand and red, white, and yellow ones in the right hand.

The *ch'ŏnshin kut*, as mentioned earlier, is performed in various styles handed down by different schools. In order to describe a *ch'ŏnshin kut* for this work, I have decided to focus on the ritual practices of Yi Sang-Sun (b. 1947) whom I met in 1993.[6] Among the Seoul area *kangshinmu*, she is the one best known for her ritual skills and knowledge of the Hanyang *kut*. Unlike most others, she has studied with several well known *kangshinmu* teachers and has mastered the ritual songs of various schools.

It is believed that the Hanyang *kut* was handed down to Yi Sang-Sun from the legendary Chŏng Kyŏng-Ok, a male shaman also known as Chŏng Chusa (died 1970), through his spirit children, Ch'oe Myŏng-Nam (spirit son) and Pak Chong-Bok (1932–2000) (spirit daughter). Yi Sang-Sun, who studied with both Ch'oe and Pak, is known to have inherited Chŏng Chusa's *munsŏ* (ritual knowledge), including songs, texts, dances, and speech patterns, as well as correct rules for preparing offerings, garments, and conducting the rituals.

A modified *ch'ŏnshin kut* is performed as the first part of the Seoul *Saenam Kut*. When it is performed as part of the Seoul *Saenam Kut*, it is referred to as *andang sagyŏng maji*, not as *ch'ŏnshin kut*. In this chapter I will discuss *ch'ŏnshin kut*, and in the following chapter I will discuss the differences between *ch'ŏnshin kut* and *andang sagyŏng maji*, as well as the second part of Seoul *Saenam Kut*. Since Yi Sang-Sun is an expert on the second part of Seoul *Saenam Kut*, chapter 10 is based on her ritual knowledge. Although Kim Yu-Gam (b. 1924), the *poyuja* (government recognized performer) of Important Intangible Cultural Property number 104, Seoul *Saenam Kut*, is a highly regarded *kangshinmu* for the *ch'ŏnshin kut*, I have chosen to discuss Yi Sang-

---

[5] Scenes from the twelve *kŏri* of Hanyang *kut* are drawn in color and explained in the manuscript *Mudang Naeryŏk* published in 1885.

[6] Yi Sang-Sun (b. 1947) was possessed by spirits at the age of fifteen and studied many years with several *myŏngmu* (well known spirit-possessed shamans) in the Seoul area. Her teachers—Kim Yu-Gam, Pak Ŏ-Jin, Pak Chong-Bok, Yi Chi-San, Yi Hong-Gi, Ch'oe Myŏng-Nam, and Ch'oe Sun-ja—have been the top ritual performers in the greater Seoul area.

Sun's *ch'ŏnshin kut* in this chapter for the sake of consistency with the following chapter.

In general the *ch'ŏnshin kut* is carried out in twelve *kŏri* (sections), which may be grouped into three parts: the first part consists of *pujŏng kŏri* for *ch'ŏngshin* (invitation of spirits), the central part consists of ten *kŏri* of *oshin* (entertainment of spirits) and *kangshin* (spirit possession), and the last part consists of *twitchŏn kŏri* as *songshin* (bidding farewell to the spirits).

Table 8
Sections of *Kut* (Ritual)

ch'ŏngshin (invitation of spirits)	1. *pujŏng kŏri*
oshin (spirit possession) and *kangshin* (spirit possession)	2. *ch'on'gung maji*
	3. *Todang kŏri*
	4. *Ponhyang kŏri*
	5. *Chosang kŏri*
	6. *Sangsan kŏri*
	7. *Pyŏlsang kŏri*
	8. *Shinjang kŏri*
	9. *Taegam kŏri*
	10. *Sŏngju kŏri*
	11. *Ch'angbu kŏri*
songshin (bidding farewell to spirits)	12. *twitchŏn kŏri*

Ch'ŏnshin kut has *anjŭn kŏri* (literally, seated sections) and *sŏn kŏri* (literally, standing sections). During the *anjŭn kŏri*, the principal *kangshinmu* seated at *changgu* sings alone, accompanying himself or herself on the *changgu*. During the *sŏn kŏri*, however, the principal *kangshinmu* moves around singing, dancing, making offerings, and delivering messages from the spirits to clients, while assisting *kangshinmu* provide drum and cymbal accompaniment, sing, make ritual offerings, help with ritual garments, and look after many detailed tasks to make the ritual progress smoothly. The *ch'ŏnshin kut* begins with *anjŭn kŏri—chudang mullim* and *pujŏng kŏri—*and the ritual continues with *sŏn kŏri* until the end.[7]

The entire *ch'ŏnshin kut* requires the participation of at least three *kangshinmu* who each perform several *kŏri* according to their ritual skills. The *tangju kangshinmu* hired by the *chegajip* (sponsors) is responsible for arranging the ritual by hiring additional *kangshinmu, chaebi* (ritual musicians), and other

---

[7] Hanyang *kut* always begin with *chudang mullim*, a preparatory ritual.

helpers, as well as reserving the ritual hall and ordering *chemul* (food offerings). The decision to assign *kŏri* to the *kangshinmu* is usually made by the *tangju kangshinmu* just before the ritual begins. The *tangju* does not automatically lead the given ritual. If there is a musically gifted *kangshinmu* hired for the ritual, the *tangju* assigns that person to lead particular *kŏri* for the day. The *tangju* has to consider the age and seniority among the hired *kangshinmu* as many are easily offended. It becomes an extremely difficult task to assign responsibilities especially if a new *kangshinmu* is hired for the occasion.

In earlier times, *pyŏlbi* (extra cash given to shamans by the audience) belonged exclusively to the shaman who performed that particular *kŏri*, but nowadays fees are split among all *kangshinmu* at the end of the *kut* regardless of who performed which *kŏri*,[8] thus reducing rivalry among *kangshinmu* wishing to perform only the more popular *kŏri*.[9]

The Hanyang *kut*, for example, begins with *pujŏng kŏri* where a seated *kangshinmu* recites prayers for about half an hour or more to invoke the spirits. It is an important recitation that few *kangshinmu* specialize in, but this *kŏri* may be scarcely noticed by clients. When a *kŏri* is performed with songs and dances and accompanied by an instrumental ensemble, clients are quick to express their enthusiasm by shouting *ch'uimsae* (cheers of encouragement)[10] (see CD track 25) or showering the *kangshinmu* with extra money.

During a ritual, the *kangshinmu* calls and entertains various spirits. Within some of the *kŏri* (sections) of the *kut*, there are smaller *kŏri* (subsections). Some of the smaller *kŏri* (subsections) are for venerated spirits while some are for lowly spirits.

If the smaller *kŏri* (subsection) is intended for venerated spirits, there are four main elements: *ch'ŏngshin* (invitation of spirits), *oshin* (entertainment of spirits), *kangshin* (spirit possession), and *songshin* (bidding farewell to spirits). It is interesting to note that the overall structure of the ritual (that is, *ch'ŏngshin*, *oshin*, *kangshin*, and *songshin* as illustrated in table 8 above) is reflected within its smaller subsections.

For instance, after the first main section, *Pujŏng kŏri*, which functions as *ch'ŏngshin* (invitation of spirits), there is the second main section, *Ch'ŏn'gung maji kŏri*, which functions as *oshin* (entertainment of spirits) and *kangshin*

---

[8] Fees for the participants (*kangshinmu* as well as musicians) are determined according to the seniority and reputation for performance skills nowadays. In general, they are grouped into four levels—beginners, average performers, good performers, and first class performers. Fees for an individual shaman or musician range from about $150 to $1,000 for a one-day ritual.

[9] *Taegam kŏri* and *ch'angbu kŏri* are the most popular *kŏri* in the Hanyang *kut*.

[10] During *musok* rituals or Korean folk music performances, the audience may participate by cheering the performers with *ch'uimsae* (encouragement), saying "*chot'a!*" (good!), "*chalhanda!*" (nice going!), or "*ŏlssigu!*" (oh, yes!).

(spirit possession). Within the *Ch'ŏn'gung maji kŏri* there are twelve smaller *kŏri* (subsections), six of which are for venerated spirits and six of which are for lowly spirits. The first of these subsections is *Ch'ŏn'gung Pulsa kŏri.*

During the *Ch'ŏn'gung Pulsa kŏri* (subsection), the shaman performs a sequence of ritual actions that can be considered as *ch'ŏngshin* (invitation of spirits), *oshin* (entertainment of spirits), *kangshin* (spirit possession), and *songshin* (bidding farewell to spirits). The shaman puts on specific ritual garments to receive and honor a specific spirit and then sings a short ritual song to invite the spirit (*ch'ŏngshin*). The shaman then sings another ritual song and performs a ritual dance to please the spirit (*oshin*). The shaman becomes possessed by the spirit and gives messages from the spirit (*kangshin*). The shaman then bids farewell to the spirit and removes the ritual garment (*songshin*).

Sharing the main elements outlined above, each *kŏri* (section) and smaller *kŏri* (subsection) is performed for specific spirits with distinct words, prayers, songs, dances, offerings, actions, and instrumental music. Within the framework of each *kŏri,* the *kangshinmu* may add personal comments or *chaedam* (witty remarks) as appropriate.

In smaller *kŏri* (subsections) for the miscellaneous lowly spirits, the elements of *ch'ŏngshin, oshin,* and *songshin* are shared, but no *kangshin* (spirit possession) takes place. The main purpose of these *kŏri* for the lowly spirits are to please them so that they will not linger on and harm anyone. The *kangshinmu* wears plain *hanbok* while calling and entertaining these miscellaneous spirits. Since no spirit possession takes place, shamans do not wear ritual garments, they do not perform ritual dances, and they do not deliver *kongsu* (messages) from the spirits during these sections. The spirits are invited, short prayers are said to please them, and they are sent away quickly.

It is important to note that some *kŏri* (sections) may be omitted or their order shifted during rituals. When the entire *kut* has to take place within two hours, the *kangshinmu* often shortens songs and dances for the venerated spirits while simply mention lowly spirits' names as an acknowledgement for their presences.

Anna-Leena Siikala, in her study of the processual structure of shamanizing séances in Inner Asia, notes that a shamanic rite is built up of action units, *actemes,* and the realization of the *acteme* in the ritual performance itself is the *act.* She states further that

> The actemes are the theme of the performance, the units carrying it forward. Thus they are functional from the point of view of the inner dynamics of the rite process rather than its manifestation. This means that the same acteme may in practice be expressed in words just as well as in movements. The actemes follow one another in an order logical to the overall course of the séance. They are grouped according to their functional context into longer periods, sequences,

while combinations of sequences make up the basic structure of the rite. (Siikala [1978] 1987:74)

One may view the structure of smaller *kŏri* (subsections) for venerated spirits in terms of actemes (action units), which correspond to the main elements of *ch'ŏngshin* (invitation of spirits), *oshin* (entertainment of spirits), *kangshin* (spirit possession), and *songshin* (bidding farewell to spirits) (see table 9).

The Preparatory Ritual, *Chudang Mullim*

Before the *ch'ŏnshin kut* formally begins, a preparatory ritual called *chudang mullim* or *chudang t'oesan* takes place.[11] During *chudang mullim*, the officiating *kangshinmu* remain inside the building to drive away malevolent spirits and their curses (*chudang sal*) and to purify the area, while clients, other *kangshinmu*, and guests remain outside the ritual hall. During *chudang mullim*, the *kangshinmu* invites the spirit of Ŏksabyŏl Kunung who is believed to have the power to protect the altar area. The *hong ch'ŏnik*, the red ritual garment of Ŏksabyŏl Kunung, is hung inside the ritual hall for its symbolic power and presence (Akamatsu and Akiba [1938] 1991, 2:135) (see plate 18).

If someone must remain inside the ritual hall because of a physical disability, he may hold onto the drum, the five-directional flags, or the ritual garment of Ŏksabyŏl Kunung while the *kangshinmu* play several phrases of *kutkŏri* and *tangak changdan* with drum (*changgu*) and cymbals (*chegŭm*) to welcome Ŏksabyŏl Kunung to the ritual hall (CD tracks 1–2). It has been a part of the musical practice among experienced shamans to begin *chudang mullim* in *kutkŏri changdan* (rhythm cycles) and make a smooth transition to the faster *tangak changdan*.

After *chudang mullim*, all are invited back into the room or ritual hall. The *kangshinmu* and the musicians sit near the altar, while others are seated facing the altar, leaving ample room for the *kangshinmu* to move about in front of the altar.

---

[11] *Chudang* refers to the ritual hall with its eight directions, namely east, west, south, north, and the directions in between (southeast, southwest, northeast, northwest) (Huhm 1980:54).

Table 9
Eight Actemes (Action Units) of Hanyang *Kut*

Ch'ŏngshin (invitation of spirits)	1.	The *kangshinmu* puts on the appropriate ritual garment to receive and honor a specific spirit.
	2.	The *kangshinmu* recites or sings a short duet (*mansubaji*) with another *kangshinmu* who sings and plays the *changgu*.
Oshin (entertainment of spirits)	3.	The *kangshinmu* sings solo songs (*t'aryŏng* and/or *noraekarak*) to please the spirits.
	4.	The *kangshinmu* performs a formalized dance (*kŏsŏng*) for the possessing spirit.
Kangshin (spirit possession)	5.	As the *kangshinmu* becomes possessed by the spirit, he or she begins to hop in one place (*tomu*). Accompanied by a percussion ensemble made up of only *kangshinmu*, he or she accelerates the pace of the hopping. When completely possessed by the spirit, the *kangshinmu* turns and stands facing the clients as the music fades.
	6.	The possessing spirit speaks through the *kangshinmu*'s mouth to the clients who stand in front of the *kangshinmu* to receive the message (*kongsu*) from the spirit. The *kangshinmu* also delivers blessings (*tŏkdam*).
Songshin (bidding farewell to spirits)	7.	The *kangshinmu* dances briefly while removing the ritual garment.
	8.	Instrumental music concludes the *kŏri*.

Ch'ŏnshin Kut

1. Pujŏng Kŏri

Ch'ŏnshin kut formally begins with *pujŏng kŏri*. During this *kŏri*, *pujŏng* (literally, pollution) is cleansed and *ch'ŏngshin* (invitation to the spirits) is extended to both *chŏngshin* (venerated spirits) and *chapkwi* (miscellaneous spirits). *Chŏngshin* include such spirits as Ch'angbu, Chesŏk, Ch'ilsŏng, Chŏnan, Hogu, Kamang, Malmyŏng, Pulsa, Pyŏlsang, Sangsan, Sanshin, Shinjang, Sŏngju, Taegam, and Todang, while *chapkwi* include Chishin, Kŏllip, Maengin, Sangmun, Sŏnang, Subi, T'ŏju, and Yŏngsan.

1.1 "Pujŏng Ch'ŏngbae"

The *kangshinmu* informs the spirits of the names of the sponsors and explains the purpose of the ritual through the song "*Pujŏng Ch'ŏngbae*." A seated *kangshinmu* sings songs, accompanying himself or herself on the *changgu*, an hourglass-shaped drum. The *kangshinmu* relays the sponsors' needs and asks the spirits to descend, to receive the offerings of the *kut*, and to help. A white sheet of paper containing information about the sponsors—their names, dates of birth, addresses, and relationship to one another—is attached to the *changgu* so that the *kangshinmu* may refer to it during the ritual if need be. Traditionally this information was provided in calligraphic form, written with a brush dipped in black ink,[12] but nowadays it is often written with a black pen or marker (see plate 36).

During *pujŏng kŏri*, the *kangshinmu* is dressed in *hanbok* (traditional Korean clothing): female *kangshinmu* wear *ch'ima* (long pleated skirt) and *chŏgori* (top) while *paksu* (male shamans) wear *paji* (trousers) and *chŏgori* (top). Both male and female *kangshinmu* wear *posŏn*, traditional white socks.

The *kangshinmu* sings "*Pujŏng Ch'ŏngbae*" first for about half an hour, using stock melodies and variations,[13] and accompanying himself or herself on the *changgu*. The rhythmic cycle used for the recitation is two sets of five-beat *pujŏng changdan* (2 + 3 or 3 + 2) with the occasional variation of adding three beats: 3 + (2 + 3) or 3 + (3 + 2) + 3 or (2 + 3) + 3 or (3 + 2) + 3. The

---

[12] The ink is produced by rubbing an ink stick (*mŏk*) on an inkstone (*pyŏru*) and mixing with a small portion of water.

[13] The *pujŏng* recitation is not sung as *noraekarak* as suggested in the two written sources: Cho Hung-youn [Cho Hŭng-Yun] (1999:17) and Kukrip (Kungnip) Munhwajae Yŏn'guso (1998:22).

kangshinmu ends the invocation song with a fast paced *hwimori changdan* (CD tracks 3–4).

While *hwimori changdan* is played, the assisting *kangshinmu* symbolically purify the ritual space by splashing clean water and *chaemul* (water mixed with ashes, salt, and red pepper powder) and by burning a piece of white paper, *soji*. Then the assisting *kangshinmu* fill the wine cups and light the candles and incense (*mansuhyang*) on the altar.

1.2 "Kamang Ch'ŏngbae," *Calling the Spirits*

The seated *kangshinmu* continues with the incantation (invitation of spirits) by singing "*Kamang Ch'ŏngbae*," still accompanying himself or herself on the drum with *pujŏng changdan*. If musicians are hired, they take their places during this recitation, getting ready to play their instruments. The *p'iri* player sits next to the *kangshinmu* at the *changgu* with the *taegŭm* and *haegŭm* players next, according to the old tradition (see plate 26). Following the incantation, the seated *kangshinmu* sings "*Kamang Noraekarak*" while the instrumentalists join in, blending with the singer's melody in heterophony (*susŏng karak*) on their instruments (CD track 5).

If a new instrumentalist has been hired for the occasion, the *kangshinmu* may form an opinion of the musician's skill while singing "*Kamang Noraekarak*," the first song in the ritual performed with melodic instrumental accompaniment. A musician may show his musicianship by performing "*Kamang Noraekarak*" well. Several musicians have told me how nervous they become whenever they are challenged to play melodic lines immediately without hesitation in whatever key a *kangshinmu* begins to sing because *kangshinmu* and musicians never rehearse songs together prior to any ritual. Sometimes the *kangshinmu* begins in one key but changes to another in midstream, keeping the musicians alert at all times.

1.3 Chinjŏk Tŭrim, *Offering of Wine to Spirits by Sponsors*

After "*Kamang Noraekarak*," the sponsors are invited to come forward to participate in *chinjŏk tŭrim* (offering of wine to spirits).[14] They fill the wine cups for the Sangsan Manura spirit[15] and do three *k'ŭn chŏl* (literally, large bows),

---

[14] *Chinjŏk tŭrim* refers to an offering of wine. When *chinjŏk* is expressed in Sino-Korean, it is written as 進爵 (*chinjak*), which refers to an act of offering wine to the king during a court banquet, *chinyŏn* (Cho H.Y. 1999:27).

[15] *Manura* may be interpreted as "wife" in contemporary Korean, but in *musok* it refers to the highest officials, for example, "kings," in old Korean (Cho H.Y. 1999:85). Sangsan

prostrating themselves three times in front of the altar while the instrumental ensemble provides the music of *Yŏmbul, Pan Yŏmbul, Kutkŏri, Nŭjŭn Hŏt'ŭn T'aryŏng,* and *Chajin Hŏt'ŭn T'aryŏng* (CD tracks 11-15, 17). If no *chaebi* (ritual musician) is hired to provide melodic instrumental accompaniment, the seated *kangshinmu* provides the *changdan* (rhythmic cycles) of *Yŏmbul, Pan Yŏmbul, Kutkŏri, Nŭjŭn Hŏt'ŭn T'aryŏng,* and *Chajin Hŏt'ŭn T'aryŏng* on the *changgu* alone. If an instrumental ensemble of *samhyŏn yukkak* (six-musician group) is hired, they play all twelve pieces of the Hanyang *Samhyŏn Yukkak* suite, beginning with *Chajin Hwanip* (CD track 6).

1.4 "Sangsan Noraekarak"

The seated *kangshinmu* sings "*Sangsan Noraekarak,*" also known as "*Changgunnim Noraekarak,*" accompanying himself or herself on the *changgu* (CD tracks 16, 18). "*Sangsan Noraekarak*" concludes *Pujŏng kŏri,* which is also the last *anjŭn kŏri* (seated part) of the ritual.

2. Ch'ŏn'gung Maji Kŏri

Ch'ŏn'gung maji kŏri is performed only during *ch'ŏnshin kut* (ritual held to usher in good fortune), not during rituals held for the sick (*pyŏng kut* or *uhwan kut*) or for the departed (*chinogwi kut*).

Ch'ŏn'gung means heaven; *maji* means welcoming. During this *kŏri,* the heavenly spirits (*ch'ŏnshin*) like Ch'ŏnjon, Pulsa, and Chesŏk are honored; thus the *Ch'ŏn'gung maji kŏri* is also referred to as Ch'ŏnjon *kŏri,* Pulsa *kŏri,* and Chesŏk *kŏri.* Ch'ŏnjon refers to the Heavenly King (Okhwang Ch'ŏnjon) revered among the religious Taoists. Pulsa refers to Buddha. Chesŏk (Hwan In Chesŏk) refers to the Heavenly Spirit, Hwan In, who sent down Hwan Ung who gave birth to Tan'gun, the legendary founder of *musok,* in the world of humans.

Incorporating the highest spirits in Taoism and Buddhism into the pantheon of *musok* is an example of syncretism. Accepting elements from other religions into *musok* was probably necessary in order to adapt and survive the days when the court and the upper-classes favored imported religions. Regardless of the various terms used to refer to this *kŏri,* the ritual is intended for Chesŏk, the highest spirit in *musok.*

The table offering for Chesŏk and Pulsa includes two candlesticks and three dishes of three-layered white rice cakes known as *cheng p'yŏn, pangmangi ttŏk* or *yong ttŏk* (see plate 31). On top of each rice cake, a white paper flower

---

Manura refers to the spirit of General Ch'oe Yŏng who is believed to reside in Tŏkmul Mountain.

(*paekryŏn*) is placed. Vegetable dishes, fruits, and a bowl of *oksu*, sacred water, are also placed on the offering table. Spoons wrapped with a bundle of uncut white thread are placed in bowls filled with uncooked rice. The number of spoons reflects the number of the sponsoring family members while the thread and rice symbolically represent wishes for long life and a plentiful harvest, respectively.[16]

The table for Pulsa and Chesŏk is always taller than the other offering tables and is placed to the far left side (one's left when facing the main altar). *Pulsajŏn* (paper sculpture cut from white mulberry paper)[17] is hung from the ceiling near the ritual table to receive the spirit of Pulsa descending from heaven (*ch'ŏn'gung*).

Within *Ch'ŏn'gung Maji Kŏri* there are twelve smaller *kŏri* (subsections). The first six subsections (2.1–2.6) are for venerated spirits while the last six (2.7–2.12) are for lowly spirits. I will explain Chŏn'gung Pulsa *kŏri* (2.1) and Chŏn'gung Kŏllip *kŏri* (2.7) in detail. For the rest of the *kŏri*, I will briefly discuss distinct features as appropriate.

2.1 Ch'ŏn'gung *Pulsa* Kŏri

Ch'ŏn'gung Pulsa *kŏri* is also known as Pulsa *kŏri* for short. It was performed outdoors in earlier days, but may be performed indoors nowadays.

2.1.1 Ch'ŏngshin *(Invitation to Spirits)*

The officiating shaman wears a long bright red skirt (*hong ch'ima*), a white pointed cowl (*kokkal* or *semosi pan kokkal*), and a long white robe fashioned after Buddhist monk's attire (*changsam*) (see plate 32). If a male shaman is officiating, he puts on a long indigo blue skirt (*nam ch'ima*) first, then adds on the red skirt. The *changsam* (robe) worn by the Korean Buddhist monks is usually light gray, but in *musok,* it is white in color and is known as *paek changsam* (white robe). The *changsam* has long, wide sleeves and is worn with

---

[16] Rice is cooked as offerings for the spirits. Uncooked rice is placed to symbolically receive blessings.

[17] I was privileged to video record the process of making various *chijŏn* (ritual paper sculptures), including *Pulsajŏn* and *nŏkjŏn*, in 1998 because a teacher shaman wished to have video recordings made for neophyte *kangshinmu* to use as reference tools in the future. In these recordings, the teacher explains the esoteric meanings of each fold and cut while a student shaman is making *chijŏn* used for Hanyang *kut*. All sacred objects made of paper are constructed at the ritual site prior to the *kut* and burned (*sogak*) at the end of the ritual.

a red belt (*hongtti*) and two long red sashes (*hong kasa*)[18] crossing over both shoulders. The shaman puts on the Buddhist prayer beads (*yŏmju*) like a necklace and tucks the ritual fan (*puch'ae*) with a long yellow ribbon into the right side of the red belt while holding a bell tree (*pangul*) with the left hand.

Pulsa kŏri begins with *mansubaji*, a duet sung by the officiating shaman (standing) and the assisting one (seated) who provides a *changgu* accompaniment for both of them. As a rule, the leading shaman sings the first phrase and the accompanist repeats the same words sung with a different melodic pattern. However, when a less experienced shaman officiates at this *kŏri*, the more experienced shaman at the *changgu* will begin the first phrase, allowing the other to repeat as a means of instruction. The two singers sing in call and response style, but the important aesthetic of this duet is in the overlapping of the melodic phrases of the two singers. Whenever one phrase is sung, the final vowel sound is held until the next singer's phrase is completed. For *mansubaji*, the principal *kangshinmu* holds a ritual fan in the right hand and a bell tree in the left, shaking the bell tree whenever the assisting *kangshinmu* sings (CD track 35).

The *kangshinmu* then dances briefly and "rides" the *muldongi*. *Muldongi* is an earthenware jar about 30 cm in diameter containing water.[19] In a sacred context, *muldongi* covered with white paper becomes a temporary sacred place for the spirits of water. The *kangshinmu*, standing on the lip of the *muldongi*, turns around once, prays to Yongshin (literally, dragon spirit, but referring to water spirits), and relays *kongsu* (message and blessings) from the spirits to the clients. The act of riding the *muldongi* is a distinctive feature of this *kŏri*.

2.1.2 Oshin *(Entertainment of Spirits)*

The shaman then sings two solo songs: "*Para T'aryŏng*" and "*Ch'ŏn'gung Maji Noraekarak*," still wearing the white *changsam* (robe).[20] The singing *kangshinmu* plays a pair of cymbals (*para*) while dancing and singing "*Para T'aryŏng*." Cymbals are played as part of the instrumental ensemble for dance accompaniment, but they are usually not used for songs. "*Para T'aryŏng*" is the

---

[18] The red sash with tinsel and decorative gold print is called *kŭmdan kasa*.

[19] In modern Korea, many *kangshinmu* perform their *kut* at *kuttang* (ritual halls) located far from their residences. In order to avoid breaking the *muldongi* (earthenware jar) in transit, some have replaced it with an aluminum pot for the same ritual purpose, as I observed on November 20, 1998.

[20] While singing "*Para T'aryŏng*," Pak In-O and his *kangshinmu* students wear plain gray hats and long robes fashioned after contemporary Buddhist monk's attire, but others usually wear white *changsam* during Hanyang *kut*.

only strophic song in the Hanyang *kut* where cymbals are used during the singing (see plate 32 and CD track 22).[21]

"*Para T'aryŏng*" is also known as "*Chungsang T'aryŏng.*" During "*Para T'aryŏng*," the *kangshinmu* holds out the cymbals to clients in order to receive extra cash offerings. Clients may place money offerings on the cymbals during or after the song when they are approached by the singing *kangshinmu*.

A brief dance follows and then "*Ch'ŏn'gung Maji Noraekarak*" is sung. Both "*Para T'aryŏng*" and "*Ch'ŏn'gung Maji Noraekarak*" end with short concluding duet songs in the fast paced *hwimori changdan* (rhythmic cycle).

The duet songs in *hwimori changdan* are sung in unison by the principal *kangshinmu* and the assisting one who plays the *changgu*, while another assisting *kangshinmu* plays cymbals.

The *kangshinmu* then dances to the instrumental accompaniment of *kut kŏri* or *t'aryŏng changdan* (rhythmic cycle) (CD track 19). The *kangshinmu* dances *tŭrŏ sukbae* and *nal sukbae* by dancing four steps toward the altar and four steps away from it.[22] *Sukbae* means greeting, while *tŭrŏ* and *nal* mean coming in and going out, respectively, suggesting the movement toward and away from the altar. Each time the *kangshinmu* moves toward the altar, he or she alternates directions (toward the altar)—toward the left side, center, and right side of the altar. While dancing, the *kangshinmu* throws the long sleeve of the *changsam* over the shoulder (*kamda*) and then releases (*p'ulda*) it toward the drum. He or she then dances holding the ritual fan in the right hand and the red sash in the left. The third set of dances is done holding the red sash in both hands while the instrumental ensemble plays *kutkŏri changdan*.

2.1.3 Kangshin *(Spirit Possession)*

When the shaman is about to be possessed by spirits, an assisting shaman senses the moment and changes the tempo of music, signaling to other musicians to change the music to *tangak changdan* (rhythmic cycle) in order to keep up with the pace of the shaman while he or she dances *tomu*, hopping in one place (CD track 20). Once possessed by the spirit, the *kangshinmu* turns around and delivers *kongsu* messages to sponsors (CD track 21).

Toward the end of singing "*Ch'ŏn'gung Maji Noraekarak*," the shaman faces the *changgu* player holding a plate filled with walnuts, chestnuts, and jujubes above the drum. While singing duets, both shamans offer the plateful of nuts to the spirits and ask for blessings (see plate 33).

---

[21] Cymbals are used sometimes for songs for Subi sung in *hwimori changdan*.

[22] If the dance begins with the right foot forward, it is in Kup'abal style from the western part of Seoul. If the *kangshinmu* dances with the left foot first, he or she is known to be trained in Kakshimjŏl, the eastern style.

Then the shaman performs *san*, a type of divination, by throwing a few nuts or fruits from the plate to the clients to see if the spirits are satisfied with the offerings. This process of tossing and counting is called *san ŭl chunda* (literally, offering the numbers) or *san* (literally, counting) for short. *San* is a type of divination where the *kangshinmu* quickly sorts out the nuts (or sometimes grains of rice, dried fruits, fresh grapes, candies, etc.) by counting them in pairs[23] to check whether the spirits are satisfied with the offerings. If none is left over (that is, the number is even), it is believed that the spirits are content. If one nut remains (that is, the number is odd), the *kangshinmu* starts over, throwing the nuts again and counting, repeating this process until the desired result is reached. By performing *san*, the *kangshinmu* is able to give clients the message that the spirits are satisfied.

To receive the nuts or fruits, men hold out their shirts and women hold their blouses or skirts out toward the *kangshinmu*. This is a traditional way of receiving nuts or fruits. For example, during *p'yebaek* (ceremony after a wedding) the bridegroom's parents throw *taech'u* (jujubes) and *pam* (chestnuts) to the newlyweds as a blessing and wish for many children, and the newlyweds hold out the front of their clothing to catch the fruits.

Throughout the ritual, whenever good fortune is ushered in and passed on to sponsors and guests by *kangshinmu*, men and women stand up as a sign of respect to the spirits possessing the *kangshinmu*. Men hold their shirts out and women hold their blouses or skirts out toward the *kangshinmu* gesturing to receive the blessings (see plate 34).

2.1.7 Songshin *(Bidding Farewell to Spirits)*

As a sign of bidding farewell to the spirits, the *kangshinmu* removes the ritual garments while dancing, keeping the plain *hanbok* (traditional outfit). An assisting *kangshinmu* folds the ritual garments neatly to be put away.

The instrumental ensemble concludes the *kŏri* by playing *kut kŏri changdan* and a short break follows.

---

[23] Although some authors state that shamans count nuts, grains, candies, etc. by groups of threes (Akamatsu & Akiba [1938] 1991, 2:139; Cho H.Y. 1999:34), it appears that this is not a common practice. I have not observed this practice in any of the rituals I attended. They always counted the nuts or other offerings in pairs. Whenever I asked shamans how they do the counting, they told me *"tulssik"* (by two).

2.2 Ch'ŏn'gung Hogu Kŏri

There are various ideas about Ch'ŏn'gung Hogu. Hogu is believed to be the spirit of a princess who died of smallpox. Hogu is considered by others to be the spirit who causes smallpox. Some think Hogu are the spirits of Koryŏ maidens captured and sacrificed by invading Chinese soldiers during the Yuan Dynasty. Others think Hogu are spirits of princesses who died unmarried, for example, the spirits of Sŏngbi, Ŭihwa Kungju, and Chŏnggyŏng Kungju (Cho H.Y. 1999:50).

The number of female spirits worshiped in *musok* is fewer than the number of male spirits. Some of the female spirits are Chishin Halmŏni, Chŏnan Puin, Hat'al, Hogu, Kyemyŏn Kakssi, Pari Kongju, and Taeshin Halmŏni.

2.2.1 *Puin* Kongsu *with Veil*

Wearing the long red skirt (*hong ch'ima*) while holding a fan in the right hand and a bell tree in the left, the *kangshinmu* lifts a large red (sometimes wine colored) veil (*nŏul, myŏnsap'o,* or *hongbo*) over the head while relaying *kongsu* (messages) from the Chŏnan Puin (noble married ladies) spirits to the sponsors. Some say the reason for covering the face is that Chŏnan Puin is a shy female spirit.

2.2.2 *Hogu* Kongsu *with* Ch'ima *(Skirt)*

The *kangshinmu* then takes off the outer red skirt (*hong ch'ima*), still wearing *hanbok* (traditional outfit), and lifts the red skirt over his or her head, covering the face to hide the "facial scars" of smallpox, while delivering *kongsu* to the clients.

2.3 Ch'ŏn'gung Malmyŏng Kŏri

Ch'ŏn'gung Malmyŏng are the spirits of shamans' ancestors. During this *kŏri*, the *kangshinmu* is dressed in plain *hanbok* (traditional clothing) and holds a fan in the right hand and a bell tree in the left while giving *kongsu* (messages from the spirits) to the clients.

2.4 Ch'ŏn'gung Shinjang Kŏri

Shinjang is short for Obang Shinjang (Five Directional Spirits). The Shinjang are military spirits who look after everything within the five directions (East, West, South, North, and Center). The *kangshinmu* puts on a blue *kugunbok* (outer garment with narrow sleeves) and dark blue *chŏnbok* (long tunic) over it. Both *chŏnbok* and *k'waeja* refer to the ritual tunic. When the tunic is worn in honor of the spirits who are associated with militant or court official spirits, it is called *chŏnbok*. He or she puts on a hat called *annulimbŏnggŏji*. For Ch'ŏn'gung Shinjang, the *kangshinmu* sings "*Ch'ŏn'gung Shinjang T'aryŏng*" while holding *obang shinjanggi* (five flags representing the Five Directional Spirits).

2.5 Ch'ŏn'gung Taegam Kŏri

Taegam are the spirits of court officials. In order to receive Taegam spirits, the *kangshinmu* dresses in the attire of a court official. He or she puts on blue *kugunbok* (outer garment), dark blue *chŏnbok* (long tunic), and *annulimbŏnggŏji* (hat). He or she sings "*Ch'ŏn'gung Taegam T'aryŏng*" to entertain Taegam spirits.

2.6 Ch'ŏn'gung Ch'angbu Kŏri

Ch'angbu is the spirit who looks after musicians and artists. The *kangshinmu* puts on *ch'angbu ŭidae*, a garment with a pink bodice and multicolored *saekdong* sleeves. *Ch'angbu ŭidae* is also known as *wŏnsam*. Holding the ritual fan, the *kangshinmu* sings " *Ch'ŏn'gung Ch'angbu T'aryŏng*" to honor Ch'angbu.

2.7 Ch'ŏn'gung Kŏllip Kŏri

Ch'ŏn'gung Kŏllip is one of the miscellaneous lowly spirits who will be invited (*ch'ŏngshin*), entertained (*oshin*), and sent away (*songshin*) in the following six smaller *kŏri* (subsections) of Ch'ŏn'gung *kŏri*. Ch'ŏn'gung Kŏllip, who is known to solicit and bring in clients for *kangshinmu* to prosper, is offered some food with prayers and sent away.

Since *kangshin* (spirit possession) does not takes place by any lowly spirit, the *kangshinmu* has no message to deliver to the sponsors. The ritual bell tree (*pang'ul*) is not used because the *kangshinmu* does not dance for the lowly spirits. The *kangshinmu* does not wear ritual clothing. The *kangshinmu* wears plain *hanbok* (traditional clothing) and holds a ritual fan (*puch'ae*) in the right hand throughout this smaller *kŏri* (subsection) as well as for the following two—Ch'ŏn'gung Maengin *kŏri* and Ch'ŏn'gung Sŏnang *kŏri*.

2.8 Ch'ŏn'gung Maengin Kŏri

The *kangshinmu* invites all Ch'ŏn'gung Maengin, the spirits who are blind. He or she says prayers for them while holding a ritual fan.

2.9 Ch'ŏn'gung Sŏnang Kŏri

The *kangshinmu* invites Ch'ŏn'gung Sŏnang, spirits known to protect the village and neighborhood. He says prayers to them while holding a ritual fan.

2.10 Ch'ŏn'gung Yŏngsan Kŏri

The *kangshinmu* invites Ch'ŏn'gung Yŏngsan, the spirits of those who died unexpectedly from accident or were murdered and became wandering spirits. The *kangshinmu* invites these spirits to comfort them with food and songs while holding *sanja* (rice cookie).

2.11 Ch'ŏn'gung Sangmun Kŏri

The *kangshinmu* prays for Ch'ŏn'gung Sangmun, spirits who are associated with death and funerals, while holding a *sanja* (rice cookie).

2.12 Ch'ŏn'gung Subi Kŏri

Subi are various lowly spirits. Sponsors kneel while the *kangshinmu* circles their heads with the *sanja*, a large crisp cookie made of rice, and throws it to a tray for countless Ch'ŏn'gung Subi, asking them to receive it as an offering and leave the ritual space.

As noted above, the *Ch'ŏn'gung maji kŏri* is made up of twelve smaller *kŏri* (subsections). During these last six smaller *kŏri* for Kŏllip, Maengin, Sŏnang, Yŏngsan, Sangmun, and Subi, prayers and food are offered by the *kangshinmu*, but no dances.

Most *kangshinmu* do not go through the entire twelve smaller *kŏri* within the *Ch'ŏn'gung maji kŏri* during a ritual. Only a few *kangshinmu* who perform the Hanyang *kut* still include all twelve smaller *kŏri*. If the ritual time is limited, the *kangshinmu* may simply mention the names of the spirits of the twelve smaller *kŏri* and go on to the next. This is why those who attend the Hanyang *kut* may not be able to easily identify all twelve smaller *kŏri* being performed. It became clear to me only when I began to assist Yi Sang-Sun who was preparing a comprehensive manual for the Hanyang *kut*.

3. Todang Kŏri

Todang kŏri is offered to the *todang* spirits protecting the neighborhood where the *chegajip* (sponsoring family) lives. For offerings to *todang* spirits, a pig's head, cow's head, or the rib cage of a cow is laid on the table. There are also twelve smaller sub *kŏri* within this *Todang kŏri*.

3.1 Todang Sanshin Kŏri

Todang Sanshin is the spirit of the mountains located in each province.[24] The *kangshinmu* begins by saluting toward the doorway, then to all four directions twice each, holding *sanjongi* (white paper sculpture, also known as *todangjongi*) in both hands. The *kangshinmu* puts on *hong ch'ima* (a red long skirt). Wearing the red *chŏnik* (outer garment fashioned after the courtier's uniform) and *pitkat* (hat with two peacock feathers), a shaman dances in *kutkŏri* and *tangak changdan*.

3.2 Todang Yongshin Kŏri

This is for Todang Yongshin (literally, Dragon Spirits) who looks after water and all the living creatures in it. The *kangshinmu* dances and speaks, still holding the *todangjongji* (which is not called *sanjongi* in this smaller *kŏri*).

---

[24] Mountain spirits are believed to reside in the mountains located in each province—Paekdu Mountain in Hamgyŏng Provinces, Myohyang Mountain in P'yŏngan Provinces, Kuwŏl Mountain in Hwanghae Province, Samkak Mountain in Kyŏnggi Province, Kyeryong Mountain in Ch'ungch'ŏng Provinces, Chiri Mountain in Chŏlla Provinces, and T'aebaek Mountain in Kangwŏn and Kyŏngsang Provinces.

3.3 Todang Kŏri

During this smaller *kŏri*, spirits of the neighborhood are entertained. The *kangshinmu* dances in *kutkŏri changdan*, holding both *sanjongi* (ritual paper) and *ch'anggŏm* (ritual trident) in the left hand and a *wŏldo* (ritual knife) in the right hand.

The *wŏldo* is a steel ritual knife with a long wooden handle. It is also called *yŏnwŏldo, ŏnwŏldo,* or *ŭnwŏldo.* With a crescent moon shaped blade, the *wŏldo* comes in various sizes averaging about 60–70 cm in length.

The set of *wŏldo* (ritual blade) and *ch'anggŏm* (ritual trident) is considered a powerful weapon used by the *kangshinmu* to fight malevolent spirits who cause sickness or misfortune. During several *kŏri* (sections) of the Hanyang *kut* (ritual), the *kangshinmu* holds the *wŏldo* in the right hand and the *ch'anggŏm* in the left to engage in a symbolic battle with evil spirits on behalf of his clients.

3.4 Todang Pugun Kŏri

The spirits of the area where the sponsors live are invited and entertained during this *kŏri*. The *kangshinmu* holds three flags (yellow, red, and white) in the left hand and the *wŏldo* (ritual knife) in the right while dancing and giving *kongsu* (messages from the spirits).

3.5 Todang Kunung (Salryung) Kŏri

The *kangshinmu* holds the *ch'anggŏm* (ritual trident) in the left hand and *puch'ae* (ritual fan) in the right. *Kunung* (militant spirits) looking after the neighborhood are entertained during this *kŏri*.

3.5.1 Sasil Seugi *with* Wŏldo

Sasil seugi is a way of detecting whether the spirits are satisfied with the ritual.[25] *Sasil* means truth and *seugi* means placing something upright. *Wŏldo sasil* is done by letting the *wŏldo* (ritual blade) stand on its own by placing the handle on the floor or on top of a plate (see plate 35). Because it is difficult to balance the ritual knife on its slim handle, if the *wŏldo* stands on its own it is believed that the spirits are extraordinarily content and people are reassured that the spirits will bestow good results for the *kut*.

---

[25] *Sasil seugi* is also called *sasŭl seugi*.

Individual *wŏldo sasil* are held on behalf of the *taeju* and *kiju*, male and female heads of the sponsoring family, respectively. Additional *wŏldo sasil* are made for the sponsors' adult children.

3.5.2 Sasil Seugi *with* Ch'anggŏm

Next *sasil seugi* is done with the *ch'anggŏm* (ritual trident) while placing a pig's head on it (see plate 4). The *ch'anggŏm,* also known as *samjich'ang*, is a ritual trident made of steel with a long wooden handle. Sizes vary, but generally they are about 60–70 cm long. The *ch'anggŏm* symbolically represents the *axis mundi*, or a cosmic tree, with its three prongs symbolizing the three elements of *ch'ŏn* (heaven), *chi* (earth), and *in* (humans). Once the trident stands on its own, the *kangshinmu* circles a wine cup counter-clockwise around the trident's handle and offers wine to the sponsor.

3.5.3 "Todang Noraekarak"

While removing the last offering from the *ch'anggŏm*, the *kangshinmu* begins to sing *"Todang Noraekarak"* and the assisting *kangshinmu* at *changgu* (drum) joins in singing the song in unison.

The *kangshinmu* is still wearing a red long skirt, a red *ch'ŏnik* (outer garment fashioned after the courtier's uniform), and *pitkat* (hat with two peacock feathers). The assisting male or female *kangshinmu* is dressed in plain *hanbok*, traditional clothing.

3.6 Todang Hogu Kŏri

The *kangshinmu* takes off the black hat (*pitkat*), red outer garment (*hong ch'ŏnik*), and red skirt (*hong ch'ima*). Wearing plain *hanbok*, the *kangshinmu* lifts the red skirt (*hong ch'ima*) above his or her head, supporting it with bell tree in the left hand and ritual fan in the right hand and gives *kongsu* (messages from spirits) to sponsors. Hogu spirits are associated with smallpox. The *kangshinmu* uses the red skirt as a veil to hide smallpox scars.

3.7 Todang Malmyŏng Kŏri

The *kangshinmu* summons the Malmyŏng spirits, the ancestor spirits of shamans. The *kangshinmu* wears plain *hanbok*, traditional Korean clothing.

Holding the bell tree (*pangul*) in the left hand and the ritual fan (*puch'ae*) in the right, the *kangshinmu* gives *kongsu* (messages from spirits) to the sponsors.

3.8 Todang Chejang Kŏri

The *kangshinmu* wears plain *hanbok* to entertain the Chejang spirit. The *kangshinmu* holds only *puch'ae*, the ritual fan, while delivering *kongsu* to the sponsors.

3.9 Todang Shinjang Kŏri

The *kangshinmu* sings "*Todang Shinjang T'aryŏng*" wearing *kugunbok* (outer garment), *chŏnbok* (tunic), and *annulimbŏnggŏji* (hat) while holding *obang shinjanggi* (the five-directional flags) for this *kŏri*. If the ritual is held at a sponsor's residence, the *kangshinmu* goes through each room with *obang shinjanggi* giving blessings and getting rid of bad influences. Then the *kangshinmu* lets the sponsors choose one flag for a brief divination. The method and interpretation of this divination is explained below in section 8.1, *kijŏm* (flag divination).

3.10 Todang Taegam Kŏri

Taegam are the spirits of court officials. The *kangshinmu* takes off *kugunbok* for this *kŏri*, still wearing the blue skirt, *chŏnbok* (tunic), and *annulimbŏnggŏji* (hat).

The *kangshinmu* offers cow's feet to the Todang Taegam spirit, as the spirit is known to enjoy meat. Holding a pair of cow's feet in both hands, the *kangshinmu* sings "*Todang Taegam T'aryŏng*" to entertain the spirit.

3.11 Todang Ch'angbu Kŏri

The *kangshinmu* puts on *ch'angbu ŭidae* (an outer garment with multiple colored sleeves) over their plain *hanbok* to honor Todang Ch'angbu spirit. When a male *kangshinmu* is performing this *kŏri*, he wears *nam ch'ima*, a long indigo blue skirt, under the *ch'angbu ŭidae*.

The *kangshinmu* sings "*Todang Ch'angbu T'aryŏng*" while holding the *puch'ae* (ritual fan) in the right hand.

3.12 Todang Kŏllip Kŏri

No song or dance is offered during this *kŏri* as Todang Kŏllip is considered one of the lowly spirits. The *kangshinmu* prays wearing plain *hanbok*, holding the ritual fan in the right hand and a dried pollack in the left. While praying for Todang Kŏllip, the *kangshinmu* places morsels of cooked rice, *ttŏk* (rice cake), and *pindaettŏk* (vegetable pancake made of mung beans) in a bowl. The *kangshinmu* circles the bowl over the heads of the sponsors and places it on the floor near the doorway.

Saying prayers in the fast-paced *hwimori changdan* (rhythmic cycle), the *kangshinmu* sends all the various lowly spirits including Todang Subi away from the ritual space during this *kŏri*.

4. Ponhyang Kŏri

Ponhyang kŏri, also known as *san paraegi*, is offered to the ancestors of shamans and sponsors. *Ponhyang* refers to the place where a family comes from. Considering Tan'gun as the progenitor of all Koreans, the symbolic *ponhyang* (birthplace) for Koreans is the mountains where Tan'gun resides as the Mountain Spirit. The offering table is filled with one incense burner, two candles, three cups filled with wine, bowls of fruits and nuts, three plates of *shiru ttŏk* (rice cakes), and two *ponhyangji* (sculptures made of white paper).

4.1 Malmyŏng Kŏri

Wearing a long indigo blue skirt (*nam ch'ima*) and green outer garment (*sŏpsu*) with white trim on the sleeves, the *kangshinmu* holds ritual paper (*ponhyangji*) and the ritual fan in the right hand and the *ponhyangji* and bell tree in the left. The *kangshinmu* calls the ancestors of shamans including Tan'gun and makes offerings on behalf of the sponsors.

4.2 Taeshin Kŏri

Taeshin spirits are known to help *kangshinmu*, empowering them with great divination skills. The *kangshinmu* wears yellow *mongduri* (outer garment) and dances, holding *puch'ae* (ritual fan) in the right hand and *pangul* (bell tree) in the left.

5. Chosang Kŏri

Chosang refers to family ancestors. In *musok*, people who died young are also considered *chosang*. Putting on the *nam ch'ima* (long indigo blue skirt) over the traditional *hanbok*, the *kangshinmu* invites the souls of the sponsors' departed relatives (up to the fourth ascending generation). New *hanbok* (traditional clothing)—*ch'ima* (skirt) and *chŏgori* (top) for female and *paji* (trousers) and *chŏgori* (top) for male ancestors—are purchased as offerings to please each *chosang* to be called and entertained during this *kŏri*. The *kangshinmu* places the new set of *hanbok* over his or her shoulder for each of the departed relatives, while calling for the soul from the symbolic *ponhyang yangsan* where *chosang* from both husband's and wife's sides of the family are believed to reside. In earlier days, only the husband's side of the family was invited for this *chosang kŏri* (Yi Sang-Sun, personal communication). But nowadays the souls of departed relatives on the wife's side are also invited during this *kŏri*. While the *kangshinmu* is possessed by *chosang* spirits, the spirits talk to the surviving relatives about things they were not able to share when they were alive.

The conversation taking place among the *chosang* and family members attending the ritual are of a personal nature. I usually do not record this *kŏri* either on audio or video tapes, respecting the sponsors' privacy. By listening to the conversation among the *chosang* and surviving relatives, one can easily surmise the purpose of the ritual—family history, relationships and/or conflicts within the family. As an observer, I often attend rituals without any prior knowledge about the sponsors but learn about them through this *kŏri* (section), because the *kangshinmu* possessed by a *chosang* talks with family members in the same voice and mien as the departed person. After each brief encounter, the *chosang* is sent away by the *kangshinmu* who cuts two pieces of cloth, one made of cotton (*mumyŏng*) and the other of hemp (*pe*), symbolizing this world and the other, respectively. By cutting the cloth, the *kangshinmu* formally separates the dead from the living and continues the ritual.

6. Sangsan Kŏri

Sangsan kŏri is also known as *San kŏri, Manura kŏri*, or *San Manura kŏri*.[26] This *kŏri* is intended to call the spirit of the historical *changgun* (military

---

[26] Sangsan refers to Tŏkmul Mountain, an important mountain where the spirit of General Ch'oe Yŏng is believed to reside. San Manura literally means mountain's highest being, like the kings and governors in old Korea. Here San Manura refers to the spirit of General Ch'oe Yŏng of the Koryŏ Dynasty, the spirit that governs Tŏkmul Mountain situated in North Korea.

general) Ch'oe Yŏng (1326–1388) who is revered among *musok* believers. General Ch'oe is known to have great power to grant any wish the *kangshinmu* may relay on behalf of the sponsors. Thus this *kŏri* is also called *changgun kŏri* or *k'ŭn* (grand) *kŏri*.

The *kangshinmu* wears *nam ch'ima* (long indigo blue skirt), blue *kugunbok* (outer garment), and blue *chŏnbok* (long tunic), fastening the ritual fan in the front. He or she adds a *nam ch'ŏnik* (blue outer garment with long wide sleeves with white trim) and *sŭl ttŭi*, a sash decorated with three pouches at the back.[27] He or she places a *k'ŭn mŏri* (large wig) on his or her head and adds a black hat called *kat*.

6.1 Chŏnan Kŏri

Chŏnan *kŏri* is an optional smaller *kŏri* performed at the beginning of Sangsan *kŏri*. Not all *kangshinmu* are possessed by the Chŏnan spirit. If a *kangshinmu* is possessed by the Chŏnan spirit, that is, the spirit of Kwan-U (Chinese Kwan-Yu), also known as Kwan-Un-Jang, then the Chŏnan *kŏri* is performed. The *kangshinmu* first puts on the ritual clothing for Sangsan—the long indigo blue skirt, *kugunbok*, *chŏnbok* (tunic), *nam ch'ŏnik* (blue outer garment with long and wide sleeves) with *sŭl ttŭi* (sash), *k'ŭn mŏri* on the head, and a black hat called *kat*. Then he or she adds *hwang ch'ŏnik* (gold colored outer garment with long wide extended sleeves) to begin Chŏnan *kŏri*. The *kangshinmu* holds red and blue flags in the left hand and *ch'ŏngryongdo* (literally, blue dragon knife) in the right hand for Kwan-U's spirit (see plate 5).

Kwan-Yu was a Chinese historic general who lived from 162 to 220 C.E. He was a mighty warrior of great repute and his story is told in one of the oldest Chinese novels, *The Romance of the Three Kingdoms*, written about 1394. In 1102 the Sung emperor of China, influenced by his Taoist advisors, received Kwan-Yu into the official religion as a duke. The story of Kwan-Yu and his rise to Kwan-Ti (Emperor Kwan, Korean Kwansŏng Chegun) is an example of a historic man's deification. Kwan-Yu became Prince in 1128, Emperor in 1594, Military Emperor in 1813, and then was deified as the God of War who protects the nation and heals the wounded. Kwan-Ti, worshipped for his integrity, is known as the god who defends the nation, civilization, and morality (Chamberlain 1997:48–55).

Kwan-U (Chinese Kwan-Yu) is one of the spirits that *musok* imported from Taoism. In 1592 when the war broke out between Korea and Japan, Korea asked China for military assistance. A Chinese army came with their belief in the Taoist spirit Kwan-Ti, God of War. After Korea defeated Japan with the help of

---

[27] Each of the three pouches contains a coin and cotton balls. The pouches are usually yellow, blue, and red.

the Chinese, Sŏnjo (r. 1567–1608), the fourteenth King of the Chosŏn Dynasty, decided to erect the first Korean shrine for Kwan-U named Tonggwan Wangmyo in Seoul in 1602.

The Chosŏn Dynasty court honored Kwan-U by designating the title "Muanwang" (King who achieved peace through military power) and presenting musical offerings at rituals held for him from 1786 until 1908. Music was selected from *Chongmyo Cheryeak* (royal ancestral ritual music) of the Chosŏn Dynasty. Lee Chae-Suk notes that all three pieces chosen for Muanwang's ritual from the eleven-piece *Chŏngdaeŏp* were those in which the *hojŏk* (conical oboe, also known as *t'aep'yŏngso*) is included in the ensemble.[28] The three pieces are namely "*Somu,*" "*Punung,*" and "*Yŏnggwan*" (Lee C.S. 1998:69). Kwan-U was also gradually accepted as one of the pantheon of spirits that *musok* believers worship. In Korea, Kwan-U is remembered on his birthday, the thirteenth day of the fifth month in the lunar calendar, as in China.[29]

6.2 Kŏsŏng *Dance*

After the *Chŏnan kŏri*, the *kangshinmu* removes the *hwang ch'ŏnik* (the proper attire for Kwan-U), keeping the ritual clothes for Sangsan spirits. In addition to the spirit of General Ch'oe, the spirits of General Yim, General Shin of P'yŏngsan of Hwanghae Province, and *yŏ changgun* (Lady General) of Halla (Han-Ra) Mountain are honored during this *kŏri*.

The *kangshinmu* begins this *kŏri* by dancing to the music provided by the instrumental ensemble. The instrumental ensemble provides slow and elegant music in the rhythm of *manura changdan*, also known as *ch'wit'ae changdan* (CD track 24).

The ritual dance steps are deliberate and dignified. The *kangshinmu* goes from side to side and forward and backward in front of the offering table. While continuing to dance this sequence of four steps of *tŭrŏ sukpae* and *nal sukpae*, the *kangshinmu* varies the dance by holding different objects in his or her hands. The *kangshinmu* first holds a hat (*kat*) in the right hand with hat strings in the left. Then the *kangshinmu* puts the hat on top of the wig, holding the long flowing sash with both hands and supporting it with a ritual fan in the right hand. The *kangshinmu* then opens the fan in the right hand and holds the sash in the

---

[28] The ritual music for Muanwang (Kwan U) was performed by an ensemble made up of one *pak* (wooden clapper), two *taegŭm* (bamboo flute), two *changgu* (hourglass-shaped drum), two vocalists, two *p'iri* (cylindrical oboe), two *haegŭm* (bowed fiddle), two *t'aep'yŏngso* (conical oboe), one *chunggo* (mid-size drum), two *taegŭm* (large gong), and one *sogŭm* (small gong) (Lee C.S. 1998:69).

[29] In China, Kwan Ti is remembered especially on the fifteenth day of the second lunar month and the thirteenth day of the fifth lunar month (Chamberlain 1997:54).

left hand. Holding one end of the sash in each hand, the *kangshinmu* then picks up the *wŏldo* (ritual knife) with the right hand and the *samjich'ang* (ritual trident) with the left.

6.3 "Sangsan Noraekarak"

After the formal dance, the *kangshinmu* places the *wŏldo* (ritual knife) on the food offerings, such as the pig's head or the cow's rib cage, as a symbolic gesture that the spirits have accepted the offerings. The *kangshinmu* then gives *kongsu* (messages from spirits) and offers wine called *myŏng chan* and *pok chan* (literally, wine for long life and prosperity) to the sponsors. The *kangshinmu* concludes the *kŏri* by singing "*Sangsan Noraekarak*." Sangsan *kŏri* is also referred to as *taenju tŭrim* (literally, offering of *taenju*)[30] referring to the entire offering of the *kŏri* performed with splendid costumes, solemn dances, and excellent music.

7. Pyŏlsang *Kŏri*

Pyŏlsang spirits belong to those who were to become king during the Chosŏn Dynasty but who faced tragic death before becoming king, for example, Yŏnsan'gun (1495–1506), Kwanghaegun (1608–1623), and Sadoseja (1735–1762). At the end of *Sangsan kŏri*, the *kangshinmu* takes off the *nam ch'ŏnik* (blue outer garment) to begin the Pyŏlsang *kŏri*. At this point, the *kangshinmu* is still wearing the long blue skirt, the *kugunbok* (military outer garment), blue *chŏnbok* (long tunic), and the *k'ŭn mŏri* (wig) from the previous *Sangsan kŏri*. He or she then takes off the black *kat* (hat), replacing it with a hat called *annulimbŏnggŏji* on top of the *k'ŭn mŏri*.[31] The offering table for Pyŏlsang *kŏri* is the same as the one that was used for the *Sangsan kŏri*.

7.1 Sasil Seugi *with* Wŏldo

Sasil seugi is a way of detecting whether the spirits are satisfied with the ritual, as described above in section 3.5.1. *Sasil seugi* with the *wŏldo* (ritual knife) takes place during this *kŏri*. This is done to verify that the spirits are content with the ritual offerings. If the *wŏldo* stands straight alone, the sponsors

---

[30] I think *taenju* may have come from *tae anju* (literally, *anju* [hors d'oeuvres served with drinks] on a grand scale).
[31] Sometimes the *kangshinmu* may change into a yellow *kugunbok* (outer garment) and black or dark brown *chŏnbok* (long tunic).

7.2 Sasil Seugi *with* Ch'anggŏm

During the *sasil seugi* with *ch'anggŏm* (trident), the *kangshinmu* places a pig's rib cage, a pig's head, several cow's feet, or a whole pig (*t'ong sasil*) on various sizes of *ch'anggŏm* (tridents), balancing the ritual trident so it will stand on its own (see plates 4 and 36) while the instrumental ensemble plays music in the rhythm of *pyŏlsang changdan* (rhythmic cycle). Sponsors and friends put extra money on top of the meat offerings during this *kŏri*.

7.3 Chakdu Kŏri

The *kangshinmu* begins to sing "*Pyŏlsang Noraekarak*" and goes toward the *changgu* (drum) while opening the *puch'ae* (ritual fan). The *kangshinmu* playing the *changgu* joins in singing "*Pyŏlsang Noraekarak*" together in unison.

A straw cutter or a fodder chopper in a secular context, the *chakdu* is used as sacred ritual twin blades by the *kangshinmu*. The most commonly used *chakdu* are made of iron. The twin blades are placed parallel, side by side, and are often wrapped together at both ends by white cloth strips. The twin blades are sharpened in silence prior to the *kut* by the shaman's helpers who place white paper, *hami*, in their mouths to avoid any pollution from talking or spitting.[32] I have observed that *hami* (white paper) is sometimes replaced by a 10,000 *wŏn* bill (about $10 in US funds, 2000) in recent years as a tip for each helper. Several *kangshinmu* told me that the sharper the edge of the *chakdu*, the more comfortable they feel standing on them. If the *chakdu* is not as sharp as it could be, they feel pain in their feet.

Possessed by a Pyŏlsang spirit during the *chakdu kŏri* (section) of the *kut*, the *kangshinmu* will stand on the sharpened edges of the twin blades of the *chakdu* with bare feet as an act of symbolic sacrifice to get rid of misfortunes (see plate 13). Not all *kangshinmu* can "ride *chakdu*" (*chakdu t'ada*), but only those who are possessed by one of the Pyŏlsang spirits, often called General Chakdu. *Chakdu* are also used in Hwanghae Province *kut*.[33]

People consider the *kongsu* (spirits' messages) delivered by a *kangshinmu* on *chakdu* to be the most powerful. Even some *kangshinmu* experienced at riding *chakdu* have told me that they are afraid to go up on *chakdu* each time

---

[32] Hwanghae Province *manshin* (shamans) use *hami* in their mouths before riding *chakdu* for similar reasons. *Hami* (but not *chakdu*) is also used in Chŏlla Province *kut*.

[33] *Chakdu* are also referred to as *pisu* in Hwanghae Province *kut* (Kim I.H. 1983:85).

before the *kut* begins. But during the *kut* when the Spirit of General Pyŏlsang possesses the *kangshinmu*, he or she instantly overcomes fear and looks forward to going onto the blades, treating the sharp edges of the *chakdu* as if they were wide wooden blocks. They have told me that they feel so elated once they are on *chakdu* that they feel like dancing. Some *kangshinmu* not only deliver *kongsu* but also write messages from the spirits while standing on the *chakdu*.[34]

Several *kangshinmu* have shared with me experiences when their feet were injured on *chakdu*. The feet may be cut if taboos are not properly observed prior to and during the *kut*. The *kangshinmu* is expected to abstain from sex for three days prior to the ritual and to cleanse themselves in the early morning of the ritual date. One thing they dread is to notice a polluted person among the onlookers while standing on *chakdu*. As soon as they spot a polluted person, *kangshinmu* can feel their bare feet being cut. People considered polluted are those who have had a recent birth, death, or surgery in the family, people who have just attended a funeral, and menstruating women. *Kangshinmu*, however, are not too worried about injuries for they firmly believe in the healing power of the spirits. They say the cut will be miraculously healed within a day or two.

Some *kangshinmu* use a *chakdu* swing. The Korean traditional swing (*kŭne*) is a wooden board suspended by two ropes. One stands on the board and holds the ropes while swinging in midair. The *kangshinmu* replaces the wooden board of the swing with *chakdu* on which he or she stands barefoot and swings very high into the air while possessed by the spirit. Among those who "ride the *chakdu* swing" made of the twin blades, Yi Sŏn-Bi (b. 1934), Kim Un-Ok (b. 1948), and Kim Chŏng-Suk (b. 1954) are well known. They are all *manshin*, spirit-possessed shamans, from Hwanghae Province.

Some *kangshinmu* climb a *chakdu* ladder made of a dozen or more single-bladed steps, while others stand placing both feet on a single blade to dance or balance on one foot on the single blade. Most *chakdu* blades are straight edged, but some are custom-made for *kangshinmu* in unique shapes. For example, Yi Chun-Yŏng, also known as Ch'onggak Tosa, a *paksu*, has created personal *chakdu* according to the spirits' instructions given to him in dreams. He has made several shapes of *chakdu*: single bladed *chakdu* in a crescent moon shape (*ch'osaengdal chakdu*), several *chakdu* with varied wavy shapes of clouds (*kurŭm chakdu*), a seven-bladed *chakdu* for Chilsŏng (Seven Stars), and a thirteen-step *chakdu* ladder (see plate 37).[35]

---

[34] I observed Ch'onggak Tosa, a *paksu*, "riding" a *ch'ilsŏng chakdu* with seven blades. The literal meaning of Ch'ilsŏng is Seven Stars. While standing on this seven-bladed *ch'ilsŏng chakdu*, he bent over to write in calligraphy what the spirit wished to convey to the sponsors of the *kut*. He also wrote spirit's messages while coming down from a thirteen-bladed *chakdu* ladder.

[35] Yi explains that the thirteen steps represent the twelve months and heaven.

Chu Chŏng-Suk (b. 1963) is known to ride *chakdu* made of 36 sharp pins. The *chakdu* has three rows of a dozen pins which are 12 cm long (Han'guk Minjok Hakhoe 1997:285). Since the *chakdu* are placed on a temporary base during the *kut*, people hold onto the handles of the ritual blades or the structure on which they are placed to provide a firm balance. Two or more people are chosen from among those considered unpolluted to hold the *chakdu*.

8. Shinjang *Kŏri*

Shinjang is a military spirit known to have power over good fortune and misfortune. In his honor, the *kangshinmu* takes off the *k'ŭn mori* (wig) and puts back on the *annulimbŏnggŏji* (hat), still wearing the long blue skirt, *kugunbok* (outer garment), and *chŏnbok* (tunic). He holds the *obang shinjanggi* (five directional flags), *wŏldo* (ritual knife) and *ch'anggŏm* (ritual trident) during this *kŏri*.

8.1 Kijŏm, *Flag Divination*

The *obang shinjanggi* (five directional flags of *Shinjang*) symbolize the Spirits of the Five Directions—east, west, south, north, and center—which are associated with five colors, each spirit with one color and one direction. The spirit of the South is associated with red, Spirit of the East with blue, Spirit of the North with green, Spirit of the West with white, and Spirit of the Center with yellow. In earlier days the Spirit of the North was associated with black, but green has replaced black.

The *kangshinmu* dances with the *obang shinjanggi*, symbolically ushering in good spirits. *Kangshinmu* also use *obang shinjanggi* for divination during the *kut*, rolling all five flags into one large bundle and asking a person to choose one of the five flagpoles. As the *kangshinmu* tucks away the flags, showing only the ends of the poles, no one, not even the *kangshinmu*, can guess which color flag is attached to which pole. As the client selects one pole, the *kangshinmu* will unwrap the whole bundle of flags, holding onto the chosen pole and separating it from the other four.

Since each color is associated with a distinct fortune, the *obang shinjanggi* serve as a divination tool for *kijŏm* (literally, flag divination). The red flag is considered auspicious; the white one, a blessing from the Heavenly Spirits. The yellow color symbolizes ancestors and is interpreted as a sign that the ancestors wish to be remembered more often by family members. The blue and green flags forewarn possible illness or death in the family, respectively. If one initially chooses a blue or green flag, the *kangshinmu* as a rule encourages the person to select one pole after another until the yellow, white or red flag is chosen.

Whenever the red flag is chosen, the ritual hall becomes filled with excitement as people rejoice for the auspicious fortune of the person.

8.2 Ch'aenggyo Pekkyŏ, *Getting Rid of Bad Forces*

For the Eastern school of Hanyang *kut*, *ch'aenggyo pekkyŏ* is performed during this *kŏri* if the sponsor is ill or facing difficulties. The sick person is seated toward the doorway covered with the *obang shinjanggi* (five directional flags), while the *kangshinmu* throws food over the patient. Foods like red beans and millet are thought to have power to get rid of problems. To overcome difficult situations, the *kangshinmu* sometimes performs *salp'uri* to get rid of *sal* (literally, curse) by using a bow and arrows.[36] The arrowheads are made of buckwheat flour dough (see plate 38). The *kangshinmu* shoots the arrows with a bow made from a branch of a peach tree.[37] A branch growing toward the east from a peach tree is chosen as it is believed to have great power to repel evil forces causing illness or troubles in life.

9. Taegam *Kŏri*

Taegam spirits are thought to have power to bestow wealth and prosperity on the sponsor's family. Taegam spirits may be generally grouped into two categories: *ut taegam* and *arae taegam* (literally, high and low officials). *Ut taegam* (high officials) include Chŏnan Taegam, Kunung Taegam, Momju Taegam, Pyŏlsang Taegam, Pyŏsŭl Taegam, Sangsan Taegam, and Shinjang Taegam, while *arae taegam* (low officials) include Pugun Taegam, Sumunjang Taegam, T'ŏ Taegam, and Todang Taegam.

The *kangshinmu* wears *nam ch'ima* (long blue skirt), *kugunbok* (outer garment), and *chŏnbok* (tunic) for low official Taegam spirits, but adds *hong ch'onik* (red outerwear with long wide sleeves) for high official Taegam spirits.

9.1 Taegam Nori

While entertaining (*nori*) various Taegam spirits, the *kangshinmu* wears a *kugunbok, chŏnbok,* and a hat called *annulimbŏngŏji.* For Kunung and Pyŏsŭl

---

[36] The term *salp'uri* is also used to refer to a section of Chindo *ssikkim kut* as well as a secular dance.

[37] Peaches are not used as part of the fruit offerings to spirits during rituals but a branch of a peach tree is used for repelling evil forces.

Taegam, the *kangshinmu* adds a *hong ch'ŏnik* (red outer garment with long wide sleeves). The *kangshinmu* sings *"Taegam T'aryŏng"* and dances (CD track 25).

Wearing plain *hanbok* the *kangshinmu* prays to Momju Taegam and Chiksŏng Taegam on behalf of the male and female sponsors, respectively.

9.2 Sulryŏk Torŭm

T'ŏ Taegam, who looks after property, is honored by way of *sulryŏk torŭm* for prosperity in business. The *kangshinmu* places a small offering table on his or her head with wine and offerings such as rice cake, fruit, pig's head, or cow's feet, then goes outside and leaves the offerings near a column or tree in the front and back of the house. I think *"sulryŏk torŭm"* comes from *"sunryŏk torŭm"* (literally, going around to inspect every corner). The *kangshinmu* sings *"T'ŏ Taegam T'aryŏng"* while going around the house.

9.3 Mugam *Dance by Sponsors and Guests of* Kut

The *mugam* dance takes place following the Taegam *kŏri* in the Hanyang *kut*, but it is not offered if the ritual is held as *pyŏng kut* or *uhwan kut* to heal the sick, because the main purpose of the *mugam* dancing is to elicit lively participation from the audience. During the *mugam kŏri*, the *chegajip* (sponsors) and guests are invited to dance in front of the altar, wearing or holding parts of the shamans' *shinbok* (ritual garments). It is believed that those who dance with the ritual garments will feel better and be blessed (see plate 39).

Traditionally various ritual garments were worn by the clients, but nowadays the *k'waeja* (long blue tunic) is offered most often because it is easy to put on and take off quickly. I have observed that some *kangshinmu* have about a dozen tunics specially made for *mugam* so that people may dance wearing them.

Since no specific dance steps are required for this impromptu dance, people express themselves freely to the instrumental music accompaniment. Fun-loving people are quick to dance anywhere to the popular rhythm of *kutkŏri changdan* (rhythmic cycle) played by any of the percussion instruments.

Occasionally unexpected spirit possession may occur while audience members are dancing *mugam* at a *kut*, as happened in the case of Yongsu's mother whose "possession was sudden and unique in its relative painlessness" as noted by Laurel Kendall (1987:59). As Yongsu's mother remembers it:

> I said, "What do you mean 'use the *mugam*?' It's shameful for me to dance like that." But the Chatterbox Mansin kept saying, "It'll give you luck. You'll be lucky if you dance." So I put on the clothes and right away began to dance

wildly. I ran into the shrine, still dancing, and grabbed the Spirit Warrior's flags. I started shouting, "I'm the Spirit Warrior of the Five Directions," and demanded money. All of the women gave me money. I ran all the way home. My heart was thumping wildly. I just wanted to die like a crazy woman. We talked about it this way and that way and decided there was no way out. So the next year I was initiated as a *mansin*. (Kendall 1987:59)

Some people are reluctant to participate in *mugam* dancing for fear of becoming involuntarily spirit-possessed, but many participate and have fun. Despite the exceptional case of spirit possession occuring during *mugam*, which may mislead one to consider the *mugam* a part of a light possession trance, as suggested by Kendall (1983: passim), people generally do not experience spirit possession while dancing *mugam*. Reviewing Kendall's work, Ch'oe Kil-Sŏng clarifies that if a person reaches an extremely agitated state by dancing *mugam*, it is caused by physical activity and not by spirit possession, because *mugam* is different from spirit possession, which as a rule is exclusive to *mudang* (Ch'oe K.S. 1989:54).

Some *musok* believers dance for their Momju Taegam (personal guardian spirits) but most people—men and women, including unmarried maidens and young brides, contrary to Kendall's informant's suggestion (Kendall 1983:235)—dance to enjoy themselves.[38]

10. Sŏngju *Kŏri*

Sŏngju, the spirit that protects the family and the household, is entertained during this *kŏri*. The *kangshinmu* wears a *hong ch'ima* (long red skirt), a *hong ch'ŏnik* (red outer garment with long wide sleeves with white trim), and a black *kat* (hat). Sŏngju *kŏri* is also known as Sŏngju Kunung *kŏri*, Sŏngju *paji*, and Sŏngju *kut*.

The *kangshinmu* sings "*Sŏngju Noraekarak*" and dances while holding a *sŏngju kunungji* (white paper) and *pukŏ*, a dried Alaska pollock, as an offering. Inside the *sŏngju kunungji* three coins are placed as an offering.

---

[38] Kendall reports that according to her *mansin* informant: "Maidens (*ch'ŏnyŏ*) who aren't married aren't supposed to dance or people will think they're wild (*sudongsuropjianhta*). Young brides (*sae saekssi*) aren't supposed to use the *mugam* either" (1983:235).

11. Ch'angbu *Kŏri*

Ch'angbu is believed to protect musically talented *kangshinmu* and their artistic talents of music and dance. For Ch'angbu, the *kangshinmu* takes off the hat and wears *tangŭi* (outer garment), which has a pink or green bodice and sleeves decorated with multi-colored horizontal stripes (*saektong*).

11.1 "Ch'angbu T'aryŏng"

Ch'angbu is known to like performing. The *kangshinmu* sings "*Ch'angbu T'aryŏng*" while holding the *puch'ae* (ritual fan). As mentioned earlier, if a male *kangshinmu* is performing, he puts on the long indigo blue skirt first before adding the *ch'angbu ŭidae,* the symbolic ritual garment for Ch'angbu. The *kangshinmu* entertains the powerful Ch'angbu spirit, asking to get rid of sickness and misfortune throughout the whole year (see plate 40).

Lyrics of the song "*Ch'angbu T'aryŏng*" illustrate how the Ch'angbu spirit will prevent ill fortune on one auspicious day of each month in the lunar calendar (CD track 28). For example, in the first month, it will be done on *taeborŭm nal* (the day of the full moon); in the third month, on the third day, *samjit nal*; in the fifth month, on the fifth day, *tano nal*; in the seventh month, on the seventh day, *ch'ilsok nal,* and so on (see conclusion for more lyrics).

11.2 "Hwangje P'uri"

If Sŏngju *kut* for a new home is performed on a grand scale, the epic song "*Hwangje P'uri*" is sung at this point by a seated *kangshinmu* who accompanies himself or herself on the *changgu* with the rhythmic cycle known as *hwangje p'uri changdan.*

11.3 Kyemyŏn Kŏri

During a *chinjŏk kut* held for a *kangshinmu*, *kyemyŏn kŏri* may be added here. The Spirit Kyemyŏn is thought to be that of Kyemyŏn Kakssi, a woman who looks after the kitchen and *ttŏk* (rice cake) storage. The *kangshinmu* sings "*Kyemyŏn T'aryŏng*," offering *ttŏk* (rice cake) to clients and onlookers before ending the *kut*. As the saying goes: "*Kyemyŏn ttŏki naolttaekkaji issŏya, kut kugyŏngŭl ta han kŏt ida*" (You have to stay until *kyemyŏn* rice cakes appear to say that you have watched the entire ritual).

After "*Kyemyŏn T'aryŏng*," the guests may leave while musicians pack their instruments. The sponsors leave without saying goodbye to anyone, knowing that they will meet the *kangshinmu* at his or her *shindang* on the third day after the ritual to pray together.

When leaving the ritual, sponsors and invited guests are not to say "goodbye" in person to the *kangshinmu* and other members of the ritual performance team. If someone says "goodbye," the *kangshinmu* or musicians tell the person to stop saying it and ask others not to bid goodbye. This custom may have originated in the Chosŏn period when courtiers often attended *kut*. Despite the fact that *kangshinmu* would be expected to bid farewell formally to the court entourage in other social situations, they were excused in this case.

12. *Twitchŏn Kŏri*

The *twitchŏn kŏri* functions as a *songshin* (bidding farewell to the spirits) to all the spirits invited to the *kut*, as well as to those who came uninvited. Here the *kangshinmu* may sing farewell, accompanying himself or herself on the *changgu*, or they may perform standing while another seated *kangshinmu* provides the *changgu* accompaniment. In earlier days, *twitchŏn kŏri* was performed exclusively by *kangshinmu* who were possessed by spirits of very low status. These *kangshinmu* were not allowed to attend the entire *kut* but came merely to perform *twitchŏn kŏri*, disappearing discreetly as soon as they had finished their parts (Pak In-O, personal communication 1993). Cho Hung-youn notes, however, that the hierarchy among shamans determined by the power of their possessing spirits (*momju*) has disappeared since World War II (Cho H.Y. 1990a:36).

Holding the ritual fan in the right hand and a dried pollock in the left, a *kangshinmu* dressed in plain *hanbok* calls back the *chapkwi* (low class spirits) like Chishin, Maengin, Sŏnang, Yŏngsan, Sangmun, and Subi who were sent away at the beginning of the *kut* through *chudang mullim*. This is to offer food, drinks, and compliments to the spirits in order not to offend them. Included in this *kŏri* are also those *chapkwi* and *chapshin* (miscellaneous spirits) who came to the ritual uninvited. The *kangshinmu* then bids farewell to all the spirits.

A performance of *twitchŏn kŏri* may last from five minutes to more than two hours. The elaborate version, known as "*Kajin Twitchŏn*," is not performed at ritual halls, but is sung at selected rituals held in sponsors' or shamans' homes for *chaesu kut*. It is seldom performed nowadays since few *kangshinmu* know the entire song. Whenever Kisaeng Paksu sings the hour and a half version of "*Kajin Twitchŏn*," *kangshinmu* gather to learn (CD track 29).[39] "*Kajin Twitchŏn*" is never performed during the *chinogwi* or *saenam kut*.

---

[39] Several *kangshinmu* have asked me for copies of my recordings, noticing that I had taped the ritual with a DAT recorder. When they get permission from the performers being recorded, I have always obliged them.

At the end of the *kut* (ritual), the *kangshinmu* throws a pair of *shink'al* (ritual knives) to the ground to see if the malevolent spirits have been expelled. The *shink'al* is a pair of brass or steel knives usually with wooden handles, their blades averaging about 30 cm long. If both blades fall pointing toward the outside of the gate of the ritual hall or the house where the *kut* takes place, it is interpreted as a sign that the malevolent spirits have perished. If both blades do not point outward, they are thrown again and again until they do point outwards. The efficacy of the *kut* being confirmed, everyone feels relieved.

Once the knives fall pointing toward the outside, *yŏngshil ŭidae* (clothing for the dead), ritual flowers, and hanging scriptures which had decorated the ritual area are all gathered and burned (*sogak*) to conclude the ritual.

Behind the Scenes

Once the *kut* is completed, the *tangju kangshinmu* (*kangshinmu* responsible for organizing the *kut*) and the *chaebi tangju* (musician responsible for organizing the musicians for the *kut*) gather to calculate the income to be shared among members of the working group. Skill and reputation determine the different scales of payments. The individual payment for invited *kangshinmu* or *chaebi* is not discussed in advance, consequently someone may be offended if they receive less money than expected.

During the ritual, *kangshinmu* and sponsors sometimes shower money (*pyŏlbi*) on musicians. This gift is kept by the individual musicians and not shared with others at the end of the *kut*. Extra money offered to *kangshinmu* during the ritual by sponsors and guests is put into the pot to be divided among the *kangshinmu* and musicians.

Sponsors, ritual participants, and guests leaving the ritual may take home some of the offerings such as fruit, meats, and rice cakes. Some refuse to take anything in order to hide from others the fact that they attended a *kut*.

CHAPTER 10

Seoul *Saenam Kut* and Music

The Seoul *Saenam Kut* is a Hanyang *kut* ritual held in the greater Seoul area to lead the souls of the departed to the next world. It is an elaborate ritual for members of the wealthy upper class. Since Seoul has been the capital of Korea for over six hundred years, the ritual garments, dance, and music of the Seoul *Saenam Kut* are greatly influenced by the court traditions of the Chosŏn Dynasty (1392–1910). The Seoul *Saenam Kut* incorporates Buddhist concepts and Taoist beliefs about the other world and elements of Confucian *chesa* (ancestor ritual) with *musok*.

Scholars agree that the meaning of "*saenam*" is yet to be discovered. Some have attempted to express *saenam* in Sino-Korean words, for example, *sanŭm* (散音) by Yi Nŭng-Hwa ([1927] 1991:182; *chirogwi* (指路鬼) or *chinhogwi* (陳胡鬼) by Yi Hŭi-Sŭng (1998:3586); and *saenam* (賽南) by Yu Man-Gong (cited in Kim S.P. 1996:40).

Saenam could be translated literally as new (*sae*) birth (*nam*). I would like to suggest that we may find the concept of *saenam* in the Seoul *Saenam Kut* ritual itself. During the ritual, families gather around a pile of rice after the recitation of the epic song "*Pari Kongju*" to learn into what life form the departed has been transformed. By examining the traces the soul leaves behind on the pile of rice, families learn that the departed is "newly born" (*saenam*) as a living creature, perhaps as a human, an animal, a snake, a bird, or a butterfly. The concepts of transformation are derived from Buddhist beliefs.

The Seoul *Saenam Kut* combines two rituals: *andang sagyŏng maji kut* and *saenam kut*. The two *kut* are intricately structured, each with twelve *kŏri* (sections),[1] and their performance is magnificent. Each *kut* begins with *anjŭn*

---

[1] The *andang sagyŏng maji kut* is reported to consist of seventeen *kŏri*: *chudang mullim, pujŏng, kamang ch'ŏngbae, chinjŏk, pulsa kŏri, todang kŏri, ch'o kamang kŏri, ponhyang kŏri, chosang kŏri, sangsan kŏri, pyŏlsang kŏri, shinjang kŏri, taegam kŏri, chesŏk kŏri, sŏngju kŏri, ch'angbu kŏri,* and *twitchŏn*, while the second part, *saenam kut,*

kŏri where the principal *kangshinmu* sits and conducts the ritual, and continues with *sŏn kŏri* where the *kangshinmu* stands and performs. *Andang sagyŏng maji* usually begins in the evening and ends in the early part of the morning. *Saenam kut*, the second part, begins after a break of a few hours.

The Seoul *Saenam Kut*, as noted, was designated as Important Intangible Cultural Property number 104 in 1996 by the national government, naming a group of performers (*poyu tanch'e*) including: Kim Yu-Gam, a shaman, as the *poyuja* ("designated performer" of the tradition); Yi Sang-Sun, another shaman, and Kim Chŏm-Sŏk, a musician, as *chŏnsukyoyuk pojoja* (assistants responsible for transmission and education); and two shamans and two musicians as *isuja* ("master artists") of this tradition. As mentioned earlier, the *poyuja* is often referred to colloquially as *in'gan munhwajae*, generally translated as "living human treasure" or "human cultural property," despite the government's attempts to discourage this practice.

The Seoul *Saenam Kut* is an elaborate ritual for the departed but the *p'yŏng chinogwi kut*, a smaller scale ritual than the Seoul *Saenam Kut*, is the most commonly held ritual for the dead in the Seoul area. I have been told that there were once two *saenam kut*—*ŏl saenam kut* and *ssanggye saenam kut*—in the Seoul area. The unique feature of the *ssanggye saenam kut* was that an immense portrait of Buddha was brought from a Buddhist temple to the *musok* ritual ground so that the portrait could be seen by people from afar. In recent years, however, the *ssanggye saenam kut* has not been performed because most of the *kangshinmu* with the ritual knowledge of this *saenam kut* have passed away and families find it too costly to sponsor such a grand scale ritual.

The Seoul *Saenam Kut*, Important Intangible Cultural Property number 104, is refined and dignified. The shaman's dance movements are slow, deliberate, and elegant, especially during the *toryŏng tolgi* (ritual circumambulation). This *kut* has many solemn sections as the shaman sings a long epic-style song, accompanying himself or herself with the *changgu* (hourglass-shaped drum) and *pangul* (bell tree). Few shamans and musicians have mastered this *kut*. Bearing in mind that over 90,000 registered *kangshinmu* (spirit-possessed shamans) are actively engaged in *musok* nowadays, the fact that only about half a dozen shamans and musicians can perform the Seoul *Saenam Kut* attests to the difficulty of learning this ritual.

---

consists of fourteen *kŏri*: *saenam pujŏng, kamang ch'ŏngbae, chungdi patsan, sajesamsŏng, malmi, toryŏng (pat toryŏng), mun dŭrŭm, yŏngshil, toryŏng (an toryŏng), sangshik, twi yŏngshil, pe tchae, shiwang kunung*, and *twitchŏn* (Kukrip Munhwajae Yŏn'guso 1998:17).

But Yi Sang-Sun, the *chŏnsukyoyuk pojoja* (teaching assistant for transmission and education) of the Seoul *Saenam Kut*, told me that *andang sagyŏng* has twelve *kŏri* as does *saenam kut*, the second part of the Seoul *Saenam Kut*.

All *kangshinmu* (spirit-possessed shamans) recognized as *poyuja*, *chŏnsu kyoyuk pojoja*, or *isuja* for the Seoul *Saenam Kut* in 1996 are female. Two *paksu* (male *kangshinmu*) were later also recognized by the government as *isuja*.

The *chaebi* (ritual musicians) recognized as *chŏnsu kyoyuk pojoja* or *isuja* for Seoul *Saenam Kut* are male. No female musicians participate as *chaebi* in Hanyang *kut*.

Table 10
The Primary Artists Designated for Important Intangible Cultural Property Number 104, Seoul *Saenam Kut*, in 1996

Title	Name	Year of birth	Role	Sex
poyuja (designated performer)	Kim Yu-Gam	1924	*kangshinmu*	female
chŏnsu kyoyuk pojoja (assistant for transmission and education)	Yi Sang-Sun	1950	*kangshinmu*	female
chŏnsu kyoyuk pojoja (assistant for transmission and education)	Kim Chŏm-Sŏk	1939	musician (*p'iri* player)	male
isuja (master artist)	Han Pu-Jŏn	1932	*kangshinmu*	female
isuja (master artist)	Kang Yun-Gwŏn	1930	*kangshinmu*	female
isuja (master artist)	Kim Chŏng-Gil[2]	1936	musician (*haegŭm* player)	male
isuja (master artist)	Hŏ Yong-Ŏp	1947	musician (*taegŭm* player)	male

When the Seoul *Saenam Kut* was designated as Important Intangible Cultural Property number 104 by the government in 1996, the *poyuja* (holder or designated performer of the cultural property) became responsible for presenting

---

[2] Kim Chŏng-Gil, although honored by the government, has decided not to participate in the performances with the group since 1997 for personal reasons.

an annual performance of the Seoul *Saenam Kut* in its original form and for teaching it to others. Twice a week, Monday and Friday evenings, Kim Yu-Gam holds classes at Seoul Chungyo Muhyŏng Munhwajae Chŏnsu Hoegwan (Seoul Training Center for the Important Intangible Cultural Properties) in Kangnam, an area located south of the Han River in Seoul. Kim teaches the basic drumming patterns to the students, most of whom are *kangshinmu* (spirit-possessed shamans). In 1990, Kim Yu-Gam taught folk singers Kim Hye-Ran and Kim Yŏng-Yim who have since then been performing Hanyang *kut* shaman ritual songs on the concert stage and produced CDs including songs from the Hanyang *kut*.[3] Nowadays, other professional singers sometimes attend the classes hoping to learn ritual songs of the Seoul area from Kim Yu-Gam for their upcoming concert appearances. A scholar from Germany has also been learning to sing and drum from Kim since the beginning of 1999.

Since most of the students are *kangshinmu* engaged in ritual practices, the motivation for coming to this school is to learn the proper Seoul *Saenam Kut*, one type of the Hanyang *kut*, as well as to be recognized as students learning it under the *poyuja*, Kim Yu-Gam. According to government regulations, a few students will be selected as *isuja* (master artists) through stiff competition after many years of training. But I have observed that some eager *kangshinmu* students have begun to call themselves *isuja* before the government officially recognizes them. They often print this information on their business cards or on signs at their *shindang* (shrines), misrepresenting themselves as *isuja* or *chŏnsuja* (disciples). People who are extremely anxious about getting titles from the government are said to suffer from "*munhwajae pyŏng*" (literally, cultural property sickness).

Kim Yu-Gam, who is honored as the *poyuja* ("designated performer") of the Seoul *Saenam Kut*, is in fact not an expert in the entire repertoire of the Seoul *Saenam Kut*. As mentioned earlier, any Hanyang *kut* needs at least three *kangshinmu* to officiate, dividing the *kŏri* (sections) according to their talents and expertise. But for the Seoul *Saenam Kut*, a minimum of five *kangshinmu* are required because everyone's specialty is different and the shared roles are interdependent. Therefore, the members of the group (*poyu tanch'e*) need to work together to sustain, transmit, and present the Seoul *Saenam Kut* in its *wŏnhyŏng* (original form).

The Seoul *Saenam Kut* consists of two parts: *andang sagyŏng maji kut* and *saenam kut*, as mentioned earlier. The first part, *andang sagyŏng maji kut*, is basically the same as the *ch'ŏnshin kut* (a type of Hanyang *kut*) held in the Seoul area to bring good luck. Because Kim Yu-Gam is the most respected *kangshinmu* for the *ch'ŏnshin kut* in the Seoul area and the oldest member of the group, she was recognized as the *poyuja* for the Seoul *Saenam Kut*, but in fact,

---

[3] Kim Hye-Ran ŭi Seoul Kut, 1993, SYNCD-052B. Kim Yŏng-Yim ŭi Sori, 1998, ARCD-005A.

Han Pu-Jŏn and Yi Sang-Sun are the real experts in the *saenam kut*, the second and distinguishing part of the Seoul *Saenam Kut*.

Enjoying the unofficial yet prestigious title of "living human treasure," Kim Yu-Gam was enthusiastic about teaching *andang sagyŏng maji kut* (the first part of Seoul *Saenam Kut*), not allowing Yi Sang-Sun, the government appointed assistant, to teach any part of the *saenam kut* (the second part of Seoul *Saenam Kut*). Some students, dissatisfied with the repetitious basic drumming lessons given by Kim for several months, urged Yi Sang-Sun to teach them privately. According to the government regulations, anyone who is recognized as *isuja* is allowed to open a studio or *hakwŏn*, a private institute, to teach (Lee Y.H. 1999:82). Yi opened a school for the Seoul *Saenam Kut* on the seventh floor of a high-rise located on Chongro (Bell Street) in downtown Seoul, and many students gather there every Tuesday and Thursday evenings.

Students who were attending both schools kept their studies with Yi Sang-Sun secret from Kim Yu-Gam, hoping to learn the pertinent song repertoires from Yi privately, while maintaining the chance of becoming the *isuja* under Kim who has the exclusive power to nominate *isuja* from the students. Unfortunately, when Kim Yu-Gam found out about this secret arrangement, she was extremely upset. As a result, some students decided not to return to Yi's school for fear of offending Kim, while others decided to leave Kim and stay with Yi, focusing on their studies. In January, 1999, Kim finally offered Yi the opportunity to teach at her school. When I left Seoul in February 1999, Yi had begun to teach four nights a week—Monday and Friday evenings at Kim's school and Tuesday and Thursday evenings at her own school, because she wished to maintain an amicable relationship with Kim but did not want to give up her own school.

Newly acknowledged *isuja* (master artists) by Kim Yu-Gam for the Seoul *Saenam Kut* are three female *kangshinmu* (Kim Ch'ung-Gang, Wŏn Ok-Hŭi [b. 1939], and Yi Kŭn-Ok), two male *kangshinmu* (Yi Sŏng-Jae [b. 1952] and Yi Yŏng-Hŭi [b. 1958]), and a musician (Yi Sŏn-Ho [b. 1953]).

Yi Sang-Sun was pleased that one of her spirit daughters, Wŏn Ok-Hŭi, was recognized as an *isuja* (master artist) by Kim Yu-Gam. Wŏn has been studying with Yi for nearly two decades but had to sever her ties with Yi in order to be nominated as an *isuja* by Kim.

1. *Andang Sagyŏng Maji Kut* (First Part of Seoul *Saenam Kut*)

Because the *andang sagyŏng maji kut* progresses as a slightly modified form of the *ch'ŏnshin kut*, I will point out some of their similarities and differences.

Both *andang sagyŏng maji kut* and *ch'ŏnshin kut* begin with *chudang mullim* (preparatory ritual) and both progress in two parts: *anjŭn kŏri* (seated sections) and *sŏn kŏri* (standing sections) where the *kangshinmu* conducts the ritual while seated or standing, respectively.

Like *ch'ŏnshin kut*, the *andang sagyŏng maji* has twelve *kŏri* (sections). Both rituals begin with *pujŏng kŏri* and end with *twitchŏn kŏri*, but variation takes place during the ten central *kŏri*. As seen in table 11, the two rituals differ in the second through fourth *kŏri*.

Table 11
The Order of *Ch'ŏnshin Kut* and *Andang Sagyŏng Maji Kut*

	Ch'ŏnshin kut	*Andang sagyŏng maji kut*
0.	*chudang mullim*	*chudang mullim*
1.	*pujŏng kŏri*	*pujŏng kŏri*
2.	*ch'ŏngung maji kŏri*	*mulgu kamang kŏri*
3.	*todang kŏri*	Pulsa/Chesŏk *kŏri*
4.	*ponhyang kŏri*	*todang kŏri*
5.	*chosang kŏri*	*chosang kŏri*
6.	Sangsan *kŏri*	Sangsan *kŏri*
7.	Pyŏlsang *kŏri*	Pyŏlsang *kŏri*
8.	Shinjang *kŏri*	Shinjang *kŏri*
9.	Taegam *kŏri*	Taegam *kŏri*
10.	Sŏngju *kŏri*	Sŏngju *kŏri*
11.	Ch'angbu *kŏri*	Ch'angbu *kŏri*
12.	*twitchŏn kŏri*	*twitchŏn kŏri*

1. *Pujŏng Kŏri*

The order and manner of performing *pujŏng kŏri* in *andang sagyŏng maji kut* is the same as the *pujŏng kŏri* of *ch'ŏnshin kut*, but the *kangshinmu* extends invitations to additional spirits of the other world during the *pujŏng kŏri* of *andang sagyŏng maji kut*. Songs like "*Kamang Ch'ŏngbae*," "*Kamang Noraekarak*," and "*Sangsan Noraekarak*" are sung in both *pujŏng kŏri*, but in *andang sagyŏng maji kut*, the song verses are modified to include the names of the spirits who will come and guide the departed soul to the other world.

During *pujŏng kŏri*, the officiating *kangshinmu* is dressed in plain *hanbok* (traditional outfit). *Pujŏng kŏri* concludes the *anjŭn kŏri* (seated section) of the *andang sagyŏng maji kut* and the *kangshinmu* stands up to continue the ritual in *sŏn kŏri* (standing sections) for the following eleven *kŏri*.

2. *Mulgu Kamang Kŏri*

During *Mulgu Kamang kŏri*, the soul of the departed will possess the *kangshinmu* and speak to the family to say personal "goodbyes." Throughout the Seoul *Saenam Kut*, the soul of the departed will appear three times to talk with the family. This is the first of the three appearances and it is referred to as *ch'o yŏngshil* (see CD track 23).

During this *kŏri*, the *kangshinmu* wears a long indigo blue skirt, *sŏpsu* (outer garment), and a *kŭn mŏri* (wig), while holding *ponhyangji* (ritual paper), *puch'ae* (ritual fan), and *panggul* (bell tree).

3. Pulsa/Chesŏk *Kŏri*

This *kŏri* is usually omitted during the *chinogwi*, a small-scale ritual held for the departed; however, if the ritual is held on a grand scale like the Seoul *Saenam Kut,* the Pulsa/Chesŏk *kŏri* is performed as part of the *andang sagyŏng maji kut*. Pulsa/Chesŏk *kŏri* is performed in place of *ch'ŏn'gung maji kŏri* of *ch'ŏnshin kut*. The main difference is that no *kangshinmu* will climb on and "ride" the *muldongi* (earthenware jar filled with water) during the Pulsa/Chesŏk *kŏri* during the *andang sagyŏng maji kut*.

4. Todang *Kŏri*

Unlike the Todang *kŏri* in the *ch'ŏnshin kut*, which is performed with twelve smaller *kŏri* (subsections), the Todang *kŏri* in the *andang sagyŏng maji kut* has only ten smaller *kŏri*. The two smaller *kŏri* that are omitted are the Todang Sanshin *kŏri* and Todang Yongshin *kŏri*.

If a ritual is held as a smaller scale *chinogwi* for the departed, the Todang *kŏri* is omitted entirely.

In the *ch'ŏnshin kut*, the Todang *kŏri* is followed by Ponhyang *kŏri*, but in the *andang sagyŏng maji kut*, the Ponhyang *kŏri* is omitted.

5. Chosang Kŏri

During *Chosang kŏri*, ancestors of the four previous generations (including parents and uncles and aunts, grandparents, great-grandparents, and great-great-grandparents) of the departed are honored. If the Seoul *Saenam Kut* is being held for a deceased *kangshinmu*, this *chosang kŏri* comes after the Sangsan *kŏri*.

Neither songs nor instrumental music are offered during this *kŏri*.

6–12. Sangsan *Kŏri* through *Twitchŏn Kŏri*

The next seven *kŏri*—Sangsan *kŏri*, Pyŏlsang *kŏri*, Shinjang *kŏri*, Taegam *kŏri*, Sŏngju *kŏri*, Ch'angbu *kŏri*, and *twitchŏn kŏri*—are performed basically the same in both the *ch'ŏnshin kut* and *andang sagyŏng maji kut* but on a smaller scale in the *andang sagyŏng maji kut* (see chapter 9).

Two important differences occur in Taegam *kŏri*. First, instead of the Momju Taegam (personal spirit for the living) in the *ch'ŏnshin kut*, the *kangshinmu* is possessed by Hajik Taegam, the spirit of the departed, in order for family members to bid farewell (*hajik*). Second, the sponsors and friends do not participate in a *mugam* (dance) during the *andang sagyŏng maji kut*.

A couple of differences occur in the last two *kŏri*. In the Ch'angbu *kŏri* of the *andang sagyŏng maji kut*, the *kangshinmu* does not offer rice cakes. In the *twitchŏn kŏri* of the *andang sagyŏng maji kut*, the Kajin Twitchŏn is not performed.

2. *Saenam Kut* (Second Part of Seoul *Saenam Kut*)

1. *Saenam Pujŏng Kŏri*

If the *saenam kut* is performed immediately following the *andang sagyŏng maji kut*, it begins with the *"Kamang Ch'ŏngbae"* song. But if the Seoul *Saenam Kut* is held as a two-day ritual and the second part takes place on the second day, the *saenam kut* will begin with the *saenam pujŏng kŏri*, inviting additional spirits—those from the other world as well as the *sajae*, spirits who guide the dead to the other world—informing them about the departed and the ritual sponsors. Then *"Kamang Noraekarak"* is sung with instrumental ensemble accompaniment.

2. *Chungdi Patsan*, Song for Chijang Posal

The *kangshinmu* sings a song called "*Chungdi Patsan*" intended especially for Chijang Posal (Sanskrit, Ksitigarbha), a Buddhist Bodhisattva who is believed to lead the dead safely to the other world.[4] This is a solo song by a *kangshinmu* who sits at the *changgu* (hourglass-shaped drum) and sings while accompanying himself or herself, calling for the spirits of the other world to come and aid the departed. The special feature of this song is in the interludes by an instrumental ensemble provided between verses. The rhythmic cycle used for this song is called *karaejo*. The *kangshinmu* completes this *kŏri* with the song "*Chungdi Noraekarak*." I heard this song for the first time at Kuksadang in March 1994 and thought it very poignant. Since *Chungdi Patsan* is rarely heard, I have included it on the accompanying CD (track 31).

3. Ttŭn Taewang (Sajae Samsŏng) *Kŏri*

Ttŭn Taewang is an honorific name for Sajae, also known as Saja—the spirits who come to guide the soul of the dead person to the other world. Sajae Samsŏng refers to three Sajae spirits, namely, Iljik Saja, Wŏljik Saja, and either Ch'ŏngjik Saja (if the deceased is young) or Hujik Saja (if the deceased is an elderly person).

Wearing an indigo blue skirt (*nam ch'ima*), a yellow outer garment (*mongduri*), and a large wig (*k'ŭn mŏri*), the *kangshinmu* sings "*Sajae Noraekarak*" and "*Chungdi Noraekarak*," followed by the "*Malmyŏng*" and "*Sajae Mansubaji*" duets.

After the duet, the *kangshinmu* makes a headband from hemp cloth (*sajae tari*) and wraps his or her head, placing paper flowers and *sajeji* (paper with money enclosed) in the headband. The *kangshinmu* tries to lighten the scene of the ritual even briefly by making *chaedam* (witty remarks) to the grieving family members (see plate 41).

The *kangshinmu* wraps a long thin piece of hemp cloth about his or her waist and around a *kŏn taegu* (dried, flattened cod), offering it as a symbolic seat for the dead to ride on to the other world. The other world is believed to be beyond a body of water. The *kangshinmu* as a psychopomp, a guide of souls to the other world, ties the dried cod on his or her back in order to carry the departed across the water to the other world (see plate 42).

The *kangshinmu* dances, gives *kongsu* (messages from the spirits), and sings "*Sajae T'aryŏng*." The *kangshinmu* calls for Sajae Samsŏng (three spirits mentioned above), asking them to take the soul of the dead safely to other world.

---

[4] Chijang Posal is Ksitigarbha, the Bodhisattva associated with death and the Underworld, known as Jizo in Japan and Ti-tsang in China.

The *kangshinmu* bids farewell here to various lowly spirits including Sŏnang, Yŏngsan, Sangmun, and Subi.

4. *Malmi Kŏri*

"*Pari Kongju*" (literally, abandoned princess) is a ritual epic song, sung during *musok* rituals throughout the Korean peninsula. *Pari Kongju* has been transmitted for generations in about fifty versions known as *Pari Tegi, Pŏri Tŏgi, Ch'il Kongju, Malmi*, and so on. In Seoul and the neighboring Kyŏnggi province *musok* rituals, *Pari Kongju* is known as *Malmi* (CD track 33).

"*Pari Kongju*" ("*Malmi*") is sung in both *chinogwi*, a ritual held for the departed among the general populace, as well as during Seoul *Saenam kut* held for the departed among the wealthy upper classes. It is rare to hear the entire song during the rituals nowadays because many contemporary *kangshinmu* shorten the song to accommodate its allotted time within the rituals. It is also sad to realize the fact that few *kangshinmu* know the song, which takes nearly two hours to perform in its entirety.[5]

"*Pari Kongju*" ("*Malmi*") and "*Hwangje P'uri*" are the two most important epic style sacred songs of Hanyang *kut*.[6] "*Pari Kongju*" ("*Malmi*") is sung for the departed, while "*Hwangje P'uri*" is sung during the *chaesu kut* held to usher in good fortune for the ritual's sponsors and their families. If one wishes to be recognized as a great *kangshinmu* in the Hanyang *kut*, he or she has to know both songs.

The story of "*Pari Kongju*" ("*Malmi*") is narrated and sung with several short stock melodies. A very brief outline of "*Pari Kongju*" ("*Malmi*") from Yi Sang-Sun's version is provided here. It must be remembered, however, that even Koreans find it difficult to understand the song text because it uses many obscure words and expressions.

The Story of Pari Kongju

The story of *Pari Kongju* begins with the great King at Sŏnhye Palace asking a diviner to choose an auspicious year for his prince's wedding date. The

---

[5] Yi Sang-Sun, the government-designated assistant responsible for transmission and training of Important Intangible Cultural Property no. 104, Seoul *Saenam Kut*, produced a recording of the entire *Pari Kongju* (*Malmi*) ritual epic song on a set of two CDs in 1999 (Asia Record) with the hope that it would become a valuable reference for her colleagues as well as for scholars who are interested in *musok* and *muak* (ritual music).

[6] Yi Sang-Sun produced a set of two CDs of *Hwangje P'uri* in 1995 on the Asia Record label.

diviner informs the King that if the wedding takes place that year, the couple will have seven daughters, but the couple would have sons if they were to marry the following year.

Disregarding the remark, the Prince gets married during that year and the couple produces six daughters. Each time they have a baby girl, they hope for a son to be born the next time. But when they realize that the seventh baby is also a girl, the couple is so upset that they decide to abandon the child. They name the baby "Pŏri degi" (literally, "the abandoned"), wrap her in cloth, place her in a jade box, and send her downstream on the Ch'ŏngch'ŏn River. An old couple named Piri Kongdŏk notice the floating box, find the baby in it, and raise the child as their own. Fifteen years later, the King and Queen, the parents of Pari Kongju (Abandoned Princess), become seriously ill. While the whole nation worries, Ch'ŏnghae Tongja, a messenger from the Blue Ocean, appears and informs people how to get sacred water to heal the King and Queen. Since it is believed that the sacred water is to be found only in the land of the dead, no one including the first six daughters offers to fetch it. As their last hope, they look for the seventh princess and find her still alive in the woods.

Asked if she would help, Pari Kongju says, "I am not really indebted to my parents or to the nation, but since my mother had me in her womb for ten months, I will go even if I might die trying." She disguises herself as a male and starts off. After many years of trials and hardship, she manages to find the sacred water. On her way back to the palace, she encounters the bier of her parents. She sprinkles the sacred water on them and they come to life again. When the parents of Pari Kongju offer to grant any of Pari Kongju's wishes, she expresses her desire to become a shaman to help and lead the departed from this world to the next, wearing *ŭnha monduri* (ritual clothing) and *k'ŭn mŏri* (decorated wig) while holding the *pangul* (bell tree) and *puch'ae* (ritual fan) (see plate 20).

Pari Kongju, *Ritual Song*

In *musok,* "*Pari Kongju*" is considered an indispensable ritual song for the dead because of its symbolic power to transport the deceased to the next world. It is believed that the departed may safely reach the fine place beyond this world by listening to the entire song of "*Pari Kongju.*" Families, relatives, and friends gather at the ritual, pray for the dead, and listen to this song, believing that Princess Pari Kongju is safely guiding the beloved to the other world.

The *kangshinmu* who sings "*Pari Kongju*" in Hanyang *kut* wears a *hong sŭran* (long red skirt), puts on an *ŭnha monduri* (floor-length ritual garment with long sleeves), and places a *k'ŭn mŏri* (ceremonial wig decorated with many jewels) and *karuma* (crown) on his or her head. *Paksu*, male *kangshinmu* (spirit-possessed shamans), wear the same ritual clothes while singing this *Pari Kongju*

(*Malmi*) song, just as female *kangshinmu* are required to wear male ritual costumes when they are possessed by male warrior spirits (see plate 6).

"*Pari Kongju*" is sung by the *kangshinmu* who accompanies himself or herself on *changgu* (hourglass-shaped drum) and *pangul* (bell tree) (CD track 33). In a small-scale *chinogwi* ritual, the *changgu* is placed in front of the presiding shaman who sits on the floor to sing. The shaman will play only one head (*kung p'yŏn*) of the *changgu* using a *kunggul ch'ae* (wooden drumstick) in the right hand while shaking the bell tree intermittently with the left hand. The *kung p'yŏn* is usually on the left side but in this case the *changgu* is turned around so that it is on the right.

As mentioned earlier, the shaman sits on a chair to sing "*Pari Kongju*." Placing a *ching* (large gong) on the floor in front of the chair first, the *kangshinmu* leans the *changgu* with one head (*ch'ae p'yŏn*) against the *ching* and secures the other head (*kung p'yŏn*) with the knees. While seated on the chair, the *kangshinmu* shakes the bell tree with the left hand and plays the drum on the *kung p'yŏn* with a *kung ch'ae* held in the right. The *hansam* (white sleeve extensions worn over wrists), *hong tti* (red embroidered belt), and *shink'al* (pair of ritual knives) are all attached to the *changgu* while *Pari Kongju* is sung in both the *chinogwi* and Seoul *Saenam kut* rituals.

In front of the drum, a table is placed on which rice is piled up, two candles are lit, and incense burns. Next to the table, a set of *hanbok* (traditional Korean clothing) and a pair of shoes belonging to the departed are placed (see plate 43).

While "*Pari Kongju*" is sung, a *saebal shimji* (small candle in the shape of a bird's foot, also known as *sebal shimji* for its three-pronged shape) is placed on top of the rice pile and lit. The *saebal shimji* is made of a long piece of white paper. The paper is first twisted to make a thin strip, then shaped into a three-footed (*sebal*) candle.

At the end of "*Pari Kongju*" the *kangshinmu* repeats prayers—"Namu Amit'abul (Sanskrit: namo' mitāyasebuddhāya)"—in *hwimori changdan*. This prayer, borrowed from the Buddhist tradition, is said in order to assist the departed to return safely to Amit'abul, the Buddha (see CD end of track 33).

At the end of the song, the *saebal shimji* (candle) is removed and family members look for traces left by the departed on the pile of rice. Discovering faint traces and interpreting them, families find comfort in knowing how their beloved has been transformed into another being.

The clothing and shoes of the departed are taken from the floor beside the offering table and placed on top of a straw mat (*totchari*) covered with two sheets. The two sheets symbolize bedding (*yo*) and covers (*ibul*), respectively. If the departed is a man, the red sheet is laid first on the straw mat, then clothing and shoes, and then the blue sheet on top. If the ritual is held for a woman, the blue sheet is laid first and the red sheet is used for covering. The whole set, referred to as *tossam*, will be carried by the family members during the following *kŏri* known as *pat toryŏng* (see plate 44).

5. Pat Toryŏng

For this *kŏri*, a gate decorated with five colors (blue, green, red, white, and yellow) is set on the ground (see plate 44). The gate, known as *kashimun* (literally, gate of thorns), represents the path that the departed has to cross in order to enter into the other world. The thorns in *kashimun* suggest the difficulty in crossing the gate. This *kŏri* is known as *pat toryŏng* as it takes place outside (*pat* or *pakk*) of the other world, before the soul can cross the gate into the other world.[7]

For *pat toryŏng*, the *kangshinmu* is dressed in the elegant ritual garment of Pari Kongju. The *kangshinmu* rolls up the first *mujigyŏn ch'ima* (underskirt) with a *kalmae maktaegi* (stick) placing the roll above the waist in order to provide fullness to the skirts. He or she puts on the second *mujigyŏn ch'ima*, *nam suran* (a long blue skirt), and *hong suran* (a long red skirt). The *kangshinmu* then puts on a *tangŭi* (long blouse fashioned after a Tang court garment) and a yellow *ŭnha mongduri* (outer garment), tying them with a *taetti* (embroidered red belt). The *kangshinmu* adds a *k'ŭn mŏri* (a large wig) and *karuma* (top part of the hair decoration) on their head, puts on a *saekdong hansam* (long multi-colored sleeve extensions) on their wrists, picks up the ritual fan and the bell tree, and begins to sing "Nŏk Noraekarak," a solo song, and *mansubaji*, a duet.

The *kangshinmu* dances slowly from the Yŏnjidang—a small altar where Chijang Posal's picture is placed (see plate 45)[8]—toward the *kashimun* gate and circumambulates the gate seven times.

Three sets of dances—*son* (hand) *toryŏng*,[9] *puch'ae* (ritual fan) *toryŏng*, and *k'al* (ritual knife) *toryŏng*—are performed while the *kangshinmu* circumambulates the *kashimun* seven times. For *son toryŏng*, the *kangshinmu* dances with elaborate hand (*son*) gestures and circumambulates the *kashimun* three times. Then the *kangshinmu* dances *puch'ae toryŏng* with the ritual fan (*puch'ae*), circumambulating the *kashimun* three times. For the last time, the *kangshinmu* circumambulates the *kashimun* once dancing *k'al toryŏng* holding the *shink'al* (ritual knives).

Family members follow the *kangshinmu*, holding candles, the *yŏngjŏng* (portrait of the departed), *wip'ae* (wooden tablets),[10] incense, a small offering table, and the *tossam*, which contains clothing and shoes of the departed between red and blue sheets. The *nŏkchŏn* (figure made of white paper where

---

[7] *Toryŏng* comes from *toryang* or *tojang* (道場) referring to a designated ritual or study area in Buddhist temples.

[8] For more about Chijang Posal, see the *Chungdi Patsan* section above.

[9] *Son toryŏng* is also known as *hansam toryŏng*.

[10] *Wip'ae* (wooden tablets) are inscribed with the name of the departed and information about the family genealogy.

the soul of the departed is resting) is placed on top of the *tossam*, then the *tossam* is lifted and carried by four people following the *kangshinmu*'s lead.

The *kangshinmu* dances in an elegant and deliberate style, advancing three steps forward and retreating one step backward, leading the entourage through the long symbolic journey. For the circumambulation, the instrumental ensemble plays *kutkŏri*, *pyŏlsang*, *kil kunak*, *kil t'aryŏng*, and *chajin kutkŏri* (CD tracks 36-38). This ritual circumambulation symbolizes Pari Kongju's escorting the departed to the other world.

6. *Mun Tŭrum* and *Yŏngshil*

The *kangshinmu* reaches the *kashimun*, the gate to the other world, to talk to the official *mun sajae* (gatekeeper), a *kangshinmu* dressed in *chŏnbok* (tunic) with flowers on the head (see plate 46). The gatekeeper plays cymbals as he or she speaks and demands a fee for the key and the services of opening the gates. A considerable amount of bribing the gatekeeper is necessary to get permission to pass the *kashimun* to the other world.

Once the *kangshinmu* passes the gate (*mun tŭrum*), a roll of hemp known as *tidil pe* (literally, stepping cloth) is laid for them to walk on toward the Yŏnjidang, the altar where the Spirit of Chijang Posal is believed to reside (see plate 47).

The *kangshinmu*, supported by sponsors on both sides, enters through the gate, carrying a table on which a *sanja* (symbolic seal) and a bolt of silk for Chijang Posal are laid, as well as a piece of paper containing the name and address of the deceased. The *kangshinmu* pleads the case for the departed at the Yŏnjidang to Chijang Posal and asks him to look after the departed. Family members then have another chance to converse with the dead person as the *kangshinmu* becomes possessed by the soul of the departed. This is the second time the dead person appears to talk with the family. It is referred to as *wŏn yŏngshil*.[11]

7. *An Toryŏng*

Now that the *kangshinmu* has crossed the *kashimun* and entered the other world, this *kŏri* is considered to be happening inside (*an*) the other world. Led by the *kangshinmu*, the same entourage of family members follows and circumambulates the offering table twelve times, symbolizing the long journey the departed must take. Above a large offering table, long cloths known as *osaek*

---

[11] *Wŏn yŏngshil* is also referred to as *pon yŏngshil*.

kurŭmtari (literally, five-colored cloud bridge) are stretched out, symbolizing a bridge from this world to the other world.

Four sets of dances—*nabi* (butterfly) *toryŏng*, *son* (hand) *toryŏng*, *puch'ae* (fan) *toryŏng*, and *k'al* (knife) *toryŏng*—are performed by the *kangshinmu*, circumambulating three times for each set of dance, accompanied by the instrumental music of *kutkŏri, kil kunak*, and *chajin kutkŏri* (CD tracks 36-38).

8. *Tossam Kŏri*

Six *kangshinmu* begin this *kŏri*. Four *kangshinmu* hold the corners of the *tossam* (red and blue sheets containing clothes of the departed), while the fifth *kangshinmu* throws ritual knives (*shink'al*) over the *tossam* to another *kangshinmu* who catches them (see figure 47).[12] The four then lift the *tossam* and the principal *kangshinmu* performs *tossam tolgi* (ritual circumambulation around the *tossam*) (see plate 48).

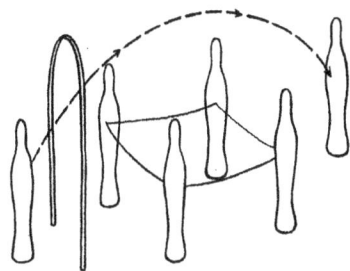

Figure 47. *Tossam Kŏri* and Ritual Knives. While four people each hold one corner of the *tossam*, the *kangshinmu* throws the ritual knives (*shink'al*) over the cloth to another *kangshinmu* who catches them.

The *kangshinmu* walks underneath the *tossam*. If the departed is male, the *kangshinmu* will go through the center and then turn to the right and come back to the starting point, outlining a figure eight (8), or the symbol for infinity (∞), each time. If the departed is female, the *kangshinmu* will turn to the left and return (see figure 48).

---

[12] The knives are not sharp.

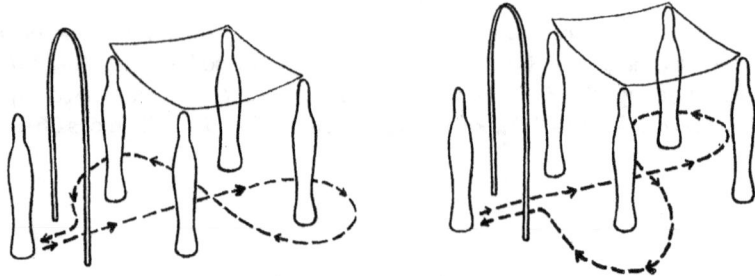

Figure 48. *Tossam* Dance. The path of the *kangshinmu* for *tossam* dance is different for a male deceased (left) and for a female deceased (right).

The *kangshinmu* repeats the figure eight (8) or infinity symbol (∞) outline of the *tossam* dance twice and then dances away from the gate and through the midway, revolving three times (see figure 49).

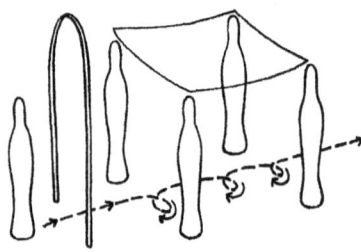

Figure 49. Ending *Tossam Kŏri*

Two *kangshinmu* then begin to sing a duet called "*Matchoa*." The principal *kangshinmu* sings holding the ritual fan and the bell tree, standing on one side of the *kashimun* gate, while the responding *kangshinmu* sings holding *sanja* (rice cookies) and *nŏkchŏn* (symbolic paper sculpture where the soul rests), standing on the other side of the gate, symbolizing the two worlds of the living and the dead separated by the *kashimun*.

9. Sangshik Kŏri

Sangshik kŏri is where a meal is offered to the departed. This kŏri amply illustrates the importance of the ancestor ritual, *chesa*, in *musok*. Most of the food offerings are dishes enjoyed by the deceased during his or her lifetime including *kimch'i*, most Koreans' favorite dish of fermented vegetables. Food and wine offerings are made also to those ancestors who had not previously received a *chinogwi kut* or *saenam kut*. During the *sangshik kŏri*, the *kangshinmu* sits on a chair and sings "*Myŏngdu Ch'ŏngbae*" while another *kangshinmu* provides *changgu* accompaniment.

10. Twi Yŏngshil Kŏri

The soul of the deceased possesses the *kangshinmu* after the *sangshik kŏri* and bids the last farewell (*twi yŏngshil*) to the family members. Picking up the *nŏkchŏn* (symbolic paper sculpture where the soul rests) with a ritual knife, the *kangshinmu* places it around the back of the neck and puts the dead person's clothing over the shoulder and sings "*Nŏk Noraekarak*."

11. Pe Karŭgi

Pe Karŭgi (literally, cutting the hemp) is a ceremonial act of bidding a formal farewell to the departed. The *kangshinmu* wears a *hong ch'ŏnik* (red outer garment) and *k'ŭn mŏri* (wig) and wraps himself or herself with a long hemp cloth. Four *kangshinmu* lift up the four corners of two long cloths, one cotton and one hemp, a long symbolic "road" from this world to the other world. Cotton cloth (*mumyŏng*) and hemp (*pe*) symbolize this world and the other, respectively. The principal *kangshinmu* splits the cloths in half with his or her body (see plate 49), holding the ritual knives (*shink'al*), which dispel negative forces and are believed to have the "magical power to comfort dead souls" (Cho H.Y. 1990:81). By splitting the cloths, this world is separated from the other world. *This kŏri* is also known as *Kil Karŭgi* (literally, separation of the roads).

12. Shiwang Kunung Kŏri

Shiwang Kunung Kŏri is the final *kŏri* of Seoul *Saenam Kut*. *Shiwang* is short for *Shiptaewang*, ten kings of *myŏngbu* (literally, dark regions).[13] *Shiwang*

---

[13] The *Shiptaewang* are: Chin'gwang Taewang, Ch'ogang Taewang, Sŏngje Taewang, Ogwan Taewang, Yŏmra Taewang, Pyŏnsŏng Taewang, T'aesan Taewang,

Kunung are guardian spirits who protect the soul from the *Shiwang* (ten kings), allowing the soul to avoid the dark regions and to reach the other world safely. The *kangshinmu*, wearing *hong ch'ŏnik* (red outerwear) and *kat* (black hat), holds the ritual fan in the right hand and dried pollack (*pukŏ*) in the left while singing another version of "*Nŏk Noraekarak*," concluding the Seoul *Saenam Kut* (CD track 34).

There is no *twitchŏn kŏri* for Seoul *Saenam Kut* because the *kangshinmu* has already sent away the uninvited and wandering spirits earlier during the *Ttŭn Taewang kŏri*.

P'yŏngdŭng Taewang, Toshi Taewang, and Odo Chŏnryun Taewang. Each king rules one designated hell: Chin'gwang Taewang rules the *hanbing chiok* (icy frozen hell); Ch'ogang Taewang, the *kŭmsu chiok* (hell filled with fierce animals); Sŏngje Taewang, the *kŏhae chiok* (hell filled with water); Ogwan Taewang, the *hangma chiok* (hell filled with devils); Yŏmra Taewang, the *toksa chiok* (hell filled with venomous serpents); Pyŏnsŏng Taewang, the *paksŏl chiok* (hell where the tongue is removed); T'aesan Taewang, the *amhŭk chiok* (hell of darkness); P'yŏngdŭng Taewang, the *ch'ŏlgang chiok* (hell made of sharp spikes); Toshi Taewang, the *p'ungsu chiok* (hell filled with wind and water); and Odo Chŏnryun Taewang, *hwat'ang chiok* (hell burning with fire).

Conclusion

While studying the Hanyang *kut,* I also attended other types of rituals conducted by ritual specialists from various regions of Korea, noticing similarities and differences. Many special features of the Hanyang *kut* that I observed reflect the court customs of the Chosŏn Dynasty (1392–1910).

Hanyang, the capital of the Chosŏn Dynasty since 1394, was the center of politics and culture. Despite the fact that shamans were not allowed to reside within the walls of Hanyang, some shamans were invited by members of the royalty to operate within the confined areas of the royal palace, as indicated in historical writings.

In present-day Seoul, the Hanyang *kut* is presented with ritual clothing, food offerings, music, and dance reflecting many of the court traditions of the Chosŏn Dynasty. Most of the ritual costumes are fashioned after the upper class courtier's clothing or military uniforms. Musical instruments used in the Hanyang *kut* are those used in court music. For example, the *changgu* (hourglass-shaped drum) and *taegŭm* (transverse flute) used in the Hanyang *kut* are the same as the ones used for *chŏngak* (court music),[1] unlike the *minsok* (folk) *changgu* and *taegŭm* used in other rituals throughout the peninsula. *Noraekarak* songs are sung only in the Hanyang *kut,* with the *changgu* accompaniment in *changdan* (rhythmic cycles) similar to those used for the *shijo* songs enjoyed by the upper classes. Ritual musicians (*chaebi*) for the Hanyang *kut* are sometimes referred to as *chŏnak,* the term used during the Chosŏn Dynasty to refer to court musicians. During the Hanyang *kut* they perform a repertoire of court and upper class music. For example, they play *Chajin Hwanip,* known in the court as *Kŏsangak,* as well as pieces from the *p'ungryu* music enjoyed by the upper classes.

Studying *musok* in the field, I have also observed a few features shared by *musok* and Inner Asian shamanism. For instance, initiatory sickness is customarily experienced by the *kangshinmu* (Korean spirit-possessed shamans) as well as by the shamans of Inner Asia. Once initiated, the neophyte shamans

---

[1] *Chŏngak* refers to music of the court and upper classes (*yangban*).

usually learn ritual songs and ritual techniques from their teachers. Most Korean shamans also learn from their *shin pumo* (spirit parents), but some carry on shamanic activities, including divination and rituals, following the spirits' instructions.

Korean and Inner Asian shamans have altars in their homes for offerings and they wear special clothing for rituals. Some of the Korean shaman's hats have feathers like those placed in some Inner Asian shamans headbands. Peacock feathers or *hosu* (tiger's white whiskers) are used for decoration of the ritual hats worn by Hanyang *kut* shamans (see plates 4 and 5). Korean terms like *paksu* and *mudang* referring to Korean shamans appear to share the same meanings as *baxsi* and *ootan*[2] in Inner Asia.

Shamans, including Korean *kangshinmu*, are regarded as healers and ritual specialists. On behalf of clients, shamans pray and hold rituals to communicate with the spirits in order to mediate ways to restore health or to overcome difficulties in life. Most shamans sing and dance to please spirits during their rituals with the accompaniment of a drum.[3] The importance of ritual drumming is shared by nearly all shamans.

Throughout the Hanyang *kut*, the *changgu* is played by a shaman who strikes the two heads of the drum with two sticks. However, when the shaman sings a long epic song during a ritual, he or she uses only one head of the *changgu*, striking it with a wooden mallet wrapped at the end with soft cloth, similar to Inner Asian shamans' drumsticks wrapped with soft furs. This musical practice of using a single head of the *changgu* in Korea is limited to the *musok* rituals in sacred context. Observing this musical practice in *musok* rituals prompts me to hypothesize that the Korean shamans' use of a single drumhead is related to the Inner Asian shamans' practice of using a single-headed frame drum for their ritual songs.

In addition to the drum, the metallic sounds of bell trees are used by Korean shamans for their ritual songs and dances. This, too, is similar to the Inner Asian shamans' musical practice of attaching jingling metal pieces to their drums, ritual clothing, or belts worn either over the neck or around the waist. Inner Asian shamans shake their drums and move their hips while singing and dancing or shake their upper bodies during trance producing metallic sounds. Based on these observations, I would like to suggest that it is reasonable to regard the Korean peninsula as an extended area where classic shamanism is practiced (see figure 50).

---

[2] *Baxsi* and *ootan* are discussed in chapter 2.

[3] Anna-Leena Siikala finds that one shared technique in shaman rituals throughout Siberia and Central Asia is rhythmic drumming, singing, and dancing. Those who do not use drums in certain regions are considered to be an exception to the rule (1987:44–45).

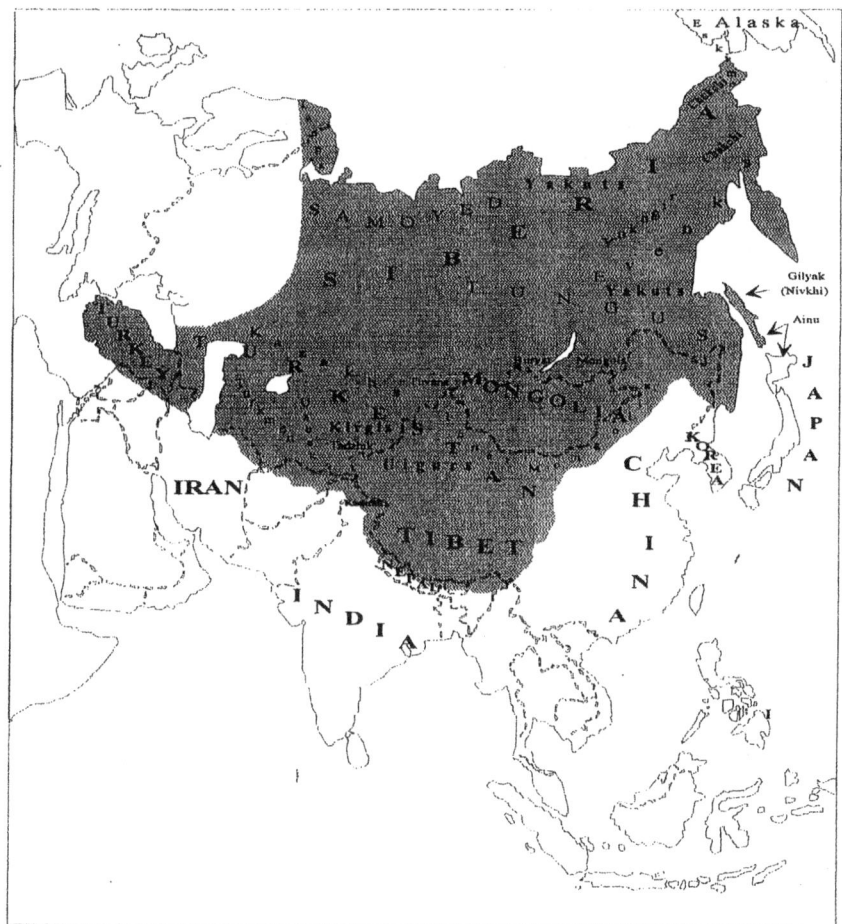

Figure 50. Map of "Classic Shamanism Areas in Asia" by Ter Ellingson

Ritual songs like *"Pujŏng Ch'ŏngbae"* and *"Kamang Ch'ŏngbae"* in the Hanyang *kut* are long prayers sung by repeating and varying several short melodies like those of the Inner Asian shaman's ritual songs, but song texts and melodies are uniquely Korean, for each music system is one way the people of a given culture conceptualize and express their world.

In China, where the *yin/yang* concept dominates, their worldview is expressed in the predominantly duple meters of their music. As Mingyue Liang observes,

> The duple rhythmic practice is culturally related in the cosmological principle of duality which is most evident in the yin-yang concept and associated

phenomenon such as moon-sun, negative-positive, etc. They likewise have their correspondences in architecture and the visual arts. (Liang 1985:25)

Discussing Venda music in South Africa, John Blacking points out that music can be analyzed and understood as tonal expressions of human experience in the context of different kinds of social and cultural organization. He provides an example of different ways in which one, two, or three drummers may produce the same surface structure of music (1973:28-31). He explains further that

> performance by combinations of two or three players of rhythms that can in fact be played by one are not musical gimmicks: they express concepts of individuality in community, and of social, temporal, and spatial balance, which are found in other features of Venda culture and other types of Venda music. (Blacking 1973:30)

In Kpelle music of Liberia, "the concept of many voices coming together as one" reveals itself in various types of multi-part musical styles including the use of hocketing (Schmidt 1984:195). Hocketing is "a practice of breaking up one melodic line through the performance of successive short fragments distributed among several players" (Hood 1971:232).

While Chinese conceptualize their world through the *yin/yang* principle (Korean *ŭm/yang*), Koreans incorporate humans as the important factor in their world filled with *ŭm/yang* elements. For example, the left head of a *changgu* drum symbolizes earth (*ŭm*), while the right one symbolizes heaven (*yang*). A *changgu* is an instrument with *ŭm/yang* components, but the full potential of *changgu* is appreciated only if a human being strikes the heads of the drum to produce sound.

This concept of three elements—*ŭm* (earth), *yang* (heaven), and humans—is expressed in the triple meters predominant in Korean music including folk, court, and *musok* ritual music. The underlying feeling of triple meters stems from the three *tchok* (literally, three sections) filling up each beat of Korean *changdan* (rhythmic cycles), expressed most frequently in *hap*, *k'ung*, and *ttak* strokes and their variations on the *changgu*. I suggest that the triple *tchok* inherent in every beat manifests the essence of the Korean worldview musically. The triple *tchok* moves constantly forward, changes, and balances the three important components.

The essence of the Korean worldview—balancing the three elements of heaven, earth, and humans—is expressed not only in music but also in visual arts, crafts, and dance. The three elements (heaven, earth, and humans) are often expressed visually in *sam t'aegŭk* or *hoeori param munyang*. *T'aegŭk* refers to the Great Absolute or Great Ultimate in Chinese philosophy, which is considered to be the source of the dual principle of *yin* and *yang*. The concept is visually expressed in Korea by the circle divided into two sections representing *yin* in blue and *yang* in red. This visual representation is referred to as *ssang* (literally, twin, i.e. dual) *t'aegŭk* in Korea. To reflect the Korean worldview of three elements, the *t'aegŭk* is also expressed as one circle but divided into three sections: red for heaven (*yang*), blue for earth (*ŭm*), and yellow for people (*in*). This visual representation is called *sam* (literally, triple) *t'aegŭk* (see plate 50).

Hoeori param munyang (literally, whirlwind pattern) has been used in folk arts and crafts. It appears to be similar to the symbol *man*, 卍, but it is different because each of the four arms has three line segments rather than two (see figure 51).

Figure 51. *Hoeori Param Munyang* (Whirlwind Pattern)

In Korea, the *kangshinmu* (spirit-possessed shamans) call spirits into their bodies during rituals. Their souls do not leave their bodies to travel to an upper or lower world as do shamans in other traditions. Based on hearsay, my family had warned me when I was six years old to keep quiet during the shaman's trance so that the *mudang*'s soul might return to his or her body during the *kut*. My mother who is now in her mid-eighties tells me that my family did not know the difference between soul journey and spirit possession at that time.

Korean shamans do not induce possession or trance states using hallucinogenic substances or offering tobacco to the spirits as is done in some other traditions. Korean shamans may give a pack of cigarettes as a gift to invited shamans, musicians, and guests. Some people have noticed Korean shamans drinking from little bottles during the rituals and several people have asked me why. The little bottles are filled with caffeinated drinks. Many people drink them to recover from fatigue at rituals as well as in other social settings.

In present-day Korea, few rituals are held in private homes, leading most people to think that *musok* is no longer practiced in contemporary Korea. But rituals held in *kuttang* (ritual halls) located on the outskirts of many cities are numerous and the number is increasing. I think it is easier for clients to sponsor a *kut* nowadays because the rituals are held privately away from their own homes and neighbors. In earlier days, the sponsoring family members prepared ritual offerings and food for guests at their home where the ritual took place. Neighbors came and participated in the ritual by sharing food and blessings. During the *kut*, shamans deliver *kongsu* (messages from spirits) to sponsors, often of a personal nature. When departed relatives possess shamans to communicate with surviving members of the family, neighbors might discover family secrets and rumors often get started. But nowadays food offerings are prepared by workers at the *kuttang* (ritual halls) and rituals may be held without one's neighbors knowing about it. I think this secured privacy is one of the factors contributing to the increase in the number of *kut*.

Shamanism, in the contemporary world, is considered by many to be a dying primitive tradition, but in the modern nation state of Korea the number of *kangshinmu* (spirit-possessed shamans) is growing. *Kangshinmu,* who are known to adapt well to any given situation, flourish nowadays utilizing modern technology. For example, dozens of *kangshinmu* offer divination and creation of talismans online from their own homepages on the internet. Some web sites advertise individual *kangshinmu*, providing photographs, biographies, and information about their specialties, as well as telephone numbers and addresses, including maps and directions to their residences.

Another thing to note is the increasing number of shamans. In earlier days, *kangshinmu* were initiated primarily in the northern part of the Korean peninsula, north of the Han River, but this is no longer true. Many spirit-possessed shamans are now being initiated throughout Korea. Even in the areas once known as *sesŭpmu tan'gol p'an* (hereditary *mudang* area), people have become more interested in hearing what the spirits have to say through *kangshinmu*. Some *mudang* choose to learn from *sesŭpmu* teachers in various regional styles of rituals, but others come to Seoul to learn from *kangshinmu* who specialize in Hanyang *kut*, Hwanghae Province *kut*, or P'yŏngan Province *kut*.

At times I have noticed that shamans who teach other shamans do not share their core knowledge and do not reveal significant techniques in order to protect their own prominence, which is reflected in their earning power. As Richard Mitchell suggests in his discussion of fieldwork, the key to successful fieldwork depends on a "special awareness of how all social actors, researchers included, choreograph concealment and disclosure" (1992:v). Shamans and musicians are constantly negotiating boundaries, guarding their ritual skills and knowledge carefully. Therefore, learning experiences for neophyte shamans as well as scholars in the field are slow and often frustrating.

Most shamans and musicians told me that they generally do not share anything important with anyone who comes around only once or twice. But when I had to ask the same question to the same shaman seven times over several years to get yet another new answer each time, I felt terribly dissatisfied. Each time we had talked during the past nine years, the shaman was aware that our conversations were being recorded. But when this shaman insisted that the seventh answer was the correct one, I could not help remembering our previous talks. I reminded the shaman of our sixth talk and how she had then also said that was the correct answer, but that did not help any. I had no choice but to wonder what the eighth answer might be, and I intend to pursue this inquiry. With modern recording technology, several government organizations and researchers have recorded wonderful performances presented as "the authentic rituals" by several shamans; however, my field experience makes me wonder whether a true authentic ritual in its entirety could be enjoyed by a public audience.

I have been assisting Yi Sang-Sun in compiling a manual for the Seoul *Saenam Kut*. Yi, a *kangshinmu*, is well respected for her performance skills and knowledge of the rituals. Yi has been designated by the government as the *chŏnsu kyoyuk pojoja* (assistant responsible for transmission and education) of the Seoul *Saenam Kut*, a type of Hanyang *kut*. The manuscript contains a large amount of information about *musok* practice. For example, Yi not only shows how to set the offering tables for spirits for large-scale rituals on different occasions, she also gives instructions for how to make offerings at home. She explains the symbolism of food offerings, ritual garments, song texts, and dance steps from the different schools of the Hanyang *kut* tradition. For this work, I have introduced the framework of *ch'ŏnshin kut* and Seoul *Saenam Kut*, but did not reveal many of the esoteric meanings I had learned from Yi, respecting her wishes to publish the work after she is designated by the government as the *poyuja* (designated performer) of the Important Intangible Cultural Property number 104, Seoul *Saenam Kut*.[4]

I feel an obligation to negotiate between the knowledge I have gained through fieldwork and the degree of disclosure to be made to others. Perhaps I am experiencing in part "the power secrecy confers and the burden it imposes," as noted by Sissela Bok (1982:xv). In the field, the help of informants for research projects is invaluable. But scholars must sort out the findings of fieldwork, distinguishing their own interpretations from those of the informants, as well as striving to overcome "their own assumptions, their own received wisdom, their own culturally conditioned viewpoint, in order to understand as clearly as possible the viewpoint of those they study" (Carrithers 1992:3).

As a native Korean, I did not expect to have any difficulty in communicating with Koreans but I was challenged to read between the lines in many situations and to avoid misunderstanding or being misunderstood, because Koreans frequently use what anthropologist Stephen Tyler calls "metamessages" (Tyler 1969:18). Tyler gives the example of how an apparently simple sentence like "it's cold in here" could mean "bring me my coat," "turn up the heat," or "you've had enough to drink and it's time to go home." The most difficult part of working with shamans for me was trying to decipher what they truly meant.

The present work, written in English, is based on fieldwork that involved communicating in Korean. Whenever I found no corresponding terms, phrases, or concepts between the two languages, I had to struggle to describe the meanings of the indigenous Korean terms for English readers. In searching for the meanings of many obscure, obsolete, or corrupted words used in *musok*, I found some but others remain unclear.

Dissatisfied with the use of foreign terms like *"musok," "mugyo,"* or "shamanism" for the Korean indigenous religion, some people have begun a movement to call it *"kut."* Observing about three hundred *kangshinmu* agreeing

---

[4] As a rule, the government designates the *chŏnsu kyoyuk pojoja* as the next *poyuja*.

to call it "*kut*" in a meeting (April 2000), I could see the potential for this term to become more widespread.

During my fieldwork, I have experienced a great deal of resistance from community people on both sides—those who are involved in *musok* and those who are not. Those involved in *musok* did not want to have an outsider looking in, while those who considered *musok* to be superstition (*mishin*) did not want me to get involved.

Some of my friends and acquaintances who objected to my interest in *musok* at the initial stage slowly came around, asking me to show them *musok* video clips or explain just what is actually going on. Several friends wanted me to take them to rituals, so I did invite them to public ritual performances put on by shamans. Afterwards several friends wished to attend *kut* in sacred context. Some are amazed I am still all right after all these years. A couple of my Christian friends told me that I had been saved because of their prayers.

I am still a Catholic. *Kangshinmu* and musicians I worked with all knew me as a Catholic. Some appreciated the fact that a Catholic cared enough to study *musok*. Others were suspicious at the beginning but came around to accept me. No *kangshinmu* suggested that I sponsor a *kut* or convert.[5] I must admit that it was a lot easier for me to be with *kangshinmu* and ritual musicians than with my Protestant friends who continually criticized my Catholic faith, pressuring me to convert to the Protestant faith.

Since the Korean government has designated several *musok* rituals as Important Intangible Cultural Properties in recent decades, the rituals have begun to serve as a resource in strengthening cultural, ethnic, and national identity. Many Koreans have found the roots of their arts, crafts, music, dance, food, clothing, customs, and beliefs in them. I met an artist who had changed his family name from "Kim" to "Mu" to convey his conviction that *mu* is the origin of Korean culture. The feelings among most Koreans toward *musok* are at best ambivalent. Some Koreans regard *musok* as a source for their ethnicity but feel uncomfortable acknowledging any of its religious elements. Some Koreans turn to shamans when desperate, but carry on with life before and afterwards without any further involvement in *musok*. Others regularly offer prayers alongside shamans and seek help from the spirits to find peace, health, and wealth for their families.

From my life's experiences, I have learned that people in general are apprehensive of what they do not understand. Fear of *musok* among people has been escalated by different degrees of "ignorance (absent knowledge), mysteries (inaccessible knowledge), and secrets (denied knowledge)" (Mitchell 1992:v). Nine years ago, I began my fieldwork among Korean shamans with considerable anxiety. I was afraid of being spirit-possessed, because every Korean I knew had

---

[5] I have met many male and female *kangshinmu* and keep in touch personally with about one hundred *kangshinmu*.

forewarned me; however, I am convinced now that no one has to worry about becoming spirit-possessed simply because they learn about *musok*, spend time with *musokin* (ritual specialists), or participate in *musok* related activities.

When I listen to the verses of songs during the rituals, I do not hear anything but blessings from spirits and ancestors. I would like to suggest to those who understand Korean to listen to the verses that *kangshinmu* sing and their kind words spoken to people. Many *kangshinmu* told me that *musok* is a religion of peace. They pray to spirits in order to receive *hwaŭi*, the peaceful solution to solve problems at hand.[6] *Musok* has always accepted other religions, including Buddhism, Confucianism, Taoism, Christianity, and various new religions, learning to cope with differences. From its early stages, *musok* has tolerated political and social oppression and survived. *Musok* is not a dying tradition despite the strong disapproval from many Koreans. *Musok* has been practiced by many Koreans for centuries and the ritual specialists of *musok* will continue to help people by asking on their behalf for *hwaŭi* (peaceful solutions) from the spirits.

By studying *musok* and Hanyang *kut*, I have uncovered some of the mystery of my ethnicity. To learn about *musok* is to learn about Korean culture and its roots. I will conclude this report of some of my findings on Korean culture with the verses from the "*Hongsu Maegi*" song in order to suggest how *musok* and Korean customs are intricately woven and mutually interdependent.

The following verses can be heard on the accompanying CD (track 28). In this recording, Yi Sang-Sun sings while accompanying herself on the *koritchak* (willow basket played with a stick) during a *ch'isŏng* (small-scale ritual) that was held in the first lunar month of 2000. If the *ch'isŏng* is offered with songs accompanied by *koritchak*, no *changgu* or *chegŭm* is used. The *ch'isŏng* ritual lasts about two hours. Yi conducts the *Hongsu Maegi Ch'isŏng* with an abridged version of the twelve *kŏri* (sections) of *ch'ŏnshin kut*. The entire ritual is performed by Yi singing alone with the *koritchak*, while the sponsors pray and receive *kongsu* (messages) from the spirits in front of the altar.

"*Hongsu Maegi*" is the latter part of a ritual song called "*Ch'angbu T'aryŏng*" that is performed during the Ch'angbu *kŏri* (section) of the *kut* (ritual). "*Hongsu Maegi*" is sung to ward off ill fortune, especially in the first lunar month of the year.[7] The song lyrics begin with the first month and end with the twelfth month. If a ritual is held later in the year, for example, in the fifth lunar month, the *kangshinmu* will sing this song beginning with the verses dealing with the fifth month and continuing through the twelfth month.

---

[6] *Hwaŭi* (literally, negotiation for peace) is often expressed as "*haŭi patnŭnda*" (receiving *haŭi*), i.e. *kangshinmu* receive instructions for how to restore peace from the spirits.

[7] *Hongsu Maegi* is also known as *Hoengsu Maegi*. *Hongsu* (torrent) or *hoengsu* (ill fortune) is prevented by the *maegi* (act of prevention). People hire *kangshinmu* in the beginning of the year to sing this song at a ritual to prevent a torrent of ill fortune.

"*Hongsu Maegi*" is sung in the rhythm of *kutkŏri changdan*, a twelve-beat rhythmic cycle, discussed in chapter 8. In the following verses, each line corresponds to one cycle of twelve beats.

> *Imal chŏmal ŭn ta kŭman tugu*
> Let me (Ch'angbu) stop talking about this and that now,

> *ilnyŏn hongsu na makko kaja.*
> prevent troubles for the coming year, and leave.

> *Ilnyŏn hamyŏnŭn yŏldu tal inde*
> (Since) there are twelve months in a year. . .

> *chŏngwŏl handal e tŭnŭn hongsu*
> For troubles in the first month,

> *chŏngwŏl ch'o (yŏl) nahŭlhal ichŏngsŏng e*
> (I will) prevent them by making offerings on the 14th day[8]

> *kŭmil tangsiru (ro)man magŏnaego,*
> with rice cakes made that day.

> *iwŏl handal e tŭnŭn hongsu nŭn*
> For troubles in the second month,

> *iwŏl taech'un e magŏnaego,*
> (I will) prevent them during the great spring days.

> *samwŏl handal e tŭnŭn hongsu nŭn*
> For troubles in the third month,

> *samwŏl Samjitnal magŏnaego,*
> (I will) prevent them on the 3rd day of the 3rd month.[9]

> *sawŏl handal e tŭnŭn hongsu nŭn*
> For troubles in the fourth month,

---

[8] *Ch'o yŏlnahŭlhal* refers to the 14th day of the 1st lunar month. In earlier days, *kangshinmu* used to leave bundles of straw in the middle of a crossroads during the night of the 14th before holding a small ritual called *hoensgu maegi* for a person who faced ill fortune.

[9] *Samjitnal* refers to the 3rd day of the 3rd lunar month when birds return from spending the winter in warmer climates.

sawŏl Ch'op'ail e magŏnaego,
        prevent them on the 8th day of the 4th month.[10]

owŏl handal e tŭnŭn hongsu nŭn
        For troubles in the fifth month,

owŏl Tano e magŏnaeso.
        (I will) prevent them on *Tano*, the 5th day of the 5th month.[11]

Yuwŏl handal e tŭnŭn hongsu nŭn
        For troubles in the sixth month,

yuwŏl Yudu e magŏnaego,
        (I will) prevent them on *Yudu*, the 15th day of the 6th month.[12]

ch'ilwŏl handal e tŭnŭn hongsu nŭn
        For troubles in the seventh month,

ch'ilwŏl hagunŭn Chilsŏknal
        (I will) choose *Chilsŏknal*, the 7th day of the 7th month,[13]

ch'ŏnsangokkyŏng ŭnhasu e
        (while) in the Milky Way of Heaven[14]

Kyŏn-U Chik-Nyŏ *nŭn sangbongshi e*
        the two lovers (Kyŏn-U and Chik-Nyŏ) meet,[15]

Ch'ilsŏngmaji ru magŏnaego,
        and offer a ritual to the Seven Star Spirits.

---

[10] The 8th day of the 4th month is the historical Buddha's birthday.

[11] *Tano* is the 5th day of the 5th lunar month when Koreans dress in new summer clothing and exchange fans as gifts.

[12] *Yudu* is the 15th day of the 6th lunar month. On that day people find the *yudu* (literally, head of streams), source of the streams, which flows toward the east, and wash their hair to keep it shining throughout the year.

[13] *Ch'ilsŏknal* refers to the 7th day of the 7th lunar month.

[14] *Ch'ŏnsangokkyŏng* comes from *ch'ŏnsang paek okkyŏng*, meaning Heaven, also known as *ch'ŏn'gung*.

[15] Kyŏn-U and Chik-Nyŏ (literally, the herd boy and weaver maiden), parted by the Milky Way, are believed to meet once a year on the night of *ch'ilsŏk* (literally 7th evening) of the 7th lunar month on a bridge formed by all the crows and magpies that have flown up to the sky to help the lovers.

p'alwŏl handal e tŭnŭn hongsu
    For troubles in the eighth month,

p'alwŏl hagunŭn Taeborŭmnal
    (I will) prevent them on the 15th day of the 8th month[16]

man chosang ch'arye ru magŏnaeso.
    by making offerings to every ancestor.

Kuwŏl handal e tŭnŭn hongsu nŭn
    For troubles in the ninth month,

kuwŏl kuilnal magŏnaego,
    (I will) prevent them on the 9th day of the 9th month.

siwŏl handal e tŭnŭn hongsu nŭn
    For troubles in the tenth month,

siwŏl sangdal e mumailnal
    (I will) select the day when nothing bad would happen

kosa chŏngsŏng ŭro magŏnaego,
    (and) offer *kosa* (a small ritual) with devotion.

tonjital e tŭnŭn hongsu nŭn
    For troubles in the eleventh month,

tonji p'uri ru magŏnaelje,
    (I will) offer *tongji p'uri* (a small ritual).

Ae-tongji, Chung-tongji, No-tongji
    Depending on when the longest night occurs this year,[17]

---

[16] The *Taeborŭmnal* (literally, great full moon day) refers to the 15th day of the 8th lunar month.

[17] *Tongji* refers to the longest night of the year in the 11th lunar month. On this day, porridge made of red beans is consumed to cast off misfortune. The color of red beans is believed to have power to repel evil forces. If *Tongji* falls at the beginning of the month, it is called *Ae-tongji*. The red bean porridge is not offered to children. But if *Tongji* falls in the middle (*Chung-tongji*) or in the latter part of the month (*No-tongji*), everyone enjoys the porridge mixed with white balls made of glutinous rice.

tongjinal ŭn tongji shi e
>(I will) select the appropriate date and time

patchuk saealshim ŭro magŏnaego,
>and make rice balls in red bean porridge.

sŏttal handal e tŭnŭn hongsu nŭn
>For troubles in the twelfth month,

Ipch'un taegil e ta makatssŭni,
>(I will) prevent them on *Ipch'un*, the first day of spring.

somun manbok rae roman saenggyŏjugo
>(Now I have made it possible)
>for ten thousand blessings to arrive,[18]

ilnyŏn hongsu ta makatssŭni
>by preventing all possible troubles from happening.

sanjin hongsu nŭn sujin hongsu
>Obstacles[19] and difficulties,[20]

nakma hongsu, kwisŏl hongsu
>falling from horses, malicious gossip,

kwanjae hongsu, ŏkulhan numyŏng hongsu
>legal troubles, false accusations,

mul hongsu, pul honsu, chech'yŏchugo. . .
>flood, fire, and so on, I will get rid of them. . .

As noted in the verses of "*Hongsu Maegi*," the *muga* (ritual song) is deeply grounded in Korean customs. The traditional holidays that Koreans celebrate in a secular context include *Sŏlnal*, the 1st day of the 1st lunar month;

---

[18] "*Somun manpokrae*" is a saying that means "through *somun* (literally, a smiling gate), ten thousand blessings will enter" and is understood as "if people are content, many blessings will be bestowed."

[19] *Sanjin hongsu* (literally meaning mountains densely packed with trees) implies too many obstacles to overcome.

[20] *Sujin hongsu* (literally meaning a river bed that is dried out) implies insurmountable difficulty.

Taeborŭmnal, the 15th day of the 1st lunar month; *Ipch'un* in February; *Samjitnal*, the 3rd day of the 3rd lunar month; *Hanshik*, the 105th day after winter solstice; *Tano*, the 5th day of the 5th lunar month; *Yudu*, the 15th day of the 6th lunar month; *Chilsŏk*, the 7th day of the 7th lunar month; *Paekchung*, the 15th day of the 7th lunar month; *Ch'usŏk*, the 15th day of the 8th lunar month; *Jungyangjŏl*, the 9th day of the 9th lunar month; *Tongji* in the 11th lunar month; and *Kumŭmnal*, the last day of the 12th lunar month. The Korean government has also designated October 3rd as *Kaech'ŏnjŏl*, a holiday for Tan'gun, the mythical founder of Korea and *musok*. But in recent years, some Korean Christians have been trying to eliminate the foundation myth of Korea by deliberately destroying statues of Tan'gun throughout the Korean peninsula.

Learning about *musok* has given me a deeper understanding of Korean culture. I consider *musok* to be one of the most important areas of study if one desires to learn about Korean culture, regardless of one's religion. By discovering how the world view of *musok* is embedded in customs and traditions of Koreans, one will attain invaluable knowledge and perspective for Korean studies.

Appendix A: Plates

Plate 1. Altar in a *Shindang* (Shrine Room). This *shindang* belongs to a *kangshinmu* (spirit-possessed shaman) whose nickname is Ssangdungi (literally, twins) because she has twin sons. Paintings of various spirits are on the walls of the *shindang*, and elaborate food offerings have been prepared for a *kut* (ritual) (see pages 14 and 67–72).

Plate 2. Divination Table. Kim Yu-Gam, a *kangshinmu*, is talking to a male client (not shown in the photograph), pointing to divination coins on the table and explaining his fortune. There is also a pile of rice on the table for divination. Her divination table shows a well worn center (see pages 14 and 69).

Plate 3. Shaman and Musician. Yim Ki-Uk, a male shaman, is singing a ritual song and playing *changgu* (hourglass-shaped drum). He wears only plain *hanbok* (traditional outfit) during this part of the ritual. Kim Chŏm-Sŏk, a ritual musician, is the sole musician (*oe chaebi*) hired for this ritual. He is playing *p'iri* (cylindrical oboe) (see page 131).

Plate 4. Todang *Kŏri*. Kisaeng Paksu, a male shaman, is wearing the ritual clothing of Todang, a male spirit, including a hat with *hosu* (tiger's whiskers). A pig's head is balanced on a ritual trident and money is placed in the pig's mouth as an offering to the spirits (see pages 49 and 208).

Plate 5. Kwan-U. Yi Sang-Sun, a female shaman, is delivering *kongsu* (messages) from Kwan-U, a Chinese military general and mythical god of war. Yi is dressed in the ritual garments of this male spirit, including a *nam ch'ima* (long indigo blue skirt), blue *kugunbok* (coat) with red sleeves, *k'waeja* (long vest), and *hwang ch'ŏnik* (golden gown with long, wide sleeves). Here the sleeves are pulled back in order to hold the *wŏldo* (ritual knife) in the right hand and the red and blue flags in the left. Yi is also wearing a *kat* (black hat) decorated with *hosu* (tiger's whiskers) (see pages 49 and 205).

Plate 6. Pari Kongju. Yi Yŏng-Hŭi, a male shaman, is wearing the elaborate ritual clothing of Pari Kongju, a female spirit, which includes *mujigyŏn ch'ima* (underskirt), *hong suran* (long red skirt with gold foil decorations), *tangŭi* (long blouse worn in the palace), *ŭnha mongduri* (yellow outer garment), and *hansam* (sleeve extensions). On his head, he has a *k'ŭn mŏri* (large wig decorated with many jewels) and *karuma* (crown). While singing the epic song "*Pari Kongju*," Yi strikes one head of the *changgu* (drum) with a stick in his right hand and shakes a *pangul* (bell tree) in his left hand (see pages 49 and 227–228).

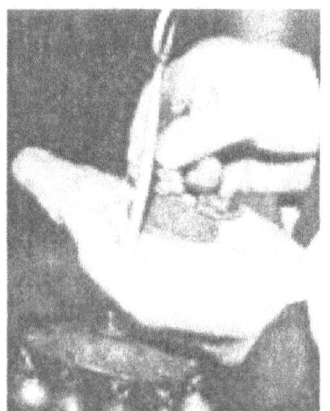

Plate 7. *Kuaebi* (Found Sacred Objects). Yim Ki-Uk, a *paksu* (male shaman), holds a *pangul* (bell tree) and divination coins that he found when he was seven years old. Yim told me that the spirits had revealed the location of these *kuaebi* to him in his dream. He found them underneath a huge rock, which is still standing near his house in Seoul (see pages 59–60).

Appendix A: Plates 253

Plate 8. *P'aldo Kut* Opening Ceremony. Hundreds of Korean shamans gather in Changch'ung Stadium in Seoul for an annual ritual sponsored by Taehan Sŭnggong Kyŏngshin Yŏnhaphoe, a national association of shamans. At the opening ceremonies, groups of shamans and ritual musicians enter with banners raised and music playing (see page 87).

Plate 9. Performance at *P'aldo Kut*. A Hanyang *kut* has been choreographed to be visually appealing to the audience in the stadium. The music is also greatly amplified. While four shamans play *chegŭm* (cymbals), Yang Hwa-Yŏng (ritual musician) plays *hojŏk* (conical oboe) instead of *p'iri* (cylindrical oboe) to increase the volume of the main melodic instrument (see page 88).

Plate 10. Members of Hyangp'unghoe (Association for Male Shamans). Ten *paksu* (male shamans) are shown here after their performance of "Seoul Ch'ŏnshin K'ŭn Kut" at Kyŏngbok Palace in 1999. The four men on the left are chaebi (ritual musicians) hired for the occasion (see page 90).

Plate 11. Altar at Musok Pojonhoe (Shaman School). The spirits are represented both in images and in calligraphy. On the left, images of the Three Buddhas and Seven Star Spirits are shown, while the Five Spirits for Five Directions and General Ch'oe Yŏng are on the right. The calligraphic characters from left to right represent the Water Spirit, Hwan In, Tan'gun, Hwan Ung, and the Mountain Spirit (see page 93).

Appendix A: Plates 255

Plate 12. Learning a Ritual Dance. Neophyte *kangshinmu* (spirit-possessed shamans) at Musok Pohonhoe (shaman school) are practicing their dance steps, holding cymbals in their hands and observing their instructor, Pak In-O, on the right (see page 94).

Plate 13. Whole Pig on *Chakdu*. Pak In-O, a male shaman, stands barefoot on *chakdu* (ritual blades) with a whole pig (*t'ong sasil*) on his shoulders as an offering to the spirits. Other shamans support the temporary structure where the blades are placed (see page 95).

Plate 14. *Honryŏng Kut* (Posthumous Wedding Ritual). Two souls are symbolically represented in human forms made of hay and dressed in wedding garments. Family members of the bride and groom gather at the ritual and pray for the peace and happiness of the couple (see page 99).

Plate 15. *Ssikkim Kut* (Ritual for the Departed). Ch'ae Chŏng-Rye, a *sesŭpmu* (hereditary *mudang*), officiates at a Chindo *ssikkim kut*, a ritual for the departed in the Chŏlla Provinces. Ch'ae leads the soul of the departed in a boat that is symbolically making its way to the other world. Ch'ae sings a ritual song while two instrumentalists (not shown in the photograph) provide musical accompaniment (see page 121).

Appendix A: Plates

Plate 16. *Suwang Kut* (Ritual for the Departed). Kim Mae-Mul, a *manshin* (spirit-possessed shaman from Hwanghae Province in North Korea), officiates at a ritual for the souls of political prisoners who had been put to death at Sŏdaemun Hyŏngmuso (West Gate Prison). Kim prostrates herself in front of the altar where the names of ninety prisoners are displayed on *wip'ae* (tablets) (see pages 121–122).

Plate 17. Blank *Wip'ae* (Tablets). Numerous blank *wip'ae* are placed around the entrance to the execution building at Sŏdaemun Hyŏngmuso (West Gate Prison) for unknown patriots and freedom fighters (see pages 121–122).

Plate 18. *Chŏngak Changgu*. Kim Yu-Gam is playing *changgu* (hourglass-shaped drum). The *changgu* used for Hanyang *kut* is the *chŏngak changgu*, which is also used for court music. It is larger in size than the *minsok changgu* used for folk music. The *hong ch'ŏnik* (red ritual garment with wide sleeves) is hung to welcome the spirit of Ŏksabyŏl Kunung (see page 187).

Plate 19. Two Shamans and Two Ritual Musicians. *Yang chaebi* refers to an ensemble of two *chaebi* (ritual musicians) hired for Hanyang *kut*. The two musicians play *p'iri* (cylindrical oboe) and *haegŭm* (two-string spiked fiddle). Here, Kim Chŏm-Sŏk is playing *p'iri* and his brother Kim Chŏng-Gil is playing *haegŭm*. Yi Sang-Sun, a *kangshinmu* (spirit-possessed shaman), is playing *changgu* (hourglass-shaped drum) while Yim Ki-Uk, a *paksu* (male spirit-possessed shaman), plays *chegŭm* (cymbals) (see page 131).

Appendix A: Plates

Plate 20. Pari Kongju. Yi Sang-Sun shakes *pangul* (ritual bell tree) in the left hand and strikes one head of the *changgu* (drum) with a stick in her right hand while singing the epic song "*Pari Kongju.*" She is wearing a yellow *ŭnha mongduri* (outer garment) and *k'ŭn mŏri* (large wig), the proper ritual attire required for Pari Kongju (Princess Pari) (see pages 125, 162, and 226–227).

Plate 21. 99-Bell *Pangul* (Bell Tree). The 99-bell tree is used by shamans from Hwanghae Province (see page 126).

Plate 22. *Koritchak* (Willow Basket). A basket woven from willow branches is used in Hanyang *kut* as a musical instrument. Kisaeng Paksu is performing *ch'isong*, a small-scale ritual. The *koritchak* is played with a stick made of paulownia wood and is sometimes used to accompany ritual songs (see page 126 and CD track 28).

Plate 23. *P'iri* (Cylindrical Oboe). Kim Chŏm-Sŏk is a *chaebi* (ritual musician) designated by the government as the *chŏnsu kyoyuk pojoja* (assistant for transmission and education) for Important Intangible Cultural Property number 104, Seoul *Saenam Kut*. Here Kim is playing the *p'iri*, a cylindrical double-reed aerophone made of bamboo (see pages 127 and 143–145).

Appendix A: Plates

Plate 24. *Haegŭm* (Fiddle). Kim Sun-Bong, a well known *chaebi* (ritual musician), is playing the *haegŭm*, a two-string spiked fiddle (see pages 128 and 142–143).

Plate 25. *Chŏngak Taegŭm* (Flute). Yi Sŏn-Ho is an *isuja* (master artist) for Important Intangible Cultural Property number 104, Seoul *Saenam Kut*. Yi is playing *taegŭm*, a transverse bamboo flute. The flute used for Hanyang *kut* is the *chŏngak taegŭm*, which is also used for court music. It is larger than the *taegŭm* used in folk music (see pages 128 and 151–152).

Plate 26. Kim Sang-Sŏl and Sam Chaebi. *Sam chaebi* (literally, three musicians) refers to an ensemble made up of p'iri (oboe), *haegŭm* (fiddle), and *taegŭm* (flute). Here Kim Sang-Sŏl, a *kangshinmu* (spirit-possessed shaman), is singing and playing *changgu* (drum), accompanied by Kim Sun-Bong (*p'iri*), Kim Chŏm-Sŏk (*taegŭm*), and Hŏ Yong-Ŏp (*haegŭm*) (see page 132 and CD track 5).

Plate 27. *Samhyŏn Yukkak* Ensemble. The *samhyŏn yukkak* ensemble consists of six musicians playing Korean traditional instruments—two *p'iri* (cylindrical oboes), *taegŭm* (transverse flute), *haegŭm* (2-string fiddle), *changgu* (hourglass-shaped drum), and *puk* (barrel drum). Here at a ritual for Tan'gun at Sajik Park in Seoul, Kim Chŏng-Gil plays *haegŭm*, Yi Sŏn-Ho plays *taegŭm*, Kim Chae-Yong plays *p'iri*, Kim Chŏm-Sŏk plays *p'iri*, Yi Sang-Sun plays *changgu*, and Peter Joon Park plays *puk* (see pages 127, 129, and 133).

Appendix A: Plates

Plate 28. Necklace with Metal Bells. When a Nepalese shaman sings and dances, they play a frame drum. In order to add metallic sounds, the shaman puts on a ritual necklace with bells over the shoulder and shakes the upper body (see pages 162 and 236).

Plate 29. Ritual Belt with Metal Bells. Nadyezhda Duvan, an Ulchi shaman from the Amur River region in Eastern Siberia, is singing and dancing while playing a frame drum. She wears *yampa* (ritual belt) with metal bells that provide metallic sounds to accompany her ritual songs (see pages 162 and 236).

Plate 30. Ritual Musicians Dressed as Court Musicians. Yi Chung-Yŏng is possessed by a spirit at the Annual *P'aldo Kut* while music is provided by a shaman playing *chegŭm* (cymbals) and nine ritual musicians playing *changgu* (drum), seven *t'aep'yŏngso* (conical oboes), and *ajaeng* (bowed zither). The *chaebi* (ritual musicians) are dressed in red clothing and black hats usually worn by court musicians (see pages 88, 129, and 179).

Plate 31. Table Offerings for Pulsa. Offerings of cooked vegetable dishes, fruits, and a bowl of *oksu* (sacred water) are placed on the table, as well as various types of *ttŏk* (rice cakes). On top of each pile of *ttŏk*, a white paper flower is placed. Two spoons wrapped in a bundle of uncut white thread are placed in a bowl filled with uncooked rice. The number of spoons reflect the number of family members who are sponsoring the ritual (see page 191).

Appendix A: Plates

Plate 32. "*Para T'aryŏng.*" Yi Sang-Sun, a *kangshinmu* (spirit-possessed shaman), is singing "*Para T'aryŏng*" while accompanying herself with cymbals (see CD track 22). Yi is wearing a *kokkal* (hat) and red *kasa* (sashes) over her white *changsam* (ritual garment fashioned after Buddhist monk's attire) (see pages 193–194).

Plate 33. Duet Song. Yi Sang-Sun, a *kangshinmu* (spirit-possessed shaman), and Yim Ki-Uk, a *paksu* (male shaman), sing "*Ch'ŏn'gung Maji Noraekarak.*" Yim provides the drum accompaniment. Yi is holding a bowl filled with jujubes and chestnuts (see page 194).

Plate 34. Receiving Blessings.
Throughout any *kut* (ritual) in Korea, whenever blessings from the spirits are delivered by a *kangshinmu*, men and women stand up to show respect for the spirit possessing the shaman. Men hold their shirts out and women hold their blouse or skirts out toward the shaman, gesturing to receive blessings. Pak In-Gyŏm, a *paksu* (male shaman) dressed in Hwanghae Province ritual garments, is delivering blessings from the spirits to the couple here (see page 195).

Plate 35. *Wŏldo Sasil*. Yi Sang-Sun checks to see if the spirits are content with the offering by balancing a large *wŏldo* (ritual knife) on top of a small dish. If the *wŏldo* stands on its own, it is understood that the spirits are content. With the *wŏldo* in place, Yi continues to pray for the sponsors. Yi is dressed in the attire of the Pyŏlsang Spirit. She is wearing a *nam ch'ima* (long indigo blue skirt), gold *kugunbok* (coat) with red sleeves, dark brown *k'waeja* (long vest), and a hat called *annulimbŏnggŏji*, decorated with peacock feathers (see pages 200 and 207–208).

Appendix A: Plates

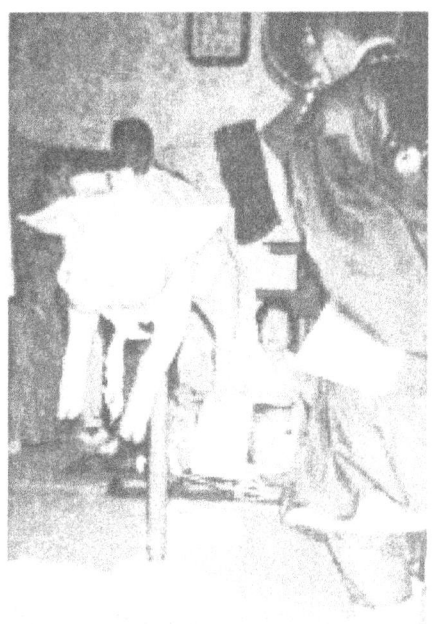

Plate 36. *Ch'anggŏm Sasil*. Pak In-O is balancing a whole pig on a *ch'anggŏm* (ritual trident) on top of a small bag filled with salt. Pak is wearing a blue skirt, blue *kugunbok* (coat), blue *ch'ŏnik* (garment with long wide white sleeves), red sash with three pouches, and *annulimbŏnggŏji* (hat). The white paper attached to the drum contains information about the sponsors. Ritual garments are arranged and hung on the left wall according to the order of the *kŏri* (sections) for the Hanyang *kut* (see pages 189 and 208).

Plate 37. Cloud-Shaped *Chakdu*. *Chakdu* (ritual blades) usually consist of two blades, but Yi Chung-Yŏng, a *paksu* (male shaman), is riding a cloud-shaped single-bladed *chakdu*. This *chakdu* is one of several custom-built *chakdu* Yi had created in shapes that the spirits revealed to him in his dreams (see page 209).

Plate 38. Arrows to Dispel Misfortune. *Kangshinmu (spirit-possessed* shamans) shoot arrows in order to get rid of misfortune. The arrowheads are made of buckwheat flour dough. The bow is made from a branch of a peach tree growing toward the east. A patient is seated in front of the altar, covered with the five directional flags (*obang shinjanggi*), and arrows are shot over her head. The number of arrows used reflect the patient's age. Kŏmsŏngdang is shooting arrows while Yim Ki-Uk is handing her the arrows as needed. Wŏn Ok-Hŏi is saying prayers (see page 211).

Plate 39. *Mugam* (Dance). Clients wearing *k'waeja* (long vests) are dancing to music provided by *sam chaebi* (ensemble of three musicians, not shown in the photo) at a private *shindang* (shrine room) of Ko Paksu in Suwŏn, Kyŏnggi Province (see pages 212–213).

Appendix A: Plates

Plate 40. *Ch'angbu Kŏri.* Yi Sang-Sun is wearing a Ch'angbu *ŭidae* (ritual garment) and holding a *puch'ae* (ritual fan) in the right hand. Two men and one woman standing on the right are sponsors of the ritual. This was part of a Seoul *Saenam Kut* held at Kyŏngbok Palace to lead the soul of Mrs. Han to the other world (see pages 121 and 214).

Plate 41. *Saje Samsŏng Kŏri.* Kim Yu-Gam is the *poyuja* (designated performer) for Important Intangible Cultural Property no. 104, Seoul *Saenam Kut,* an elaborate ritual for the departed. Kim Yu-Gam tries to lighten the scene even briefly by making *chaedam* (witty remarks) to the grieving family members during the Seoul *Saenam Kut.* She has a headband with paper flowers and *sajeji* (paper with money enclosed) in the headband (see pages 121 and 225).

Plate 42. Shaman as a Psychopomp. The other world is believed to be beyond a body of water. Chu Pok-Hŭi has tied a dried, flattened cod to her back as a symbolic seat for the soul of the departed to ride to the other world (see page 225).

Plate 43. Pari Kongju. Yi Sang-Sun is the *chŏnsu kyoyuk pojoja* (assistant for transmission and education) for Important Intangible Cultural Property no. 104, Seoul *Saenam Kut*. Yi is singing the sacred epic song "*Pari Kongju*" at a ritual held for the departed. Yi is dressed in a *hong suran* (red long skirt with gold foil decoration) and *ŭnha mongduri* (yellow garment). For much of the "*Pari Kongju*" song, the *kangshinmu* wears a *k'ŭn mŏri* (large wig decorated with many jewels), but when the verses are about the delivery of the seven princesses, the *kangshinmu* takes off the wig and places it on a small table near two large candles and a pile of rice. The clothing and shoes of the departed are laid between the mourning husband and the *kangshinmu* (see page 228).

Appendix A: Plates

Plate 44. *Kashimun* (Gate of Thorns). The clothing and shoes of the departed are wrapped in sheets (*tossam*) and carried by family members. Yi Sang-Sun, wearing the formal attire of Pari Kongju, leads the group in a ritual circumambulation around the *kashimun* (gate of thorns), which represents the path to the other world (see pages 228 and 229).

Plate 45. Yŏnjidang. The Yŏnjidang is a small altar with Chijang Posal's picture, paper lotus flowers, and food offerings. Chijang Posal (Sanskrit, Ksitigarbha) is a Buddhist Bodhisattva who is believed to lead the dead safely to the other world (see page 229).

Plate 46. *Mun Sajae* (Gatekeeper). Wŏn Ok-Hŭi, an *isuja* (master artist) for Important Intangible Cultural Property no. 104, Seoul *Saenam Kut*, is dressed as the *mun sajae* (gatekeeper) in *chŏnbok* (tunic) with paper flowers in her headband. She plays cymbals as she speaks and demands a fee for the key and the services of opening the gate to the other world (see page 230).

Plate 47. Crossing the *Kashimun* (Gate). Yi Sang-Sun, supported by ritual sponsors on both sides, enters through the gate, carrying a table on which a *sanja* (symbolic seal) and a bolt of silk for Chijang Posal are laid, as well as a piece of paper containing the name and address of the deceased. A roll of hemp known as *tidil pe* (literally, stepping cloth) is laid for them to walk on toward the Yŏnjidang, the altar where the spirit of Chijang Posal is believed to reside (see page 230).

Appendix A: Plates 273

Plate 48. *Tossam Tolgi* (Ritual Circumambulation). Four assisting *kangshinmu* are lifting the *tossam* (sheets containing clothing of the departed). Yi Sang-Sun will perform a ritual circumambulation under the *tossam*, outlining a figure eight (8), or the symbol for infinity (∞) (see pages 231–232).

Plate 49. *Pe Karŭgi*. *Pe karŭgi* (literally, cutting the hemp) is a ceremonial act of bidding farewell to the departed. By splitting the cloth, this world is separated from the other world (see page 233).

Plate 50. *Sam T'aegŭk*. The essence of the Korean worldview—balancing the three elements of heaven, earth, and humans—is expressed not only in music but also in visual arts, crafts, and dance. The three elements (heaven, earth, and humans) are often expressed visually in *sam t'aegŭk*. *T'aegŭk* refers to the Great Absolute or Great Ultimate in Chinese philosophy, which is considered to be the source of the dual principle of *yin* and *yang*. To reflect the Korean worldview of three elements, the *t'aegŭk* is also expressed as one circle but divided into three sections: red for heaven (*yang*), blue for earth (*ŭm*), and yellow for people (*in*). This visual representation is called *sam* (literally, triple) *t'aegŭk* (see page 239). Photo by Chung Su-Mi [Chŏng Su-Mi].

Appendix B: CD Notes

The recordings on this audio compact disc were made during ritual performances of Hanyang *kut* in Seoul, Korea after I received permission to record from the *kangshinmu* (spirit-possessed shamans), *chaebi* (ritual musicians), and ritual sponsors involved.

Chudang Mullim
1. *Kutkŏri* 0:11 (see pages 169–170 and 187)
2. *Tangak* 0:15 (see pages 171–172 and 187)
Yi Myŏng-Ok: *changgu* (drum); Yi Yŏng-Hŭi: *ching* (gong); Yi Yŏng-Hŭi's spirit daughter: *chegŭm* (cymbals)

Pujŏng Ch'ŏngbae
3. *Pujŏng changdan* 1:58 (see pages 172 and 189–190)
4. *Hwimori changdan* 0:55 (see pages 173 and 190)
Kim Yu-Gam: voice and *changgu*; anonymous: *chegŭm*

5. *Kamang Ch'ŏngbae Noraekarak* 3:54 (see pages 157, 174, and 190)
Kim Sang-Sŏl: voice and *changgu*; Kim Sun-Bong: *p'iri* (oboe); Kim Chŏm-Sŏk: *taegŭm* (flute); Hŏ Yong-Ŏp: *haegŭm* (fiddle)

Chinjŏk by *samhyŏn yukkak* ensemble
6. *Chajin Hwanip* 2:44 (see pages 25, 127, 129, 174 and 191)
7. *Seryŏngsan* 2:23 (see pages 25, 127, and 175)
8. *Samhyŏn Todŭri* 3:19 (see pages 25 and 127)
9. *T'aryŏng & Pyŏlgok T'aryŏng* 3:02 (see pages 25, 127, and 170)
Kim Sun-Bong: *changgu*; Kim Chŏm-Sŏk: *p'iri*; Hŏ Yong-Ŏp: *p'iri*; anonymous: *taegŭm*; anonymous: *ajaeng*; anonymous: *puk* (drum)

10. *Pyŏlgok T'aryŏng* by *yang chaebi* ensemble 2:50 (see page 170)
Kim Chŏm-Sŏk: *taegŭm*; Kim Chŏng-Gil: *haegŭm*; Yim Ki-Uk: *changgu*; anonymous: *chegŭm*

Chinjŏk by *sam chaebi* ensemble
11. *Yŏmbul* 0:23 (see pages 165, 175, and 191)
12. *Pan Yŏmbul* 0:26 (see pages 165, 176, and 191)
13. *Kutkŏri* 0:13 (see page 191)
14. *Nŭjŭn Hŏt'ŭn T'aryŏng* 0:18 (see page 191)
15. *Chajin Hŏt'ŭn T'aryŏng* 0:08 (see pages 171 and 191)
16. *Sangsan Noraekarak* 0:12 (see page 191)
Yi Sang-Sun: voice and *changgu*; Kim Sun-Bong: *p'iri*; Kim Chŏm-Sŏk: *taegŭm*; Hŏ Yong-Ŏp: *haegŭm*; anonymous: *chegŭm*

Chinjŏk and *Sangsan Noraekarak* by *yang chaebi* ensemble
17. *Pan Yŏmbul, Kutkŏri, Nŭjŭn Hŏt'ŭn T'aryŏng, Chajin Hŏt'ŭn T'aryŏng* 0:49 (see page 191)
18. *Sangsan Noraekarak* 2:57 (see pages 157, 174, and 191)
Yim Ki-Uk: voice and *changgu*; Kim Chŏm-Sŏk: *p'iri*; Kim Chŏng-Gil: *haegŭm*

Pulsa kŏri
19. *Kutkŏri* 2:14 (see pages 165, 169, and 194)
20. *Tangak* 0:31 (see pages 165, 171, and 194)
21. *Kongsu* 0:35 (see page 194)
22. *Para T'aryŏng* 2:16 (see pages 125, 156, 169, and 194)
Yi Sang-Sun: voice, *pangul* (bell tree), *para* (cymbals); Kim Yu-Gam: *changgu*; Kim Chŏm-Sŏk: *p'iri*; Hŏ Yong-Ŏp: *taegŭm*; Kim Chŏng-Gil: *haegŭm*; anonymous: *chegŭm* during *Kutkŏri* & *Tangak*

23. *Ch'o Yŏngshil* 1:51 (see page 223)
Yi Sang-Sun: voice

24. *Ch'wit'ae* 3:56 (see pages 165, 177, and 206)
Kim Chŏm-Sŏk: *p'iri*; Kim Chŏng-Gil: *haegŭm*; Ham Kwang-P'il: *changgu*; anonymous: *chegŭm*

25. *Taegam T'aryŏng* 3:57 (see pages 156, 169, 185, and 212)
Ham Kwang-P'il: voice and *changgu*; Kim Chŏm-Sŏk: *p'iri*; Kim Chŏng-Gil: *haegŭm*; anonymous: *chegŭm*

Ssang hojŏk

26. *Kutkŏri, Kkot Banga T'aryŏng* 2:22 (see pages 25, 127, 130, and 169)
27. *Chajin T'aryŏng* 1:17 (see pages 25, 127, 130, and 171)
Kim Chŏm-Sŏk: *hojŏk* (conical oboe); Hŏ Yong-Ŏp: *hojŏk*; Kim Sun-Bong: *changgu*; anonymous: *puk*; anonymous: *chegŭm*

28. *Ch'angbu T'aryŏng* 3:31 (see pages 126, 169, 214, and 243–247)
Yi Sang-Sun: voice and *koritchak* (willow basket)

29. *Twitchŏn* 3:37 (see pages 157 and 215)
Ham Kwang-P'il: voice and *changgu*; Kim Tong-Ho: voice

Chungdi Patsan

30. *Kamang Ch'ŏngbae* 0:34 (see pages 27 and 224)
31. *Chungdi Patsan* 3:03 (see pages 27 and 225)
32. *Chungdi Noraekarak* 0:48 (see pages 27, 157, 174, and 225)
Yi Sang-Sun: voice and *changgu*; Kim Sun-Bong: *p'iri*; Kim Chŏm-Sŏk: *taegŭm*; Hŏ Yong-Ŏp: *haegŭm*

33. *Pari Kongju* 6:17 (see pages 27, 125, 162, and 226–228)
Pak Chong-Bok: voice, *changgu*, and *pangul*; anonymous: *chegŭm*

34. *Nŏk Noraekarak* duet 1:03 (see pages 125, 157, 174, and 234)
35. *Sajae Mansubaji* 2:43 (see pages 125, 157, and 193)
Yi Sang-Sun: voice and *pangul*; Yim Ki-Uk: voice and *changgu*; Kim Sun-Bong: *p'iri*; Kim Chŏm-Sŏk: *taegŭm*; Hŏ Yong-Ŏp: *haegŭm*

Toryang

36. *Kutkŏri* 0:22 (see pages 230 and 231)
37. *Kil kunak* 3:15 (see pages 178, 230, and 231)
38. *Chajin Kutkŏri* 0:10 (see pages 171, 230, and 231)
Kim Sun-Bong: *p'iri*; Kim Chŏm-Sŏk: *taegŭm*; Hŏ Yong-Ŏp: *haegŭm*; Yim Ki-Uk: *changgu*

Glossary of Korean Terms

aedong kija (애동기자 祈者) Neophyte, term of endearment.
aekmaeki (액맥이) A ritual held to prevent misfortune.
ajaeng (아쟁 牙箏) A bowed zither.
ak in (악인 樂人) A musician.
Amit'abul (아미타불 阿彌陀佛) Sakyamuni, the historical Buddha.
an anp'akk kut (안안팍굿) Literal meaning, inside/outside *kut*. Refers to the *chinogwi kut*, which takes place inside the ritual hall and on the ground outside the hall.
andang sagyŏng maji (안당사경맞이) The first part of the *saenam kut*.
anjŭn kŏri (앉은 거리) Ritual in which the officiating *mudang* sits and prays.
ant'aek kŏri (안택거리) Ritual for the house.
anullimbŏnggŏji (안울림벙거지) A Chosŏn Dynasty military officer's hat. Also known as *chŏnrip*. Worn with *chŏnbok* and *kugunbok* for Shinjang, Pyŏlsang, and Taegam *kŏri*.
chabara (자바라) A pair of cymbals.
Ch'ach'aung (차차웅 次次雄) Refers to the king during the reign of King Namhae (4–24 AD), the second king of the Shilla period.
ch'ae (채) A thin bamboo stick used with the *changgu* (hourglass-shaped drum). Also known as *yŏl ch'ae*.
ch'ae p'yŏn (채편) The right head of the *changgu* (drum).
chaebi (재비/잽이) Musicians who perform for *musok* rituals. Also refers to professional instrumentalists in secular contexts. For example, *kayagŭm chaebi*, for a professional *kayagŭm* (12-string zither) performer. According to Kim Ki-Su, *chaebi* comes from *ch'abi* (差備 literally, getting ready) (Kim K.S. 1972:90).
chaebi tangju (재비 당주 堂主) The musician responsible for securing other musicians for a ritual.
chaedam (재담 才談) Witty remarks.
chaein (재인 才人) Literally, a talented person. Refers to entertainers and male musicians in the hereditary *musok* tradition.
chaemul (잿물) Sacred water mixed with ashes of burnt paper.

chaesu (재수 財數) Good luck. Good fortune.

chaesu kut (재수굿 財數굿) A *kut* to usher in good fortune. Also known in Seoul area as *ch'ŏnshin kut*.

chagŭn halmŏni (작은 할머니) Literally, younger grandmother. Refers to the *ching* (large gong) player in Hwanghae Province *kut*.

Chajin Hwanip (자진 환입 還入) A piece of music with a sixteen-beat rhythmic cycle. Also known as *Chajin Hanip* (자진 한잎, 삭대엽 數大葉).

chajin yŏmbul (자진 염불 念佛) A six-beat rhythmic cycle.

chakmyŏng (작명 作名) Creating an auspicious name.

chakdu (작두 斫刀 [작도]) A straw cutter or a fodder chopper in secular context. In *musok*, some *kangshinmu* (spirit-possessed shamans) stand barefoot on the sharp edges of the twin blades of the *chakdu* during the *kut*.

chan kkot (잔꽃) Paper flowers thought to represent a spoon and a pair of chopsticks. They are placed on top of *ttŏk* (rice cakes) stacked in layers as offering to the spirits for their enjoyment during the *kut* (National Research Institute of Cultural Properties of Korea 1998:165).

Ch'angbu (창부 倡夫/唱婦) The spirit who looks after musicians and performers.

changdan (장단 長短) Literally, long and short. Refers to rhythmic cycles.

changgo (장고 杖鼓/長鼓) An hourglass-shaped drum. See *changgu*.

ch'anggŏm (창검 槍劍) Ritual trident.

changgu (장구) Standard name for the hourglass-shaped drum.

changgu (장구 獐狗) *Changgu* expressed in different Sino-Korean characters (Chin 1993:19).

ch'anggŭk (창극 唱劇) Musical drama in which the performers sing in *p'ansori* style (Killick 1998:535).

changgun (장군 將軍) The spirit of a military general.

changsam (장삼 長衫) Refers to a Buddhist monk's robe. The white robe known as *paek changsam* (white robe) or *so changsam* (plain robe) is worn with a red belt (*hongtti*) and red sash (*hong kasa*) for the *musok* ritual. It is worn for Chesŏk *kŏri*, Chŏn'gung Ch'ilsŏng *kŏri*, and Pulsa *kŏri*.

chapkwi (잡귀 雜鬼) Sundry ghosts.

che (제 祭) A ritual. *Chai* in Chinese.

cheaekch'obok (제액초복 除厄招福) Eliminating misfortune and inviting blessings.

chedangmaji (제당맞이) A *kŏri* (section) performed only in the *chinjŏk kut* held by spirit-possessed shamans for their own celebrations.

chegajip (제가집 祭家집) A family who sponsors a *kut*.

chegŭm (제금 提琴) A pair of cymbals.

cheja (제자 弟子) Literally, a student or disciple. A euphemism for *mudang*.

cheja (제자 祭者) Literal meaning, one who conducts the ritual.

chemul (제물 祭物) Ritual offerings.

chesa (제사 祭祀) A ritual for ancestors.

Glossary

Chesŏk (제석 帝釋) Chesŏk refers to the Heavenly Spirit, Hwan In Chesŏk, who sent down Hwan Ung who gave birth to Tan'gun, the legendary founder of Korea.

Chiha Yŏjanggun (지하여장군 地下女將軍) One of the statues of the village guardians. The female general looking after the Underworld. See also Ch'ŏnha Taejanggun.

chihwa (지화 紙花) Ritual flowers made of paper. Also known as *muhwa* and *chohwa*. Flowers embody symbolic meanings and are created for ritual offerings, but are also occasionally used as hair ornaments.

Chijang Posal (지장보살 地藏菩薩) Ksitigarbha, the Bodhisattva associated with death and the Underworld (Walraven 1994:101). Chijang Posal took a vow not to enter Nirvana until he had personally rescued every inhabitant of the lower realms (J. Covell 1992:107). Known as Jizo in Japan and Ti-tsang in China.

chijŏn (지전 紙錢) Ritual articles made of white paper. Folded to create certain forms or cut with scissors to make specific designs. *Chijŏn* created in the form of birds, lanterns, candles, tassels, human figures, and so on, have their own esoteric meanings and purposes. For example, paper fences are used to create sacred areas in the ritual hall, while *nŏkjŏn,* shaped like a human figure, is said to shelter the dead soul temporarily during the *kut*. The use of *chijŏn* may be described to outsiders, but the esoteric meanings contained in certain folds, designs, and cut-outs are considered sacred and are guarded by *kangshinmu*.

chilsŏk (칠석 七夕) The 7th day of 7th month in lunar calendar.

Ch'ilsŏng (칠성 七星) The seven stars of the Great Bear (Ursa Major). Big Dipper.

Ch'ilsŏng halmŏm (칠성할멈 七星할멈) A woman diviner.

ch'ima (치마) A traditional woman's pleated skirt. In *musok*, the floor-length red (*hong*) and blue (*nam*) *ch'ima* are used. If the bottom part of the skirt is decorated with *kŭmbak* (plated in gold foil), the skirt is called *sŭran*, or *taeran* if the *kŭmbak* is done in two rows. During the ritual, the dark blue skirt is worn for the spirits associated with courage and war, the red one for the spirits promoting peace and harmony. *Paksu*, male shamans, wear blue *nam ch'ima* before adding other ritual garments.

ching (징 鉦) A large gong. See also *taegŭm* (대금 大金).

chinjŏk (진적 進爵 [진작]) An offering of wine. Comes from *chinjak* referring to the wine offerings to kings at banquets held during the Chosŏn Dynasty.

chinjŏk kut (진적굿 進爵굿 [진작굿]) A spirit-possessed shaman's *kut* held to celebrate his or her career as a shaman.

chinogwi kut (진오귀 굿) A *kut* held for the deceased in Seoul and Kyŏnggi Province.

chipshin kut (집신굿 集神굿) A ritual held to gather all the spirits together.

Chishin (지신 地神) The spirit of the earth.

ch'isŏng (치성 致誠) A small-scale ritual.
chŏ (저 笛) Bamboo flute. See *taegŭm*.
ch'ŏ olligi (처올리기) A part of the *kut* in the *sesŭpmu* (hereditary *mudang*) tradition.
ch'o pujŏng (초부정 初不淨) A purifying act performed at the beginning of a *kut*.
Ch'oe Yŏng Changgun (최영장군 崔瑩將軍) A historic general (1326–1388) of the Koryŏ Dynasty.
chŏgori (저고리) A Korean traditional woman's blouse or man's shirt.
chohwa (조화 彫花) Flowers made of cut paper. Also known as *chihwa* or *muhwa*.
choimjul (조임줄) Ropes used for tuning the *changgu* (hourglass-shaped drum).
ch'ŏlhakka (철학가 哲學家) Literally, a philosopher. A euphemism for a diviner.
ch'ŏllik (철릭) Ritual outer garment worn with a belt. See *ch'ŏnik* (天翼).
ch'ŏllyuk (철륙) See *ch'ŏnik* (天翼).
chŏmbok (점복 占卜) Diviner or divination.
chŏmjaengi (점쟁이 占쟁이) A diviner.
chŏmsa (점사 占辭) Divination.
chŏmsang (점상 占床) A divination table.
chŏmsŏng (점성 占星) Astrology.
chomu (조무 助巫) A shaman assisting at a ritual.
ch'ŏn (천 天) The sky or heaven.
chŏnan (전안 殿內) A shrine.
chŏnbok (전복 戰服) A long ritual tunic, fashioned after the Chosŏn Dynasty royal uniform (Kim Y.S. 1999:37). Also known as *k'waeja*.
chong (종 鐘) A bell.
chŏngak (정악 正樂) Genre of music enjoyed by upper class people.
chŏngak changgu (정악장구 正樂長鼓) *Changgu* used in court music and the Hanyang *kut*.
chŏngak taegŭm (정악대금 正樂大笒) Bamboo flute used in court music and the Hanyang *kut*.
ch'ŏngbae (청배 請拜) An invitation.
Chŏnggamrok (정감록 鄭鑑錄) A book written by Chŏnggam (정감 鄭鑑) and Yi Shim (이심 李沁) in 1785.
chŏnghwasu (정화수 井華水) Clean water offered to the spirits.
chŏngpuin (정부인 貞夫人) A title awarded to wives of civic and military officers of the second *p'um* (rank) by the Chosŏn court from 1417. Formerly, *hyŏnpuin* (현부인 縣夫人).
ch'ŏngryongdo (청룡도 青龍刀) Literally, blue dragon's knife. Refers to a large ritual knife.
chŏngshin (정신 正神) Literally, correct spirits. Refers to venerated spirits worshipped during the ritual.

Glossary

ch'ŏngshin (청신 請神) An invitation for the spirits.
chŏngsŏng (정성 精誠) Earnest devotion or sincere dedication.
ch'ŏngsong mudang (청송무당 請誦巫堂) A musically talented *mudang* who is invited by other *mudang* to sing and dance.
Ch'ŏn'gun (천군 天君) The Heavenly Prince.
ch'ŏn'gung (천궁 天宮) Heaven.
Ch'ŏnha Taejanggun (천하대장군 天下大將軍) One of the statues of the village guardians. Literal meaning, the great general under heaven. See also Chiha Yŏjanggun.
ch'ŏnik (천익 天翼) Ritual outer garment, also known as *ch'ŏllyuk* or *ch'ŏllik*. A floor-length outer garment with long sleeves with white trim extending to the floor. It is fashioned after the Chosŏn Dynasty military officers' uniforms. The garment is created in three colors—red (*hong*), gold (*hwang*), and blue (*nam*)—and worn for specific spirits during the rituals.
Ch'ŏnjon (천존 天尊) The Heavenly Being.
ch'ŏnmin (천민 賤民) Base people. The lowest of four classes of people during the Chosŏn Dynasty.
chŏnnae (전내 殿內) A diviner.
chŏnrip (전립 戰笠) A ritual hat used in Pyŏlsang *kŏri* since the Koryŏ period (Yi S.J. 1998 (2):25). Also known as *anullimbŏnggŏji*.
Ch'ŏnshin (천신 天神) Heavenly spirits.
ch'ŏnshin kut (천신굿 薦新굿, 薦神굿) A Hanyang *kut* for good fortune.
chŏnsu kyoyuk pojoja (전수교육보조자 傳授[受]教育補助者) Assistant responsible for transmission and education of Important Intangible Cultural Properties.
chŏnsuja (전수자 傳授[受]者) Disciple.
ch'ŏnyŏ mudang (처녀무당 處女巫堂) Literal meaning, a virgin *mudang*. Refers to an unmarried woman *mudang*.
ch'op'ail (초파일 初八日) The 8th day of the 4th lunar month. Buddha's birthday.
chŏpshin (접신 接神) An act of spirit possession.
chosang (조상 祖上) Ancestors.
Chosŏn (조선 朝鮮) The last dynasty (1392–1910) in Korea, also known as Yi (이 李) Dynasty.
Chosŏn Minjujuŭi Inmin Konghwaguk (조선민주주의인민공화국 朝鮮民主主義人民共和國) Official name of North Korea.
chŏttae (젓대) General term for flutes. Refers to *taegŭm*.
Chu Yŏk (주역 周易, [역경 易經]) The ancient Chinese divination manual (Chinese *Yi Ching*).
chudang sal (주당살 周堂煞) Curse caused by malevolent spirits remaining in a ritual area.
ch'uimsae (추임새) Shout of encouragement.
chumu (주무 主巫) The officiating *kangshinmu*.

chun kŏri (준거리 準巨里) Part of a *kut* where the audience may participate in dancing. For example, *mugam kŏri* in the Seoul area or the *norŭm kut*. (Ch'oe 1981:151)

chungin (중인 中人) Literally, middle people. One of the four classes of people during the Chosŏn Dynasty.

Chŭngsangyo (증산교 甑山敎) A new religion founded in 1901 by Chŭngsan (1871–1909). His legal name, Kang Il-Sun 강일순 姜一淳.

Ch'unhyangjŏn (춘향전 春香傳) A secular epic song. One of the *p'ansori* repertoire.

dhâranî (다라니) Buddhist incantation.

haegŭm (해금 奚琴) A two-string fiddle.

hajik (하직 下直) A farewell.

haksŭpmu (학습무 學習巫) Apprenticed *mudang*.

halmŏni (할머니) Grandmother.

hami (하미) White paper placed between the lips to prevent pollution (spitting or improper speech).

han (한 恨) Grief, unresolved feeling, etc.

han t'ŭl (한틀) Literally, one set. Refers to the trio ensemble of *p'iri*, *haegŭm*, and *taegŭm*. See also *sam chaebi*.

Hananim (하나님) The Heavenly God (The Only God).

hanbae (한배) A musical phrase based on breathing.

hanbok (한복 韓服) Korean traditional clothing.

Han'gang (한강 漢江) Han River.

Han'guk Minsok Shinmun (한국민속신문 韓國民俗新聞) *Korean Folk Newspaper* published in Seoul by Taehan Sŭngkong Kyŏngshin Yŏnhaphoe.

hansam (한삼 汗衫) Long white sleeve extensions that cover the hands. Used for the circumambulation during *saenam kut*.

Hansŏng (한성 漢城) Former name of present-day Seoul. See Hanyang.

Hanŭnim (하느님) The Heavenly God.

Hanyang (한양 漢陽) Former name of present day Seoul. The nation's capital since 1394 from the beginning of the Chosŏn Dynasty, except for 1399–1405 when the kings designated Kaesŏng as the capital (Kim J.K. 1978:14).

Hanyang *kut* (한양굿 漢陽굿) A *kut* from the greater Seoul area.

hoengsu magi (횡수막이 橫數막이) A ritual held to avoid misfortune.

Hogu Pyŏlsang Mama (호구별상마마 胡口別相媽媽) Spirit known to spread smallpox.

Hogu Pyŏlsŏng (호구별성 戶口別星, 胡鬼 [호귀]別星) Spirit known to spread smallpox.

hoguk pulgyo (호국불교 護國佛敎) Korean Buddhism. Developed to protect the nation.

hojŏk (호적 胡笛) Conical oboe. Also known as *t'aep'yŏngso*.

hŏju kut (허주굿 虛主굿) Ritual held prior to the initiation *kut*.

hong ch'ima (홍치마 紅치마) A red long pleated skirt worn for Pulsa, Chesŏk, San, Todang, Malmi, and Toryŏng *kŏri*. During the Hogu *kŏri*, the *kangshinmu* uses it as a veil, lifting it over his or her head and holding it in front of the client.

hong ch'ŏnik (홍천익 紅天翼) A red ritual garment with extended white sleeves. Also referred to as *hong ch'ŏnrik, hong ch'ŏllik*, or *hong ch'ŏllyuk*. The *ch'ŏnik* in red with extended white sleeves is fashioned after the outfit of *tanghagwan*, a military officer of the Chosŏn Dynasty. The *hong ch'ŏnik* is worn with the hat (*pitkat*) for Sanshin Kunung, Pyŏsŭl Taegam, and Sŏngju *kŏri*.

hong kasa (홍가사 紅袈裟) Red sash.

hong kat (홍갓) Red hat used during Kunung *kŏri*. Also known as *churip*.

hong suran (홍수란 紅繡襴) Red long skirt with *kŭmbak* (plated in gold foil).

hong tti (홍띠) Red belt.

hongsu (홍수 洪水) Torrent or flood.

honryŏng kut (혼령굿 婚靈굿) A ritual held to marry two souls.

hosemi (호세미) *Mudang* in Northeastern Hamgyŏng Provinces.

hosu (호수 虎鬚) Literally, tiger's whiskers. Refers to white feathers in shaman's ritual hat.

hubo (후보 候補) Candidate.

hunjang (훈장 訓長) Literally, a teacher. Refers to male shaman.

hwabon (화본 畵本) Literally, silk used to paint on. Refers to *musok* paintings.

hwang ch'ŏnik (황천익 黃天翼 *hwang ch'ŏllyuk* or *hwang ch'ŏllik*) The *ch'ŏnik* in gold color symbolizes Heaven or aristocracy. It is worn with a gold crown for the Heavenly King, Kwansŏng Chegun, or the spirits of historic kings.

Hwangje p'uri (황제푸리 皇帝푸리) An epic song sung during the *ch'ŏnshin kut*.

hwaraengi (화랭이) See *hwarang*.

hwarang (화랑 花郞) Literal meaning, flower boys. Originally referred to young aristocratic warriors of the Shilla Kingdom. In *musok* may refer to male *mudang* or hereditary musicians in the southern provinces.

hwaŭi (화의 和議, 和宜) Negotiation for peace. Reconciliation.

hyodo (효도 孝道) Filial piety.

hyŏpsu (협수 夾袖) Ritual garment with bodice in black, blue, green or yellow and red sleeves. Lined with red cloth. Worn usually with a sash.

hyungbae (흉배) A decoration on ritual clothing.

imo (이모 姨母) Mother's younger or older sister.

indari (인다리 人橋 [인교]) Literal meaning, a human bridge. In *musok indari* refers to the suffering of shamans losing loved ones. If a candidate refuses to become a shaman at his or her calling, his or her family members may experience serious illness or die until he or she accepts the fate of becoming a shaman.

in'gan munhwajae (인간문화재 人間文化財) Literal meaning, a human cultural property. Refers to the designated performer for an Important Intangible Cultural Property.

injŏng (인정 人情) *ŭl ssŭda*. Money offered at a ritual to symbolically help with expenses for the deceased on the way to the other world.

Inwangsan (인왕산 仁王山) Mountain in Seoul where Kuksadang is located.

isuja (이수자 履修者) Literally, someone who completed the course. Refers to master artists appointed by the government for an Important Intangible Cultural Property.

Kaech'ŏnjŏl (개천절 開天節) Literally, the day of heaven's opening. Refers to October 3rd, the national holiday commemorating Tan'gun.

kaek kwi (객귀 客鬼) Wandering spirits.

Kakshimjŏlbon (각심절본 覺心寺本) Rituals handed down from the Kakshimjŏl area in Seoul.

kalttae (갈대) Literally, reed. Refers to *taegŭm*, bamboo flute.

kamang (가망 感應 [감응]) Spirits.

kangshin (강신 降神) Spirit possession or spirit intrusion.

kangshin kut (강신굿 降神굿) Initiation ritual for a spirit-possessed shaman. Also known as *naerim kut*.

kangshin pyŏng (강신병 降神病) Spirit sickness.

kangshinmu (강신무 降神巫) Spirit-possessed shaman.

kangyak (강약 强弱) Literally, strong and weak. Refers to dynamics in music.

kasa (가사 袈裟) A pair of long sashes fashioned after Buddhist monks' attire. Red ones (*hong kasa*) are worn for the Pulsa *kŏri* in Hanyang *kut*. In Hwanghae Province *kut* a red one (*hong kasa*) and a green one (*ch'ŏng kasa*) are worn for the Ch'ilsŏng *kŏri*.

kat (갓 [입자 笠子]) Black hat for a man.

kayagŭm (가야금 伽倻琴) A twelve-stringed plucked zither.

ki (기 氣) Energy or cosmic breath.

kidae (기대) Musically trained *haksŭpmu* (apprenticed *mudang*).

kija (기자 祈子) Praying for a son.

kija (기자 祈者) Literal meaning, a person who prays.

kijanim (기자님 祈者님) Literal meaning, a person who prays. *Nim*, an honorific.

kijŏm (기점 旗占) Divination done with five directional flags.

kiju (기주 祈主) A female sponsor of a *kut*.

kimch'i (김치) Spicy fermented vegetable.

kimu (기무 技巫) A musically trained *mudang*.

kimul (기물 器物) Ritual objects.

kisaeng (기생 妓生) Female entertainers trained in music, art, and poetry.

kkwaenggwari (꽹과리) Small gong.

koehwangji (괴황지 槐黃紙) Yellow paper used for amulets.

Koguryŏ (고구려 高句麗) An early Korean kingdom (37 B.C.E.–668 C.E.).

Glossary

koin (고인 鼓人) Musician.
kokkal (고깔) White pointed cowl. Also known as *semoshi pan kokkal*.
Kŏllip (걸립 乞粒) The souls of dead beggars (Lee 1981:116). Spirits known to bring in clients.
kolsang (골상 骨相) Divination based on facial bone structure.
komo (고모 姑母) Father's older or younger sister.
kŏn taegu (건대구 乾大口) Dried cod.
kongguri ch'ae (공구리채) A wooden drumstick used to play a drum *(changgu)* for outdoor or ritual music.
konghang (공항 空港) Airport (formerly, *pihaengjang*, 비행장 飛行場).
kongin (공인) A musician.
kongjang (공장 工匠) An artisan.
kongju (공주 公主) A princess.
kongsu (공수 空唱) A spirit's words spoken through a shaman.
kŏri (거리 巨里) Section of a *kut* (ritual).
koritchak (고리짝) A willow basket. Used in *musok* to hold clothing for the ancestors or as a percussive musical instrument for small-scale rituals. Also known as *tonggori*.
Koryŏ (고려 高麗) Koryŏ Dynasty (918–1392).
kosa (고사 告祀) A small-scale ritual.
kuaebi (구애비) Ritual objects discovered by neophyte shamans.
kugunbok (구군복 具軍服, 舊軍服) A Chosŏn Dynasty military officer's uniform. A black, blue or brown coat-like garment with red sleeves and red lining.
kukmu (국무 國巫) A *mudang* hired by the court.
kŭkrak [*kŭngnak*] (극락 極樂) Paradise.
Kuksadang (국사당 國師堂) A ritual hall located in Seoul.
kukt'aeminan (국태민안 國泰民安) Peace for the nation and her people.
kŭmdan kasa (금단가사 錦端架裟) Red sash with tinsel and decorative golden print.
kŭmŏ (금어 金魚) A painter who specializes in Buddhist related images.
k'ŭn halmŏni (큰 할머니) Literally, older grandmother. Refers to a female *changgu* player in Hwanghae Province rituals.
k'ŭn mŏri (큰머리) A ceremonial wig decorated with jewelry. See *man*.
kŭne (그네) A swing.
kung an kut (궁안굿 宮內 [궁내]굿) Ritual held at the court.
kung pat kut (궁밖굿 宮外 [궁외]굿) Ritual held outside the court.
kung p'yŏn (궁편 宮鞭) Left head of the *changgu* (hourglass-shaped drum).
kunggul ch'ae (궁굴채) A wooden drumstick used to play *changgu* for outdoor or ritual music. Also known as *kongguri ch'ae*.
kunghap (궁합 宮合) Compatibility between two people.
Kungnip Kugakwŏn (국립국악원 國立國樂院) National Center for Korean Traditional Performing Arts.

Kunung (군웅 軍雄) The spirits of war heroes.

kup'abalbon (구파발본 舊擺撥本) A ritual handed down from the Kup'abal area of Seoul.

kurŭm (구름) Clouds.

kut (굿) A large scale *musok* ritual incorporating music and dance.

kut p'ae (굿패) Ritual group.

k'waeja (쾌자 快子) Comes from *kwaeja* (괘자 掛子). A long tunic fashioned after the military uniform of the Chosŏn Dynasty. Also known as *chŏnbok*. Worn by *mudang* throughout Korea, including *sesŭpmu* (hereditary *mudang*). In the Hanyang *kut*, the *k'waeja* appears in two colors—blue and black: blue for Shinjang and Taegam *kŏri*, black for Pyŏlsang and T'ŏ Taegam *kŏri*. Black *k'waeja* are often replaced by brown ones nowadays.

kwangdae (광대 廣大) Musicians. A euphemism for a hereditary *mudang*.

kwansang (관상 觀相) Divination based on facial features.

Kwanseŭm Posal (관세음보살 觀世音菩薩) In Sanskrit, Avalokitesvara. Also known as Kwanŭm.

Kwanŭm (관음 觀音) In Sanskrit, Avalokitesvara.

Kwan-Un-Jang (관운장 關雲長) Chinese warrior (162–220 C.E.) whose spirit is worshipped in *musok*. His birth name was Kwan-U, 관우 關羽.

kwi (귀 鬼) Evil spirits.

kyeja (계자 係者/繼者) Literally, one who continues the tradition. Refers to *kangshinmu*.

kyŏk (격 覡) Refers to male *mudang*.

kyŏngch'al (경찰 警察) Police (formerly *sunsa*, 순사 巡査).

kyŏngjangi (경장이 經장이) One who specializes in reciting sutras.

kyŏngmyŏnjusa (경면주사 鏡面朱砂) Powdered red cinnabar pigment.

Kyŏngsŏng (경성 京城) Seoul was referred to as Kyŏngsŏng during the Japanese occupation. Pronounced Keijō in Japanese.

Kyugonshiŭibang (규곤시의방) A cookbook written by Lady Chang of Andong (1598–1681).

maenggyŏk (맹격 盲覡) A blind male *mudang*.

maengin (맹인 盲人) A blind person.

maji (마지 摩旨) A rice offering.

maji (마지 麻紙) Literally, papers made of hemp. Refers to *musok* paintings.

makkŏli (막걸리) Wine made from rice, barley, wheat, or potatoes.

Malmi (말미 末尾) Refers to *Pari Kongju* (Princess Pari), an epic song sung during the *chinogwi kut* held for the departed in the greater Seoul and Kyŏnggi areas.

malmun (말문 말門) Literally, word gate. The first message from the spirits spoken through a neophyte's mouth is interpreted as the opening of the *malmun* of a shaman.

man (만) A ceremonial wig decorated with jewelry. See *k'ŭn mŏri*. It is worn during Sangsan, Pyŏlsang, *Malmi*, and *Toryŏng kŏri* in Seoul *kut*.

Glossary

Man (만 卍) A Buddhist emblem. Sanskrit Suastika.

manmulsang (만물상 萬物商) Literally, a shop that sells ten thousand items. Refers to shops that sell the religious goods of *musok*.

Manmyŏng (만명 萬明, 卍明) Ancestors of spirit-possessed shamans. Sometimes refers to the spirit of General Kim Yu-Shin's mother.

manshin (만신 萬神/卍神) Literally, ten thousand spirits. Refer to a spirit-possessed shaman believed to control ten thousand spirits. Preferred term among the *mudang* from Hwanghae Province. Sometimes used as a derogatory term for a shaman who believes in ten thousand spirits, particularly from a monotheist's point of view.

mansubaji (만수바지) Duet song.

mansuhyang (만수향 萬壽香) Incense. A brand name that has come to be used as a generic term (cf. Kleenex for tissues).

miko (日語, 巫女) A Japanese shaman.

Minbi (민비 閔妃) Queen Min, the patron of *musok*. Also respectfully referred to as Myŏngsŏng Hwanghu, 명성황후 明成皇后 (1851–1896).

min'gan shinang (민간신앙 民間信仰) Religion of (folk) people.

minyo (민요 民謠) Folk songs.

mishin (미신 迷信) Superstition. Derogatory term for *musok* practice.

mokt'ak (목탁 木鐸) A wooden idiophone (Chinese *muyu* 木魚) made in the shape of a fish. Struck with a wooden mallet.

momju (몸주) Body-governing spirit.

mongduri (몽두리 蒙頭里) A yellow outer garment fashioned after the attire of ladies in the Chosŏn Dynasty court. It is worn for the *Taeshin, Malmi*, and *Toryŏng kŏri*. Also referred to as *ŭnha mongduri*.

mu (무 巫) The Korean indigenous religion. Also refers to female *mudang*.

mu ŭi (무의 巫儀) A *musok* ritual.

muak (무악 巫樂) Ritual music.

Muanwang (무안왕 武安王) Honored title for Kwan-U, the Kwan-Un-Jang.

mubok (무복 巫服) Ritual garment.

mubult'ongshin (무불통신 無不通神) Power to communicate directly with spirits.

much'ŏn (무천 舞天) Literally, dance to heaven. Refers to a ritual.

mudang (무당 巫堂) A ritual specialist.

muga (무가 巫歌) Ritual songs used in *musok*.

mugam (무감 巫感 or 舞觀 [무관]) The part of the *kut* where clients are encouraged to dance wearing or holding pieces of the shaman's ritual clothing.

mugu (무구 巫具) Ritual objects used in *musok*.

Mugyo (무교 巫敎) Literally, *mu* religion.

mugyŏk (무격 巫覡) Spirit-possessed male shamans.

mugyŏng (무경 巫經) Incantations.

muhwa (무화 巫畵) *Musok* paintings.

muja (무자 巫子/巫者) Literally, a person who practices *mu*. Refers to male shamans.

mujang (무장 巫裝) Ritual garment.

mujigyŏn (무지견 無地絹) White fabric without patterns.

mukkuri (무꾸리) Divination.

muldongi (물동이) Water jar.

mumyŏng (무명 木綿 [목면]) Cotton cloth.

munhwajae (문화재 文化財) Important Intangible Cultural Property.

Munmuwang (문무왕) The 30th King of Shilla Kingdom (r. 661–681) who united the three Kingdoms: Shilla, Paekche, and Koguryŏ.

munsaje (문사제 門使者 [문사자]) Gatekeeper.

munsŏ (문서 文書) Literally, document. Refers to knowledge of rituals.

munyŏ (무녀 巫女) Female shamans.

muryŏng (무령 巫鈴) A set of ritual bells.

mushindo (무신도 巫神圖) Sacred painting of the spirits.

musok (무속 巫俗) The indigenous belief system of Korea.

Musok Pojonhoe (무속보존회 巫俗保存會) The Musok Preservation Association. The formal name of the school for spirit-possessed shamans in Seoul.

musokdo (무속도 巫俗圖) Sacred painting of the spirits.

musokin (무속인 巫俗人) Literally, a person who practices *musok*. Usually refers to *mudang*, the ritual specialists, not *musok* believers in general.

myŏlgong (멸공 滅共) The elimination of communism.

myŏng ch'ang (명창 名唱) Well known singers.

myŏngbu (명부 冥府) The underworld.

myŏngchan pokchan (명잔복잔 命盞福盞) Wine for long life and prosperity.

myŏngdari (명다리 命橋[명교]) Literally, a life bridge. Constructed from long pieces of cloth. Refers to a symbolic "bridge" for long life.

myŏngdo (명도 明圖) A brass mirror.

myŏngdu (명두 明斗) A diviner possessed by the spirit of a deceased child.

myŏngham (명함 名銜) Business or calling cards.

myŏngin (명인 名人) Well known artists or artisans.

myŏngmu (명무 名巫) Well known *mudang*.

myŏnsap'o (면사포 面紗布) Veil.

naerim kut (내림굿) An initiation ritual for a spirit-possessed shaman.

naerin mudang (내린무당 巫堂) Spirit-descended shaman.

naeryŏk pongji (내력봉지 來歷封紙) Covered bowls filled with grain used for divination at an initiation ritual.

nam ch'ima (남치마) A long indigo blue skirt, considered the most essential piece of clothing for the *kangshinmu*. For the Hanyang *kut*, the *nam ch'ima* is worn for *Chosang, Changgun,* Pyŏlsang, Shinjang, Taegam, and *Toryŏng kŏri. Paksu*, male shamans, put on *nam ch'ima* before adding on the ritual garments.

nam ch'ŏnik (남천익 藍天翼) Also known as *nam ch'ŏnrik* and *nam ch'ŏllyuk*. It is a dark blue garment with extended white sleeves fashioned after the uniform of the *tangsanggwan*, a military officer of the Chosŏn Dynasty. It is worn with *sultti* (belt with three pouches attached), also known as *sŭltti* for the *changgun* (military general) spirits during Sangsan *kŏri*.

Nam Yi (남이 南怡) A well known general (1144–1168) of the Chosŏn Dynasty who died young because of false accusations.

Namdaemun (남대문 南大門) South Gate in Seoul.

namgyŏk (남격 男覡) Male *mudang*.

nammu (남무 男巫) Male *mudang*.

Namsan (남산 南山) Mountain in Seoul where the original Kuksadang was located. Once known as Mokmyŏk San (목멱산 木覓山).

Namu Amit'abul (나무아미타불 南無阿彌陀) Buddhist prayer.

nangjung (낭중 郎中) Male *mudang*. Term used during Chosŏn Dynasty.

naramudang (나라 무당 巫堂) *Mudang* hired by the court.

narye (나례 儺禮) Annual exorcism of the court during the Koryŏ Dynasty.

nogaba (노가바: 노래가사바꾸어부르기) Singing by changing lyrics for a given melody.

noja (노자 路資) Literally, money for the road. Refers to the expenses for the soul traveling to the other world.

nŏul (너울) Veil.

nunch'i (눈치) Social sense.

Obang Shinjang (오방신장 五方神將) Spirits of the Five Directions.

obang shinjanggi (오방신장기 五方神將旗) Five flags symbolizing the Spirits of the Five Directions.

odong (오동 梧桐) Paulownia tree.

ohaeng (오행 五行) The five elements.

Okch'ugyŏng (옥추경 玉樞經) A Taoist prayer.

Ŏksabyŏl Kunung (억사별군웅 億士別軍雄) The spirit who removes malevolent spirits during the *chudang mullim* held before the *kut* begins. Also known as Sangsan Kunung (상산군웅 上山軍雄).

oksu (옥수 玉水) Sacred water.

ŏn wŏldo (언월도 偃月刀) A large ceremonial battle blade.

osaek kurŭmtari (오색 五色 구름다리) Literally, five-colored cloud bridge. Refers to long five-colored cloth hung in the ritual area.

oshin (오신 娛神) Entertaining the spirits.

osimi (오세미) *Mudang* in northeastern Hamgyŏng Provinces.

paek changsam (백장삼 白長衫) White ritual garment fashioned after the Buddhist monk's robe.

paekji (백지 白紙) White mulberry paper.

Paekma Shinjang (백마 신장 白馬神將) The Militant Spirit that rides a white horse.

paekryŏn (백련 白蓮) White paper flower.

paji (바지) Trousers.

paksa (박사 博士) A spirit-possessed male shaman. In secular context, Ph.D.

paksu (박수 博數) A spirit-possessed male shaman.

p'alch'ŏn (팔천 八賤) Base people who work in eight different occupations: artisans (*kongjang* 공장 工匠), Buddhist monks (*sŭngryŏ* 승려 僧侶), butchers (*paekjŏng* 백정 白丁), female entertainers (*kisaeng* 기생 妓生), funeral attendants or pallbearers (*sangyŏ kkun* 상여꾼 喪輿꾼), musicians (*kwangdae* 광대 廣大), private slaves (*sanobi* 사노비 私奴婢), and shamans (*mudang* 무당 巫堂).

p'aldo (팔도 八道) Literally, eight provinces. Refers to all of Korea in earlier years.

p'algwanhoe (팔관회 八關會) Festival of Eight Vows.

pangsaengje (방생제 放生祭) A ritual releasing of fish, eels, turtles, and so on, back to the water.

pangul (방울) Bell or bell tree.

p'ansori (판소리) Solo epic singing with *puk* (drum) accompaniment.

p'ansu (판수 判數) A blind male diviner.

para (바라) Large cymbals.

Pari Kongju (바리 공주 公主) Epic song about Princess Pari. Also known as *Malmi*.

p'at (팥) Red beans.

pe (베 麻布[마포]) Hemp cloth.

pe karŭgi (베가르기) Cutting the hemp cloth. Also known as *kil karŭgi*.

pigabi (비가비 非甲이) Musicians who are not born into *sesŭpmu* (hereditary *mudang*) families (southwestern tradition).

pihaengjang (비행장 飛行場) Old word for airport. Now *konghang*.

p'iri (피리 觱栗 [필율]) A cylindrical oboe made of bamboo.

pisu (비수 匕首) Literally, a dagger. Refers to the double-bladed fodder chopper on which the *manshin* stands barefoot in the Hwanghae Province tradition.

Pitkat (빗갓) A black hat decorated with *hosu* (tiger's whiskers). Worn for Sanshin, Kunung, and Sŏngju *kŏri*. Also known as *kat*.

poksa (복사 卜士/卜師) A male diviner.

ponhyang (본향 本鄉) A native place.

pŏpsa (법사 法師) A man specializing in the recitation of sutras.

posal (보살 菩薩) Literal meaning, a *bodhisattva*. Refers to a female *mudang*.

poyu tanch'e (보유단체 保有團體) Literally, a retaining group. Refers to the government designated performing group of an Important Intangible Cultural Property.

poyuja (보유자 保有者) Literally, holder or retainer. Refers to the artists designated by the government as the performers of an Important Intangible Cultural Property.

puch'ae (부채 扇 [선]) Fan.

p'udak kŏri (푸닥거리) Small-scale healing ritual.

Glossary

pujak (부작 符作) An amulet in three-dimensional form.
pujŏk (부적 符籍) Talisman in two-dimensional form.
pujŏng (부정 不淨) Pollution.
pukŏ (북어 北魚) Dried pollock, used in *musok* as an offering.
Pulsŏl Ch'ŏnji P'alyanggyŏng (불설천지팔양경 佛說天地八陽經) A Buddhist prayer.
Pulsŏl ch'ŏnsugyŏng (불설천수경 佛說千手經) A Buddhist prayer.
p'ungmul (풍물 風物) Outdoor ensemble percussion instruments and *hojŏk* (conical oboe).
p'ungsu (풍수 風水) Literally, wind and water. Refers to geomancy.
puri (부리) Family roots. Refers to ancestor spirits of a given family.
p'yebaek (폐백 幣帛) Formal greetings of the bride and groom to their families.
pyŏlbi (별비 別費) Extra money offered by clients during the ritual.
pyŏng kut (병굿 病굿) A healing ritual.
pyŏngch'ang (병창 竝唱) Singing solo, accompanying oneself on a string instrument.
saebal shimji (새발심지) Paper candle in the shape of a bird's foot. Also known as *sebal shimji*.
saekdong hansam (색동 한삼 汗衫) Long white sleeve extensions with multi-color stripes worn by Pari Kongju during *Toryŏng kŏri*.
saet'ani (새탄이 새타니) Literal meaning, a person riding birds. Refers to *mudang*.
saja (사자 使者) A spirit believed to lead the deceased to the other world.
Saje (사제) See *saja*.
saju (사주 四柱) Literally, four columns. Information of one's birth: time, date, month, and year.
sal (살 煞) Sudden misfortune (cf. curse).
salman (살만 薩滿) Borrowed from the transliterated Chinese word for *shaman*.
salp'uri (살푸리 煞푸리) Removal of *sal*.
sam chaebi (삼재비) A trio of musicians playing *p'iri, taegŭm,* and *haegŭm*.
Sambul Chesŏk (삼불제석 三佛帝釋) Refers to the three Buddhist figures—Sakyamuni, Avalokitesvara, and Mahasthamaprata in Sanskrit. Amit'abul (아미타불 阿彌陀佛), Kwanseŭm Posal (관세음보살 觀世音菩薩), and Taeseji Posal (대세지보살 大勢至菩薩) in Korean.
samgang oryun (삼강오륜 三綱五倫) *Samgang* (三綱), three cardinal human relationships, between ruler and subject (군위신강 軍爲臣綱), father and son (부위자강 父爲子綱), and husband and wife (부위부강 夫爲婦綱), reinforced by *oryun* (오륜 五倫), the five moral imperatives of righteousness (의리 義理) between sovereign and subject (군신 君臣), proper rapport (친애 親愛) between father and son (부자 父子), separation of functions (분별 分別) between husband and wife, sequence of birth (차서 次序) between elder and younger brothers (장유 長幼), and faithfulness (신의 信義) between friends (붕우 朋友).

Samguk Yusa (삼국유사 三國遺事) *Memorabilia of the Three Kingdoms* written in 1193 by Buddhist monk Iryŏn (1209–1289) (일연 一然). Also known as *Legends and History of the Three Kingdoms of Ancient Korea*.

samhyŏn yukkak (삼현육각 三絃六角) An ensemble of six musicians playing two *p'iri, taegŭm, haegŭm, changgu,* and *puk*. Also, the repertoire performed by this ensemble.

samil ch'isŏng (삼일치성 三日致誠) Small ritual held on the third day after a *kut*.

samjae (삼재 三才) The three elements of the world: heaven, earth, and humans.

samjae p'allan [p'alnan] (삼재팔난 三災八難) Refers to hardship in life. Literally, three disasters and eight difficulties. The three disasters are caused by fire, water, or wind; the eight difficulties, by hunger, thirst, cold, heat, water, fire, knife, and war.

samjich'ang (삼지창 三枝槍) A ritual trident.

samjitnal (삼짓날) The third day of the third month in the lunar calendar.

samu (사무 師巫) Refers to *mudang*. Shows respect.

samulnori (사물놀이 四物놀이) Literally, playing four things. Refers to a percussion ensemble of four instruments: *changgu, ching, kkwaenggwari,* and *puk*.

san jum (산줌 算줌) Literally, offering the counting. Refers to divination by way of counting fruits, grains of rice, candies and so on by pairs to determine if the spirits are satisfied. If the number is even, it is interpreted as meaning that the spirits are content.

sangmun (상문 喪門) Lowly spirit lurking around the dead.

sangshik (상식 上食) Offering food for ancestors.

sani (사니) Hereditary musician.

sanja (산자) Large cookies made of rice.

sanjin (산진 山盡) Mountain packed with trees.

sanjo (산조 散調) Instrumental folk solo genre developed in the 19th century.

sant'ong (산통 算筒) Box filled with divination sticks.

saŏ (사어 死語) Literally, dead word. Obsolete argot.

sarye ch'isŏng (사례치성 謝禮致誠) Literally, small ritual to thank the spirits. Refers to small-scale ritual held on the third day after a *kut*. Also known as *samil ch'isŏng*.

sasil (사실 查實) Literally, examining the truth. Refers to an act of divination during *kut*.

sebal shimji (세발심지) Paper candle in the shape of three legs. Also known as *saebal shimji*.

sesŭpmu (세습무 世襲巫) A hereditary *mudang*.

seyogo (세요고 細腰鼓) Another name for *changgu*.

shihwayŏnp'ung (시화연풍 時和年豊) A peaceful and plentiful time.

shijo (시조 時調) A short lyric poem.

shimbang (심방) Term for *mudang* used on Cheju Island.

Glossary

shin (신 神) Spirit. The character "shin" is "made up of the radical shi 示 'an omen,' and the phonetic shen 신(申)" (Wu 1991:3).
shin abŏji (신아버지 神아버지) A spirit father.
shin chason (신자손 神子孫) Spirit children.
shin kyo (신교 神敎) Religion of spirits.
shin ŏmŏni (신어머니 神어머니) A spirit mother.
shin pumo (신부모 神父母) Spirit parents.
shin ŭl purinŭn saram (신을 부리는사람) Person who controls the spirits.
shinawi (시나위) Instrumental ensemble music in the *sesŭpmu kut*.
shinbang (신방 神房) Sacred room. See *shindang*. Also refers to male shaman.
shinbok (신복 神服) Ritual garment.
shindang (신당 神堂) A sacred room where the shaman's altar is placed.
shin'gu (신구 神具) Ritual objects.
Shinjang (신장 神將) Militant spirit (Lee 1981:110).
shinjang (신장 神裝) Ritual garment.
shinjang halmŏm (신장할멈 神將할멈) Old female diviner possessed by the Shinjang Spirit.
shink'al (신칼 神刀 [신도]) A set of ritual knives. Used for dancing and symbolic fighting with *kwi* (malevolent spirits) that cause sickness or misfortune.
shinmyŏng (신명 神明) A deity or divinity.
shinryŏng (신령 神鈴) A set of ritual bells.
shinryŏng hwabon (신령화본 神靈 畵本) Paintings of spirits.
shinsang (신상 神像) Paintings of spirits.
shinsŏn (신선 神仙) Refers to the Taoist immortal beings.
shint'ak (신탁 神託) A spirit's words spoken through a shaman. Also known as *kongsu*.
shint'ongryŏk (신통력 神通力) Power to communicate with spirits.
ship taewang (십대왕 十大王) The Ten Kings of the other world—Chin'gwang Taewang (진광대왕 秦廣大王), Ch'ogang Taewang (초강대왕 初江大王), Songje Taewang (송제대왕 宋帝大王), Ogwan Taewang (오관대왕 伍官大王), Yŏmra Taewang (염라대왕 閻羅大王), Pyŏnsŏng Taewang (변성대왕 變成大王), T'aesan Taewang (태산대왕 泰山大王), P'yŏngdŭng Taewang (평등대왕 平等大王), Toshi Taewang (도시대왕 都市大王), and Odo Chŏnryun Taewang (오도전륜대왕 五道轉輪大王).
shiwang (시왕 十王) Short for *ship taewang*, the Ten Kings of the other world.
sogak (소각 燒却) Burning things after the ritual.
sŏgi (서기 西紀) Gregorian calendar.
sogŭm (소금 小金) Small gong. Refers to *kkwaenggwari*.
soji (소지 燒紙) Literally, burning paper. Refers to the purifying act of burning sacred paper.
soju (소주 燒酒) Distilled hard liquor.
Sŏkchŏn (석전 釋奠) Ritual held for Confucius and Confucian scholars.

sokkot (속곳, 속옷) Long baggy women's underwear.
sŏn kŏri (선거리) Literally, standing section. Refers to the parts of the ritual in which the officiating *mudang* stands, unlike *anjŭn kŏri* (literally, seated section) in which the *mudang* sits.
Sŏnang (서낭 城隍 [성황]) Tutelary spirits.
sŏn'ga (선가 仙家) Old term referring to a spirit-possessed shaman, used during the Koryŏ period (918–1392) (Yun & Lee 1987:19).
songshin (송신 送神) Bidding farewell to the spirits.
Sŏngsu (성수) This word comes from Sŏngsuk (성숙 星宿), one of the spirits in *musok*.
sŏn'gwan (선관 仙官) A spirit-possessed *mudang* born into an upper class family.
sŏnmudang (선무당 선巫堂) Inexperienced *mudang*.
sŏnp'ung (선풍 仙風) Old term referring to a spirit-possessed shaman, used during the Koryŏ period (Yun & Lee 1987:19).
sŏnsaengnim (선생님 先生任) Teacher.
sŏpsu (섭수) An outer garment made with a gold or green bodice and red sleeves. Gold *sŏpsu* are worn for Pyŏlsang but blue ones for *Shinjang* or *Momju Taegam*. For Ponhyang *kŏri*, green *sŏpsu* with white trim (*kkŭttong*) are worn. Also known as *kugunbok*.
ssanggoljuk (쌍골죽 雙骨竹) A type of bamboo tube.
ssuksu (쑥수 熟手 [숙수]) A person who specializes in arranging the offerings on the altar for the ritual.
subi (수비 隨夫/ 隨陪 [수부 / 수배]) Lowly spirits.
sujin (수진 水盡) Dried out river bed.
sukmu (숙무 熟巫) Musically trained spirit-possessed *mudang*.
sukpae (숙배 肅拜) A formal greeting.
sulryŏk torŭm (술력 巡歷 [순력] 도름) Literally, inspecting every corner.
sultti (술띠) A belt with three pouches worn with blue *ch'ŏllik* during the Sangsan *kŏri*.
sŭnbang (슨방) Term for *mudang* on Cheju Island.
sup'alyŏn (수팔연 水波蓮 [수파련]) Paper flowers placed on the offering table.
sŭpdŭkmu (습득무 習得巫) Apprenticed *mudang*.
suran (수란 繡란) A long skirt with *kŭmbak* (plated in gold foil) trim.
susang (수상 手相) Divination based on the shape of hand and lines of palms.
susŏng karak (수성가락 隨聲가락) Melodies played by instruments accompanying songs like *kasa, kagok,* or *shijo* in the *chŏngak* repertoire.
sŭsŭng (스승) Literally, a teacher. *Mudang* in Hamgyŏng Provinces.
tabang (다방 茶房) Teahouse.
taeanju (대안주 大按酒) Great offering of food and drink.
taeborŭmnal (대보름날) Full moon in the first month of the lunar calendar.
taedong kut (대동굿) *Kut* held for the community.

taegam (대감 大監) The protector of the home (Lee 1981:123) and the great overseer.

t'aegil (擇日) Selecting an auspicious date.

taegŭm (대금 大笒) A transverse bamboo flute.

taegŭm (대금 大金) A large gong. Refers to *ching*.

Taehan Min'guk (대한민국 大韓民國) Official name of the Republic of Korea or South Korea.

Taehan Sŭnggong Kyŏngshin Yŏnhaphoe (대한승공경신연합회 大韓勝共敬神聯合會) Literally, Korean Spirit Worshippers' Association for Victory Over Communism. Refers to an association for shamans.

taeju (대주 大主) A male sponsor for a *kut*.

t'aeju mudang (태주무당 太主巫堂) Diviner possessed by the T'aeju spirits.

t'aenghwa (탱화 幀畵) Buddhist paintings. Refers also to *musok* paintings. Also known as *hwabon*, *hwabun*, or *yŏngbon*.

taenju (댄주 大按酒 [대안주]) Literally, food served with drink on a grand scale. Refers to Sangsan *kŏri* in Hanyang *kut*.

t'aep'yŏngso (태평소 太平簫) A conical oboe.

Taeseji Posal (대세지보살 大勢至菩薩) In Sanskrit, Mahasthamaprata.

Taeshin (대신 大神) The ancestor spirit of *kangshinmu*. Also known as Taeshin Halmŏni.

taeshin k'al (대신칼 大神刀[대신도]) A pair of ritual knives decorated with tassel made of white paper strips.

taesu taemyŏng (대수대명 代數代命) Transferring misfortune elsewhere.

tangak (당악 堂樂) Ritual music. Also refers to a rhythmic cycle used in Hanyang *kut* music.

tanggolle (당골레) Refers to hereditary *mudang*.

tanggol p'an (당골판) Area designated for a hereditary *mudang*.

tangju (당주 堂主) *Mudang* responsible for overseeing the entire *kut*.

tan'gi (단기 檀紀) The Korean traditional calendar. Its beginning corresponds to the year 2333 B.C.E.

tan'gol (단골) In secular context, *tan'gol* refers to a regular customer or client in a business relationship. In *musok*, *tan'gol* refers to the *mudang* one regularly patronizes, especially in the hereditary tradition.

tan'golle (당골레) Hereditary *mudang*.

tangŭi (당의 唐衣) Ritual garment fashioned after Tang court costumes.

Tan'gun (단군 檀君) The mythical founder of Korea.

Tano (단오 端午) The 5th day of the 5th lunar month.

t'apsang (탑상) A ritual for installing the altar.

t'aryŏng (타령 打令, 打鈴) A shaman song.

t'aryŏng (타령 妥靈) Refers to the ritual offering of song and dance practiced since the Koryŏ period (918–1392) (Yi Nŭng-Hwa [1927] 1991:180).

T'ojŏngpigyŏl (토정비결 土亭秘訣) Divination manual written by T'ojŏng, (legal name, Yi Chi-Ham 이지함) about 450 years ago.

tŏkdam (덕담 德談) Blessings. Good wishes.
tokkyŏng chŏmbok (독경점복 讀經占卜) Recitation of prayers and divination.
tokkyŏng poksul (독경복술 讀經卜術) Recitation of prayers and divination.
tomu (도무 跳舞) Dancing while jumping up and down in one spot.
tongja mudang (동자무당 童子巫堂) A *mudang* possessed by the Tongja (boy) Spirit.
tongji (동지 冬至) The longest night of the year.
tongjŏn (동전 銅錢) Brass coins.
tongmaeng (동맹 東盟) Chumong founder-worship of Koguryŏ (37 B.C.E.–668).
toryŏng tolgi (도령 돌기 道場 [도장] 돌기) Circumambulation.
tosa (도사 道士) Enlightened Taoist or teacher.
tosa (도사 道師) Literally, a Taoist teacher.
t'osaebi (토새비) Male *mudang* in Hamgyŏng Provinces.
tossam (돗쌈) Bundle wrapped in straw mat.
totchari (도짜리) Straw mat.
tti (띠) Belt.
ttŏk (떡) Rice cake.
Ttŭn Taewang (뜬대왕 大王) An honorific for Saja.
uhwan kut (우환굿 憂患굿) Healing ritual.
ŭidae (의대 衣帶) Clothes and belts.
ŭmyang (음양 陰陽) Yin and yang in Chinese. The dual cosmic forces.
ŭnha mongduri (은하몽두리 銀河蒙頭里) Outer garment worn by Pari Kongju.
ŭnŏ (은어 隱語) Argot. Used exclusively among group members.
wip'ae (위패 位牌) Wooden tablets.
wŏldo (월도 月刀) Crescent moon shaped ritual knife.
wŏn (원) The Korean monetary unit.
wŏnhyŏng (원형 原形) Original form.
wŏnsam (원삼 圓衫) Floor-length outer garment with a pink or green bodice (*kil*) and multi-colored sleeves. Pink *wŏnsam* is worn for Hogu and green for Ch'angbu *kŏri*.
yakryŏngsu (약령수 藥靈水) Sacred water received from the spirits by Pari Kongju.
yaksu (약수 藥水) Literally, medicinal water. Refers to sacred water.
yangban (양반 兩班) Elite class of Chosŏn Dynasty.
yangjung (양중 兩中) Male *mudang*. Term used during Chosŏn Dynasty.
Yi Ch'a-Don (이차돈 異次頓) His legal name, Pak Yŏmch'ok (박염촉 朴厭觸) (?–528 C.E.).
Yi Dynasty (이 李) Also known as the Chosŏn Dynasty (1392–1910).
yŏlch'ae (열채) Bamboo stick used for the right head of *changgu*.
yŏmju (염주 念珠) Buddhist prayer beads.
yŏmu (여무 女巫) Female *mudang*.
yŏndunghoe (연등회 燃燈會) Lotus lantern festival held during Koryŏ Dynasty.

yŏnggo (영고 迎鼓) Literally, spirit-invoking drums. Refers to the harvest festival of Puyŏ (18 B.C.E–660).
yŏngjŏng (영정 影幀) Portrait.
yŏngmae (영매 靈媒) One who can communicate with spirits.
yŏngsan (영산 靈山) The mountain of dead souls (Lee 1981:116). Refers to spirits who faced unexpected deaths.
yŏngshil (영실 靈室) Dead souls.
Yongshin (용신 龍神) Literally, the dragon spirit.
yŏnwŏldo (연월도 烟[煙]月刀) Crescent moon shaped ritual knife.
yŏpchŏn (엽전 葉錢) Brass coins.
Yubulsŏn (유불선 儒彿仙) Confucianism, Buddhism, and Taoism.
Yudu (유두 流頭) The 15th day of the 6th lunar month.

References

Akamatsu, Chijo and Takashi Akiba. 1991. *Chosŏn Musok ŭi Yŏn'gu* [Research on Korean *musok*]. Translated from Japanese into Korean by Sim U-Sŏng. Seoul: Tongmunsŏn. Originally published in Japanese in two volumes, 1937–38.

Akiba, Takashi. 1987. *Chosŏn Musok ŭi Hyŏnji Yŏn'gu* [Field research on Korean *musok*]. Translated from Japanese into Korean by Ch'oe Kil-Sŏng. Taegu: Kyŏngbuk Inswaeso. Originally published in Japanese, 1950.

Biederman, Hans. 1992. *Dictionary of Symbolism.* Translated by James Hulbe. NY: Facts On File.

Bishop, Isabella Bird. [1898] 1970. *Korea And Her Neighbors: A Narrative of Travel, with an Account of the Recent Vicissitudes and Present Position of the Country.* Reprint, Seoul: Yonsei University Press.

Blacking, John. 1973. *How Musical Is Man?* Seattle: University of Washington.

Bok, Sissela. 1982. *Secrets: Ethics of Concealment and Revelation.* NY: Pantheon Books.

Bourguignon, Erika. 1976. *Possession.* Corte Madera, CA: Chandler & Sharp Publishers, Inc.

Buswell, Robert E. Jr. 1997. "Monastery Lay Association in Contemporary Korean Buddhism: A Study of the Puril Hoe." In *Religion and Society in Contemporary Korea*, edited by Lewis R. Lancaster and Richard K. Payne, 101–126. Berkeley: University of California, Institute of East Asian Studies, Center for Korean Studies.

Carrithers, Michael. 1992. *Why Humans Have Cultures: Explaining Anthropology and Social Diversity.* Oxford: Oxford University Press.

Central Daily Newspaper Ltd., ed. 1998. *Korean Business Directory 1998–1999.* Seattle: The Central Daily Newspaper Ltd.

Ch'a Ok-Sung. 1997. *Han'gukin ŭi Chonggyo Kyŏnghŏm: Mugyo* [Religious experiences among Koreans: *Mu* religion]. Seoul: Sŏgwangsa.

Chamberlain, Jonathan. 1997. *Chinese Gods.* Selangor Darul Ehsan, Malaysia: Pelanduk Publications.

Chang, Sa-Hun. 1991. *Dictionary of Korean Music.* Seoul: Segwang Ŭmak Ch'ulp'ansa.

Chang, Sŏng-Man. 1992. *Musok Ko* [About *musok*]. Seoul: Minsan.

Chin, Kwang-Sŏk. 1993. "Hŭng gwa Mŏt ŭi Sŏl Changgu: Kim O-Ch'ae Sŏnsaeng" [Aesthetics of drumming of Kim O-Ch'ae]. *Kut* 6:3–26.

Chin, Soo-Young. 1989. "The Role of Ritual for Korean American Elderly." In *Frontiers of Asian American Studies*, edited by Gail M. Nomura, Russell Endo, Stephen H. Sumida, and Russell C. Leong, 127–139. Pullman, WA: Washington State University Press.

Cho, Cha-Ryong. 1996. *Shin ŭl T'aekhan Namja* [A man who chose the spirits]. Seoul: Paeksong.

Cho, Hung-youn (Hŭng-Yun). 1990. *Han'guk ŭi Mu* [Korean *mu*]. Seoul: Chŏngŭmsa.

———. 1997. *Mu: Han'guk Mu ŭi Yŏksa wa Hyŏnsang* [*Mu*: history and present form of Korean *mu*]. Seoul: Minjoksa.

———. 1999. *Hang'uk ui Shamanism* [Korean shamanism]. Seoul: Seoul National University Press.

Chodron, Thubten. 1992. *Taming the Monkey Mind*. Leicestershire, England: Tynron Press.

Ch'oe, Chun-Shik. 1996. *Han'guk Chonggyo Iyagi: Han'gukin ŭi Maŭmŭl Pijŭn Mu, Yu, Pul, To* [Tale about Korean religions: Mu, Confucianism, Buddhism, and Taoism, which formed Korean minds]. Seoul: Hanul.

Ch'oe, Kil-Sŏng. 1981. "Mudang ŭi Yŏksa: '*Mudang Naryŏk*' e Kwanhayŏ" [History of *mudang*: on '*Mudang Naryŏk*']. In *Han'guk ŭi Mudang*, 69–80. Seoul: Yŏlhwadang.

———. 1989. *Han'guk Min'gan Shinang ŭi Yŏn'gu* [Research on Korean folk belief]. Taegu: Kyemyŏng Taehakkyo Ch'ulp'anbu [Kyemyŏng University Press].

———. 1990. *Han'guk Musok ŭi Yŏn'gu* [Research on Korean *musok*]. Seoul: Asea Munhwasa.

———. 1992. *Han'guk Musokji* [Journals on Korean *musok*]. 2 vols. Seoul: Asea Munhwasa.

Ch'oe, Tong-Hyŏn. 1994. *P'ansori ran Muŏt in'ga* [What is *p'ansori*?]. Seoul: Tosŏ Ch'ulp'an Editor.

Choi, Chong-Min. 1983. "Hwanghaedo Kut ŭi Ŭmak" [Ritual Music in Hwanghae Province]. In *Hwanghaedo Naerimkut* [Initiation ritual in Hwanghae Province], Han'guk ŭi Kut [Korean rituals], vol. 1, 97–106. Seoul: Yŏlhwadang.

Choi, Chungmoo. 1987. "The Competence of Korean Shamans as Performers of Folklore." Ph.D. diss., Department of Folklore, Indiana University, Bloomington.

———. 1989a. "The Artistry and Ritual Aesthetics of Urban Korean Shamans." *Journal of Ritual Studies* (University of Pittsburgh) 3 (2): 235–249.

———. 1989b. "The Recruitment of Shamans in Korea: The Symbiosis Between Cultural Idiom and Performing Arts." In *Shamanism: Past and Present*, edited by M. Hoppal and O. von Sadowszky, vol. 2, 283–294. LA: Fullerton International Society for Trans-Oceanic Research.

———. 1997. "Hegemony and Shamanism: The State, the Elite, and Shamans in Contemporary Korea." In *Religion and Society in Contemporary Korea*, edited by Lewis R. Lancaster and Richard K. Payne, 19–48. Berkeley: University of California, Institute of East Asian Studies, Center for Korean Studies.

Choi, Hŏn. 1995. "Seoul ŭi Chaesu Kut kwa Chinogwi Kut" [*Chaesu kut* and *chinogwi kut* in Seoul]. In *Han'guk ŭi Kut* [Korean rituals]: *Korean Shaman Music*, edited by

Yi Yun-Gyŏng, 9–34. Vol. 29 of *Anthology of Korean Traditional Music*. Seoul: The National Center for Korean Traditional Performing Arts.
Chŏng, Pyŏng-Ho. 1992. *Minsok Kihaeng* [An account of traveling through folklore]. Seoul: Nunpit.
Chu, Kang-Hyŏn. 1997. "Uri Munhwa ŭi Susukkekki" [Mystery (riddles) of our culture]. Seoul: Hankyŏre Shinmunsa.
Chung, Sung Sook. 1998. "The Impact of Yin and Yang Ideology in the Art of Korean P'ansori Tradition: An Analytical Study Based on the Late Mme. Pak Nok-Ju Version of P'ansori Hŭngbo-ga." Ph.D. diss. in Ethnomusicology, University of California, Santa Barbara.
Clark, Charles Allen. [1932] 1961. *Religions of Old Korea*. Seoul: Society of Korea.
Clements, Forrest E. [1932] 1965. "Primitive Concepts of Disease." In *American Archaeology and Ethnology*, edited by A. L. Kroeber, Robert H. Lowie and Ronald L. Olson. Berkeley: University of California Press. 32 (2): 185–252.
Coleman, Craig S. 1996. *American Images of Korea: Korea and Koreans Portrayed in Books, Magazines, Television, News Media, and Film*. Seoul: Hollym.
Cooke, Peter. 1980. "Heterophony." In *The New Grove Dictionary of Music and Musicians*. London: Macmillan Publishers Ltd. 8:537–538.
Covell, Alan Carter. 1986. *Folk Art and Magic: Shamanism in Korea*. Elizabeth, NJ: Hollym International Corp.
Covell, Jon Carter. 1992 (1981). *Korea's Cultural Roots*. Elizabeth, NJ: Hollym International Corp.
Czaplicka, M.A. 1914. *Aboriginal Siberia: A Study in Social Anthropology*. Oxford: The Clarendon Press.
Deuchler, Martina. 1980. "Neo-Confucianism: The Impulse for Social Action in Early Yi Korea." *The Journal of Korean Studies* 2:71–111.
Dioszegi, Vilmos. 1968. "The Problems of the Ethnic Homogeneity of Tofa (Karagas) Shamans." In *Popular Beliefs and Folklore Tradition in Siberia*, edited by Dioszegi, 239–329. Bloomington: Indiana University.
———. 1978. "Pre-Islamic Shamanism of the Baraba Turks and Some Ethnogenetic Conclusions." In *Shamanism in Siberia*, edited by V. Dioszegi and M. Hoppal, 2 (1): 83–167. Budapest: Akademiai Kiado.
Dournon, Geneviève. 1992. "Organology." In *Ethnomusicology: An Introduction*, edited by Helen Myers, 245–300. The Norton/Grove Handbooks in Music. NY: W.W. Norton & Company.
Duvan, Nadyezhda. 1996. "The Ulchi World View as Told to and Translated by Jan Van Ysslestyne." In *First Fish First People: Salmon Tales of the North Pacific Rim*, edited by Judith Roche and Meg McHutchison, 90–99. Seattle: University of Washington Press.
Eliade, Mircea. 1964. *Shamanism: Archaic Techniques of Ecstasy*. Translated from French by Willard R. Trask. Bollingen Series 76. Princeton: Princeton University Press.

———. 1987. "Shamanism." In *The Encyclopedia of Religion*, edited by M. Eliade, 13:201–208. NY: Macmillan Publishing Co.

Ellingson, Ter. 1974. "Musical Flight in Tibet." *Asian Music* 2:3–43.

———. 1987. "Drums." In *Encyclopedia of Religion*, edited by M. Eliade, 4:494–503. NY: Macmillan Publishing Co.

———. 1996. "Classic Shamanism Areas in Asia." Map handout for *Trance and Spirit Possession* seminar, University of Washington.

Finnegan, Ruth. 1977. *Oral Poetry: Its Nature, Significance and Social Context*. Cambridge: Cambridge University Press.

Firth, Raymond. 1958. "Religion in Social Reality." In *Reader in Comparative Religion: An Anthropological Approach*, edited by W. A. Lessa and E. Z. Vogt, 124–133. Evanston, Illinois: Row, Peterson and Company.

Friedson, Steven M. 1996. *The Dancing Prophets: Musical Experience in Tumbuka Healing*. Chicago: University of Chicago Press.

Gaster, Theodor H. 1987. "Amulets and Talismans." In *The Encyclopedia of Religion*, edited by Mircea Eliade, 1:243–246. NY: Macmillan Publishing Co.

Gennep, Arnold van. 1960. *The Rites of Passage: A Classic Study of Cultural Celebrations*. Chicago: The University of Chicago Press.

Guillemoz, Alexandre. 1983. *Les Algues, Les Anciens, Les Dieux: La Vie et la Religion d'un Village de Pecheurs-Agriculteurs Coreens* [Seaweed, ancestors, gods: life and religion of a fishing-agricultural village in Korea]. Paris: Le Leopard d'Or.

———. 1998. "What do the *Naerim Mudang* from Seoul Learn?" In *Korean Shamanism: Revivals, Survivals, and Change*, edited by Keith Howard, 73–89. Seoul: Royal Asiatic Society Korean Branch.

Ha, Man-Su. 1992. *Haengsa Yogŏl* [The manual for ritual]. Seoul: Minsan.

Haft, Nina Otis. 1992. "Initiation into Ecstasy: An Interview with Hi-ah Park, Korean Mudang." *Shaman's Drum* 26 (winter): 36–45.

Han'guk Chonggyo Sahoe Yŏn'guso, ed. 1991. *Han'guk Chonggyo Munhwa Sajŏn* [Dictionary for Korean religion and culture]. Seoul: Chipmundang.

Han'guk Kojŏn Yongŏ Sajŏn, eds. 1991. *Han'guk Kojŏn Yongŏ Sajŏn* [Dictionary for old Korean]. Seoul: Shinhŭng Inswae Chushik Hoesa.

Han'guk Minjok Hakhoe, ed. 1997. *Han'guk ŭi Myŏngmu* [Famous shamans in Korea]. Seoul: Mundŏksa.

Han'guk Minsok Taesajŏn P'yŏnch'an Wiwŏnhoe, ed. 1991. *Han'guk Minsok Taesajŏn* [Extensive Korean folk dictionary]. Seoul: Minjok Munwhasa.

Han'guk Munhwa Sangjing Sajŏn, eds. 1996. *Han'guk Munhwa Sangjing Sajŏn*. [Dictionary for Korean cultural symbols]. Seoul: Tonga Ch'ulp'an.

Harner, Michael J. 1973. *The Jivaro: People of the Sacred Waterfalls*. Garden City, NY: Anchor Press/Doubleday.

Harvey, Youngsook Kim. 1983. "Korean *Mudang*: Socialization Experiences of Six Female Shamans." Ph.D. diss. in Anthropology, University of Hawaii.

Heyman, Alan. 1983. "The Ritual Song of the God Sonnim." *Korea Journal* 23 (11): 50–57.

———, ed. 1993. *The Traditional Music and Dance of Korea*. Seoul: Korean Traditional Performing Arts Center.
Hobsbawm, Eric. 1983. "Introduction: Inventing Traditions." In *The Invention of Tradition*, edited by Eric Hobsbawm and Terence Rangers. Cambridge: Cambridge University Press.
Hogarth, Hyun-key Kim. 1995. "Reciprocity, Status and the Korean Shamanistic Ritual." Ph.D. diss. in Social Anthropology, The University of Kent, Canterbury.
Hood, Mantle. 1960. "The Challenge of Bi-Musicality." *Ethnomusicology* 4 (2): 55–59.
———. 1971. *The Ethnomusicologist*. NY: McGraw-Hill Book Co.
Howard, Keith. 1990. *Bands, Songs, and Shamanistic Rituals: Folk Music in Korean Society*. Seoul: Royal Asiatic Society Korean Branch.
———. 1996. "Preservation and Presentation of Korean Intangible Cultural Assets." In *Methodologies for the Preservation of Intangible Heritage: Final Report of the Policy Meeting on the Development of Methodology for the Preservation of Intangible Heritage*, edited by The Korean National Commission for UNESCO, 85–14. Seoul: Office of the Cultural Properties of the Republic of Korea in cooperation with UNESCO.
———. 1998a. "Korean Shamanism Today." In *Korean Shamanism Revivals, Survivals and Change*, edited by K. Howard, 1–14. Seoul: Royal Asiatic Society, Korea Branch.
———. 1998b. *A Study of Musical Instruments in Korean Traditional Music*. Seoul: The National Center for Korean Traditional Performing Arts.
Huhm, Halla Pai. 1980. *Kut: Korean Shamanist Rituals*. Seoul: Hollym International Corp.
Hulbert, Homer B. [1906] 1969. *The Passing of Korea*. Seoul: Yonsei University Press.
Hwang, Lu-si. 1990. *P'aldo Kut* [*Kut* from eight provinces]. Seoul: Taewŏnsa.
———. 1992. *Han'gukin ŭi Kut kwa Mudang* [Korean rituals and ritual specialists]. Seoul: Munŭmsa.
———. 1997. "The Kut in Contemporary Shamanism." In *Korean Cultural Heritage: Thought and Religion*, edited by Jongwon Kim, 2:198–205. Seoul: Samsung Moonhwa Printing Co.
———. 1995. "Han'guk Musok ŭi T'ŭksŏng" [Special features of Korean *musok*]. In *Han'guk ŭi Musok Munhwa* [Korean *musok* culture], Han'guk Munhwa Sŏnjip [Korean culture] Series, no. 2, edited by Kim Yŏl-Gyu et al., 29–59. Seoul: Pakijŏng.
Iryŏn [Il-Yŏn] (1206-1289). 1972. *Samguk Yusa: Legends and History of the Three Kingdoms of Ancient Korea*. Translated by Ha T'ae-Hung and Crafton K. Mintz. Seoul: Yonsei University. Compiled in 1285.
Izumi, Seich. 1969. "Mudang Naeryŏk" [History of *mudang*]. *Toyo Bunka (Asian Culture)*. Tokyo. 46–47 (March): 55–74.
Janelli, Roger L. and Dawnhee Yim Janelli. 1982. *Ancestor Worship and Korean Society*. Stanford, CA: Stanford University Press.
Jary, David and Julia Jary. 1991. *The Harper Collins Dictionary of Sociology*. NY: Harper Perennial, A Division of Harper Collins Publishers.

Kang, Tong-gu. 1998. "Traditional Religions and Christianity in Korea." *Korea Journal* 38 (3): 96–127.
Kaufmann, Walter. 1967. *Musical Notations of the Orient: Notational Systems of Continental East, South, and Central Asia*. Bloomington: Indiana University Press.
Kendall, Laurel. 1983. "*Mugam*: The Dance in Shaman's Clothing." In *Korean Folklore*, edited by The Korean National Commission for UNESCO, 224–238. Seoul: The Sisa-yong-o-sa Publishers, Inc.
———. 1987. *Shamans, Housewives, and Other Restless Spirits: Women in Korean Ritual Life*. Honolulu: University of Hawaii Press.
———. 1988. *The Life and Hard Times of a Korean Shaman*. Honolulu: University of Hawaii Press.
Killick, Andrew P. 1998. "The Invention of Traditional Korean Opera and the Problem of the Traditionesque: *Ch'anggŭk* and its Relation to *P'ansori* Narratives." Ph.D. diss. in Ethnomusicology, University of Washington, Seattle.
Kim, Chin-Yŏng and Hong T'ae-Han. 1997. *Sŏsa Muga: Pari Kongju Chŏnjip* [The epic songs: complete selection of Princess Pari]. Seoul: Minsokwŏn.
Kim, Chongsuh. 1993. "Eastern Learning: An Overcoming of Religious Pluralism." In *Reader in Korean Religion*, edited by Kim Chongsuh, 223–243. Seoul: The Academy of Korean Studies.
Kim, Chong-Tŏk, ed. 1989. *Hanyang Sŏn Kŏri* [Hanyang Kut]. Seoul: Minsan Ch'ulp'an.
Kim, Duk-Hwang. 1988. *A History of Religions in Korea*. Seoul: Daeji Moonhwa-sa.
Kim, Hyung-chan [Hyŏng-Ch'an]. 1977. "The History and Role of the Church in the Korean American Community." In *The Korean Diaspora: Historical and Sociological Studies of Korean Immigration and Assimilation in North America*, edited by Hyung-chan Kim, 47–63. Santa Barbara, CA: ABC-Clio, Inc.
———. 1996. *Tosan An Ch'ang-Ho: A Profile of a Prophetic Patriot*. Seoul: Tosan Memorial Foundation.
Kim, In-Hoe. 1983. "Naerim Kut, Sŏngsukhan Ingyŏk ŭi Kudojarosŏ ŭi Chŏnhwan" [Initiation ritual, transformation into a religious leader with mature personality]. In *Hwanghaedo Naerimkut* [Initiation ritual in Hwanghae Province], Han'guk ŭi Kut: [Korean rituals], vol. 1, 75–96. Seoul: Yŏlhwadang.
Kim, John K. 1978. *Old Hanyang, New Seoul: A Guide to Korea's Fastest Growing Metropolis*. Seoul: Eastern Media.
Kim, Ki-Su. 1972. *Kugak Ipmun* [Introduction to Korean traditional music]. Seoul: Han'guk Kojŏn Ŭmak Ch'ulp'ansa.
Kim, Kŭm-Hwa. 1995. *Kim Kŭm-Hwa ŭi Mugajip* [Ritual song collection of Kim Kŭm-Hwa]. Seoul: Munŭmsa.
Kim, Mun-Gi. 1987. *Han'guk ŭi Pujak: Tan ŭi Misul Pujak ŭl T'onghaesŏbon Kich'ŭng Munhwa* [Korean amulets: searching for the base culture through the arts in amulets]. Seoul: Porimsa.
Kim, Nak-pil. 1993. "Taoism in Korea: A Brief Introduction." In *Reader in Korean Religion*, edited by Kim Chongsuh, 99–137. Seoul: The Academy of Korean Studies.

Kim, Sŏn-P'ung. 1996. "Seoul Saenam Kut." In *Seoul Saenam Kut: Muhyŏng Munhwajae Palgul Ki/Yenŭng Chosa Yŏn'gu Pogosŏ* [Seoul Saenam *kut*: Research report on discovery of artists for Intangible Cultural Properties], no. 227, 35–55. Seoul: Munhwajae Kwalliguk.

Kim, T'aegon [Kim T'ae-Gon]. 1974. "Shaman Chants." In *Survey of Korean Arts: Folk Arts*, edited by National Academy of Arts. Seoul: National Academy of Arts. 1 (3): 115–133.

———. 1979. *Han'guk Mugajip 4: Han'guk Musok Ch'ongsŏ 1*. [Korean ritual song collections 4: Korean *musok* series 1]. Seoul: Chipmundang.

———. 1981. *Han'guk Musok Torok: Han'guk Musok Ch'ongsŏ 3* [Collection of photographs of Korean *musok*: Korean *musok* series 3]. Seoul: Chipmundang.

———. 1983. "Shamanism in the Seoul Area." In *Korean Folklore*, edited by The Korean National Commission for UNESCO, 266–292. Seoul: The Si-sa-yong-o-sa Publishers, Inc., Korea and Pace International Research Inc., USA.

———. 1989. *Han'guk ŭi Musok Shinhwa: Han'guk Musok Ch'ongsŏ 7*. [Myths in Korean *musok*: Korean *musok* series 7]. Seoul: Chipmundang.

———. 1991. *Han'guk ŭi Musok* [Korean *musok*]. Seoul: Taewŏnsa.

———. 1993a. *Musok kwa Yŏng ŭi Segye* [*Musok* and the spirit world]. Seoul: Han'ul.

———. 1993b. *Paintings of Shaman Gods of Korea*. Seoul: Yŏlhwadang.

———. 1998. *Korean Shamanism—Muism*. Korean Studies Series, no. 9. Translated by Chang Soo-Kyung. Seoul: Jimoondang Publishing Co.

———, ed. 1976. *Han'guk Mugajip 2: Han'guk Musok Ch'ongsŏ 1* [Korean ritual song collections 2: Korean *musok* series 1]. Seoul: Chipmundang.

———. 1978. *Han'guk Mugajip 3: Han'guk Musok Ch'ongsŏ 1* [Korean ritual song collections 3: Korean *musok* series 1]. Seoul: Chipmundang.

———. 1979. *Han'guk Mugajip 4: Han'guk Musok Ch'ongsŏ 1*. [Korean ritual song collections 4: Korean *musok* series 1]. Seoul: Chipmundang.

———. 1991. *Han'guk Musok Yŏn'gu: Han'guk Musok Ch'ongsŏ 4*. [Research on Korean *musok*: Korean *musok* series 4]. Seoul: Chipmundang.

———. 1992. *Han'guk Mugajip 1: Han'guk Musok Ch'ongsŏ 1* [Korean ritual song collections 1: Korean *musok* series 1]. Seoul: Chipmundang.

Kim, Uichol and Sang-Chun Choi. 1995. "Indigenous Form of Lamentation, *Han*: Conceptual and Philosophical Analyses." In *Korean Cultural Roots: Religion and Social Thought*, edited by Ho-Youn Kwon, 245–266. Chicago: Integrated Technical Resources.

Kim, Young-ho. 1993. "Buddhism in Korea: Traditions in Syncretic Thought and Self-Enlightenment." In *Reader in Korean Religion*, edited by Kim Chongsuh, 1–61. Seoul: The Academy of Korean Studies.

Kister, Daniel A. 1999. *Sarm ŭi Drama: Kut ŭi Chonggyojŏk Sangsangryŏk Yŏn'gu* [Life drama: searching for religious imagination of rituals]. Seoul: Sŏgang University Press.

Korea Times Ltd., ed. 1996. *Korean Business Directory of Washington 1998–1999*. Seattle: The Korea Times Ltd.

Korean Overseas Culture and Information Service. 1997. *Facts about Korea*. Seoul: Ministry of Culture and Tourism.

Kukrip [Kungnip] Munhwajae Yŏn'guso, ed. 1998. *Seoul Saenam Kut: Chungyo Muhyŏng Munhwajae Che 104 Ho* [The Important Intangible Cultural Property no. 104]. Seoul: Kukrip Munhwajae Yŏn'guso.

———. 1998. *Namhaean Pyŏlshin Kut: Chungyo Muhyŏng Munhwajae Che 82-Ra Ho*. [The Important Intangible Cultural Property no. 82-ra]. Seoul: Kukrip Munhwajae Yŏn'guso.

Lee, Bo-hyung [Yi, Po-Hyŏng]. 1973. "Shamanist Music." In *Survey of Korean Arts: Traditional Music*, edited by National Association of Arts, 175–180. Seoul: National Academy of Arts.

Lee, Chae-Suk, Yi Sŏng-Ch'ŏn, Kim Chŏng-Ja, Kang Sa-Jun, Hwang Chun-Yŏn, Yim Mi-Sŏn, Kim Chŏng-Su, Yi Sang-Gyu, Kwŏn To-Hŭi, and Song No-Yŏn. 1998. *Chosŏnjo Kungjung Ŭirye wa Ŭmak* [Court rituals and music during Chosŏn Dynasty]. Seoul: Seoul National University.

Lee, Hye-Ku. 1957. "Muak Yŏn'gu: Ch'ŏngsugol ŭi Todang Kut" [Studies on shaman ritual music of neighborhood *kut* in Ch'ŏngsugol]. In *Han'guk Ŭmak Yŏn'gu* [Studies on Korean music], 164–182. Seoul: Sumundang.

Lee, Jung young. 1981. *Korean Shamanistic Rituals: Religion and Society 12*. Hague: Mouton Publishers.

Lee, Ki-Baik. 1984. *A New History of Korea*. Translated by Edward Wagner and Edward Shultz. Cambridge: Harvard University Press.

Lee, Kwang Kyu. 1988. "The Practice of Traditional Family Rituals in Contemporary Urban Korea." *Journal of Ritual Studies*. Pittsburgh, PA: University of Pittsburgh [Dept. of Religious Studies]. 3 (2): 167–183.

Lee, Kwang Kyu and Youngsook Kim Harvey. 1973. "Teknonymy and Geononymy in Korean Kinship Terminology." *Ethnology* 12 (1): 31–46.

Lee, Kwang Kyu and Walter H. Slote, eds. 1993. *Overseas Koreans in the Global Context*. Seoul: Seoul National University.

Lee, Peter H., ed. 1981. *Anthology of Korean Literature*. Honolulu: University of Hawaii Press.

Lee, Peter H., D. Baker, Y. Ch'oe, H. Kang, and H. Kim, eds. 1993. *Sourcebook of Korean Civilization: Vol. 1. From Early Times to the Sixteenth Century*. NY: Columbia University Press.

———, eds. 1996. *Sourcebook of Korean Civilization: Vol. 2. From the Seventeenth Century to the Modern Period*. NY: Columbia University Press.

Lee, Sang-Sook and G.D. Sibley. 1981. "Talismans: The Art of Fortune." *Korean Quarterly*. 2 (3): 27–33.

Lee, Yong-Hak. 1999. *Muhyŏng Munhwajae Chŏnsŭng, Pojon Hwalsŏnghwa Pangane Kwanhan Yŏn'gu: Kukga Chungyo Muhyŏng Munhwahae Chedorŭl Chungshimŭro* [A study on revitalizing Intangible Cultural Property: its transmission and preservation-focus on Important Intangible Cultural Property system]. MA thesis in General Administration, Yonsei University, Seoul.

Lewis, I.M. 1989. *Ecstatic Religion: A Study of Shamanism and Spirit Possession*. London: Routledge.

Liang, Mingyue. 1985. *Music of the Billion: An Introduction to Chinese Musical Culture*. NY: Heinrichshofen Edition.

Lim, Jae-Hae. 1999. "Kut ŭi Chuch'e rŭl T'onghaebon Kut ŭi Yangsang gwa Hyŏnshil Inshik" [Understanding appearance and reality of rituals through ritual's sovereignty]. In *Han'guk Musokhak*, edited by Han'guk Musok Hakhoe, 95–140. Seoul: Han'guk Musok Hakhoe.

Lord, Albert B. 1965. *The Singer of Tales*. NY: Atheneum.

Lowie, Robert H. 1958. "Shamans and Priests Among the Plains Indians." In *Reader in Comparative Religion: An Anthropological Approach*, edited by W. A. Lessa and E. Z. Vogt, 411–413. Evanston, Illinois: Row, Peterson and Company.

Lyu, Kingsley K. 1977. "Korean Nationalist Activities in Hawai'i and the Continental United States, 1900–1945, Part 1: 1900–1919." *Amerasia Journal* 4 (1): 23–90.

Maskarinec, Gregory G. 1995. *The Ruling of the Night: An Ethnography of Nepalese Shaman Oral Text*. Madison: The University of Wisconsin Press.

Michell, Richard G. Jr. 1993. *Secrecy and Fieldwork: Qualitative Research Methods Vol. 29*. Newsbury Park, CA: Sage Publication.

Minjok Munhwasa, ed. 1991. *Han'guk Minsok Tae Sajŏn* [Extensive Korean folk dictionary]. Seoul: Minjok Munhwasa.

Mun, Kyu-P'il, ed. 1997. *Han'guk ŭi Musokin* [Musok practitioners in Korea]. Seoul: People Bank.

———. 1997. *Hanŭn P'ulgo Tŏk ŭn Ssak'o* [Vent grudge but accumulate virtue]. Seoul: People Bank.

Munwha Kongbobu, Munwhajae Kwanriguk, ed. 1985. *Chungyo Muhyŏng Munwhajae Haesŏl: Ŭmak P'yŏn* [Explanations on the Important Intangible Cultural Properties: music section]. Seoul: Munhwajae Kwanriguk [Kwalliguk].

Munhwajaech'ŏng, ed. 1999. *Chungyo Muhyŏng Munhwajae Hyŏnhwang* [Current situation of the Important Intangible Cultural Properties]. Seoul: Munhwajaech'ŏng.

Nan-Gok. 1885. *Mudang Naeryŏk* [History of *mudang*].

NCKTPA. 1999. *Korean Traditional Music Yearbook 1998*. Seoul: The National Center for Korean Traditional Performing Arts.

NIV Hanyŏng Haesŏl Sŏnggyŏng, eds. 1998. *NIV Hanyŏng Haesŏl Sŏnggyŏng*. (New International Version: Bible in Korean and English with explanations). Seoul: Agape Ch'ulp'ansa.

Noh, Tong-Eun. 1995. *Han'guk Kŭndae Ŭmaksa 1* [Korean music history in recent years 1]. Seoul: Han'gilsa.

Ŏmun'gak, ed. 1994. *Han'guk Munye Sajŏn* [Dictionary for literature and art]. Seoul: Ŏmun'gak.

Paden, William E. 1994. *Religious Worlds: The Comparative Study of Religion*. Boston: Beacon Press.

Paik, Lak-Geoon [Nak-Chun]. 1969. Foreword to *The Passing of Korea*, by Homer B. Hulbert. Seoul: Yonsei University Press.

Pak, Chŏng-Jin. 1993. "Uri Shidae Chaein ŭi Kyebohak 2" [Genealogy of contemporary musicians]. *Munhwa Yesul* [Culture and art] (October): 24–38.
Pak, Hwang. 1994 (1987). *P'ansori Yibaeknyŏnsa* [Two hundred year history of *p'ansori*]. Seoul: Sasayŏn.
Pak, In-O. 1990. *Chŏnt'ong Hanyang Kut Kŏri* [Traditional Hanyang *kut*]. Seoul: Musok Pojonhoe.
Pak, Yong-Suk. 1988. "Hoehwa Rosŏbon Musokhwa" [Musok images through paintings]. In *Han'guk ŭi Minsok Yesul* [Korean folk arts], edited by Chae-Hae Yim, 334–344. Seoul: Munhak kwa Chisŏngsa.
———. 1993. "Tosang Ŭrosŏŭi Mushindo wa kŭ Hoehwasŏng [Images of musok spirits as paintings]." In *Han'guk Mushindo: Paintings of Shaman Gods of Korea*, edited by T'aegon Kim, 39–62. Seoul: Yŏlwhadang.
Paper, J. 1997. *The Spirits Are Drunk: Comparative Approaches to Chinese Religion*. NY: State University of New York Press.
Park, Hung-Ju [Pak Hŭng-Ju]. 1991. *Kut*. Seoul: Kut Yŏn'guso.
———. 1999. "Sam T'aegŭk ŭn Samshin ŭi P'yosang [*Sam t'aegŭk* as the symbol of Samshin]." *Yesul Segye* [Art world] 109 (10): 77–85.
Park, Mi-Kyung [Pak Mi-Gyŏng]. 1996. *Han'guk ŭi Musok kwa Ŭmak* [Korean *musok* and music]. Seoul: Sejong Munhwasa. Translated by Yun Hwa-Jung. Originally published in English in 1985. *Music and Shamanism in Korea: A Study of Selected Ssikkŭm-gut Rituals for the Dead*. Ph.D. diss., UCLA.
Pegg, Carole. n.d. *Song of the Soul: Performing Mongolian Identity*. Ph.D. diss., Dept. of Social Anthropology, University of Cambridge.
Philippi. 1982. *Songs of Gods, Songs of Humans: the Epic Tradition of the Ainu*. San Francisco: North Point Press.
Pihl, Marshall R. 1994. *The Korean Singer of Tales*. Cambridge, MA: Havard University Press.
Potapov, L.P. 1968. "Shaman's Drums of Altaic Ethnic Group." In *Popular Beliefs and Folklore Tradition in Siberia*, edited by V. Dioszegi, 205–234. Bloomington: Indiana University.
Pratt, Keith and Richard Rutt. 1999. *Korea: A Historical and Cultural Dictionary*. Richmond, Great Britain: Curzon.
Ramstedt, G.J. 1949. *Studies in Korean Etymology: Suomalais-Ugrilaisen Seuran Toimituksia XCV*. Helsinki: Suomalais-Ugrilainen Seura.
Reichl, Karl. 1992. *Turkic Oral Epic Poetry: Traditions, Forms, Poetic Structure*. NY: Garland Publishing Inc.
Reinhard, Johan. 1976. "Shamanism and Spirit Possession: The Definition Problem." In *Spirit Possession in the Nepal Himalayas*, edited by J. Hitchcock and R. Jones, 12–20. New Delhi: Vikas Publishing House Ltd.
Rinchen, Yongsiyebu. 1977. "Noms de chamanes et des chamanesses en mongol." *L'Ethnographie* 74–5:148–53. Quoted in Caroline Humphrey, 1996, *Shamans and Elders: Experience, Knowledge, and Power Among the Daur Mongols* (Oxford: Clarendon Press), 322.

Rouget, Gilbert. 1985. *Music and Trance: A Theory of the Relations between Music and Possession.* Translated from the French by Brunhilde Biebuyck. Chicago: The University of Chicago Press.
Ryu, Sang-Ch'ae. 1992. *Minŭi wa Muŭi* [Folk medicine and shamanic healing]. Seoul: Sŏhaemunjip.
Ryu, Tong-Sik. 1989. *Han'guk Mukyo ŭi Yŏksa wa Kujo* [History and structure of Korean *mu* religion]. Seoul: Yonsei University.
Sasamori, Takefusa. 1997. "Therapeutic Rituals Performed by Itako (Japanese Blind Female Shamans)." *The World of Music* 39 (1): 85–96.
Schechner, Richard. 1988. *Performance Theory.* Revised and expanded edition. NY: Routledge.
Schmidt, Cynthia E. 1984. "Interlocking Techniques in Kpelle Music." In *Studies in African Music*, vol. 5 of *Selected Reports in Ethnomusicology*, 195–216.
Seo, Maria K. 1998. "*Kangshinmu*, Spirit-Possessed Shaman of Korea." In *Shaman, Jhankri and Nele: Music Healers of Indigenous Cultures*, edited by Helen Zelon, 76–79. NY: Ellipsis Arts.
Seoul T'ŭkbyŏlsi Munhwajae Wiwŏnhoe, ed. 1995. *Seoul Musok P'yŏn: Seoul Minsok Taekwan 2* [About Seoul area *musok*: overview of Seoul area folklore 2]. Seoul: Samsŏng Ch'ulp'ansa.
Shirokogoroff, S.M. [1935] 1980. *Psychomental Complex of the Tungus.* NY: AMS Press, Inc.
Siikala, Anna-Leena. 1987. *The Rite Technique of the Siberian Shaman.* Helsinki: Academia Scientiarum (1978). Fennica. PF Communication No. 220.
Sim, U-Sŏng, ed. 1988. *Madang Kut Yŏnhŭibon: Muhyŏngmunhwajae Mijijŏngjongmok* [The scenario for *madang kut*: intangible cultural properties not designated by the government]. Seoul: Kip'ŭnsaem.
Simmel, Georg. 1950. *The Sociology of Georg Simmel.* Translated by Kurt H. Wolff. NY: The Free Press.
Si-sa-yŏng-ŏ-sa, ed. 1996. *Si-sa Elite Korean English Dictionary.* Seoul: Si-sa-yŏng-ŏ-sa.
Slobin, Mark. 1976. *Music in the Culture of Northern Afghanistan.* Tucson, AZ: The University of Arizona Press.
Slote, W.H. 1993. "Koreans Abroad in Therapy: Implications for the Homeland." In *Overseas Koreans in the Global Context*, edited by K. K. Lee and W. H. Slote, 61–80. Seoul: Seoul National University.
Smith, Jonathan Z. 1994. *The Harpercollins Dictionary of Religion.* San Francisco: Harper Collins Publishers.
Song, Do-Young. 1998. "*Noraebang*: A Case Study of Cultural Industry and Mode of Cultural Consumption." *Korea Social Science Journal* 25 (1): 97–125.
Sŏng, Kyŏng-Rin and Yi Po-Hyŏng. 1992. *Paebaengi Kut: Muhyŏngmunhwajae Chijŏngchosabogosŏ* [Report on Intangible Cultural Properties], no. 156. Seoul: National Research Institute of Cultural Properties of Korea.
Sorensen, Clark W. 1989. "Introduction." *Journal of Ritual Studies.* Pittsburgh, PA: University of Pittsburgh [Dept. of Religious Studies]. 3 (2): 155–165.

Sullivan, Bruce M. 1998. *Historical Dictionary of Hinduism: Historical Dictionaries of Religions, Philosophies, and Movements, No. 13*. Lanham, MD: The Scarecrow Press, Inc.

Sun, Soon-Hwa. 1992. "The Vocational Socialization of the Korean Shaman." *Korea Journal* 32 (3): 86–102.

Taehan Sŭnggong Kyŏngshin Yŏnhaphoe, ed. 1991. *Kyŏngshin 20 Nyŏnsa Hwabo* [Photographs of 20 year history of Kyŏngshin Association]. Seoul: Taehan Sŭnggong Kyŏngshin Yŏnhaphoe.

Troshchanski, V.F. 1902. *The Evolution of the 'Black Faith' (Shamanism) of the Yakut*, 118. Kazan. Quoted in M.A. Czaplicka, 1914, *Aboriginal Siberia: A Study in Social Anthropology* (Oxford: The Clarendon Press), 198.

Turnbull, Colin. 1990. "Liminality: A Synthesis of Subjective and Objective Experience." In *By Means of Performance: Intercultural Studies of Theatre and Ritual*, edited by R. Schechner and W. Appel, 50–81. Cambridge: Cambridge University Press.

Turner, Victor. 1969. *The Ritual Process: Structure and Anti-Structure*. Chicago: Aldine Publishing Company.

———. 1992. *Blazing the Trail: Way Marks in the Exploration of Symbols*. Tucson & London: The University of Arizona Press.

Tylor, Stephen A., ed. 1969. *Cognitive Anthropology*. NY: Holt, Rinehart and Winston, Inc.

Vitebsky, Piers. 1995. *The Shaman: Voyages of the Soul Trance, Ecstasy and Healing from Siberia to the Amazon*. London: Macmillan in association with Duncan Baird Publishers.

Walraven, Boudewijn. 1985. *Muga: The Songs of Korean Shamanism*. Dordrecht: ICG Printing.

———. 1994. *Songs of the Shaman: The Ritual Chants of the Korean Mudang*. London: Kegan Paul International.

———. 1998. "Interpretations and Reinterpretations of Popular Religion in the Last Decades of the Chosŏn Dynasty." In *Korean Shamanism: Revivals, Survivals, and Change*, edited by Keith Howard. Seoul: Royal Asiatic Society Korean Branch. 5:55–72.

Warren, C. and B. Laslett. 1980. "Privacy and Secrecy: A Conceptual Comparison." In *Secrecy: A Cross-Cultural Perspective*, edited by S. K. Tefft. NY: Human Sciences Press.

Wu, Bing-an. 1989. "Shamans in Manchuria." In *Shamanism: Past and Present*, edited by Mihaly Hoppal and Otto von Sadovzky. LA: Fullerton International Society for Trans-Oceanic Research. Part 2:263–269.

Wu, Jing-Nuan, trans. 1991. *Yi Jing*. Washington, DC: The Taoist Center.

Yang, Jongsung [Chong-Sŭng]. 1994. *Folklore and Cultural Politics in Korea: Intangible Cultural Properties and Living National Treasures*. Ph.D. diss., Department of Folklore, Indiana University, Bloomington.

---. 1995. "Mudang Munhwa ŭi Chŏnt'ong: Kangshinmu Chŏnsŭnggo" [Tradition of mudang culture: consideration of transmission of kangshinmu]. In *Pigyo Minsokhak* [Comparative folklore], 75–89.

---. 1998. "Pangul go: Musok ŭl Chungshim ŭro" [Consideration of bells: focusing on their use in musok]. *Saenghwal Yŏn'gu* [Research on living] 2 (1): 119–126.

1999a. "Seoul Kut." In *Han'guk ŭi Musok* [Musok in Korea], 21–84. Seoul: National Folk Museum.

1999b. "Han'guk Mushin ŭi Ch'eje wa Ch'egye [System and order of Korean *musok* spirits]." In *Shamanism ŭi Pigyo Munhwaron* [Comparative cultural discourse on shamanism], 4–18. Seoul: Institute of Cross-Cultural Studies, Seoul National University.

Yi, Chae-Gon. 1996. *Seoul ŭi Min'gan Shinang* [Folk belief in Seoul area]. Seoul: Paeksan Ch'ulp'ansa.

Yi, Chŏng-yŏng. 1983. "Shamanistic Thought and Traditional Korean Homes." In *Korean Folklore*, edited by The Korean National Center for UNESCO, 193–210. Seoul: The Si-sa-yong-o-sa Publishers, Inc., Korea.

Yi, Du-Hyun. 1988. "Role Playing Through Trance Possession in Korean Shamanism." In *Shamanism: The Spirit World of Korea*, edited by R. W. I. Guisso and C.S. Yu, 162–180. Berkeley, CA: Asian Humanities Press.

Yi, Hŭi Sŭng, ed. 1998. *Kugŏ Taesajŏn* [Korean dictionary]. Seoul: Minjung Sŏrim.

Yi, Ki-baek. 1970. *New Lectures on Korean History*. Seoul: Ilchogak.

Yi, Kyu-Wŏn. 1997. *Uriga Chŏngmal Arayahal Uri Chŏnt'ong Yein Paek Saram* [One hundred traditional artists we should know about]. Seoul: Hyŏnamsa.

Yi, Nŭng-Hwa. [1927] 1991. *Chosŏn Musokko* [On Korean *musok*]. Translated by Yi Chae-Gon. Seoul: Tongmunsŏn.

---. [1959] 1977. *Chosŏn Togyosa* [History of Korean Taoism]. Translated by Yi Chong-Ŭn. Seoul: Posŏng Munhwasa.

Yi, Po-Hyŏng. 1982a. "Han'guk Muŭisik ŭi Ŭmak" [Korean ritual music]. In *Han'guk Musok ŭi Chonghapjŏk Koch'al* [Overview of Korean *musok*], edited by In-Hoe Kim et al., 209–230. Seoul: Minjok Munwha Yŏn'guso, Koryŏ Taehakkyo.

---. 1982b. "Kyŏngsŏ T'origwŏn ŭi Muga Minyo." In *Na Un-Yŏng Paksa Hoegap Kinyŏm Nonmunjip*, 173–186. Seoul: Segwang.

---. 1985. "Hamgyŏngdo Kut ŭi Ŭmak" [Ritual music in North and South Hamgyŏng Provinces]. In *Hamgyŏngdo Mangmuk Kut: Pe rŭl Kalla Chŏsŭnggil ŭl Takkajunŭn Kut* [Mangmuk *kut* in Hamgyŏng Provinces: a ritual leading the dead to the other world by way of cutting *pe* (symbolic hemp cloth)], Han'guk ŭi Kut [Korean rituals], vol. 8, 104–107. Seoul: Yŏlhwadang.

---. 1993. "Han'guk Musok Ŭmak" [Korean ritual music]. In *Seoul Chinogwi Kut: Han'guk ui Kut Series No. 20*, edited by Yŏlhwadang. Seoul: Yŏlhwadang.

Yi, Sŏng-Jae. 1997. *Chaemi Itnŭn Kuak Killajabi* [Fun-filled guide for Korean traditional music]. Seoul: Media.

Yi, Wŏn-Sŏp. 1996. *Shinjŏm ŭi Myŏngin* [Well known *kangshinmu* diviners]. Seoul: Pitsaem.

———. 1999. *Han'guk ŭi Mudang* [Korean *mudang*]. Seoul: Blue Family.
Yim, Tong-Gwŏn. 1986. "Sungshin kwa Hyŏpdong ŭi Chang, Hyangt'oshinje" [Hyangt'oshinje, the site for spirit worship and cooperation]. In *Ŭnsan Pyŏlshin Kut* [Korean *kut*: Ŭnsan Pyŏlshin *kut*], Han'guk ŭi Kut [Korean rituals], vol. 9, 74–92. Seoul: Yŏlhwadang.
Yŏlhwadang, ed. 1983–1993. *Han'guk ŭi Kut* [Korean rituals] in 20 volumes. Seoul: Yŏlhwadang.
Young, Barbara Elizabeth. 1980. *Spirits and Other Signs: The Practice of Divination in Seoul, Republic of Korea*. Ph.D. diss. in Anthropology, University of Washington.
Yu, Ch'ang-Sun. 1998. *Yijoŏ Sajŏn* [Dictionary of terms used during the Yi Dynasty]. Seoul: Yonsei University.
Yun, Myung-Won. 1999. *A Study of Musical Instruments in Korean Traditional Music*. Translated by Park Il-Woo. Seoul: The National Center for Korean Traditional Performing Arts, Ministry of Culture and Tourism.
Yun, Seung-Yong. 1997. "Outline of Religious Culture." In *Religious Culture in Korea*, edited by Hollym International Corp., 7–37. Elizabeth, NJ: Hollym International Corp.
Yun, Sŏk-Un. 1978. *Han'guk Muakko* [On Korean traditional dance music]. Seoul: Tonghaktang.
Yun, Yŏl-Su, ed. 1994. *Kŭrim ŭro Ponŭn Han'guk ŭi Mushindo* [Korean spirits seen through paintings]. Seoul: E-Ga Book Publisher.
Zerańska-Kominek, Slawomira. 1992. "The Turkmen Bakhshy: Shaman and/or Artist." In *European Studies in Ethnomusicology: Historical Developments and Recent Trends. Selected Papers Presented at the VIIth European Seminar in Ethnomusicology, Berlin, October 1–6, 1990*, edited by M.P. Bauman, A. Simon and U. Wegner, 303–316. Wilhelmshaven, Germany: Florian Noetzel Verlag.
Zozayong, Horay. 1982. *Guardians of Happiness: Shamanistic Tradition in Korean Folk Painting: 1882–1983*. Seoul: Emileh Museum.
———. 1994. *Guardians of Happiness: Shamanistic Tradition in Korean Folk Painting*. Seoul: Emileh Museum.

Index

actemes, 186–187, 188
aerophones, 24, 136. See also *hojŏk, p'iri, taegŭm, t'aep'yŏngso*
ajaeng (bowed zither), 130, 178
Akamatsu, Chijo & Takashi Akiba
   chipshin kut, 62 n. 8
   Chosŏn Musok ŭi Yŏn'gu (Research on Korean *Musok*), 182
   mudang (etymology), 39
   mugyŏng (prayers and incantations), 41
   musicians, 138 n. 5
   naeryŏk pongji (divination containers used for the neophyte), 62
   paksu (etymology), 46
   red *ch'ŏnik*, 187
   ritual songs, 7
   san divination, 195 n. 23
   Seoul *kut*, 181
   sukmu (musician *kangshinmu*), 45 n. 34
Akiba, Takashi, 7
altar, 69–71, 93, 236
amulets, 72–74
analytical *haksŭpmu*, 80
ancestors. See *chosang*
andang sagyŏng maji kut (ritual), 183, 217, 221–224
anjŭn kŏri (seated section of ritual), 65, 157, 184
apprenticed *mudang*. See *haksŭpmu*
argot, See *ŭnŏ* and *saŏ*
association for male shamans, 90–91
association for shamans, 83–90

baxsi (male shaman), 47, 236
bell tree, 125–126, 193, 228. See also *pangul*
bells, 125–126, 130. See also *pangul*
bi-musicality, 109

Biederman, Hans, 42–43
Bishop, Isabella Bird, 38 n. 27
Blacking, John, 238
body-governing spirit, 36. See also *momju*
Bok, Sissela, 241
Bourguignon, Erika, 135
Buddhism, 32–37, 37 n. 26, 41, 43, 45, 68 n. 6, 72, 74, 93, 191
Buswell, Robert E. Jr., 45 n. 35

Carrithers, Michael, 241
Catholic faith, 36 n. 23, 51 n. 47, 59 n. 4, 81 n. 31
Central Daily, 79 n. 28
Ch'a, Ok-Sung, 5
chabara (cymbal),125. See also *para*
Ch'ae, Chŏng-Rye, 121
ch'ae p'yŏn (right head of *changgu* drum), 161
   for "*Pari Kongju*," 161, 228
chaebi (ritual musician), 3, 101–102, 235
   as drummers for *samhyŏn yukkak* ensemble, 129
   for Hanyang *kut*, 138–180 passim
chaebi tangju (musician responsible for hiring other musicians for a ritual), 102, 216
chaedam (witty remarks), 95, 225
chaesu kut (ritual for good luck), 24, 99, 181. See also *ch'ŏnshin kut*
chakdu (ritual blades), 89, 95, 208–210. See also *pisu*
Chamberlain, Jonathan, 205, 206 n. 29
Chang, Pyung-Kil [Pyŏng-Gil], 181
Chang, Sa-Hun, 133 n. 8
Chang, Sŏng-Man, 64, 100 n. 5, 131
Chang, Soo-Kyung [Su-Gyŏng], 5 n. 7
changdan (rhythmic cycles), 164–178, 238
changdan used in Hanyang *kut*
   chajin hŏtŭn t'aryŏng, 191

315

changdan (rhythmic cycles) *(continued)*
   chajin hwanip, 174, 235
   ch'wit'ae, 165, 177, 206
   dodûri. See *yômbul*
   hwangje p'uri, 214
   hwimori, 165, 173, 190, 194, 203
   karaejo, 225
   kil kunak, 177–178, 230
   kutkôri, 169–170, 187, 191, 194, 199, 212, 230
      for *mugam* dance, 212
      for song accompaniment, 159
   mansubaji. See *kutkôri*
   manura, 206. See also *ch'wit'ae*
   noraekarak. See *shijo*
   nûjûn hôtûn t'aryông, 191
   ôtmori, 172
   pan yômbul, 176, 191
   pujông, 189
   pyôlsang, 170–171, 177, 178, 208, 230
   seryôngsan, 175
   shijo, 158, 173–174
   tangak, 171–172, 187, 194, 199,
   t'aryông, 170. See also *pyôlsang*
   yômbul, 175, 191
changgo (drum), 123. See also *changgu*
ch'anggôm (ritual trident), 200–201, 208, 210
changgu (hourglass-shaped drum), 123–125
   changgu heads, 228
   chôngak changgu (used in Hanyang *kut*), 123–124, 235
   for "*Pari Kongju*," 156, 162
   for *samhyôn yukkak* (six-musician ensemble), 129
   four main strokes, 168
   ideographs, 123, 125
   minsok changgu (used in folk music), 124, 235
   notation, 167–178
   Northwestern Province style drumming, 136–137
   p'ungmul changgu (used for ritual by secular musician), 124
   symbolism, 124
ch'anggûk (drama sung in *p'ansori* style), 105
chap kwi (malevolent spirits), 36, 189, 215
chap shin. See *chap kwi*
chegajip (clients), 4, 22–23, 82, 139, 212
   mugam dance, 139, 212–213
chegûm (cymbals), 65, 94, 125, 130, 136, 165, 187

chegûm (cymbals) *(continued)*
   for song accompaniment, 125, 194
chegûm notations
   for *kutkôri changdan* (rhythmic cycle), 170
   for *pan yômbul changdan*, 176
   for *pyôlsang changdan*, 171
   for *tangak changdan*, 172
chesa (ritual for ancestors), 217, 233
Chijang Posal, 225, 229, 230
Ch'ilsông. *See also* Seven Star Spirits
Chin, Kwang-Sôk, 125
Chin, Soo-Young, 180 n. 21
Chindo Island *ssikkim kut*, 109, 121,161
ching (large gong), 25, 42, 65, 103, 127, 130
   for "*Pari Kongju*," 162, 228
chinjôk kut (ritual celebration by shaman), 25, 103–104, 133
chinogwi kut (ritual for the departed), 99, 103. See also *saenam kut*
ch'isông (small ritual for good fortune), 77, 103, 126
Cho, Cha-Ryong, 16 n. 2, 89, 137
Cho, Hung-Youn [Hûng–Yun],
   changgu head, 124 n. 1
   chinjôk, 190 n. 14
   ch'ônik, 76 n. 23
   female spirits, 196
   Hanyang *kut*, 155
   hierarchy among shamans, 215
   Important Intangible Cultural Properties, 27, 27 n. 21
   manura, 190 n. 15
   mu, 5, 5 n. 6
   pujông song, 189 n. 13
   san divination, 195 n. 23
   shink'al, 233
   symbolism of musical instruments, 7
      changgu, 124
      chegûm, 125
      pangul, 125
      p'iri, 128
      taegûm, 129
Chodron, Thubten, 37 n. 26
Ch'oe, Chun-Shik, 35
Ch'oe, Kil-Sông, 5, 22, 41, 181 n. 2, 213
Ch'oe, Nam-Ôk, 83–84
Ch'oe, Nam-Sôn, 5
Ch'oe, Tong-Hyôn, 164 n. 13
chohwa (paper flowers), 104, 191–192, 225
Choi, Chong-Min, 126
Choi, Chungmoo, 44, 64 n. 10

Choi, Hôn, 156
chômbok, 41. See also divination
chômjaengi, 41. See also diviner
chônak (instrumentalist), 138, 235. See also *chaebi*
chônan (shrine), 67. See also *shindang*
Chông, Pyông-Ho, 105
chôngak changgu (drum used in Hanyang *kut*), 124, 235
chôngak taegûm (flute used in Hanyang *kut*), 128–129, 235
Chônggamrok (divination manual), 52
chôngganbo (traditional musical notation system), 166, 168
ch'ôngryongdo (literally, blue dragon ritual knife), 205
chôngshin (venerated spirits), 36, 157, 189
ch'ôngshin (invitation to spirits), 184–188, 189
ch'ôngsûng mudang (musician-shaman hired for *kut* performance), 65, 138
chônnae (shaman who does not sing or dance), 26, 45, 65
ch'ônshin kut (ritual for good fortune), 99, 181–216 passim
  actemes, 186–187, 188
  andang sagyông maji (the first part of Seoul *Saenam kut*), 183, 217, 221–224
  comparison of *ch'ônshin kut*, 182
chônsu kyoyuk pojoja (teacher appointed by government), 118
  for Seoul *Saenam Kut*, 218–221
chônsuja (student learning a cultural property), 118
chordophones, 136. See also *ajaeng, haegûm, kayagûm, kômun'go*
chosang (ancestors), 36, 224
Chosôn Dynasty
  eight types of work, 43
  four social classes, 43
  Hanyang (capital), 7, 7 n. 9
Christian faith, 37, 37n. 25, 44, 70, 79 n. 27, 80, 81 n. 31
Chu Yôk (Book of Changes), 52. See also *Yôk Hak*
chudang mullim, 187, 222
ch'uimsae (cheers), 114, 163, 185
chumu. See *tangju*
"Chungdi Patsan," 26n 19, 156, 225
circumambulation, 218, 229–231
Clark, Charles Allen, 5, 38n. 27, 40, 76n 22
Clements, Forrest E., 56, 58, 61

clients, 78–83 passim
coins for divination. See *yôpchôn*
Coleman, Craig S., 30
Confucianism, 12, 32–34, 37, 217
Cooke, Peter, 159 n. 8
cultural properties, 116–119
cymbal dance, 95
cymbals used in Buddhist ritual. See *para*
cymbals used in *kut*. See *chegûm*

dance by clients. See *mugam* dance
dance by shamans. *See* ritual dance
designated performer for Important Intangible Cultural Properties. See *poyuja*
Deuchler, Martina, 37
Dioszegi, Vilmos, 56, 65
divination, 41, 52–53, 62, 78, 80, 85
diviner, 41, 52–53
  how to find them, 78–83 passim
drum (Inner Asian shaman drum), 65, 135, 161–162, 165, 236
drum (Korean barrel drum). See *puk*
drum (Korean hourglass-shaped drum). See *changgu*
drum notation, 167–178
drum sticks, 65, 236
  for *changgu*, 94, 161, 165, 228
  for *puk*, 127
Dournon, Geneviève, 42 n. 32
duet songs. See *mansubaji* and *noraekarak*
Duvan, Nadyezhda, 68, 68 n. 5, 162

Eliade, Mircea, 55, 60, 98, 160
Ellingson, Ter, 42, 135, 161, 237 (map)
ensembles for Hanyang *kut*, 130–134
epic songs in sacred and secular contexts, 159–164

fan. See *puch'ae*
fees for ritual performers, 130, 185
female *mudang* (ritual specialist), 5. See also *sesûpmu*
female spirits, 196, 206, 214
female sponsor for a ritual, 82, 201
Finnegan, Ruth, 160
Firth, Raymond, 58
five colored ritual flags. See *obang shinjanggi*
five directional ritual flags,187. See also *obang shinjanggi*
Five General Spirits for five directions. *See* Obang Shinjang Spirit

flags advertising *musok* practice, 80
flute. See *taegûm*
folk music, 105–106
folk religion, 6. See also *min'gan shinang*
folk singer/*haksûpmu*, 42. See also Kim Hye-Ran and Pak Chông-Uk
folk songs. See *minyo*
foreign scholars, 7, 19–20, 85 n. 38
fortune-telling. See divination
frame drums, 135, 161, 236
Friedson, Steven M., 135

Gaster, Theodor, 72
Gennep, Arnold van, 58
geononymy, 50
gods and spirits in *musok*, 35–36
gong. See *ching, kkwaenggwari,* or *sogûm*
government designated cultural properties. See *munhwajae*
grain, symbolic meaning, 62, 67, 192
Guillemoz, Alexandre, 51 n. 49, 83 n. 35, 92 n. 43

Ha, Man-Su, 64
Ha, T'ae-Hung & Crafton K. Mintz, 31 n. 6
haegûm (fiddle), 108, 128
Haft, Nina Otis, 63 n. 9
haksûpmu (apprenticed *mudang*), 4, 40–42
  ritual, 106–113
  ritual garments, 77
Han, Pu-Jôn, 27, 219, 221
han t'ûl (trio ensemble), 132. See also *sam chaebi*
Han, Yông-Sô, 132, 147
hanbok (Korean traditional clothing), 49, 77, 189, 204
  for the departed, 75, 204, 228
Han'guk Minjok Hakhoe (Association for Korean Studies), 79 n. 29, 210
Han'guk Musok Hakhoe (Association for Korean Shamanistic Studies), 6
Han'guk Shamanism Hakhoe (Korean Society for Shamanism Studies), 6
Hanyang, 7, 7 n. 9
Hanyang *kut*, 6–7, 155, 181–234 passim
  instrumental ensemble, 130–134
  musical instruments, 123–130
  songs, 156–163. See also *muga*
Hanyang *Samhyôn Yukkak*, 133
Harner, Michael J., 41 n. 30
harvest rituals, 32

Harvey, Youngsook Kim
  ch'ôngsûng mudang, 138 n. 4
  meeting shamans, 22 n. 7
  nunch'i, 64 n. 10
  suyông ômoni, 60 n. 6
  symptoms of spirit sickness, 59
  teknonymy and geononymy, 50
healing experience, 58, 83–84
healing ritual, 59, 99
hereditary *mudang*. See *sesûpmu*
hereditary *mudang* rituals, 104–106, 121
heterophony, 138, 159, 190
Heyman, Alan, 33 n. 13, 161, 163
Hô, Yong-Ôp, 27, 141, 145–146, 219
Hobsbawn, Eric, 178, 178 n. 18
hocketing, 238
hoeori param munyang (whirlwind pattern), 239
Hogarth, Hyun-Key Kim
  cymbal, 137
  gate crashing, 22 n. 8
  Kim Kum-Hwa, 19–20
  sadae sasang, 20 n. 4
  Taehan Sûnggon Kyôngshin Yônhaphoe, 48, 48 n. 42, 83 n. 35
hojôk (conical oboe), 3, 24, 110, 129–130, 206.
  See also *t'aep'yôngso*
hongsu maegi (small ritual to prevent misfortune), 103, 243–247
honryông kut (posthumous wedding ritual), 99
Hood, Mantle, 109, 166, 238
Howard, Keith, 36 n. 21, 57, 107 n. 29, 116–117, 124 n. 1
Huhm, Halla Pai, 100, 137, 187 n. 11
Hulbert, Homer B., 34–35, 38 n. 27
human cultural asset. See *poyuja*
human cultural property, 46, 218. See also *poyuja*
hwabon, 71. See also sacred paintings
Hwan In, 31, 35, 93, 191
Hwan Ung, 31, 35, 93, 191
Hwang Lu-Si, 99 n. 1, 99 n. 2, 100 n. 4, 119 n. 46, 137
Hwanghae Province ritual bells, 126
Hwanghae Province ritual drumming, 136
hwaûi (peaceful solution), 243
Hyangp'unghoe (male shaman association), 90–91, 182

I Ching (Book of Changes), 52. See also *Yôk Hak*

Index

idiophone. See *ching, kkwaenggwari, koritchak,* and *mokt'ak*
Ilyon [Il-Yôn, Monk Iryôn], 31
Important Intangible Cultural Properties, 6, 116–121
   governing law, 6, 116–119 passim
   performers. See *poyuja*
   performing group. See *poyu tanch'e*
   rituals, 118
indari (literally, human bridge), 59
in'gan munhwajae, 46, 218. See also *poyuja*
in-groups, 27. See also *kut p'ae*
initiation ritual, 61, 63. See also *naerim kut*
Inner Asian shamanism, 5
   acteme theory by Siikala, 186–187
   altars, 236
   drums, 65, 161–162, 135, 236
   initiatory sickness, 60, 235
   musical practice, 64–65, 160–162, 236–237
instrumental ensemble for ritual, 130–134
instrumentalists for rituals, 104, 138–140. See also *chaebi*
instruments used by *haksûpmu*, 41–42
instruments used by *kangshinmu*, 123–127
instruments used for *kut*, 123–130. See also
   ajaeng, changgu, chegûm, ching, haegûm, hojôk, kkwaenggwari, koritchak, para, p'iri, puk, taegûm, and *t'aep'yôngso*
Intangible Cultural Properties, 6, 116–119
isuja (artist for a cultural property), 118
   for Seoul *Saenam Kut*, 219
Izumi, Seich, 40, 182

jaesu kut, 8. See also *chaesu kut*
Janelli, Roger & Dawnhee Yim Janelli, 99 n. 3
Jary, David & Julia Jary, 23 n. 10
jinogwi kut, 8. See also *chinogwi kut*

kaek kwi (wandering spirit), 18
kalttae (flute), 129. See also *taegûm*
Kang, Tong-Gu, 31 n. 9
Kang, Yun-Gwôn, 27, 219
kangshin (spirit possession), 55–56, 61–63, 136, 185–187
kangshin kut (initiation ritual), 60. See also *naerim kut*
kangshinmu (spirit–possessed shamans in Korea), 4–5, 40, 44–51, 55–56, 67–83
   fees for ritual performers, 185
   how to find them, 78–83

kangshinmu (continued)
   liminal experience, 57–66 passim
   musical practice, 135–138
   musical training, 8, 64–65, 91–96
   ritual manuals, 64
   TV appearance, 88–90
kangshinmu kut (ritual officiated by spirit-possessed shamans), 97–104, 181–234
   how *kôri* are assigned for *kut*, 185
Kanji (Sexagenary Cycle), 52
karaoke, 180
kari kut (ritual for shamans), 104
Kaufmann, Walter, 166
kayagûm (12-string plucked zither), 121
Kendall, Laurel,
   iron ornament, 48 n. 41
   mugam, 212–213, 213 n. 38
   ritual garment, 48, 49
ki (energy), 168
kidae (musician trained for shaman ritual songs), 41, 137
kija (shaman), 51. See also *kangshinmu*
kijôm (divination with ritual flags), 210–211
kiju (female ritual sponsor), 82, 201
Killick, Andrew, 163 n. 12
Kim, Ch'an-Sôp, 147–148
Kim, Chôm-Sôk, 24, 27, 133, 141, 143–145, 218, 219
Kim, Chông-Gil, 26, 27, 141, 144, 145, 219
Kim, Chong-Tôk, 64
Kim, Chongsuh, 34 n. 15
Kim, Ch'un-Gang, 108, 111, 221
Kim, Duk-Hwan, 5
Kim, Hye-Ran, 106–109, 111, 220
Kim, Hyung-Chan, 79 n. 27, 114 n. 40
Kim, In-Hoe, 5, 63 n. 9, 208 n. 33
Kim, Ki-Su, 155, 157 n. 5, 166 n. 15
Kim, Kûm-Hwa, 19–20, 46, 119, 161
Kim, Mae-Mul, 121–122
Kim, Mun-Gi, 72
Kim, Nak-Pil, 52 n. 52
Kim, Sôn-P'ung, 27, 27 n. 21, 217
Kim, Sun-Bong, 142–143
Kim, T'aegon
   kemshimbach'im, 103
   Kyôngshin Yônhaphoe, 83
   muga, 7, 160–161
   musok, 5, 5 n. 7
   sacred painting, 72
   Seoul *kut*, 181
   sesûpmu/tan'gol, 78 n. 26

Kim, T'aegon *(continued)*
  spirits and grains, 62
  spirits classified, 36
Kim, Ui-Chol & Sang-Chun Choi, 64 n. 10
Kim, Yong-Ho, 33
Kim, Yŏng-Yim, 220
Kim, Yu-Gam, 27, 50, 109, 111, 124, 161, 183, 218–221
kimch'i, 233
kimul (ritual receptacle), 68
Kister, Daniel A., 32
kkwaenggwari (small gong), 41, 127, 130, 162
koehwangji (paper used for amulet), 73
koin (musician), 104
kongsu (message delivered from spirits), 23, 25, 94, 105, 119, 137, 188, 193, 208, 239
Korea, 6, 29–30
  foundation myth, 31–32
  provinces, 86 n. 39
Korea Times, 79 n. 28
Korean Overseas Cultural and Information Service, 30, 34
Korean shaman. *See kangshinmu*
Korean shamanism, 6. *See also mu* or *musok*
Korean traditional clothing. *See hanbok*
kôri (sections) in various Hanyang *kut*, 181–234 passim
  ch'aenggyô pekkyô, 211
  chakdu kôri, 208–210
  Ch'angbu *kôri*, 182, 214, 222, 224
  changgun kôri, 204–205. *See also* Sangsan *kôri*
  Chesôk *kôri*, 182, 223
  chinjôk tûrim, 190–191
  chônan kôri, 205–206
  ch'ôn'gung maji kôri, 182, 191–199, 222
  chosang kôri, 182, 204, 222,
  chudang mullim, 187, 222
  Hogu *kôri*, 182, 196
  Kôllip *kôri*, 197, 203
  k'ûn kôri, 204–205. *See also* Sangsan *kôri*
  kurûng kôri, 182
  Kyemyôn *kôri*, 214–215
  malmi kôri, 162, 226–228
  malmyông kôri, 182, 196
  manshin malmyông kôri, 183
  Manura *kôri*. *See* Sangsan *kôri*
  mugam kôri for the clients, 212–213
  mulgu kamang kôri, 222, 223
  mun tûrum, 230
  pe karûgi, 233

kôri (sections) *(continued)*
  ponhyang kôri, 182, 203, 222
  ponhyang malmyông kôri, 203
  pujông kôri, 25, 184, 189–190, 222, 224
  Pulsa/Chesôk *kôri*, 223
  Pyôlsang *kôri*, 182, 207–210, 222
  San *kôri*. *See* Sangsan *kôri*
  San Manura *kôri*, 182. *See also* Sangsan *kôri*
  Sangsan *kôri*, 182, 204–205, 222
  sangshik kôri (food offering for ancestors), 233
  Shinjang *kôri*, 182, 197, 210–211, 222
  Shiwang Kunung *kôri*, 233–234
  Sôngjo *kôri*, *See* Sôngju *kôri*
  Sôngju *kôri*, 182, 213, 222
  sulryôk torûm, 212
  Taegam *kôri*, 182, 211–213, 222
  Taeshin *kôri*, 182, 203
  Todang *kôri*, 199–203
  tossam kôri, 231–232
  TtûnTaewang *kôri*, 225–226
  twitchôn kôri, 157, 182, 215–216
  yôngshil kôri, 223, 230, 233
koritchak (basket), 103, 126, 130
kôsông dance, 188, 206–207
kosu (drummer), 163
kuaebi (retrieved ritual objects), 59–60
Kukrip Munhwajae Yôn'guso, 7, 77, 189 n. 13, 218 n. 1
Kuksadang (ritual hall), 23, 24, 101
kûmô (monk painters), 72
kung p'yôn (left head of a drum), 161
kunggul ch'ae (drum stick), 94, 124, 162, 166, 228
  for "Pari Kongju," 162, 228
kunghap (compatibility), 52
kut (ritual), 3, 4, 6, 97–122
  by *kangshinmu*, 99–104
  etymology, 97–98,
  for neighborhood, 100
  mudang kut, 3
  p'ungmul kut, 3
  regional variations, 6–7, 98–99, 155
  seasonal rituals, 100
kut, large-scale ritual with music and dance, 3, 4,
  andang sagyông maji, 217, 221–224
  an'taek kut, 100
  chaesu kut, 99
  Changmal Todang *Kut*, 98
  Cheju Ch'ilmôri *Tang Kut*, 118
  chinjôk kut, 75, 104

Index

kut, large-scale rituals *(continued)*
  chinogwi kut, 99, 103, 162
  ch'ŏlmul kut, 110
  ch'ŏnshin kut, 181–216
  Hahoe Pyŏlshin *Kut*, 98
  honryŏng kut (posthumous wedding ritual), 99
  hwan'gap yŏt'am (ritual for 60 year old person), 103
  kangshin kut (initiation ritual). *See* naerim *kut*
  Kuri Kalmae *Todang Kut*, 119
  Kyŏnggi *Todang Kut*, 118
  maŭl kut for neighborhood, 99
  Momyŏk San Tae Ch'ŏnje, 120
  naerim kut (initiation ritual), 60–63
  Nam Yi *Changgun Kut*, 119, 143
  Namhaean *Pyŏlshin Kut*, 77, 118
  nara kut, 85, 99
  Ômmiri Changsûngje (*p'ungmul kut*), 98
  P'aldo Kut, 85–88, 104
  P'ilbong Tangsanje (*p'ungmul kut*), 98
  p'ungmul kut by secular musicians, 3, 98
  pyŏng kut (healing ritual), 59, 99
  P'yŏngsan *Sonorŭm Kut*, 118
  seasonal *kut*, 100
  Seoul *Saenam Kut*, 118, 217–234 passim
  Sôhaean Paeyŏnshin Kut and Taedong Kut, 118, 119
  son kut, 161
  Sôngju *kut*, 100
  sosŭl kut, 104
  ssikkim kut, 109, 121, 161
  Sudong *Pyŏlshin Kut*, 98
  suwang kut, 121–122
  taedong kut, 98–99, 119
  Tonghaean Pyŏlshin Kut, 118
  ture kut, 98
  Ûnsan *Pyŏlshinje*, 118
  Wido Ttibae Nori, 99, 118
  Yôngdûng Kut, 99
kut, small-scale ritual without dance, 3, 77, 101, 130
  aekmaegi (ritual to prevent ill fortune), 102
  ant'aek kut (ritual for the new home), 100
  chari kôji (cleansing ritual for the dead), 103
  chipkashim (cleansing ritual for the dead), 102
  ch'isŏng (ritual asking for good fortune), 77, 103

kut, small-scale rituals *(continued)*
  hôju kut (ritual for shamans to be), 60, 103
  hongsu maegi (ritual to prevent misfortune), 103
  kemshimbach'im (small ritual after child birth), 103
  kilje (street ritual for the dead), 103
  pangsansje, 103
  pison (small ritual asking for good fortune), 77, 102, 103
  p'udak kôri (healing ritual), 102
  sarye ch'isŏng (ritual on the third day following a large *kut*), 102
  sonbibim (prayers offered), 102
  yŏngjang ch'igi (healing ritual), 102
  yôt'am (ritual held prior to the wedding), 103
kut as parody, 113–116. *See also "Paebaengi Kut"*
kut as theater production, 111–113
kut by folk singers, 106–111 passim. *See also haksûpmu kut*
kut by hereditary *mudang*, 77, 104–106
kut by secular musicians. *See p'ungmul kut*
kut by shamans (*kangshinmu*), 99–106, 181–234
kut for good luck. *See chaesu kut* or *ch'ŏnshin kut*
kut for healing. *See* pyŏng *kut*
kut for neighborhood, 100
kut for new home. *See* Sôngju *kut* or *an'taek kut* (small-scale)
kut for the departed. *See also chinogwi* or *saenam kut*
kut in various provinces, 6, 86, 155
kut p'ae (ritual group), 95, 138
Kut Yôn'guso (*Kut* Research Institute), 6
kuttang (ritual hall), 84, 101, 239
kuûm (onomatopoeic words), 166
Kwan-U, 205–206
kwangdae (musician), 43, 163
kwi shin (malevolent spirit), 3, 56, 58, 103
kyeja (shaman), 51
Kyŏng *t'ori* (musical dialect of Kyŏnggi Province), 109
kyŏngjangi (sutra reader), 41, 44, 45
Kyŏngshin Yŏnhaphoe (association for shamans), 83. *See also* Taehan Sûnggong Kyŏngshin Yŏnhaphoe
Kyŏngsô *t'ori* (musical dialect of Kyŏnggi and northwestern provinces), 156
Lee, Chae-Suk, 206, 206 n. 28
Lee, Hye-Ku, 157 n. 5

Lee, Jung-Young, 40, 161, 181
Lee, Ki-Baek, 32, 32 n. 11, 33
Lee, Kwang-Kyu, 30, 50
Lee, Kwang-Kyu & Youngsook Kim Harvey, 50
Lee, Peter
   Chosŏn, 29 n 2
   Hwang Chin-I, 112 n. 39
   Korean language, 98
   Samguk Yusa, 31 n. 6
   shijo, 158 n. 7
   Tan'gun, 31
Lee, Sang-Sook & G.D. Sibley, 72
Lee, Yong-Hak, 118, 119 n. 44, 221
Lewis, I.M., 55, 57
Liang, Mingyue, 39–40, 237–238
Lim, Jae-Hae, 4 n. 2, 98
liminal experience for Korean shaman, 57–66
   liminal, 60–65
   postliminal, 66
   pre-liminal, 58–60
living cultural treasure, 46. See also *poyuja*
living human treasure, 218, 221. See also *poyuja*
Lord, Albert B., 160
Lowie, Robert H., 41
Lyu, Kingsley K., 30 n. 5

male clients, 5, 48, 82, 201
male *kangshinmu*, 5. See also *paksu*
male ritual sponsors. See *taeju*
male shaman. See *paksu*
male shaman association. See Hyangp'unghoe
malevolent spirits, 3. See also *kwi shin*
man (Swastika symbol), 42, 239
manmulsang (*musok* specialty shop), 73
manshin (shaman), 40, 43, 45–46, 119, 126
   etymology & ideographs, 43
mansubaji (duet songs), 137, 157, 159, 188, 193, 229
mansubaji song accompaniment, 159. See also *kutkôri changdan*
Maskarinec, Gregory G., 41 n. 30
mediumistic *kangshinmu*, 80
melodic variation. See *susông karak*
messages from spirits. See *kongsu*
metallic objects in rituals, 125–126, 162, 236
metamessages, 241
min'gan shinang (folk religion), 6, 44
minsok ûmak (folk music), 105–106
minyo (folk songs), 107

mirror, brass, 59, 68
miscellaneous spirits, 36
mishin (superstition), 3, 43, 242
Mitchell, Richard G. Jr., 240, 242
mokt'ak (wooden fish idiophone), 41
monju (body governing spirit), 36, 61, 215
monthly offering, 82
mu, 3–4, 5, 39. See also *musok*
mu practitioners, 4. See also clients
muak (ritual music), 155–163 passim
mubok (ritual garments), 74–77, 187–234 passim. See also *shinbok* or *shinjang*
mudang (ritual specialist), 3–5, 38–53 passim
   apprenticed *mudang*. See *haksûpmu*
   etymology, 39–40
   hereditary *mudang*. See *sesûpmu*
   ideographs, 39–40
   mudang who does not sing or dance, 45. See also *chônnae*
   spirit-possessed *mudang*. See *kangshinmu*
Mudang Naeryôk, 182
muga (ritual songs), 156–162 passim
muga (ritual songs) used in Seoul Saenam Kut
   "Ch'angbu T'aryông," 197, 202, 214, 243
   "Changgunnim Noraekarak," 191
   "Ch'ôn'gung Maji Noraekarak," 193–194
   "Ch'ôn'gung Shinjang T'aryông," 197
   "Chungdi Noraekarak," 225
   "Chungdi Patsan," 26 n. 19, 156, 225
   "Chungsang T'aryông," 194
   "Hongsu Maegi," 243–247
   "Hwangje P'uri," 156, 162, 214, 226
   "Kajin Twitchôn," 215
   "Kamang Ch'ôngbae," 156, 222, 224, 237
   "Kamang Noraekarak," 190, 222, 224
   "Kôsangak," 235
   "Kyemyôn T'aryông," 214
   "Malmi," 226–228. See also "*Pari Kongju*"
   "Matchoa," 232
   "Myôngdu Ch'ôngbae," 233
   "Nôk Noraekarak," 229, 233, 234
   "Para T'aryông," 125, 156, 193–194
   "Pari Kongju," 75, 156, 161–162, 226–228
   "Pujông Ch'ôngbae," 189, 237
   "Pyôlsang Noraekarak," 208
   "Sajae Noraekarak," 225
   "Sajae T'aryông," 225
   "Sangsan Noraekarak," 191, 207, 222
   "Sôngju Noraekarak," 213
   "Shinjang T'aryông," 157, 197
   "Taegam T'aryông," 158, 197, 212

muga (ritual songs) *(continued)*
  "*T'ô Taegam T'aryông*," 212
  "*Todang Ch'angbu T'aryông*," 202
  "*Todang Noraekarak*," 201
  "*Todang Shinjang T'aryông*," 202
  "*Todang Taegam T'aryông*," 202
mugam dance (for clients), 139, 212–213
mugyo (shamanism), 5. See also *mu* or *musok*
mugyôk (male shaman), 46. See also *paksu*
mugyông (incantation), 41, 65
muhwa, 71. *See* sacred paintings
muhyông munhwajae (intangible cultural property), 6, 116–119
muism, 5. See also *mu* or *musok*
muldongi (ritual water jar), 193, 223
mumyông (cotton cloth), 204, 233
Mun, Kyu-P'il, 73, 80 n. 29
munhwajae (cultural properties), 116–119 passim
Munhwajae kwanriguk. *See* Munhwajaech'ông
munhwajae pohobôp (laws protecting cultural properties), 6, 116–118
munhwajae pyông (illness), 220
Munhwajaech'ông (Bureau of Cultural Properties), 116
munsô (correct rules for *musok* practice), 96, 183
muryông (ritual bell). See *pangul*
mushindo, 71. *See also* sacred paintings
musical dialect. See *t'ori*
musical training for spirit-possessed shamans, 8, 64–65, 91–95
musicant/musicated, 135–136
musicians for Hanyang *kut*. See *chaebi*
musok, 4–6, 35–38. See also *mu*
musok believers. See *shindo* or clients
Musok Pojonhoe (school for spirit-possessed shamans), 91–96 passim
musokin (shaman), 51. See also *kangshinmu*
myôngdo (brass mirror), 59, 68

naerim kut (initiation ritual), 60–63, 78
naeryôk pongji (divination mode for neophyte shaman), 62
Nan-Gok, 182, 182 n. 4
nara kut, 99
National Center for Korean Traditional Performing Arts, 7–8, 164
neophyte, 57–66 passim
new religions of Korea, 34
nogaba method, 157

Noh, Tong-Eun (Tong-Ûn), 157, 157 n. 6
noraebang (karaoke room), 180
noraekarak, 156–159, 235. See also various *noraekarak* song titles under *muga*
noraekarak changdan notation. See *shijo changdan* notation.
notation system. See *chôngganbo*
nunch'i (social sense), 64

o chaebi (five musician ensemble), 131
obang shinjanggi (five colored ritual flags), 94, 197, 202, 210–211
oboe, conical. See *hojôk* or *t'aep'yôngso*
oboe, cylindrical. See *p'iri*
odong (paulownia wood), 123, 130
oe chaebi (solo *p'iri* player), 131–132
Office of Cultural Properties, 117
ohaeng (five elements), 52
oksu (sacred water), 66, 67, 69, 192
onomatopoeic words, 166
ootan, 236
original form. See *wônhyông*
oshin (entertaining spirits), 185–187
outdoor percussion ensemble music. See *p'ungmul kut*

Paebaengi Kut, 113–116
Paden, William, 35 n. 20
Paik, Lak-Geoon [Paek Nak-Chun], 34 n. 17
Pak, Chong-Bok, 26, 27, 137, 183
Pak, Chông-Jin, 140
Pak, Chông-Uk, 106–107, 110
Pak, Hwang, 164 n. 14
Pak, In-O, 64, 93
  shaman school, 91–95
Pak, Ô-Jin, 137
Pak, Yong-Suk, 5, 52 n. 50, 71
paksu (male shaman), 46–49, 236
  association, 90–91
  etymology, 46–47
  ideographs, 46
  in *Paebaengi Kut*, 115–116
  ritual garments, 48–49, 227–228
p'alch'ôn (8 jobs considered lower class), 43
P'aldo (8 provinces), 86 n. 39
pangul (ritual bell tree), 68, 125–126, 156, 157, 162, 193, 223, 228
p'ansori (secular epic song), 105–106, 113, 163–164
p'ansori repertoires, 163, 163 n. 13
p'ansori singers, 163, 164, 164 n. 14

p'ansu (blind diviner), 41, 44, 45
pantheon of gods, 35–36
Paper, J., 48
paper objects used in *kut*
    candle, 228
    flowers, 104, 191–192, 225
    nôkchôn, 229, 232, 233
    ponhyangji, 203, 223
    pulsajôn, 192
    sanjongi, 199, 200
    sôngju kunungji, 213
para (cymbals), 94, 125, 156, 193–194
para ch'um (cymbal dance), 95
paraji (duet songs). See *mansubaji*
"*Pari Kongju*," 156, 162, 226–232
    outline of the song, 226–227
    ritual garment, 75, 227–228, 229
    tossam dance, 231–232
Park, Chông-Jin, 140
Park, Hûi-A, 63n 9
Park, Hûng-Ju, 6, 43
Park, Mikyung [Pak Mi-Kyông], 7, 161
participant observer, 23, 64
pe (hemp), 204, 233
Pegg, Carole, 160
pentatonic scale, 156
percussion instruments, 79. See also *changgu,*
    chegûm, ching, kkwaenggwari,
    koritchak, mokt'ak, puk
persons considered polluted, 209
Philippi, 160
pigabi (non-hereditary musician), 104
Pihl, Marshall R., 33, 163, 164
p'iri (cylindrical oboe), 24, 127–128
pisu (sacred blades), 110, 119, 208n 33. See
    also *chakdu*
poksa (male diviner), 44, 45, 47
pôpsa (male sutra reader), 41, 180
posal (female ritual practitioners), 41, 45
posthumous wedding ritual. See *hon'ryông kut*
Potapov, L.P., 65
poyu tanch'e (performing group for cultural
    property), 117
    Seoul *Saenam Kut*, 218
poyuja (designated performer for cultural
    property), 46, 117–119
    Seoul *Saenam Kut*, 50, 218, 219, 241
poyuja hubo (next in line for *poyuja*), 118
Pratt, Keith & Richard Rutt, 29 n.1, 33 n. 12, 48
priest, 41. See also *sesûpmu*
provinces of Korea, 86 n. 39

pseudonyms for shamans, 49–51
puch'ae (ritual fan), 68, 94, 193, 223, 229–231
pujak, 72. See also amulets
pujôk, 72. See also amulets
puk (double-headed barrel drum), 41–42, 127,
    129
p'ungmul kut (ritual by secular musicians), 3, 98,
    165
p'ungmul p'ae (musician group for *p'ungmul*
    kut), 98
p'ungsu (geomancy), 52
pyôlbi (extra cash contribution), 119, 185, 216
pyông kut (healing ritual), 59, 99
Pyông'an Province style ritual drumming, 136–
    137
pyôngch'ang (singing and accompanying oneself
    on a string instrument), 105

Ramstedt, G.J., 97
Reichl, Karl, 47, 160
Reinhard, Johan, 5, 56
research organizations on *musok*, 6
rhythmic cycles. See *changdan*
rhythmic pattern, 24. See also *changdan*
Rinchen, Yongsiyebu, 39
ritual. See *kut* (large-scale and small-scale) and
    p'ungmul kut
ritual blade for shaman to ride on barefoot. See
    chakdu or *pisu*
ritual dance, 94, 194
    circumambulation, 229–231
    kôsông dance, 188, 206–207
    tomu dance, 136, 188, 194
    tossam dance, 231–232
ritual garments. See *shinbok, shinjang,* and
    mubok
ritual group. See *kut p'ae*
ritual hall. See *kuttang*
ritual jar filled with water. See *muldongi*
ritual knife. See *ch'ôngryongdo, shink'al* or
    wôldo
ritual manuals for Hanyang *kut*, 64, 93
ritual music ensemble, 130–134
ritual music practice and change, 178–180
ritual musician. See *chaebi*
ritual prayers. See *mugyông* and *tokkyông*
ritual receptacles. See *kimul*
ritual songs. See *muga* for song titles
    duet songs. See *mansubaji, noraekarak*
    epic songs, 159–164
    strophic songs, 156–157

ritual speech patterns, 94–95
ritual specialist. See *mudang, kangshinmu,* and *sesûpmu*
ritual sponsors. *See* clients, *chegajip, kiju,* or *taeju*
ritual trident. See *ch'anggôm* or *samjich'ang*
Rouget, Gilbert, 135
Ryu, Sang-Ch'ae, 73
Ryu, Tong-Sik [Yu Tong-Shik]
  mu (etymology), 39
  mugyo, 5
  haksûpmu, 41 n. 31
  Sangsan pugun kut, 181 n. 3
  Seoul *kut,* 181
  spirits' power, 36
  yaksu, 69 n. 11

sa chaebi (four musician ensemble), 131
sacred paintings, 71–72
sacred room. See *shindang*
saenam kut (second part of Seoul *Saenam Kut*), 224–234 passim
saju (birth information), 14, 52, 102
sal (curse), 211
salp'uri (ritual eliminating *sal*), 211
sam chaebi (trio musicians), 108, 131, 132, 142
sam t'aegûk (the great ultimate embodying three elements), 238, 239
samgang oryun (three bonds and five relationships), 37
Samguk Yusa (Memorabilia of the Three Kingdoms), 31
samhyôn yukkak (six musician ensemble), 129, 131, 133–134, 191
samjae (three elements: heaven, earth, humans) 3, 38, 201, 238
samjich'ang (ritual trident), 201. See also *ch'anggôm*
samulnori (percussion group), 106, 110
san (divination), 195
sani (hereditary musicians), 139, 141
sanjo (instrumental solo genre), 106, 121
sant'ong (divination box), 69
saô (argot no longer used), 22
Sasamori, Takefusa, 44
sat'uri (regional dialect), 109
Schechner, Richard, 97, 106
schéma of *rites de passage,* 58
Schmidt, Cynthia E., 238
seasonal rituals, 100
sections of *kut.* See *kôri*

Seo, Maria K., 58
Seoul *Saenam Kut,* 7, 26–27, 118, 217–234
  etymology, 217
  government designated performers, 219
  ideograph, 217
sesûpmu (hereditary ritual specialist), 4, 7, 40
sesûpmu rituals, 104–106
shaman, 4–5, 6, 56–58
  defined by Reinhard, 5, 56
  etymology, 56–57
shaman, hired to lead a ritual. See *tangju*
shaman, Korean, 4–5. See also *kangshinmu*
shaman associations. *See* Taehan Sûnggong Kyôngshin Yônhaphoe
shaman association for male shamans. *See* Hyangp'unghoe
shaman school, 91–96
shamanism, 6, 55–56
shijo (classic poem), 158
shijo changdan notation, 173–174
shimbang (shaman in Cheju Island), 35, 40–41, 44, 77
shin abôji (spirit father), 60, 64
shin ômôni (spirit mother), 60, 64, 88
shin pumo (spirit parent), 64, 91, 92, 236
shinawi (instrumental music in *sesûpmu kut*), 106
shinbok (ritual garment), 48–49, 74–77, 189–234 passim
shinbyông (spirit sickness), 58–59
shindang (sacred room/shrine/ritual hall), 66, 67–71, 90–91
  Alaska Halmôni, 70
  Hyangp'unghoe members, 90–91
  Mrs. A, 14
shindo (*musok* believer), 78–83. *See also* clients and sponsors
shin'ga, 156. See also *muga* and ritual songs
shin'gamul (adversity forced on neophyte), 59, 60
shinjang (ritual garment), 74. See also *shinbok*
shink'al (ritual knife), 59, 216, 228, 231, 233
shinryông (ritual bells), 59. See also *pangul*
shinryông hwabon, 71. *See also* sacred paintings
shinsach'ambae (attending Shinto services), 34
shint'ak, 137. See also *kongsu*
Shintoism, 34
shint'ongryôk (power to communicate with spirits), 83
Shirokogoroff, S.M., 57
shrine. See *shindang* or *kuttang*

Siberian shaman, 68, 162
Siikala, Anna-Leena, 57, 186–187, 236 n. 3
Sim, Woo-sung [Wu-Sông], 113, 114
Simmel, Georg, 85
Slobin, Mark, 161 n. 9
Slote, W.H., 12
Sô, Chông-Bôm, 80, 137
Sô, T'ae-Sôk, 161
soe sori (metallic sound), 125
sogak (ritual burning), 192n. 17, 216
sogûm (small gong), 127. See also *kkwaenggwari*
soji (burning of ritual paper), 39, 190
sôn kôri (standing section of a ritual), 65, 184, 218
Song, Do-Young, 180 n. 22
Sông, Kyông-Rin & Yi Po-Hyung [Po-Hyông], 114
songshin (farewell to spirits), 185–187, 215
"*Sônt'aek [Choice]*," a theater production of *kut*, 111–113
Sorensen, Clark W., 43
sosûl kut (ritual for new shaman), 104
soul journey, 55
soul loss, 55
specialty shop, 64, 75. See also *manmulsang*
spirit father. See *shin abôji*
spirit intrusion, 56, 58, 61
spirit mother. See *shin ômôni*
spirit parents. See *shin pumo*
spirit-possessed shaman. See *kangshinmu*
spirit possession, 55–56, 60–63
spirit sickness, 58–59, 60
spirits, 3, 35, 36
spirits (female), 196, 206, 214
spirits (malevolent spirits). See *kwi shin*
spirits (miscellaneous spirits). See *chap kwi* or *chap shin*
spirits, venerated in Hanyang *kut*
   Big Dipper Star-Spirit, 93. See also Ch'ilsông
   Buddha, 71. See also Pulsa
   Ch'angbu, 189, 197, 214
   Chesôk, 35, 36, 62, 189, 191, 192
   Ch'ilsông, 36, 67, 72, 93, 103, 189
   Chônan, 189
   Ch'ônjon, 191
   Hogu, 36, 62, 189, 196
   Kamang, 189
   Kunung, 36, 62, 200
   Malmyông, 189, 196, 201

spirits *(continued)*
   Obang Shinjang (Five Directional Spirit), 36, 72, 93, 197
   Ôksabyôl Kunung, 187
   Pulsa, 73, 189, 191, 192
   Pyôlsang, 36, 189, 207–209
   Sajae Samsông, 225
   Sambul Chesôk, 67, 93
   San Manura Spirit, 36
   Sangsan Manura, 189, 190–191. See also San Manura
   Sanshin (Mountain Spirit), 62, 72, 93, 189
   Sanshinryôngnim, 73. See also Sanshin
   Seven Star Spirits, 36, 67, 68, 72, 93. See also Ch'ilsông
   Shinjang, 189, 197
   Shiptaewang, 233–234
   Shiwang, 233–234
   Sôngju, 36, 189, 213
   spirits, miscellaneous, 189, 197–198
   Taegam, 36, 189, 211
   Todang, 189, 199–203
   Ttûn Taewang. See Sajae Samsông
   Yongshin, 62, 93, 193
sponsors for ritual, 22. See also *chegajip, taeju, kiju*
ssang changgu (pair of drums), 137
ssang hojôk (pair of conical oboes), 130
ssang t'aegûk (ûm/yang symbol), 239
ssikkim kut in Chindo, 109, 121
ssoeni (non-hereditary musicians), 139
stock melodies, 156, 189
strophic songs, 156–158
Sullivan, Bruce M., 42
Sun Soon-Hwa, 51 n. 49, 83
superstition, 3, 43, 80, 242
susông karak (melodic variations), 138, 159, 190
sutra readers, 41. See also *kyôngjangi* and *pôpsa*
sutra reading. See *tokkyông*
swastika, 42. See also *man*
symbolism
   of colors, 73, 80, 210, 239
   of cloth (cotton and hemp), 204
   of divination materials, 62, 210
   of musical instruments
      changgu, 124, 168
      chegûm, 125
      haegûm, 128
      p'iri, 128
      taegûm, 129
   of *samjich'ang* (ritual trident), 201

Index

syncretism, 191

t'aegŭk (the great ultimate), 238–239
taegŭm (flute), 128–129, 235
taegŭm (large gong), 127
Taehan Sŭnggong Kyŏngshin Yŏnhaphoe, 83–90, 84 n. 35, 84 n 36, 104
taeju (male ritual sponsor), 82, 201
t'aenghwa, 72. See also sacred paintings
t'aep'yŏngso (conical oboe), 129–130, 179. See also *hojŏk*
taesudaemyŏng (misfortune disposed to other object), 102
talisman, 72–74
tanggol mudang, 104. See also *sesŭpmu*
tangible cultural property, 116–117
tangju musician (responsible for hiring other musicians for a ritual). See *chaebi tangju*
tangju shaman (hired to lead *kut*), 101–102, 130, 184–185, 216
tan'gol, 78–79, 82. See also clients
tan'gol mudang. See *sesŭpmu* and *tanggol mudang*
tan'golp'an (neighborhood designated for *tan'gol mudang*), 78, 240
tangshim (food served at ritual hall), 101
Tan'gun, 31–32, 35, 71, 93, 191, 203, 248
Tan'gun Chosŏn, 32
Taoism, 33, 41, 191, 205
t'apsang (ritual for installing a sacred room), 67–68
t'aryŏng changdan for *t'aryŏng* songs, 159. See also *kutkŏri changdan*
tchok (section), 169, 238
teknonymy, 50
Ten Commandments, 37, 37n 25
three elements. See *samjae*
Three Kingdoms, 33
T'ojŏng Pigyŏl, 52
tŏkdam (blessing), 94, 188
tokkyŏng (sutra reading), 41, 162, 180
tokkyŏng chŏmbok (sutra reading and divination), 41, 43
tokkyŏng poksul (sutra reading and divination), 45
tomu (dance of spirit possession), 136, 188, 194
t'ori (musical dialect), 109, 115, 156
toryŏng dance (circumambulation), 218, 229–231
an toryŏng, 230–231

toryŏng dance *(continued)*
k'al toryŏng, 229, 231
nabi toryŏng, 231
pat toryŏng, 229–230
puch'ae toryŏng, 229, 231
son toryŏng, 229, 231
tossam (mat holding clothing and shoes of the departed), 228
tossam kŏri, 231–232
trance, 55, 60
trio instrumental ensemble. See *sam chaebi*
triple meters, 169
triplets, 169
Troshchanski, V.F., 39, 47
Turnbull, Colin, 63
Turner, Victor, 51 n. 48, 57, 66
twi p'uri (gathering after an event), 180
Tylor, Stephen A., 241

udagan, 39
uhwan kut (healing ritual). See also *pyŏng kut*
ŭm/yang (two elements), 52, 168, 238
ŭnŏ (argot), 21

van Gennep, Arnold, 58
variation on a melody. See *susŏng karak*
Vitebsky, Piers, 47

Walraven, Boudewijn, 5 n. 5, 31 n. 6, 156 n. 2, 161
wandering spirit, 18. See also *kaek kwi*
Warren, C. & B. Laslett, 85
willow basket. See *koritchak*
wŏldo (ritual knife), 200–201, 207–208, 210
wŏnhyŏng (original form), 6, 117–119
wŏnhyŏng for Seoul *Saenam Kut*, 220
World Wide Web advertisement, 80, 80 n. 30
Wu, Bing-an, 57
Wu, Jing-Nuan, 52 n. 50

Yang, Jongsung [Chŏng-Sŭng]
hierarchy of spirits, 36
isuja, 118n. 43
learning experience, 36 n. 22
Paebaengi Kut, 114
Pak In-O, 92
pangul, 126
yang chaebi, 178
yampa (ritual belt used by Siberian shaman), 162
yang chaebi (two musician ensemble), 131, 178
Yi, Chŏng-Yŏng, 140 n. 9

Yi, Chun-Yŏng, 178–179, 209
Yi, Hui-Sung, 40 n.28, 217
Yi, Kyu-Wŏn, 137, 137 n. 3
Yi, Nûng-Hwa
   Chosŏn Musokko (Korean Musok), 4 n. 1
   dang (etymology), 40
   kut (etymology), 97
   paksu (etymology), 46
   saenam (etymology), 217
   shin kyo, 5
   t'aryŏng, 156 n. 3
Yi, Po-Hyŏng, 7, 109, 114, 162
Yi, Sang-Sun, 26, 27, 49, 62, 74, 111, 158, 124, 131, 137, 182–183, 199, 218, 219, 221, 241
Yi, Sôn-Ho, 151–152, 221
Yi, Sông-Jae, 91, 120, 121, 221
Yi, Wŏn-Sôp, 59 n. 3, 79, 80 n. 29
Yi, Yŏng-Hûi, 103, 221
Yim, Ki-Uk, 59–60, 90, 91, 104, 131
Yim, Suk Jay, 5
Yim, Tong-Gwŏn, 138 n. 5
yin/yang. See *ûm/yang*

Yôk Hak (The Book of Changes), 52
yôksulga (diviner), 52–53
yôngjông (portrait), 229
yôngshil (ancestor speaking through *kangshinmu*), 230
   ch'o (first) *yôngshil*, 223
   pon, or *wôn* (main) *yôngshil*, 230
   twi (last) *yôngshil*, 233
yôngshil ûidae (clothing for the departed), 216
yôpchôn (divination coin), 14, 69
Young, Barbara Elizabeth, 80
yuhyông munhwajae (tangible cultural property), 116–117
Yuk Kap, 52
Yun, SeongYong, 34
Yun, Sôk-Un, 168
Yun, Yôl-Su, 72

Zeranska-Kominek, Slawomira, 47
zither, bowed. See *ajaeng*
   plucked. See *kayagûm*
Zozayong, Horay, 35 n. 18, 35 n 19

For Product Safety Concerns and Information please contact our EU
representative GPSR@taylorandfrancis.com
Taylor & Francis Verlag GmbH, Kaufingerstraße 24, 80331 München, Germany

www.ingramcontent.com/pod-product-compliance
Lightning Source LLC
Chambersburg PA
CBHW071759300426
44116CB00009B/1144